DEDICATION

I would like to dedicate this book to my lovely wife, Barbara, who influenced and inspired me to write it. Also, to my lovely daughter Missy and her husband James Cahill, and to their children, Noah and Calley—all of them make me a very proud father, and grandfather. And to my mother, Ann Mills, who passed away as we completed this book. She dedicated her life to nurturing me, and encouraged me to plant those first seeds and nurture them, to help me enjoy the ecosystem all around. May that nurturing rub off onto you, as a gardener in the great state of Nevada.
—Linn Mills

I would like to dedicate this book to my wife Shirley for her patience and prodding. And to our children Kyle, Erin, and Lori and her husband Chad, who were amazed that Dad was writing a book. I also dedicate this book to my mother, Margaret Campbell Post, who was very excited when I told her I was writing a book. She passed away at the age of 99 just as I began to write.
—Dick Post

ACKNOWLEDGMENTS

I OWE A DEBT OF GRATITUDE to countless individuals and groups whose teachings, reassurances, and plain hard work helped to bring this book into being. This book would not have been written were it not for the chain of circumstances that led Cool Springs Press's Roger Waynick and Hank McBride to me; they showed enough of an interest and faith in me to choose me as one of their authors. And of course, my thanks for the ever-diligent and persistent encouragement from Billie Brownell, who read and edited the entire manuscript. She made it what it is: the first statewide gardening book for Nevada.

How can I ever thank my coauthor Dick Post enough? Dick was my State Horticulturist and became my mentor when I started with the University of Nevada Cooperative Extension as a vegetable specialist. He assisted me as I moved to Las Vegas in 1976 to learn more about gardening in the desert. We worked together on many projects over the years. (It has been a difficult task to bring the diverse Nevadan climates together into one book; Dick and I also had a difficult time whittling down the number of plants to the allotted amount for this book.)

This book is a reflection of all the people and situations that have affected my life. There is no way to include all who had a hand in helping me in my career to bring about the writing of this book. With that in mind, I will only mention the many organizations I have worked with over the years that have been of great assistance to me. Within each organization are untold numbers of people who helped me. I won't mention all the names for fear of omitting some who have done so much on my behalf.

Working at the Desert Demonstration Gardens has allowed me to come in contact with hundreds of people who visit the Gardens. To all the volunteers and staff of the Gardens, I owe an immense debt of gratitude, with special appreciation for the knowledge shared by Peter Duncombe, Gardens Director.

I will be forever grateful to Nevada Cooperative Extension for opening the gate to allow me to preach the gospel of gardening in southern Nevada. A special thanks goes to my superiors, peers, and

The What, Where, When, How & Why
of Landscape Gardening in Nevada

NEVADA
Gardener's
Guide

Linn Mills   Dick Post

COOL
SPRINGS
PRESS

Nashville, Tennessee
A Division of Thomas Nelson, Inc.
www.ThomasNelson.com

Published by Cool Springs Press, a Division of Thomas Nelson, Inc.,
P.O. Box 141000, Nashville, Tennessee 37214

Mills, Linn.
    Nevada gardener's guide / Linn Mills and Dick Post.
        p.   cm.
    Includes bibliographical references and index.
    ISBN 1-888608-97-8 (pbk. : alk. paper)
    1. Landscape plants -- Nevada. 2. Landscape gardening -- Nevada.
    I. Post, Dick. II. Title.
  SB407 .M57 2001
  635.9'0973--dc21

                                                     2001005386

First Printing 2001
Printed in the United States of America
10 9 8 7 6 5 4 3

Managing Editor: Billie Brownell
Horticultural Editor: Dennis Swartzell
Production Artist: S. E. Anderson

On the cover (clockwise from top left): Blanket Flower (Dency Kane, photographer),
Pindo Palm (Thomas Eltzroth, photographer), Golden Barrel Cactus (Charles Mann,
photographer), Penstemon (Charles Mann, photographer)

Visit the Thomas Nelson website at: www.ThomasNelson.com

Acknowledgments

secretaries. They saw a spark in this shy individual as they assisted me with the programs we initiated.

Gratitude goes out to the many who have assisted me in the community to provide accurate gardening information. They include Southwest Trees and Turf, Mojave Water Management, UNLV Arboretum, the Southern Nevada Landscape Architects Chapter, the Nevada Landscape Association, Nevada Federation of Garden Clubs, Golf Course Superintendents Association, the Southern Nevada Arborist Group, the Nevada State Department of Agriculture, and local horticulture distributors.

A special thanks goes to Dennis Swartzell of the UNLV Arboretum, who proofed the book for Horticultural accuracy, and who provided some of the text. A big thanks to Dr. Bob Stauffer for his comments and reviews of many of the chapters that transformed them into this, the book you're about to read.

Southern Nevada exploded from 200,000 people in the '60s to 1.4 million in the new millennium. Thanks is too pale a word for the encouragement and steady support of the *Las Vegas Review Journal* and KLAS TV 8 for allowing me to take the gospel of desert gardening to the ever-growing Las Vegas Valley. Very few would have ever known me had it not been for mass media.

And last, but certainly not least, my thanks to you, the reader, for having the confidence in me to use this book to help you have the best landscape ever.

—Linn Mills

I MOST LIKELY WOULD NEVER HAVE COMPLETED THIS BOOK without the help of my daughter Erin, who did all the research and writing of the plant entry introductions. It made the writing go much faster for me.

Linn Mills proved to be a valued colleague. We have had an interesting time deciding on what plants to review and what might grow

ACKNOWLEDGMENTS

where, and I think we managed to bring together a comprehensive view of gardening throughout Nevada. Linn brings life and animation to his lectures and his writing, and it has been a pleasure working with him on this book.

I would like to thank my many colleagues, particularly Wayne Johnson at the University of Nevada Cooperative Extension. We have collaborated on many projects over the years which are the foundation of my gardening experiences. I have had the opportunity to work with a great number of individuals, organizations, and communities to help them develop their gardening ideas for the good of their communities. Together we have built demonstration gardens and arboretums, and have enjoyed the fun of gardening.

For 25 years I taught ornamental horticulture at the University of Nevada, giving me the opportunity to watch my students develop their interest in horticulture. I have enjoyed their help and friendship over the years.

For thirty-two years, I have the most fun in my life as the Nevada Gardener, belting out the word on gardening throughout Northern Nevada. My thanks to KSRN, KGVM, and CPTL for putting up with my last-minute production, and for allowing me to do live shows from the beaches of the Pacific to the National Zoo in Washington, D.C., and from pay phones in not-so-glamorous parking lots of gas stations during my travels.

How can I ever thank the staff at Cool Springs Press? I don't think they thought Linn and I would be such a challenge. Thanks to Roger Waynick and Hank McBride. Billie Brownell was very patient with us and was both our drill sergeant and mentor, who gave us constant encouragement from the beginning through completion of the book.

—Dick Post

NEVADA Gardener's Guide

CONTENTS

INTRODUCTION

GARDENING IN NEVADA IS A CHALLENGE. We have wide variations in climate, changes in elevation, generally poor soils, and very dry conditions. Most visitors to the state are drawn to Nevada by gambling and bright lights of the casinos rather than by plants and beautiful gardens. They often go home without ever noticing that people garden here. But they do.

The first opinion of those making their first visit to Nevada is that it is hilly and covered with sand dunes. This couldn't be further from the truth. There are a series of mountain ranges going from north to south with high, broad valleys between them. To most of those who visit, Nevada is a vast emptiness of what appears to be barren land—that's why Highway 50 is known as the loneliest road in America. You don't see many folks traveling on it, and towns are few and far between. Well, there are some sand dunes, and even a sand mountain, and for a while camels did roam the hills. (They were used in Virginia City and then let go, and a few survived for a while in the wild.) Gardeners now have to fend off wild horses instead.

What has always intrigued us is that in each of the abandoned mining towns across the state there are some types of plants that survived for a hundred years or so on their own. Perhaps a Peach, Rhubarb, or maybe an Iris that was planted in just the right spot—a quiet reminder of what the pioneers felt they needed to survive.

Nevada is 313 miles wide (east to west) and 483 miles long (from north to south), and it is the seventh largest state. An interesting fact about Nevada is that the Federal Government owns 87 percent of the land, which is also one of the reasons development is sparse or nonexistent. Nevada lies within the Great Basin, with a small part of the southern end of the state in the Mojave Desert. The Great Basin extends from the Sierra Nevada Range on the western border into Utah on the eastern border. There are mountain ranges alternating between flat basins from one side of the state to the other.

Introduction

Within the Great Basin, there is not a stream or river originating in Nevada that leaves the state and flows to an ocean. The Humboldt River is the longest river with a continuous flow, and it starts in the northeastern part of the state and ends in a sink in western Nevada. The Truckee River starts at Lake Tahoe (which is shared with California), and flows from the mountains through Reno to end up out in the desert in Pyramid Lake. In the southern part of the state, the Colorado River travels along the border between Arizona and Nevada. Lake Mead, formed by Hoover Dam on the Colorado, is shared with Arizona.

The plants of the Great Basin are rather diverse. In the mountains, from west to east, they range from Jeffery Pine to Piñon Pine/Juniper forests in the dry interior. Sagebrush, Rabbit Brush, and Greasewood make up most of the shrubs. The imported Cheat Grass has invaded much of the grassland; it is highly flammable and a major cause of wildfires. In the southern part of the state, Yucca, Cacti, Creosote Bush, and Mesquite are a few of the native species.

NEVADA CLIMATE

To identify the hardiness of plants in this book, we have included a plant hardiness zone map adapted from the USDA Plant Hardiness Map (page 232), and have identified six zones for winter hardiness. The Heat Zone Map (page 231) was developed according to summer heat regions and relates to average high temperatures during the summer. The three heat regions are hot, high desert, and mountainous.

The climate of the state is as variable as the plants. Summer temperatures range from 105 degrees Fahrenheit in Las Vegas, the hot region (elevation, 2162 feet), to a brief high of 87 degrees Fahrenheit in Ely, the mountainous region (elevation, 6253 feet), and 95 degrees Fahrenheit in Reno, the high desert region (elevation, 4404 feet) in between. There is a wide fluctuation from daytime to nighttime temperatures in many communities as well. Reno, for example, may get to 95 degrees Fahrenheit during the day and drop to 50 degrees Fahrenheit at night. In June, Dick once experienced 100 degrees Fahrenheit during the day, and it froze that night. Las Vegas might drop 30 degrees in all. During the winter, the average temperature of Las Vegas is 55 degrees Fahrenheit with a low of 15 degrees Fahrenheit. In Ely, the average is 37 degrees Fahrenheit, and the low was minus 27 degrees Fahrenheit. Reno's average is 47 degrees Fahrenheit in the winter and the lowest temperature was minus 16 degrees Fahrenheit.

The growing season also varies greatly. Las Vegas has 265 days, Ely, 75 days, and Reno has 133 days. All the towns at elevations of over 6,000 feet, such as Eureka and Austin, will be the same as Ely, and frost has been know to occur anytime during the summer.

Precipitation differs greatly throughout the state as well. In the low-elevation areas or the hot region of southern Nevada around Las Vegas, the annual precipitation is four inches. In most of the valleys or high desert regions of the rest of the state, the annual precipitation is about eight to nine inches, and in the mountainous regions (those areas above 5000 feet), up to twenty inches. In parts of the Sierra Nevada Range, over two hundred inches of precipitation fall annually.

NEVADA GARDENING

Discussing gardening in Nevada would not be complete without discussing the soil. We refer to Nevada soils as mineral soils that are low in organic matter and nutrients. They are somewhat alkaline, and many are saline as well; both of these factors will affect the growth of plants.

SOILS

The soil of Nevada is generally clayey and poorly drained. When you are preparing the soil it is always a good idea to mix in organic mulch. In most cases, three inches worked into the soil works well,

Introduction

but this needs to be repeated year after year. Some plants may require a lighter soil, so add much more mulch to the soil for those plants.

You need to test the soil for salts and alkalinity. Check with your local Cooperative Extension Office to get an average figure for your community. If the soil is alkaline (a pH of 8.5 or greater), you need to add something, such as sulfur, to acidify the soil. Alkalinity of the soil tends to make iron unavailable, even though soil tests will not show a deficiency. In some plants, iron deficiency shows up on the new leaves as yellowing between the veins of the leaves, and bright green veins. If the soil test shows that salts are high, the only solution is to water your plants with water low in salts. There is no chemical solution for this problem. (Watering can be a problem in Nevada because some of our water is salty, too.)

NUTRIENTS

Plant nutrients are needed for good growth. Nitrogen is lost very rapidly from the soil here, and phosphorus is often low as well. Most Nevada soils will test high for potassium, so it is usually not a limiting factor for plant growth. Fertilizers are salts, so it is better to apply slightly less than recommended rather than more. We recommend a preplant fertilizer that has between 10 and 16 percent nitrogen and close to equal amounts of phosphorous and potassium. This is considered a balanced fertilizer. Combinations of bone meal, blood meal, fish emulsion, and others will give about the same results.

It is convenient to fill a one-pound coffee can with the balanced fertilizer (for example, 15-15-15) and spread the contents evenly over one-hundred square feet of garden—the equivalent of a square that measures ten feet on each side. There are many water-soluble fertilizers available on the market. We prefer one that is complete and balanced, such as 20-20-20. This means that it contains 20 percent nitrogen, 20 percent phosphorous, and 20 percent potassium.

Fresh animal manure can be used, but don't apply it any deeper than two inches per year or salt injury may occur. Packaged steer manure contains up to 10 percent salt and negligible amounts of nutrients, and it can burn plants if used in large amounts.

PLANTING

It is important when planting tree and shrubs to take a little extra time when preparing the planting hole. The best way is to dig a hole with the sides sloping in toward the bottom. Make the hole at least three times the diameter of the rootball and only as deep as the rootball to allow for better drainage and to loosen the soil for root growth into the native soil. If the sides of the hole are shiny after digging the soil, take a garden rake and scratch up the sides well before planting. There is some controversy about using soil amendments or organic matter in the backfill used to cover the rootball. The danger is that if there is more mulch than soil and the soil is poorly drained, water movement from the highly organic soil to the clay may stop completely. A little mulch, such as one part mulch to five parts soil, will not cause a problem. The important thing is to mulch around the plant after planting to keep the soil cooler and to slow evaporation.

WATERING

Irrigation of the garden is important because we just don't get those nice afternoon showers as many parts of the country do. Most of the water comes from deep wells for both domestic and municipal users. When we were evaluating the amount of water a plant uses in various parts of Nevada, we found that an acre (a football field is about an acre) of plants requires water to a depth of four feet to supply the water needs in western Nevada. This will vary a little for the high desert and mountainous parts of the state, and in southern Nevada, plants will require twelve feet of water.

Introduction

To supply that need, various water districts have developed schedules to supply the amount required and hopefully not overwater or underwater the garden. In the hot region of southern Nevada in November, December, January, and February, water the lawn two days a week, three times a day, for four minutes at a time. In the spring and fall—including March and April and then September and October—water four days a week, three times a day, for four minutes each time. In the summer—May, June, July, and August—water seven days a week, three times a day, for four minutes each time. For plants in winter, water one day a week, once a day, for twelve minutes. In spring and fall, water two days a week, once a day for twelve minutes, and in the summer, water three days a week, once a day for twelve minutes. If you have two-gallon-per-hour emitters, water for an hour each time, and if they emit one gallon per hour, water two hours each time.

In the Reno area, lawns generally don't need water between the middle of November and the middle of March. In April and May apply three-fourths of an inch of water twice a week; on June 1, one-half inch twice a week; July and August, one inch twice a week; and for September and October, back to one-half inch twice a week. In Carson City, watering is allowed every other day. Refer to the irrigation schedules in the appendices.

To ease watering demands, try to place plants with the same watering needs together, such as Petunias and Marigolds. Yucca and Pansies do not mix well because Pansies prefer a moderate amount of water and Yucca, low to none at all.

We used high, medium, and low as designations of water use for the plants in each chapter. If you live in a hot region like Las Vegas, follow the Las Vegas guide, or double the inches of water recommended. In the high desert and mountainous regions, the water guide for Reno is the one to follow.

PLANT PESTS

One of the advantages of having a very dry climate is that many diseases and insects do not bother our plants. Check your plants on a weekly basis for insects and diseases. All plants seem to get aphids at one time or another. Spider mites, which are almost microscopic, need to be scouted out as well. The mites like hot, still air, so look for them in the summer. Most of the time, if you see an insect on the plant, you can wash it off with a good stiff spray of water. If not, you need to identify the insect and use the control for that pest. There are both organic and chemical control materials available. It is also important to keep your plants healthy and to not let them become drought stressed.

Wind is something that you need to be aware of. During the summer the wind will come up at about 2:00 in the afternoon and will last into the evening. This is very common in all the valleys across the state. In Las Vegas, the wind starts around 10:00 in the morning. The wind is hot and dry and can stress plants in a matter of hours. If a plant is listed as a high water user, it needs to have protection from the wind.

PLANTING DATES

The planting dates vary from valley to valley. In Las Vegas the last killing frost in the spring is in early March, and the growing season ends with the first frost in early November. In Ely, the last frost in the spring is around the middle of June and the first frost in the fall occurs around the first of September. Reno's last spring frost is around the middle of May, and the growing season ends about the first of October.

WILDFIRES

In most all of the communities of Nevada, wildfire is a concern as new housing developments encroach on range and forested areas. It

Introduction

is important in fire-prone areas to choose plants carefully and to reduce the vegetation around homes. Dead plants and grasses are very flammable and must be removed. Shrubs don't have to be removed, but cluster them so there is space between the groupings. It is wise to have a defensible space around your home in these areas; this means a minimum of thirty feet cleared of all brush. Grass is a good plant to use in the defensible-space area.

PLANTS IN THE BOOK

How did we select the plants for this book? Well, some of them are just-plain-neat plants and some are plants that we have in our own yards. My (Dick's) yard is a jungle of everything from trees to shrubs, waterfalls, lilypads, and some flowers. The idea I had when I started was to see the lights of the city below me and to have the feeling that I was out in the woods. I overdid the last part—the bunny farm in the backyard supplies the compost, and the dog runs off the raccoons. Well, some of the time. The other selection guideline we used was whether or not you could find all these plants in the nurseries and garden centers within certain geographic limits. You won't find Palm Trees in the garden centers of Ely, for example.

Once you get over the look of the soil and get the sprinkler system installed, it's amazing how many plants grow in Nevada, and how intriguing the home landscapes can be. No matter whether you live in the hot, dry Mojave Desert of southern Nevada, or on the mountainside in Austin where the old-fashioned Yellow Rose prevails, you can enjoy gardening in Nevada.

H O W   T O   U S E   T H I S   B O O K

E ACH ENTRY IN THIS GUIDE provides you with information about a plant's characteristics, habits, and basic requirements for growth. The Plant Profile box at the top of the page summarizes some of the primary characteristics such as mature height and spread, bloom period and color if applicable, hardiness zones (the zone in which the plant is winter hardy), sunlight and water needs, and a few additional benefits. Each entry is also identified by the initials of its author.

LIGHT REQUIREMENTS

Each plant's light requirements (the amount of sunlight suitable for the plant's needs) are indicated by the following symbols. It is possible a plant can grow or thrive in more than one range of sunlight.

Full Sun   Partial Shade   Shade

WATER REQUIREMENTS

We indicate each plant's need for water, whether it is high, medium, or low, by showing one of the following icons.

High   Medium   Low

How to Use This Book

BENEFICIAL CHARACTERISTICS

Some of the additional beneficial characteristics of many of the plants we recommend are shown by the following symbols:

 Attracts Butterflies

 Long Bloom Period

 Attracts Hummingbirds

 Old-Fashioned Plant

Produces Edible Fruit

 Supports Bees

Has Fragrance

Drought Resistant

 Produces Food for Wildlife

Provides Shelter for Birds

Good for Cut Flowers

Good Fall Color

Did You Know?

Many plant entries end with a "Did You Know?" box that offers information about a plant's uses, nomenclature, history, or other information that is little known or just plain interesting!

CHAPTER ONE

Annuals

ANNUALS BY DEFINITION are plants that complete their life cycles within a year and then die. In nature the life cycle begins at the start of the growing season when the seed germinates. Marigolds, Petunias, and Zinnias are just some examples. Annuals grow large enough to produce flowers and then seeds for the next generation. Generally speaking, annuals mean *color*!

Annuals have been part of gardening for thousands of years. The Chinese created flower gardens, and China is believed to be where the Chrysanthemum originated. In Babylon, Persia, Egypt, and Greece, annuals were featured at the homes of the wealthy. Flowers were not valued in the Middle Ages, but interest reemerged because plants could be valuable for food, medicine, and other practical purposes. Even later, biological expeditions were organized to seek out new and rare flowers. During this period, flowers were introduced into Europe from Brazil, Mexico, Australia, Japan, China, and even the United States. This led to the crossing of new and interesting varieties.

Annuals can be *hardy*, *half-hardy*, or *tender*. These terms indicate the temperature ranges that various annual seeds need in order to germinate (or sprout) and grow successfully, and the plant's ability to endure freezing or sub-freezing temperatures after sprouting. These two separate criteria account for the seeming paradox of some annuals, such as the Sunflower, whose seeds survive outdoors in regions of sub-freezing winters but germinate after the last frost and produce tender plants. In this case, the seed is hardy but the plants themselves are not. Plant hardiness terms provide the two most important dates to know: the last expected frost in the spring and the first anticipated frost in the fall.

Annuals are specialists at producing seeds. They invest their energy in making as many seeds as possible during the growing

Chapter One

season and then die, often from exhaustion. They bloom more quickly, more freely, and longer than any other types of plants.

Because of their brilliant colors, annuals instantly transform a drab landscape into a refreshing scene. They represent a good starting point for the first-time gardener. You can easily correct any mistake made with annuals, and they are so versatile! Annuals provide an opportunity to grow a plant as large as your house (thinking of Sunflowers), to produce pleasant or weird color combinations, to grow edible flowers for the dinner table, or to provide an array for cut-flower arrangements.

Annuals lend themselves to container gardening as well. As home lots have become progressively smaller and buildings take priority over open spaces, many people will never have access to a full-fledged garden. But we still have window ledges, front steps, balconies, and backyards. This presents a new challenge—to become gardeners without gardens. Growing annuals in containers becomes an innovative way of doing so. We now have compact annuals, which are ideal for containers. Garden centers stock easy-to-handle soil and pottery that blends with the plant to produce a rather pleas- ing effect. Almost every style of gardening that can be expressed in a full-size garden can be replicated in a container garden.

And don't forget wildflowers—they add an exciting dimension to gardens. We all know how dramatic they are in the desert; they can also have a dramatic effect in your yard. But to duplicate a desert environment, be sure to stay away from planting everything in straight rows.

Because annuals can form a basic component of any landscape design, they are often overlooked in the planning process—but they shouldn't be, as they offer so much color and variety to any garden.

Ageratum

Ageratum houstonianum

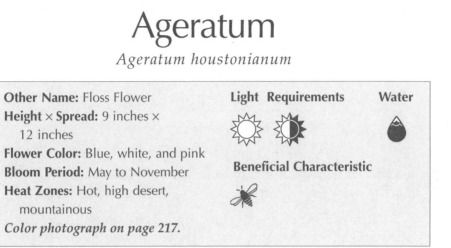

Other Name: Floss Flower	Light Requirements	Water
Height × Spread: 9 inches × 12 inches		
Flower Color: Blue, white, and pink		
Bloom Period: May to November	Beneficial Characteristic	
Heat Zones: Hot, high desert, mountainous		
Color photograph on page 217.		

Ageratum, sometimes called Floss Flower, is a great little flowering plant for edging the flower bed. The blooms have a fuzzy appearance and are produced in dense clusters that cover the entire plant from late spring into November. They are available mainly in shades of blue, but can be found in white and occasionally in pink. The Ageratum most commonly used is a dwarf cultivar called 'Blue Mink' that only grows to 9 inches high and spreads to about 12 inches in diameter. The foliage is about an inch in diameter and somewhat heart-shaped. They grow best in full sun, but in the hot region you'd better give them part shade, particularly during the hottest part of the day. (DP)

REGIONAL TIPS

Ely, which is in the mountainous region, has late spring frosts—you don't want to plant here before the first of June. Reno is located in the high desert, so you need to plant after May 15 if you want to avoid frost. Las Vegas is located in the hot region, so Ageratum can be planted here as early as February and again in the fall.

WHEN, WHERE, AND HOW TO PLANT

In the high desert and mountainous regions of the state, Ageratum should be planted after the last spring frost. The best way to plant Ageratum is to use bedding plants—its seeds will never develop if seeded directly into the garden. If you want to start your own indoors to transplant to the garden, figure on about seven weeks from sowing the seed to having a plant mature enough for transplant. Because Nevada's soils are low in organic matter and also alkaline you'll need to add organic mulch to the soil. Add 4 to 6 inches of mulch to the soil surface and till it in to a depth of 6 inches;

also add (at the same time as the mulch) the contents of a 1-pound coffee can full of a complete fertilizer containing between 10 and 16 percent nitrogen to every 100 square feet of garden. Space the plants about 8 to 10 inches apart when you transplant them, digging the holes just as deep as the rootball. Place the plant in the hole, cover with soil, and water.

CARE AND MAINTENANCE

Ageratums are carefree. After they have been planted, mulch around them with about an inch of compost. This will help keep the soil from drying out too fast and help reduce weeds as well. They need about 2 1/2 inches of water weekly, so daily watering with a drip-mist system or twice a week with a sprinkler is adequate. Use a water-soluble fertilizer once a month, according to directions, for better growth.

LANDSCAPE MERIT

Ageratum is an excellent plant for edging the flower bed or as mass plantings in flower borders. Because of its height it should be planted toward the front of the bed so taller flowers will not hide it.

ADDITIONAL SPECIES, CULTIVARS, OR VARIETIES

If you are looking for a pink Ageratum, consider 'Pinky Improved', which grows to 8 inches high. 'Summer Snow' is, as you might have guessed, a white-flowered Ageratum. Try 'Blue Danube' for the best display of lavender/blue flowers.

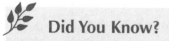

Did You Know?

I prefer the new hybrids to the old types. On the old types, new flowers open up below the brown, dried-up blooms. The new hybrids bloom above the old, spent flowers.

Calendula

Calendula officinalis

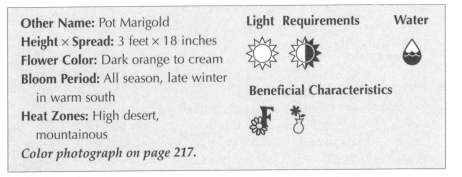

Other Name: Pot Marigold
Height × Spread: 3 feet × 18 inches
Flower Color: Dark orange to cream
Bloom Period: All season, late winter in warm south
Heat Zones: High desert, mountainous
Color photograph on page 217.

Light Requirements

Water

Beneficial Characteristics

Calendulas are very attractive flowering plants, with double or semi-double disklike flowers. The blooms grow to between 2 to 4 inches in diameter and come in shades of dark orange to cream, with the centers of the flowers often darker. The leaves are long and narrow and slightly sticky with a spicy fragrance; they can get as tall as 3 feet but most will be shorter. In the hot regions, Pot Marigolds are a welcome addition to the garden of late fall and early spring, but they don't do well at all during the hottest part of the year. The increased heat of the hot regions causes the flowers to be distorted. They will, however, tolerate dry soils even though they don't like the heat. In the high desert and mountainous regions they add lots of flowers from spring through midsummer. You can extend their flowering period by removing the spent blooms. (DP)

Regional Tips

Calendulas can be planted from seed sown directly in the soil in the fall in the hot regions of the Las Vegas area, or grown from transplants.

When, Where, and How to Plant

Plant Calendula in the spring and early summer for the high desert and mountainous regions. They tolerate temperatures slightly below freezing, and Calendulas can be planted from seed. If the soil is about 70 degrees Fahrenheit, they will take about five days to germinate. If the soil is left undisturbed, they have been known to reseed themselves in the hot regions and some of the warmer regions of the high desert. In the high desert and mountainous regions it is much more reliable to purchase Calendula bedding plants. If Calendula is directly seeded into the garden, it will never make it to flowering size. You can sow the seed inside, and in seven weeks you will have a bedding plant ready to be transplanted to the garden. For the best show, plant Calendulas in full sun or part shade. While they are not fussy about the kind of soil they require, you will get much better growth and flowers if you prepare the soil prior to planting. Add 3 inches of organic mulch and mix into the upper 5 inches of soil. The addition of a complete fertilizer goes a long way toward production of sturdy plants and lots of flowers.

Care and Maintenance
Calendulas don't require any special care and don't have pest problems. (It is even claimed that they repel ants!) While they will survive drought conditions, they will bloom much better if they receive a medium amount of moisture water twice a week to a soil depth of 6 inches. They also will do better if they get light applications of a water-soluble fertilizer every few weeks during the growing season.

Landscape Merit
Calendulas can be used as a mass planting, or planted in mixed beds. In our demonstration gardens, we used the drift approach to blend them in with other annuals. They also make excellent plants for containers. Because of their height, Calendulas make great plants for use in the center of the bed and also as accent plants. But use them sparingly as accents because they can overpower the bed. They are excellent for cut flowers and they last for a long time.

Additional Species, Cultivars, or Varieties
It is hard to find specific varieties in the garden centers, so you are limited to what is available. Seed catalogs offer a wide selection of varieties.

Flowering Kale and Cabbage

Brassica oleracea acephala

Height × Spread: 10 to 15 inches ×
  10 to 15 inches
Flower Color: Blue-green leaves;
  white, pink, red, magenta,
  or purple middle leaves (blooms
  are not ornamental)
Bloom Period: Summer (leaves)
Heat Zones: Hot, high desert,
  mountainous
Color photograph on page 217.

Light Requirement

Water

Beneficial Characteristic

Flowering Kale and Cabbage are really not flowering plants at all, but colorful foliage plants. They are considered hardy annuals, and in the warmest parts of the state they will grow outside all winter long. Even in the rest of Nevada they will continue to grow into the early winter and generally aren't killed until the temperatures dip into the teens. In fact, the foliage color will be better after the first light frost of the fall. The foliage of both Flowering Cabbage and Kale is a dark bluish-green as it matures, and the new foliage that develops in the center of the plant has various shades of red, white, magenta, pink, and purple. Viewed from above, they look like giant double roses. The difference between the Flowering Cabbage and Kale is that Kale has a slightly looser head of leaves than does Cabbage, and the leaves are ruffled more on the edges. You can use the center of the plant for a colorful, flowerlike table decoration. The leaves can be used in salads as well. (DP)

REGIONAL TIPS

Flowering Kale and Cabbage are planted in the fall in the hot regions of Nevada. Planting around September 15 yields larger leaves than planting later. In the high desert and mountainous regions they are best adapted for spring, late summer, and fall. These plants are heat sensitive and will not form leaves, but will bolt (go to seed) during the hottest part of the summer.

When, Where, and How to Plant

The only time to plant Flowering Kale and Cabbage is in the fall. For one thing, they "flower" better then. They also don't like summer heat. I have tried them in the Reno area in the summer, and they just don't do that well, even though our average temperature is about 72 degrees Fahrenheit. You can start them from seed, but it is easiest to get bedding plants. I like the 6-inch-pot size so I have an instant display. Flowering Kale and Cabbage can be planted almost anywhere, growing best in well-drained, organic soils and spaced 10 inches apart. If they are planted into containers, use houseplant soil mix—it drains well and yet is easy to keep moist. If you are planting them into the garden, dig the hole as wide as the rootball and just a little deeper, working at least 6 inches of organic compost into the top 8 inches of soil. Place the rootball in the hole and fill in soil around the rootball. They don't require much fertilizer, but if you work a fertilizer containing 10 to 16 percent nitrogen into the soil at time of planting, you get the best results.

Care and Maintenance

When the temperature is over 80 degrees Fahrenheit, watch out for aphids on the plants. This is even truer if the plants are not getting enough water and become stressed, which is why it is important to keep the soil moist. Remove dry leaves.

Landscape Merit

I have seen Flowering Kale and Cabbage planted as carpet beds using the different-colored plants to form the pattern. Some have been very elaborate, while others just spell out a greeting. They also work well in large containers, especially when other flowers are combined with them.

Gazania

Gazania species

Height × Spread: 10 inches ×
12 inches
Flower Color: Yellow, orange, white,
rose, pink, and some bicolors
Bloom Period: Late spring to early
summer; some throughout summer
Heat Zones: Hot, high desert,
mountainous
Color photograph on page 217.

Light Requirement

Water

Beneficial Characteristic

Gazanias are rather interesting plants that respond very well to sunlight. The flowers fold up at night and they even fold up on overcast days. The flowers are single and daisylike, though you can find some that are semi-double. They can be striped with contrasting shades of orange-rust or yellow. The leaves of Gazanias are long, deeply lobed, and feathery looking; dark green on the upper surface and somewhat silvery underneath. Most Gazanias form clumps or mounds to about 10 inches high and about as wide. In the hot regions of southern Nevada they grow as perennials, but in the high desert and mountainous regions they are grown as annuals. While they flower best in the late spring and early summer, they will flower off and on throughout the growing season. (DP)

REGIONAL TIPS

In the hot regions they can be planted almost anytime except during the coldest months of December and January.

WHEN, WHERE, AND HOW TO PLANT

Plant Gazanias anywhere they will get lots of sun. If you live in the hot regions of southern Nevada, plant them where you can leave them undisturbed for about three to four years if you are growing them as perennials. In the rest of the state, plant them after the last frost in the spring. Gazanias can grow in most soils and take a minimum amount of water once they are established. They can be planted from seed in the Las Vegas area, but purchasing them as bedding plants means you will have flowers much sooner than if you try to start them from seed. (In the rest of the state the only way to go is to use bedding plants.) They can also be divided about every three years in the spring, and you can make cuttings of them in the fall and grow them in a sunny window over winter and plant them back out in the garden during spring. Before you plant, mix the contents of a 1-pound coffee can full of a complete fertilizer between 10 to 16 percent nitrogen into 100 square feet of garden. (An example is a square 10 feet by 10 feet.) At the same time apply a layer of organic mulch to a depth of about 3 inches, and till both the mulch and the fertilizer into the soil.

CARE AND MAINTENANCE

Gazanias are easy to care for and don't have any pest problems. You do have to pay attention to frost, as they will freeze when temperatures get into the mid-20s. In the Ely, Eureka, and Austin areas they will not do very well because of generally cold soils throughout the growing season. In the hot regions, clumping Gazania die out very quickly from root rot if they are overwatered. Try planting the trailing varieties.

LANDSCAPE MERIT

They are ideal for those hot, bright spots in the garden and are particularly good in those narrow parking strips that are normally hard to maintain. Gazanias are great in level spots in the garden, as filler plants between shrubs, in flower beds, and as a ground cover. They are used in color bowls with a combination of other annual flowers.

ADDITIONAL SPECIES, CULTIVARS, OR VARIETIES

A few of the clumping Gazanias that are worth trying are 'Aztec Queen', a bicolor; 'Copper King'; and 'Burgundy'. One of the varieties that will remain in bloom even on dark, cloudy days is 'Moonglow'. Trailing Gazanias you might try include 'Sunglow' and 'Sunburst'.

Geranium

Pelargonium hortorum

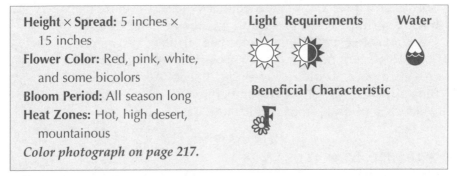

Height × Spread: 5 inches ×
  15 inches
Flower Color: Red, pink, white,
  and some bicolors
Bloom Period: All season long
Heat Zones: Hot, high desert,
  mountainous
Color photograph on page 217.

Light Requirements

Water

Beneficial Characteristic

Geraniums were once one of those old-fashioned plants that very few people grew. For the most part, plants were passed around as slips from one gardener to another. Now they are available from seed. One of the goals of the plant breeders was to develop a cultivar that could be started from seed and bloom before everyone else's. One of those cultivars was called 'Sooner'. If I remember my story correctly, it did bloom sooner, but the breeder's favorite football team was in Oklahoma. Geraniums have interesting foliage as well as attractive flowers. Zonal Geraniums have dark lines on the leaves, making them attractive even when they are not in bloom. The leaves are round and the flowers are clusters up to 4 or more inches in diameter. The individual flowers are about 3/4 inch in diameter, but some have blooms larger than 1 inch. Once Geraniums start to bloom they continue blooming throughout the season, and all have a spicy fragrance. (DP)

REGIONAL TIPS

Geraniums grow everywhere in the state. They start out a little sensitive to cold in the spring but by fall they will survive temperatures to slightly below freezing.

WHEN, WHERE, AND HOW TO PLANT

Geraniums can be planted out in the garden after the last killing frost. They do best in full sun but will still flower well in partial shade. In the hot regions, provide some afternoon shade. I've had very good success with both morning sun and a southwestern exposure that gets really hot. They can be grown in any part of Nevada, particularly when planted in containers. At elevations over 6,000 feet, containers allow you to bring them in if it looks like a frost. You can plant Geraniums from seed if you start them in March, but the best way is to purchase them as bedding plants and transplant directly into the garden. (I prefer the 4-inch pots because they have already started to bloom—you get instant color.) They really need a soil high in organic matter to do their best, so spread 6 inches of organic mulch on the soil along with some fertilizer and till to a depth of 6 inches. When transplanting them to the garden, space them about 12 inches apart; but if you are designing a container garden, Geraniums look best planted about 8 inches apart.

CARE AND MAINTENANCE

Geraniums are easy to care for and generally have few pest problems. There is a worm that attacks the flower buds just as they are starting to bloom. The only thing I've found to control this insect is a systemic insecticide. The other pest to which Geraniums are susceptible is dodder. This is a parasitic plant that has yellow stems that twine around the host's leaves and stems. The only control for dodder is to get the infested plants out of the garden and into the trash as soon as possible—don't put infested plants in your compost pile! Water Geraniums twice weekly and use a water-soluble fertilizer once a month, according to directions.

LANDSCAPE MERIT

Geraniums are effective when used in flower beds and containers, and are excellent in flower pots on the patio or as an accent at the front door. (They are one of the major plants that fill the various pots and whiskey barrels around the Post yard.) Ivy Geraniums also work very well in hanging baskets.

Lobelia

Lobelia erinus

Height × Spread: 8 inches × 8 inches, some trailing to 1 foot
Flower Color: Mainly light blue to violet, some pink or white
Bloom Period: Early summer until frost
Heat Zones: Hot, high desert, mountainous
Color photograph on page 217.

Light Requirements

Water

*L*obelia erinus is an annual with flowers very similar to Salvia, only smaller. The flowers are about ⅓ inch across, with the predominant color a light blue. The compact varieties grow to about 6 inches in height and just as wide. The ones I like the best are the trailing Lobelias. A 12-inch basket full of these flowers is outstanding for any outdoor living area, whether it's the deck, patio, or even the front stoop. They can also be used as a ground cover plant in planters. Once you see a pot full of Lobelias overflowing the container, you'll want them every year. (DP)

REGIONAL TIPS

In the hot regions such as the Las Vegas area they will do a little better under shady conditions, and can also be planted in early spring. Lobelias take a little extra care in the high desert of Nevada because they are more heat sensitive.

WHEN, WHERE, AND HOW TO PLANT

In the northern—high desert and mountainous—region of the state, plant Lobelias after the last killing frost in the spring. They grow equally well in full sun or partial shade, with the best location being where they get morning sun and protection from the afternoon sun. (The hottest time of the day is around 4:00 p.m.) They are great for edging but need to be planted about 6 inches apart. Because of their moisture requirement, they should not be planted with flowers that like a drier site. Lobelias can be started from seed, but it takes two months to get a good, sturdy transplant, and they need to be started indoors. But it's best to plant them as bedding plants. Lobelias like good, rich soil with lots of organic matter. If planting in a container, the best soil will be a houseplant mix that drains well yet retains moisture. (I put at least 6 plants in a 12-inch basket for the end result of solid color.) If planting them into the garden, add a layer of organic mulch to a depth of at least 3 inches and mix thoroughly into the top 6 inches of soil. Adding a complete fertilizer between 10 to 16 percent nitrogen also helps; use a 1-pound coffee can filled to the brim for every 100 square feet of garden.

CARE AND MAINTENANCE

Lobelias have very few pests, but aphids can be a problem, particularly if the plants get stressed. If they are planted in containers, fertilize with a water-soluble fertilizer about every month throughout the growing season. And, oh yes, a reminder: They need to be watered once a day (twice daily when temperatures are in the 100s) when container grown.

LANDSCAPE MERIT

Lobelias add a nice contrast to the garden or to hanging baskets with delicate flowers and fine foliage.

ADDITIONAL SPECIES, CULTIVARS, OR VARIETIES

The most popular of the compact Lobelias is 'Crystal Palace' with deep blue flowers; it makes a great little edging plant for flower beds. 'Rosemond' has red flowers, 'White Lady' has white, 'Blue Cascade' is the easiest of the trailing Lobelias to find in the garden centers, and 'Sapphire' is also a nice one. There are also some perennial Lobelias that are not that widely used: One is the Cardinal Flower, which grows to 4 feet tall and is very hardy, but is a bog plant, so it's not adapted to the desert; another is *L. syphilitica,* which is also very hardy but requires substantial water to survive.

Marigold

Tagetes erecta

<table>
<tr><td>

Height × Spread: 3 feet × 18 inches
Flower Color: Yellow to gold,
    orange, rust, and even white
Bloom Period: Early summer to frost
Heat Zones: Hot, high desert,
    mountainous
Color photograph on page 217.

</td><td>

Light Requirement

Beneficial Characteristic

</td><td>

Water

</td></tr>
</table>

Marigolds used to be one of those flowers that could be used anywhere in the garden as long as you wanted yellow-orange flowers. Now there is a true white Marigold called French Vanilla Hybrid that grows to 2 feet high and has 3-inch blooms—the blooms range in size from 2 inches up to over 4½ inches. *T. erecta* is divided into French and American types. The American is the tallest and gets up to 3 feet high with full, double flowers. The French Marigolds are medium to dwarf in size. They grow to between 10 and 12 inches high and feature single or double flowers. They can be used for cut flowers and have a very strong scent that tends to make some people sneeze, but a scentless one has now been developed. The foliage is lacelike and dark green in color. They are favorites throughout Nevada and will grow anywhere. (DP)

REGIONAL TIPS

Marigolds are not hardy at all, so watch out for those late frosts in the mountainous and high desert regions.

WHEN, WHERE, AND HOW TO PLANT

This is one plant often replanted because of late frosts. It's also the first annual to be lost to frost in the fall. In the Las Vegas area it's safe to plant them in early spring, and in late spring everywhere else. Plant them in full sun. Marigolds are easy to plant from seed, and while they will often start when seeded directly into the garden, they do much better started indoors and transplanted into the garden after the last frost in the spring. No special soil preparation is needed to grow them, but as with any garden, you get the best results when organic mulch is tilled into the soil. In the cooler parts of Nevada they will self-seed when the spring is mild. Because most

Marigolds are hybrids, you are going to be in for a surprise when the seed from last year's crop starts to flower. Some of the flowers will revert to the traits of the parents and you will see orange and yellow fuzz balls in the garden. This is particularly true if the seed is from plants that grew from plants that grew from those planted two years ago.

CARE AND MAINTENANCE

Marigolds are very easy to care for. They don't have any insect or disease problems and, particularly in the cooler regions of the state, require only a medium amount of water. Because of their odor, they are considered natural insect repellents.

LANDSCAPE MERIT

Marigolds adapt anywhere in the garden. They can be planted in drifts with other flowers or planted in beds of Marigolds only. As with any planting, place the taller plants in the back of the bed and the shorter ones in the front. Dwarf Marigolds make a good edging for flower beds and can also be used in containers.

ADDITIONAL SPECIES, CULTIVARS, OR VARIETIES

Some varieties of the American Marigolds are 'Climax', 'Perfection', and 'Lady'. French hybrids, *T. patula*, include 'Grand Prix', 'Jaguar', and 'Bonanza'. There are also some specialty Marigolds that are interesting to have in the garden. One of these is Irish Lace, *T. filifolia*. It has been around for a long time but is still a neat little plant, with fine, lacy, dark-green foliage making a great little round mound to 6 inches tall, and with tiny white flowers in the summer and fall.

Moss Rose

Portulaca grandiflora

Height × Spread: 6 inches × 16 inches	Light Requirement	Water
Height × Spread: 6 inches × 16 inches **Flower Color:** Red, pink, orange, yellow, white, and pastel colors **Bloom Period:** Early summer to frost **Heat Zones:** Hot, high desert, mountainous *Color photograph on page 217.*	☼	◐

Moss Rose got its name from the shape of the flower—when it opens, it looks like the blossom of single rose. The flowers grow to 2 inches in diameter and are single for the most part, but there are a few varieties that form double flowers. The colors of the flowers are clear and bright shades of red, white, yellow, orange, and pink; there are even some in pastel shades. The growth of the plant is somewhat trailing with reddish branches, and the succulent leaves are tubular and get up to an inch long. Moss Rose is another flower that has to have full sun in order to bloom. The flowers close in the late afternoon and open again with the morning sun. For as delicate as the flower looks, Moss Rose is tough and takes the heat and dry conditions well. (DP)

REGIONAL TIPS

Moss Rose is a great plant for all the regions of the state, and it will tolerate not only the heat but a little cool temperature as well.

WHEN, WHERE, AND HOW TO PLANT

Moss Roses love it hot and don't grow very well until the soil warms up, so plant them after the last frost in the spring. In the cooler part of the state the temperature drops to the low 50s, resulting in slow germination. If you want to start Moss Roses from seed (even though transplants are best), plan on about seven weeks when growing them indoors, from the sowing of the seed to growth of a sturdy transplant. They will grow in any type of soil but grow best in somewhat sandy, well-drained soil. Prepare the soil by adding 3 inches of mulch and mixing it thoroughly into the garden soil. Mix in a complete garden fertilizer that contains between 10 and 16 percent nitrogen at the time of tilling; the contents of a 1-pound coffee can filled with a complete fertilizer, for 100 square feet of garden, is plenty. Use a formula between 10 to 16 percent nitrogen.

CARE AND MAINTENANCE

Moss Roses are pretty carefree. They are considered very drought tolerant in most places, but in all areas in Nevada they need a good soaking about once or twice a week or even three times a week in the hot regions.

LANDSCAPE MERIT

It is the ideal flower for those hot spots in the garden such as dry banks, rock gardens, and small, sunny pockets. Moss Rose plants also make a great little ground cover. Because of their trailing habit they are ideal for hanging baskets, and are also great when planted in shallow terra-cotta bowls placed on the patio.

ADDITIONAL SPECIES, CULTIVARS, OR VARIETIES

A few of the varieties available are 'Magic Carpet', 'Sunglo', and 'Sunkiss'. The 'Giant Radiance' series is known for semi-double flowers that will grow to over 2 inches across.

Did You Know?

Moss Roses have a very close relative that is one of the black sheep of the garden. Purslane, P. oeracea, is a very hard weed to eliminate, with its succulent tubular leaves and a habit of spreading out like a mat. Rather than bright, multicolored flowers, Purslane has tiny yellow flowers producing thousands of seeds. It's best to hoe them out before they go to seed, but you also have to nearly vacuum the garden afterward, because any leaves left behind will be a newly rooted plant in a few days. If you're adventuresome, the leaves make a fair substitute for watercress in your summer salad, with a similar biting taste.

Pansy

Viola × wittrockiana

Height × Spread: 4 to 9 inches × 12 inches	**Light Requirements**	**Water**
Flower Color: White, purple, red, orange, and yellow; dark face		
Bloom Period: Early spring to late fall	**Beneficial Characteristic**	
Heat Zones: High desert, mountainous		
Color photograph on page 217.		

Pansies are cheerful additions to Nevada's gardens, taking the cold of winter and starting to flower early in the spring. While they are considered annuals, in the northwestern part of the state they will often persist for two or three years. The older varieties of Pansies were heat sensitive and subject to attack from mites, but newer varieties have resistance to heat. In the hot region of southern Nevada they are used as a winter flower, but they have problems as soon as the summer heat sets in. Pansies are best known for their "faces." Though the flower may be white, red, orange, purple, or yellow, it's the dark blotch in the center that look like the eyes and a mouth everyone looks for. The plants only get to about 9 inches high but can easily spread to over 12 inches, with the flowers 2 to 3 inches in diameter. The foliage is dark green and the leaves are spade-shaped with rounded teeth. (DP)

REGIONAL TIPS

Pansies are best adapted to the cooler parts of the high desert and to all of the mountainous regions. At high elevations like Ely and Eureka, spring planting will be the most successful. In southern Nevada they have to be planted in the late fall after temperatures have dropped below 80 degrees Fahrenheit.

WHEN, WHERE, AND HOW TO PLANT

Plant Pansies in the fall in the northwestern and southern parts of the state and they'll start flowering in early spring. They cannot be successfully planted from seed sown directly into the garden, so it is best to plant them as transplants, which are most readily available in the early spring. Pansies can be planted most anywhere. If they have morning sun, they will be happy all summer long because they will be protected from the hot afternoon sun. Pansies like a good, rich soil that has a lot of organic matter in it. For Nevada gardens this means applying a 4- to 5-inch layer of organic mulch to the soil and mixing it into the top 6 inches. It is a good idea to apply a complete fertilizer at the same time so both the organic matter and the fertilizer will be worked into the soil. Fill a 1-pound coffee can full of a complete fertilizer that contains between 10 and 16 percent nitrogen and apply it to 100 square feet of garden. Place the plants 6 inches apart. Dig the hole as deep as the rootball, cover with soil, and give it a good soaking after planting.

CARE AND MAINTENANCE

Pansies need moist soil to do their best. Use a water-soluble fertilizer about every three weeks during the growing season for best growth and flowering; mix according to directions on the label. Some of the heat-tolerant varieties will grow with less water. Pansies do have insect and disease problems when they get heat stressed—both powdery mildew and spider mites attack when it gets hot. The new heat-resistant Pansies are not as susceptible and will usually make it through the summer. The Violas, Pansies without faces, also have better heat resistance.

LANDSCAPE MERIT

Use them anywhere in the garden. At home Pansies end up in planters, whiskey barrel–halves, and flowerpots, and scattered around in flower beds.

ADDITIONAL SPECIES, CULTIVARS, OR VARIETIES

The 'Universal' variety is one of the heat-resistant types; 'Pacific Giant' is an old variety with large flowers but no heat resistance.

Petunia

Petunia × hybrida

Height × Spread: 10 to 18 inches × 18 inches	Light Requirement	Water

Height × Spread: 10 to 18 inches × 18 inches

Flower Color: Violet, pink, red, purple, yellow, white, and bicolors

Bloom Period: Late spring to first frost

Heat Zones: Hot, high desert, mountainous

Color photograph on page 217.

Light Requirement

Water

Beneficial Characteristic

Petunias are the universal flowers for Nevada. They grow almost any-where and will provide lots of color throughout the entire growing season. The traditional Multifloras are always an excellent choice and can be found in over fifteen color combinations with flowers that are solid color to bicolor. While their flowers are a little smaller, they have a lot more of them. The flowers completely cover the foliage when in full bloom. The Grandifloras have larger flowers that are single and double as well. They also come in all the Petunia colors. The single flowers on Petunias are funnel-shaped, opening up into a wide brim. The doubles look somewhat like carnation flowers. Another popular type is the Cascade, which has long stems that will flow over the sides of a container or over the edge of a retaining wall. They have the largest single flowers, 5 inches across. The leaves are broad and a good, solid green, but a little on the sticky side—a small problem in windy, dusty spots because the dust has a tendency to stick to the leaves. (DP)

REGIONAL TIPS

In the hot regions, plant them from late fall to early winter, and in the rest of Nevada, plant after the last spring frost.

WHEN, WHERE, AND HOW TO PLANT

Plant Petunias as bedding plants. Petunia seeds are so small that it is hard to grow your own, so transplanting is best. Once established, they can withstand a light frost. They will grow best in full sun, in almost any (including alkaline) soil. They grow better if the soil has been amended with an organic mulch applied 3 inches deep and tilled into the soil. Work in some fertilizer at the same time. Space the plants about 15 inches apart, dig all the holes a little deeper than the rootballs, then toss the plants in the holes, cover the roots with soil, and give them a good soaking afterwards. Pinch the terminal bud after you plant to force more buds, resulting in bushier plants.

CARE AND MAINTENANCE

Petunias need a moderate amount of water and once established they will do fine on two good soakings a week. Fertilize them about every three weeks throughout the growing season with a water-soluble fertilizer mixed according to directions. One of the most important things to do is to remove the flowers as they wilt to keep Petunias looking fresh. Pinch off the old blooms or they will turn into straggly stems with a flower here and there. Pinching off old blooms not only makes the plants look better, but they will continue to flower until frost. If you don't, they will have only a few flowers at the ends of the flower stalks. Petunias have few pest problems. Verticilium wilt will kill them if planted in the same spot, and dodder attacks them also, but it is rare. (Dodder is a parasitic plant, a dark yellow thread twining through and over the plants; you must pull up the infected plants and destroy them.)

LANDSCAPE MERIT

Petunias are very versatile and fit anywhere in the garden. In our demonstration garden we plant them in drifts of solid colors. They are also great in hanging baskets, beds, and planter boxes. One popular use of Petunias is in color bowls: 14-inch shallow containers filled with a variety of flowers including Petunias. When purchased in 4-inch pots, they provide instant color.

Phlox

Phlox drummondii

	Light Requirement	Water
Other Name: Annual Phlox **Height × Spread:** 6 to 20 inches × 10 to 15 inches **Flower Color:** White, pink, red, and bicolors **Bloom Period:** Early summer to frost **Heat Zones:** Hot, high desert, mountainous *Color photograph on page 217.*	☀	💧

Phlox have clusters of showy flowers covering the entire plant throughout the growing season. The individual flowers are only about an inch in diameter, but the flower clusters are 4 inches in diameter. They are available in a variety of colors that include mauve, light and dark red, pink, white, crimson, peach, buff, yellow, and purple-blue. Some varieties have contrasting colors in the center of the flowers (for example, white with a tinge of red in the center). The foliage of this plant is covered with sticky hairs. Phlox grows as high as 20 inches, and there is a dwarf variety which grows only to 6 inches high. (DP)

REGIONAL TIPS

They can survive the winter as long as the temperature doesn't fall below 0 degrees Fahrenheit.

WHEN, WHERE, AND HOW TO PLANT

Plant after the last frost in the spring in the high desert and mountainous regions, and in fall in the hot regions of Nevada. Phlox will withstand hot temperatures, but when it is hot, don't expect the flowers to last very long. This outstanding plant blooms best when placed in full sun. Phlox grows best in a well-drained soil with lots of organic matter yet will tolerate almost any soil. But the plants are no exception to the benefits of good soil preparation: add at least 3 inches of organic mulch to the soil and till in to a depth of 6 inches. Because they are heavy feeders, add the contents of a 1-pound coffee can of a complete fertilizer with 10 to 16 percent nitrogen for every 100 square feet of garden soil, tilled in at the same time as mixing in the mulch. (This amount of fertilizer adds about 1 pound of actual nitrogen per 100 square feet.) You can start them from seed, but I guess my impatience shows when it come to planting seed, because I would rather get them at the garden shop and transplant them into the garden so I can enjoy the flowers much sooner. Space them about 10 inches apart and dig the holes as deep as the rootballs and a little wider. Drop the plant in the hole, cover the rootball with soil, and give it a good soaking.

CARE AND MAINTENANCE

These plants don't require any special care. Water them to a depth of 6 inches two times a week for best growth and flowering. If the temperatures are over 100 degrees Fahrenheit, water them three times a week. They will continue to flower better if you pinch off the spent flowers, thus forcing them to produce new growth.

LANDSCAPE MERIT

The plants are great additions to flower beds and border plantings. One of the neatest plantings I have seen was a row of tall Phlox planted in front of a brick wall of an old mansion in Virginia City. The taller ones are very effective when planted in groups or clusters of the same color. Dwarf varieties are nice when used in color bowls: shallow bowls 14 inches in diameter filled with a variety of flowers. Dwarf types also make good edging plants in the flower bed, because they don't get over 6 inches high.

Scarlet Sage

Salvia splendens

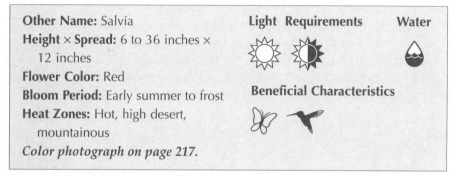

Other Name: Salvia	Light Requirements	Water
Height × Spread: 6 to 36 inches × 12 inches		
Flower Color: Red		
Bloom Period: Early summer to frost	Beneficial Characteristics	
Heat Zones: Hot, high desert, mountainous		
Color photograph on page 217.		

S carlet Sage is one of the best red flowers you can find for the garden. They flower on spikes extending above the foliage, with tubular-shaped flowers that flare out at the ends. Other Salvia species not only come in red, but in purple, white, lavender, salmon, and pink. The foliage is bright green. There are some very good dwarfs that don't grow any higher then 5 inches; they are very reliable and will bloom throughout the summer until frost. (DP)

REGIONAL TIPS

Scarlet Sage looks hot and likes it hot as well. It grows equally well in the hot, high desert, and mountainous regions.

WHEN, WHERE, AND HOW TO PLANT

Plant them during mid-spring, in the cooler regions of the state, and early spring in the warmer regions. They can be started from seed sown directly in the garden, but in the high desert and mountainous regions it's better to use bedding plants. They are tolerant of intense heat, so they are great for the hottest spots of the garden. Scarlet Sage does best in a well-drained soil with lots of organic matter. When preparing the soil, add a 6-inch layer of organic mulch to the soil and till in to a depth of 6 inches. Because the plants are also considered heavy feeders, add fertilizer before tilling in the organic mulch so it will all be mixed into the soil at the same time. The easiest way to add the fertilizer is to fill a 1-pound coffee can to the top with a complete fertilizer containing 10 to 16 percent nitrogen and apply to 100 square feet of garden. (If all you can find is 20-20-20 fertilizer, fill the can half full for every 100 square feet.) Plant them about 8 to 10 inches apart. I dig the holes first so they are a little wider than the rootball of the plant, but the same depth. I toss one in each hole, backfill around the roots, and after I've planted them, I give them all a good soaking.

CARE AND MAINTENANCE

They don't require any special care and don't have any pest problems. Scarlet Sage is tolerant of some drought, but the plants will flower better if they get a deep watering of about 3 inches a week.

LANDSCAPE MERIT

Scarlet Sage can be used anywhere in the garden. Because it is a spike flower, use it as an accent. Dwarf varieties are often used in the center of color bowls, and when they are surrounded with Petunias and dwarf Annual Phlox, they really stand out. They also look great in planter boxes and whiskey barrels. Because they will flower in areas with part shade, I use them as a solid planting under my Oak tree.

ADDITIONAL SPECIES, CULTIVARS, OR VARIETIES

There are a number of varieties available from seed. A couple are: 'Flare', growing 20 inches high, with bright, clear-red flowers; and 'St. John's Fire', a dwarf variety that has red flowers.

Did You Know?

There are a lot of other Salvia *species that are used for landscaping, but they are often hard to find. Some are woody shrubs such as Mexican Bush Sage. This plant is not hardy in the north, however. The Garden Sage,* Salvia officinalis, *is the Sage you use for seasoning the Thanksgiving turkey dressing.*

Snapdragon

Antirrhinum majus

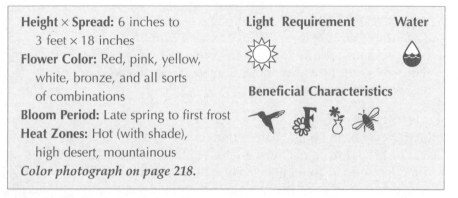

Height × Spread: 6 inches to 3 feet × 18 inches	Light Requirement	Water
Flower Color: Red, pink, yellow, white, bronze, and all sorts of combinations		
Bloom Period: Late spring to first frost	Beneficial Characteristics	
Heat Zones: Hot (with shade), high desert, mountainous		
Color photograph on page 218.		

Snapdragons are the fun flowers of the garden. The typical flowers start tubular-shaped at the stems and are topped off with upper and lower "jaws." However, if you look at the flowers of the double-flowered Snapdragons, they take on the appearance of bell flowers. Then to confuse things even more, Butterfly Snapdragons look somewhat like Azalea flowers. They come in a variety of colors, including red, yellow, white, pink, orange, and some bicolor combinations. They are available in dwarfs like 'Tom Thumb', which never gets higher then 6 inches, to the 'Double Supreme' that grows to 30 inches high. Snapdragons are spike flowers, and the flowers are above the foliage. Of all the varieties, I still like the old 'Rocket' best. As a kid, I had a quarter acre of them that I used to supply all the neighborhood parties. (I even caught a professor's wife picking them at 2:00 in the morning—but that's another story.) (DP)

REGIONAL TIPS

In the hot regions of the state, Snapdragons need part shade during the hottest part of the day. Snapdragons can be perennials but are usually treated as annuals. In my garden they will often survive the winter, but they generally don't flower all that well the second year.

WHEN, WHERE, AND HOW TO PLANT

In the hot regions, plant Snapdragons in the early fall before the nighttime temperatures drop below 50 degrees Fahrenheit, and they will flower for most of the winter. In the other regions, plant them in the late spring. If you want to have a ready supply of cut flowers, plant them in rows where they get lots of sunlight. Snapdragons grow best in a good, rich soil. Spread a 3-inch layer of organic mulch over the soil along with 1 pound of a complete fertilizer per 100 square feet, and till the mulch and fertilizer into the top 6 inches of soil. They can be started from seed, but the best way to plant them is as bedding plants. I don't make a lot of fuss over transplanting. Just dig the hole, toss in the rootball, fill around the rootball with soil, and move on to the next plant, spacing them about 15 inches apart.

CARE AND MAINTENANCE

Snapdragons are easy to take care of. Because they are somewhat heavy feeders, apply a water-soluble fertilizer about every three weeks during the growing season, mixed according to directions. Apply 1 inch of water twice a week in the cooler regions or water daily during the heat of summer in the hot regons.

LANDSCAPE MERIT

The tall ones are great accent plants. I like to plant them in groups toward the back of the bed with shorter plants around them. The dwarfs make good edging plants and are a nice contrast with other edging plants, like Alyssum. I also plant them in containers along with lower-growing flowers. If you have children (or are just young at heart), plant them where children can reach out and touch them and squeeze the throats so that the "jaws" of the flowers will open.

ADDITIONAL SPECIES, CULTIVARS, OR VARIETIES

Some of the tall Snapdragons are 'Pinnacle' and 'Rocket'. Dwarf varieties include 'Tom Thumb', 'Floral Carpet', and 'Magic Carpet'. If you want to try one of the bell-flowered types, try 'Bright Butterflies'. 'Madame Butterfly' (30 inches tall) and 'Sweetheart' (12 inches tall) are azalea-flowered types.

Stock

Matthiola incana

Height × Spread: 12 to 30 inches × 8 to 12 inches **Flower Color:** White, cream, pink, lavender, red, and purple **Bloom Period:** Spring to early fall; winter in hot regions **Heat Zones:** Hot (in winter), high desert, mountainous *Color photograph on page 218.*	**Light Requirements** ☀ ◑ **Beneficial Characteristics** ✿ ⚘ 🐝	**Water** 💧

Stocks are perennials that are grown as annuals. They flower on spikes in loose clusters ranging in height from 12 inches to 3 feet. The flowers are either single or double and can be up to an inch in diameter. They bloom in red, white, cream, pink, purple, and lavender. The blues and reds have purple highlights that make them appear to glow, and all have a very nice fragrance that is spicy sweet. The fact that they have a good fragrance and that they keep well makes them one of the best cut flowers, and one that turns up in the Post house from time to time. Stocks have large, oblong leaves that grow to over 4 inches long. (DP)

Regional Tips

Stocks are king in Las Vegas where they flourish in the hotel gardens all winter long, providing the temperatures don't dip too low. You don't want to plant them too late in the fall, because flower development will be delayed; they have a tendency to grow but not bloom if nights get too cold.

When, Where, and How to Plant

In all but the hot parts of the state Stocks are planted in the early spring. They do withstand a moderate amount of frost, growing best in the cooler part of the growing season and generally not flowering when the temperatures climb over 90 degrees Fahrenheit. The shorter Stocks show up in color bowls that appear in the garden centers in early May. They prefer full sun but will tolerate partial shade, and they need a soil with good drainage, because they can get root rot if it is poorly drained. They do best when planted in slightly alkaline soil. Because Nevada soils are notoriously low in organic matter, add 6 inches of organic mulch to the surface, along with the contents of a 1-pound coffee can filled with a complete fertilizer containing 10 to 16 percent nitrogen. Mix it thoroughly into the top 6 inches of soil. Stocks can be started from seed indoors and transplanted out to the garden, but it is easier to purchase bedding plants and transplant them directly into the garden. Space the tall ones 10 inches apart and the short ones 8 inches apart. After planting, give them a good soaking.

CARE AND MAINTENANCE
Give Stocks one inch of water twice a week. Don't overwater, because of their susceptibility to root rot. They need lots of nutrients to really do their best, so apply a water-soluble fertilizer about every three weeks, mixing the fertilizer according to directions. Also, remove spent flowers.

LANDSCAPE MERIT
Stocks can be planted anywhere. You will find them doing equally well in planters, raised beds, border plantings, and even containers. They also make excellent accents in the garden.

ADDITIONAL SPECIES, CULTIVARS, OR VARIETIES
There are many varieties of Stocks to choose from. The double 'Giant' and 'Column' Stocks are unbranched and excellent for cutting. The 'Giant Imperial' is branched, as is the 'Ten Weeks' Stock, which is the parent of the annual varieties. *Mathiola longipetala bicornis*, the 'Night Blooming' Stock, only grows to 12 inches high and has small, single flowers that curl up during the day and come out at night. They are very good for edging and, true to their name, they are even more fragrant in the evening.

Sunflower

Helianthus annuus

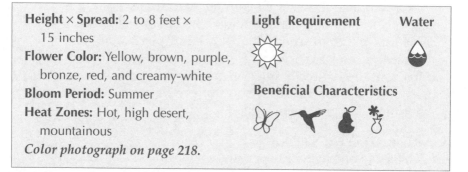

Height × Spread: 2 to 8 feet ×
 15 inches
Flower Color: Yellow, brown, purple,
 bronze, red, and creamy-white
Bloom Period: Summer
Heat Zones: Hot, high desert,
 mountainous
Color photograph on page 218.

Light Requirement

Water

Beneficial Characteristics

Sunflowers have become really popular, and there are literally dozens of varieties to choose from. They are particularly fun for kids. The big game with my kids was to see who could raise the tallest Sunflower. If the flower heads were huge, that was okay too. They produce large, disklike flowers with the ray petals radiating out from a brown center. Most Sunflowers have single flowers, but doubles are available. The traditional color is yellow, but you can get them in shades of orange, red-brown, and mahogany, as well as creamy-white, purple, and bronze. A few have tinges of differing colors on the petals. 'Strawberry Blonde' is a good example of this. Each petal starts out from the center as yellow, blending to a rose color, then back to yellow at the tip. The first thing that strikes you about Sunflowers, besides how tall they get, is the size of the flowers. The one we are most familiar with always shows up at the county fair flower show—it has flowers that grow to over 1½ feet in diameter. Sunflowers range in height from 15 inches up to 8 feet, and flower size can vary from the large-flowered down to those 3 inches across. The roasted seeds, by the way, make a great snack. The problem is that the birds aren't choosy and seem to know when seeds are ready, just before we do. (DP)

REGIONAL TIPS
Sunflowers can be grown throughout Nevada. In the hot regions, plant in early spring.

WHEN, WHERE, AND HOW TO PLANT
Sunflowers like lots of sunlight. They are planted from seed sown in the spring according to directions on the package label. They will grow in almost any soil, but they will grow better if you add some

organic mulch to the soil and work it in. They don't require much fertilizer. Once they have germinated, thin them to about 2 feet apart.

CARE AND MAINTENANCE

Sunflowers need 2 inches of water a week once they start to flower, even though they are tolerant of heat and drought. The taller varieties need to be staked, particularly if they are growing in a windy spot. As you are fertilizing other flowers during the summer, you can fertilize them as well.

LANDSCAPE MERIT

There is a Sunflower for almost any situation. The tall ones make great background plants as well as temporary windbreaks. If you are planting them for the birds, plant where you can observe the birds with little disturbance. Some of the varieties are fantastic for cut flowers, so plant them where you can harvest the flowers without ruining the display in the garden. The dwarf varieties are ideal for border plantings and can even be used in containers. 'Indian Blanket' is one that is pollen-free and was developed to be used as a cut flower.

ADDITIONAL SPECIES, CULTIVARS, OR VARIETIES

Now you can get a Sunflower for every purpose. If you want dwarfs, try 'Mini-sun' or 'Elf'. If you like to feed the birds then you must try 'Soraya', which is, by the way, the first Sunflower ever to become an All-America Selections Winner. 'Sunset' and 'Tangina' also attract birds. 'Go Bananas' with this one as a cut flower, or try 'Parasol Mix'. If you want to eat the seeds, then 'Mammoth' is the one for you.

Sweet Alyssum

Lobularia maritima

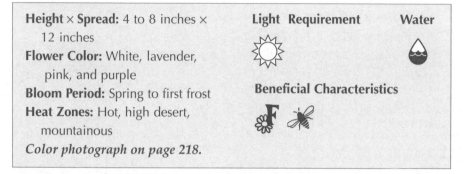

Height × Spread: 4 to 8 inches ×
    12 inches
Flower Color: White, lavender,
    pink, and purple
Bloom Period: Spring to first frost
Heat Zones: Hot, high desert,
    mountainous
Color photograph on page 218.

Light Requirement

Water

Beneficial Characteristics

Sweet Alyssum is one of the most reliable edging plants you can get for Nevada gardens. The plants are very tolerant of cold temperatures and when the winters are mild they will continue to flower late into the fall. They form very nice low-growing ground cover plants, with lance-shaped foliage that grows about ½ to 1 inch long, and tiny flowers with four petals in tight clusters. When Sweet Alyssum is in bloom all you can see are the flowers. The most common flower color is white, but you can also get them in pink, lavender, and purple. One of the most interesting things about this flower is how sensitive it is to sunlight. If half the plant is in the sun and the other half is in the shade, only the side in the sun will have flowers. It will flower, however, if it gets a little light shade. The flowers have a slight fragrance and attract bees to the garden. (DP)

REGIONAL TIPS
They will do very well in the Las Vegas area through most of the winter, acting more like perennials.

WHEN, WHERE, AND HOW TO PLANT
Plant in full sun. Sweet Alyssum can be planted in the spring as bedding plants; in the warmer parts of the state they will often reseed themselves. Sweet Alyssum is easy to start from seed in the hot regions, but seeding directly into the soil is usually disappointing for gardeners in the cooler regions of Nevada. They might germinate, but because of the cool nighttime temperatures, flowering is delayed—so use bedding plants and transplant them into the garden. They will grow in most soils, but all plants fare better if you add 3 inches of organic material to our tight desert soils, tilled in to a

depth of 6 inches. Though Alyssums are not heavy feeders, they will get off to a better start if you incorporate some general-purpose fertilizer into the soil at the same time you till in the mulch.

CARE AND MAINTENANCE
Sweet Alyssum is very carefree and is not bothered by garden pests. By the end of the summer, flowering might start to slow down, so give the plants a light shearing and in a short time you'll be enjoying a new crop of flowers. They can withstand some drought and hot weather. For best growth give them 1 inch of water at least twice a week.

LANDSCAPE MERIT
Because of its height, use Sweet Alyssum as a ground cover, as well as an edging plant in the flower bed. It makes a great rock garden plant. If you have pavers or flagstone pathways, it is very attractive as filler between them. Use Sweet Alyssum in planters and containers and hanging baskets and let the plants drape over the sides. It's also very common for use in color bowls when used with other plants.

ADDITIONAL SPECIES, CULTIVARS, OR VARIETIES
The old standby is the 'Carpet of Snow', which grows to between 2 and 4 inches tall. It has been around for a long time. 'Rosie O'Day' is another one that has been around for a while and is also very reliable. It has deep lavender to pink flowers.

Sweet Pea

Lathyrus odoratus

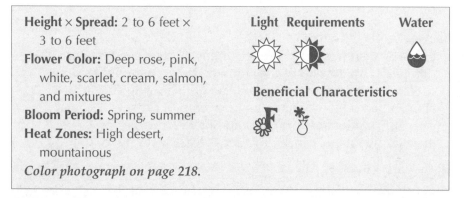

Height × Spread: 2 to 6 feet × 3 to 6 feet

Flower Color: Deep rose, pink, white, scarlet, cream, salmon, and mixtures

Bloom Period: Spring, summer

Heat Zones: High desert, mountainous

Color photograph on page 218.

Light Requirements

Water

Beneficial Characteristics

Sweet Peas start flowering in the spring and continue throughout the summer. They are either bush types or climbers. The advantage of the bush types is that they get 2 feet high, and they don't require a trellis. The climbers do need a trellis to climb on and get to 6 feet tall. Flowers are almost 1 inch in diameter and come in red, scarlet, white, salmon, cream, blue, purple, and amethyst. The flowers are typically pea-shaped with an upright petal and two side petals. Most of the varieties have a good fragrance and are excellent as cut flowers. I know local gardeners who produce them in greenhouses in the winter to sell to the local florists. (DP)

REGIONAL TIPS

Sweet Peas don't do well in hot weather, so in the regions around Las Vegas plant them in the late fall and early spring. They do particularly well in places like Ely.

WHEN, WHERE, AND HOW TO PLANT

Plant them in the spring in the high desert and mountainous regions. The bush types can be planted most anywhere, including beds and containers. Because they need more water than most other plants, limit them to a few places in the garden so it will be easier to apply extra water as needed. The vining types need some kind of support to climb on; provide a trellis or let them go on strings. In the high desert, string is by far the best because it doesn't get hot and injure the stems as wire will. Plant Sweet Peas from seed; you rarely find transplants at the garden centers. Soak the seeds for a couple of hours before sowing them. (It also helps to use a legume germination starter for better germination.) Give them a spot in full sun, in an organic soil—add at least 6 inches of organic mulch to the soil and work it in; then apply the contents of a 1-pound coffee can filled with a complete fertilizer containing between 10 and 16 percent nitrogen, spread it over 100 square feet of garden, and till in with the mulch. Sow the seeds about 1 inch deep and space them about 2 inches apart. I have found that a mixture of one-half peat moss and one-half sand to cover the seeds really works well to prevent rot. When the seedlings are about 6 inches high, thin them to 6 inches apart. Keep the soil moist after planting.

CARE AND MAINTENANCE
Sweet Peas need lots of water, so in the high desert give them 1 inch of water every day. Slugs attack them; if slugs are a problem in your yard, set out slug bait around the plants. To keep the plants blooming, cut the flowers about every other day and remove all the seedpods. Hot days bring on powdery mildew, which looks like flour on the leaves. Use an appropriate fungicide labeled for use in powdery mildew treatment.

LANDSCAPE MERIT
Sweet Peas are one of the few flowers that add delicate, pastel colors to the landscape and are known for their fragrance.

ADDITIONAL SPECIES, CULTIVARS, OR VARIETIES
Perennial Sweet Peas, *L. latifolius*, are also grown throughout Nevada. They are found in older gardens and are very hardy, with magenta-colored flowers. This is another flower that often will persist in abandoned mining camps, particularly if it gets started next to a stream.

Verbena

Verbena × hybrida

Height × Spread: 6 to 8 inches × 12 inches	**Light Requirement**	**Water**
Flower Color: White, pink, red, purple, blue, and various combinations.		
	Beneficial Characteristics	
Bloom Period: From early summer to late fall		
Heat Zones: Hot, high desert, mountainous		
Color photograph on page 218.		

Verbena is one of the nicest low-spreading flowers you can find. The flowers are in flat clusters that develop to 3 inches in diameter, and many Verbena varieties have a white eye in the center of the flower, formed by the corolla tube where the petals attach to it. The blooms may be a rich red, pink, purple, or blue and even combinations. They flower from early spring to late fall. The plants only grow to 12 inches at the most but will spread to over 2 feet if given the room. The leaves are bright-green to gray-green and are serrated, or saw-toothed. Leaves are about 2 to 4 inches long and oblong in shape. (DP)

REGIONAL TIPS

Verbena is grown as an annual throughout most of the state, but in the hot regions it lasts as a perennial.

WHEN, WHERE, AND HOW TO PLANT

Plant Verbenas in the spring. While they are considered half-hardy, most gardeners have the best results when they plant them after the last frost in the spring—particularly true of the high desert and mountainous regions. They like it hot, so plant them in full sun for best flowering; they flower hardly at all in the shade. Verbenas grow best in a well-drained soil. For best growth add 3 inches of organic mulch to the soil and till in to a depth of 6 inches. Verbenas respond to heavy fertilization, so apply the contents of a 1-pound coffee can of a complete fertilizer containing between 10 and 16 percent nitrogen per 100 square feet of garden. Verbenas are a little hard to start from seed, so it is best to use bedding plants and transplant out to the garden. Plant them about 2 feet apart if they are being used as a ground cover. For an instant look, plant them about 12 inches apart. Dig the holes as deep as the root-balls and a little larger in diameter, then drop the plants in the holes, covering the roots with soil as you go. After planting, give them a good soaking.

CARE AND MAINTENANCE

Verbenas are very drought tolerant but are susceptible to powdery mildew if they get stressed for too much water. Give them 1 inch of water twice a week. Powdery mildew looks like a thin layer of flour on the leaves at first, then the leaves die. Verbenas don't have any insect pest problems.

LANDSCAPE MERIT

There is really no end of places to plant Verbena as long as it is in a sunny spot. Because of its low-growing habit and spreading nature, it makes a wonderful ground cover that can be used on slopes, for draping over walls, in hanging baskets, and even in the rock garden. Plant in the color baskets in combinations of all different flowers. Verbena makes a great edging plant and can also be planted in borders.

ADDITIONAL SPECIES, CULTIVARS, OR VARIETIES

A few varieties available are 'Tickled Pink', 'Blue Lagoon', 'Quartz Burgundy', which was an All-America Selection in 1999, and 'Sand'. A perennial species called Peruvian Verbena, *V. peruviana*, grows in the warmer regions of Nevada and will persist in the Reno area for a few years unless the temperature dips below 0 degrees Fahrenheit. It's a very fine ground cover that forms a flat mat of foliage and has magenta-colored flowers.

Zinnia

Zinnia elegans

Height × Spread: 6 inches to
2 feet × 18 inches

Flower Color: Red, white, yellow,
orange, lavender, purple, and pink

Bloom Period: Early summer to fall

Heat Zones: Hot, high desert,
mountainous

Color photograph on page 218.

Light Requirement

Water

Beneficial Characteristics

Zinnias are one of my most favorite flowers, but that wasn't always the case. Twenty-something years ago in my trial gardens, they would look great until about the end of July, then powdery mildew would attack them and I would have to pull them out. The new hybrids give us disease-free plants all season long. Zinnia flowers are from 1 inch in diameter for dwarf types to over 5 inches on the standard-size plants. Flowers come in all colors but blue and include red, yellow, white, orange, lavender, purple, and pink. Some of the varieties like 'Whirligig' are bicolor. The flower forms include single, double, cushion, semi-double, and cactus types with quilled petals, and large-flowered types have Dahlialike blooms. The plants range in height from 6 inches to over 2 feet, with foliage a bright green. They make excellent cut flowers that will last for a long time in flower arrangements. The more you cut the flowers, the more flowers you are going to get, and the plants become bushier. (DP)

REGIONAL TIPS

In the hot regions like Las Vegas they can be planted in late winter to early spring, and after frost in the high desert and mountainous regions.

WHEN, WHERE, AND HOW TO PLANT

Zinnias are planted in the spring. Plant them in a spot were they will get full sun and a little breeze for air circulation. Zinnias germinate very fast from seed and can be planted directly into the garden in most all regions; the only drawback is you have to wait about six weeks for the flowers. Bedding plants are the way to go. They will grow in almost any soil but do best in one that is well drained. Add a 3-inch layer of organic mulch to the soil and till it in to a depth of 6 inches. Space tall varieties about 18 inches apart and the dwarf varieties at about 12 to 15 inches. Dig the holes as deep as the rootballs and a little wider, toss the plants into the holes, and finish by covering the rootballs with soil. After planting, give them a good soaking.

Care and Maintenance
Zinnias don't require very much care and are generally pest-free. Plant the newer resistant varieties to avoid powdery mildew. Even though they like the hot weather, you don't want to let them wilt, so give them 1 inch of water twice a week. They will bloom much better if you fertilize them about every three weeks with a water-soluble fertilizer mixed according to directions. Pinch off the spent blooms.

Landscape Merit
Zinnias are wonderful plants anywhere you want to use them. The taller ones are adapted to border plantings and easily mix with other flowers to make a very colorful display. The dwarf ones like 'Peter Pan' can be used as edging plants, plus they work very well in containers and color bowls—shallow containers from 12 to 14 inches in diameter.

Additional Species, Cultivars, or Varieties
If you are looking for tall Zinnias, try 'Oklahoma' or 'Giant-Flowered Mix'. The 'Dahlia-Flowered' Mix is also good. Dwarf varieties include 'Small World' and 'Lilliput'. For a nice, big single flower, try 'Pinwheel'.

CHAPTER TWO

Bulbs

AFTER A LONG, DREARY WINTER, it's great to be able to experience the sunshine of spring. But sunshine comes in several forms. It can be the warm rays of a spring morning or the refreshing colors and fragrances of spring bulbs. Indoors or outdoors, bulbs can transform the gray colors of winter into the yellow, red, and purple colors of spring.

Bulbs represent a great opportunity for involving children in a gardening experience. In school or at home, a bulb provides a long relationship between a child and a plant. And what a great opportunity for teaching and learning. Bulbs can cause a whole different world to bloom for kids.

When growing bulbs, planning is very important. The variety selection, bulb storage, planting location, fertilization, pest control, and other aspects of management all come into play to make this choice a successful growing experience.

What child or adult would not be spellbound by the array of bulbs that are available in a mail-order catalogue? What a great opportunity to focus on the use of color in the environment, as this is a rare opportunity to see a photo of final results while still in the early planning stage of a project. In the home or in the garden, bulbs can be color-coordinated with their surroundings, and they also provide the opportunity to shift or change colors on a daily basis. Make a place to "test" proven bulbs in every home or garden, especially if you involve children.

Bulbs offer the opportunity to obtain maximum beauty from a minimum amount of space. Whether it's a mass of bulbs growing in the fields of Holland or an isolated windowbox, bulbs brighten any day, in any spot. What a great opportunity to produce a gift that shows love and care to someone confined to a home or a wheelchair.

Chapter Two

Bulbs have a unique ability to transform an area into a tapestry of springtime magic. For best results, start with a design. Just three different colors can yield a unique design: place these bulbs in clusters or scatter them throughout a given area; or place the taller bulbs in the back or middle of a bed; or place the shorter varieties on the edge or in front of plants. For maximum visual impact, select bulbs that bloom at the same time. If you mix early-, mid-, and late-blooming varieties together, the look will be less dramatic. Also, go for successions of blooms to make the season last longer. Once the spring bulbs peak, use other plants to utilize and maintain color in an area. There is a flowering bulb to suit every taste and every garden purpose.

Many diseases and insects do not affect bulbs. In most cases, you can remove by hand damaged foliage and foliage affected by fungus. Be aware that Neem oil, which is widely used for disease and insect control, can damage some flowers in the bud stage.

The term "bulb" is often used loosely, as many bulbous plants are not true bulbs. True bulbs have pointed tops, short underground stems on basal plates, and new growth called *bulblets* that form offshoots of the parent bulb. Amaryllis, Grape Hyacinth, and Daffodils are true bulbs because they grow from enlarged buds with modified leaves called *scales*. Included in the family of "bulbous" plants that are not "true bulbs" are those produced from corms, rhizomes, and tubers. Gladiolus is an example of a corm.

Crocus

Crocus species

Crocuses bring the blooms that begin to wipe winter away from our minds. They are a burst of color at such a surprising time and come with such cheerful colors of blue, yellow, and white; and now Crocus corms come in a medley of designs, ranging from solid colors to stripes. Each flower contains a simple cluster of petals above a short stem surrounded by green or variegated spiky foliage. Crocuses are the first to bloom, so plant a crowd of them in a rock garden to wake it up for the season ahead. The colorful bloom's delicate size and knifelike foliage contrast nicely with the rocks. Create an exciting early-spring bed by planting a multicolored row of Crocuses in front of your evergreen shrubs, which will serve as a lush backdrop when the small flowers bloom. You can also plant a bunch with your perennials, annuals, and Irises, or cluster the corms near early-blooming shrubs. (LM)

REGIONAL TIPS

In the south, plant Crocuses on the north and east side of the home to give them more of a chance to stay in the rest period. In the north, plant them so they get 6 to 8 hours of direct sunlight.

WHEN, WHERE, AND HOW TO PLANT

Buy firm, plump corms as soon as they appear on the nursery shelves in the fall. If you purchase prepackaged ones, feel each to ensure its firmness; avoid those that are soft to the touch. In the early fall, enrich the onsite soil with organic matter and some bone meal. Dig a hole 4 to 5 inches deep and wide enough for all the corms. To enhance the show of blooms next spring, always plant a dozen or more of one kind. To create a more natural look and avoid a military form, toss a handful across the bed and plant where they land, but keep them at least 2 inches apart. Firmly place soil around the corms with the ends pointing up. In the north, cover the planted area with mulch and in the south, plant Alyssum or Pansies over them. The flowers will give you color through the winter until the Crocuses push up through them to take on that naturalized look.

CARE AND MAINTENANCE

Keep the soil moist until the ground freezes in the north, but in the south, water through the winter. As the weather warms, water more often. To get better blooms and larger bulbs for the next season, feed them with a bulb fertilizer just as their leaves peek through the snow or ground. After the blooming season, do not remove the foliage until it dies down. The leaves are replenishing the bulblets in the ground. Because Crocus blooms so early in the spring, it has no serious pest problems.

LANDSCAPE MERIT

What better way to decorate a border planting? Plant them among rocks and with other flowers, but whatever you do, they look prettier by the dozen (or more).

ADDITIONAL SPECIES, CULTIVARS, OR VARIETIES

There are thousands of varieties to select from. To ensure success, order from catalogs early or purchase Crocus corms as soon as they arrive at the nursery.

Daffodil

Narcissus × hybrids

Other Name: Narcissus	**Light Requirements** **Water**
Height × Width: 18 inches × 10 inches	
Flower Color: Yellow, peach, white, and other colors	**Beneficial Characteristic**
Foliage Color: Deep green	
Bloom Period: Spring	
Zones: 4 to 8	
Color photograph on page 218.	

Daffodils are the trumpets in the symphony of flowers that shout "Spring is here!" They come in all sizes from ankle- to knee-high, and the trumpets of these flowers are typically 1 to 3 inches in diameter. Choose a spring garden color ranging from pure-white blooms to the traditional golden yellow to fiery red and orange flowers. Add a little glamour by ringing the tree in front of your home, and listen to the comments people make when they notice the circle of color. Toss a handful or two between small shrubs, and plant them where they fall to grow them the way nature would. Line a flower bed with a row of red-cupped and tangerine-colored petals to provide a bold foreground for evergreen shrubs. Tuck some around rocks and see how well they naturalize among the stones. (LM)

REGIONAL TIPS

In the north, plant bulbs in September or immediately after purchase. In the south, add more chilling hours to the already prechilled bulbs because of our warm weather. Unchilled Daffodil bulbs will not flower properly. Place bulbs in a well-marked bag (some people have eaten bulbs, mistaking them for onions and garlic!), and put in the refrigerator for six to eight weeks prior to planting.

WHEN, WHERE, AND HOW TO PLANT

As a general rule, choose large, double-nosed Daffodils that are firm. Avoid Daffodils that are soft, bruised, or moldy, although those with loose, papery coverings are fine. In the south, plant your Daffodils on the north and east side of a home to give them some relief from the afternoon sun and winds. Always plant a dozen or more of one kind of bulb to enhance the color impact, but avoid planting in straight rows to achieve a more natural look. Plant them in a well-drained soil that has been enriched with organic matter, down to about a foot deep. Remove 6 to 8 inches of soil and place the bulbs so the tips are pointing up, spacing at least 3 inches between each bulb. Replace the soil and firm it around the bulbs. At this point you can mulch over them or plant annuals such as Alyssum or Pansies. (The annuals give color through the winter and the bulbs push through for a more naturalized look.) Water well after planting and keep soil moist.

CARE AND MAINTENANCE

In the south where the winters are so dry, keep the growing area moist. As the weather warms, water more often. To get better blooms and larger bulbs for the next season, feed them just as their leaves peak through the snow or ground with a nitrogen-type fertilizer. Leave the foliage on the bulbs until they die down to develop new bulblets for next year. If you see leaves and flowers turning a pale silver to brown, you have thrips. Remove the infested plant parts or use insecticidal soap.

LANDSCAPE MERIT

Daffodils perform wonderfully in containers, and since we pay more attention to them in containers, plant the bulbs closer together. Or plant them along borders or in among ground covers or to fill in until a new landscape matures. I have found Daffodils show off better if planted with more of their own kind.

ADDITIONAL SPECIES, CULTIVARS, OR VARIETIES

There are thousands of Daffodils to choose from. The trick is to select early for the quality bulbs at the nursery or order them from a catalog.

Gladiolus

Gladiolus hybridus

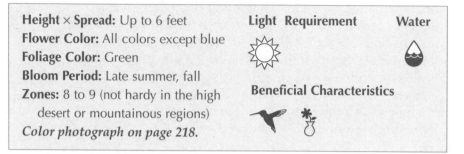

Height × Spread: Up to 6 feet
Flower Color: All colors except blue
Foliage Color: Green
Bloom Period: Late summer, fall
Zones: 8 to 9 (not hardy in the high desert or mountainous regions)
Color photograph on page 218.

Light Requirement

Water

Beneficial Characteristics

Gladiolus has spectacular flowers in red, yellow, orange, peach, white, purple, magenta, and even green. The leaves of Gladiolus are shaped like swords that are about 2 inches wide and about 2 feet long. The blooms can grow up to 8 inches in diameter, and you can expect to have twelve to fourteen flowers in bloom at the same time, flowering on tall spikes up to 5 feet high. What is really interesting to me about Gladiolus flowers is the way they open. The flower buds at the bottom of the spike open first, followed sequentially by the others, up to the tip of the spike. What I like to see when I'm judging Gladiolus is the bottom third of the spike in full bloom, the middle third half-open, and the top third still a tight bud. If you are going to use them in your own flower arrangements, use this "third" rule; your arrangement will look fantastic for a longer period of time. (DP)

REGIONAL TIPS

In the high desert and mountainous regions, the corms need to be dug in the fall and stored in a place where they'll stay above freezing temperatures. In the hot regions of the state they can be left in the ground all year long.

WHEN, WHERE, AND HOW TO PLANT

In the high desert and mountainous regions, plant them in the spring after frost. Start planting in January in the hot regions and continue planting about every three weeks to ensure a continuous show throughout the growing season. If the main reason you are growing Gladioli is for cut flowers, then just plant them in rows where they will get full sun. They will grow in most soils, but an addition of 4 to 6 inches of organic mulch to the soil will provide much better growth. Mix in a 1-pound coffee can full of a complete fertilizer that has between 10 and 16 percent nitrogen at the same time you mulch. Gladioli are started from corms, which are compressed stems with paper scales. This will cover 100 square feet. Use only good, healthy, solid corms, plant them four times deeper than they are wide, and space them about 6 inches apart. Give them a good soaking after planting, and in about eight weeks you will see some flowers.

CARE AND MAINTENANCE

Gladioli have some pest problems. Soilborne insects and bulb rot can be reduced by dusting the bulbs with a fungicide-insecticide before planting. Another pest to watch for is thrips. This insect will cause white streaks on the leaves and can distort the flowers. Control them with a pesticide registered for control of thrips. Give Gladioli an inch of water at least twice a week and fertilize them during the growing season with a water-soluble fertilizer about every month, according to the directions on the label.

LANDSCAPE MERIT

Gladioli are welcome additions in flower beds and border plantings. Because of their spike flowers, they make very good accents.

ADDITIONAL SPECIES, CULTIVARS, OR VARIETIES

Some varieties to try include 'Summer Glow', which has yellow flowers with a purple throat, and 'Angel Wings' with ivory flowers. 'Valencia' is a magenta-and-white bicolor. If you need to have a green one, then you will have to plant 'St. Patrick's'.

Grape Hyacinth

Muscari species

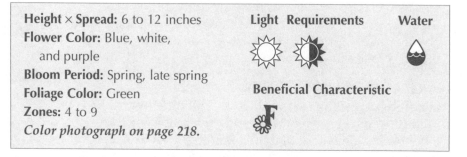

Height × Spread: 6 to 12 inches	Light Requirements	Water
Flower Color: Blue, white, and purple		
Bloom Period: Spring, late spring		
Foliage Color: Green	Beneficial Characteristic	
Zones: 4 to 9		
Color photograph on page 218.		

If you are looking for a spring-flowering bulb that is very reliable and easy to grow, look no further. Grape Hyacinth is what you're looking for. It has deep green, straplike foliage coming out from the plant's base. The flower stalks grow slightly above the foliage, from 6 to 12 inches, and flowers crowd together and cover all sides of the stalk. The flowers are shaped like miniature Swiss cowbells: small at the opening and ballooning out in the center. Blue is the most popular color, but you can find them in white and purple as well. They start flowering near the mid-spring and remain in bloom for about two weeks. You can leave them in the garden for years and they will continue to produce more bulbs and spread. Grape Hyacinths are true bulbs. (A true bulb has a small basal stem covered with compressed leaf scales making up the body of the bulb.) (DP)

REGIONAL TIPS

Grape Hyacinth is best adapted to the high desert and mountainous regions because of the high chilling required for development of the flower bud.

WHEN, WHERE, AND HOW TO PLANT

Plant Grape Hyacinth in the fall before the ground freezes. If you try planting them in the spring, as with most spring-flowering bulbs, you end up getting lots of leaves but no flowers. If this happens, just leave them in the garden and next year they will bloom. They grow in full sun or part shade, so plant them under trees and tall shrubs. For the most part, Grape Hyacinths will bloom long before the leaves on the trees come out and shade them. They grow best in soils with good drainage. Prepare the soil by adding a 3- to 4-inch layer of organic mulch to the soil. After applying the mulch, mix it all into the top 6 inches of soil. Plant the bulbs about 2 to 3 inches apart and 2 inches deep. After planting, give them a good soaking.

CARE AND MAINTENANCE

Grape Hyacinths are easy to care for. You can plant them in the fall and ignore them all winter and expect them to come up in the spring and burst into flower. If the winter is on the dry side, give all your spring-flowering bulbs a good soaking about once a month. Water them about an inch every two weeks when they start to flower for better-looking plants and flowers. No fertilizer is needed at the time of planting because everything they need is stored in the bulbs. The only fertilizer my Grape Hyacinths get is what I apply to the annuals I plant around them in the spring.

LANDSCAPE MERIT

I use Grape Hyacinth as an edging plant around all my flower beds. The only problem is making sure I leave enough room to plant the annuals after the Grape Hyacinths die down. They also make great rock garden plants. And of course, they are wonderful planted with Tulips and Daffodils.

ADDITIONAL SPECIES, CULTIVARS, OR VARIETIES

Species of Grape Hyacinth to try include *Muscari armeniacum*, which has flowers that are blue and scented. *M. comosum* has greenish-purple-tipped flowers and *M. botryoides* 'Album' has white flowers.

Tulip

Tulipa species

Do children still draw, color, and paste Tulips on the school windows? We sure did when I was in elementary school. It was from this beginning that I developed my love for Tulips. When I think of Tulips, I think of *spring* and *color*. What is more striking than a bed of Tulips in their commanding hues? I look forward to the catalogs, and almost drool over the colorful photos, imagining how they will look that next spring. (Bulb catalogs are a treat; they come during the dog days of summer so I can enjoy them in an air-conditioned room.) Tulips grow ankle high and even above the knees and bloom from early spring into summer. Breeders now have perennial Tulips you only have to plant once every five years. And their fragrance fills the wintry air to make the dreary winter blues quickly disappear. (LM)

REGIONAL TIPS

In southern Nevada, add more chilling hours to the already prechilled bulbs because of the our warm weather. (A lack of chilling will cause the blooms to remain down in the foliage.) Place the bulbs in a well-marked bag and put in a refrigerator for six to eight weeks before planting. In the north, plant bulbs in September or immediately after purchase.

WHEN, WHERE, AND HOW TO PLANT

Plant Tulips in northern Nevada after purchase and in southern Nevada after chilling them. Choose firm bulbs. Avoid bulbs that are damaged, soft, or moldy and those that have emerging green shoots. Plant Tulips in a spot with southeast exposure to provide partial shade; blooms overexposed to the sun have a shortened flowering cycle. Plant Tulips in a well-drained soil enriched with organic matter and some bone meal mixed in to about a foot deep. Remove 6 to

8 inches of soil and place the bulbs so the tips are pointing up, keeping at least 3 inches between each bulb. Replace the soil and firm it around the bulbs. Always plant a dozen or more of one kind of bulb to enhance the show. To avoid a formal look, toss the bulbs and plant them where they land. In the south, plant annuals over the bulbs for color through the winter, and in the north mulch over them.

CARE AND MAINTENANCE

You need to keep the soil moist around the bulbs. That means southerners must water through the winter and northerners until the ground freezes. As the weather warms, water more often. We used to tell people they don't need to fertilize bulbs, but research reveals we will get better blooms and larger bulbs for next season if we feed them with nitrogen as leaves peek through the ground. Fight the tendency to remove foliage after bloom; it helps develop growth of new bulblets in the ground. There are no pest problems with Tulips.

LANDSCAPE MERIT

Decorate a border planting, or mix Tulips among rocks with other flowers. But to really draw attention to Tulips, plant them in quantity.

ADDITIONAL SPECIES, CULTIVARS, OR VARIETIES

There are over three thousand different varieties to choose from; get to the nursery early to make the best choices.

Did You Know?

A virus in the soil sometimes causes the appearance of Tulips with unusual streaks. At one time, an infected bulb sold for $30,000 due to the craving for streaked Tulips.

CHAPTER THREE

Cacti

CACTI ARE AMONG the strangest plants on our planet. They offer an incomparable wealth of shapes, magnificent blossoms, and bizarre spines. They awaken in us the desire to collect and to create—these flowering plants that over a period of centuries have had to adapt themselves to sunny, hot, and dry locations. They developed highly original shapes, such as column- and barrel-shaped forms to decrease evaporation from their surfaces; in order to be able to store water for drought periods, they developed heaviness or thickness of flesh; for protection against sunlight, they developed rosettes and leaves that are reduced to spines, waxy surfaces, cork-like coatings, or silvery, hairlike coverings.

Cacti represent the ideal plants for a desert environment, as they survive on the less-than-ideal conditions of heat and dryness. Faced with surviving where rains are few and far between, these plants root extensively and often quite shallowly so that they might absorb every drop of precious moisture. These water-misers of the plant world plump up their waxy-skinned bodies and hold moisture very efficiently.

Cacti need good drainage. To enhance drainage even more, plant them on higher ground. When planting, be sure to allow adequate space to accommodate their mature sizes. In any desert landscape design, always slip in cacti or use them as accent plants.

Cacti end up in our gardens because of our love for them—no one plants them for fruit production. Although fruit comes along on some cacti, like the Opuntias, it is more a novelty item. You may find cacti fruit sold as "Pitayas" in some markets.

The large genus of *Opuntia* is divided into two major groups: those with flattened joints and those with cylindrical joints (or sections). Plants in the *Opuntia* group that includes the Prickly Pear and

Chapter Three

Cholla also have tiny, barbed hairs (called glochids) located at the base of the spine clusters. These are easily overlooked, but they are potentially more troublesome than the spines.

For gardening purposes it is both reasonable and practical to group drought-tolerant plants together. Even if their original homes differ, they generally will settle down to one method of cultivation and thrive by it. But some plants may refuse to produce flowers consistently. Gardeners who have the time, skill, or patience may be able to modify the environment so that flowers come forth.

When using cacti in the garden, keep them away from your walkways and from children's play areas, but close enough to show off their blooms. Use them as accent plants, as they make such bold statements, but don't plant cacti just for the sake of adding them if they don't fit your tastes. These plants are too precious to waste. They have been the survivors of the desert for centuries, so you should decide ahead of time that they will survive a chosen place in your landscape.

Beavertail Cactus

Opuntia basilaris

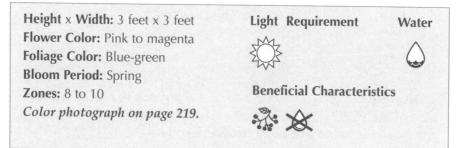

Height x **Width:** 3 feet x 3 feet
Flower Color: Pink to magenta
Foliage Color: Blue-green
Bloom Period: Spring
Zones: 8 to 10
Color photograph on page 219.

Light Requirement

Water

Beneficial Characteristics

From the *Opuntia* genus come the ever-popular Beavertail Cactus, Cow's Tongue, Purple Pancake, Engelmann's, Porcupine, Hedgehog Prickly Pears, Teddy Bear, Silver and Staghorn Chollas, and the list goes on. Beavertail is one of my favorites as it is so pleasing and there are so many used today. It gets knee-high and sprawls out 3 feet in a rambling style. The bluish-green, heart-shaped pads with spines (glochids) develop a crosshatched pattern that reminds me of quilts Mother made. Cactus flowers are perfect and awe-inspiring when emerging in spring. Look how every petal is precisely shaped and colored. Only the artist in the sky can do it. Beavertails have the drinking habits of camels; they survive a long time between irrigation and still look robust. The Opuntias are native to the Southwest, but you'll find them transplanted around the world. The Opuntias known as Cholla produce thorns, which are troublesome if they latch onto you; they make effective barriers to deter people at property edges. (LM)

REGIONAL TIPS

The Opuntias are only hardy enough to grow in southern Nevada.

WHEN, WHERE, AND HOW TO PLANT

Plant from nursery containers anytime it is hot or whenever someone gives you pads. They will grow in any soil provided they have good drainage and full sun. Blend some organic matter in the soil prior to planting to enhance drainage. Use tongs and heavy gloves when handling the pads, as they do bite back. Pull the soil back, plant the rootball or place the bottom half of the pad in the ground, and firm the soil around it. Water weekly throughout the first summer.

Care and Maintenance

These Cacti will survive our annual rainfall, but to bring out their lushness and beauty, supplement rainfall monthly. Water even more prior to bloom in the spring. If we have a long dry spell, water twice a month with 2 gallon-per-hour emitters running for 2 hours. Opuntias do not require any fertilizer supplements but a cupful of ammonium sulfate in the early spring will add a touch of luster to the landscape. There is no need for pruning other than to remove damaged pads. If the Opuntia becomes overgrown, remove the out-of-line pads and give them to friends. Cochineal scale, evident by white, fluffy stuff on the pads, is the only pest that bothers Opuntias. Wash them off with a strong jet of water.

Landscape Merit

Use them as accents, specimens, barriers, in desert settings; in fact, they become a very dominant, bold statement in landscapes.

Additional Species, Cultivars, or Varieties

O. acicularis, or Bristly Prickly Pear, has large pads with prominent dots covering the pads with orange-reddish blossoms. *O. engelmannii*, or Engelmann's Prickly Pear, has bright yellow flowers followed by fruit loved by birds. *O. ficus-indica*, or Tuna Cactus, has large pads that are relatively free of spines with yellow cup-shaped flowers along the pads turning into fruit harvested by people, birds, and animals. *O. violaceae* 'Santa Rita', or Purple Pancake Cactus has flat, rounded pads that turn purple when it's cold, bringing a new look to the landscape. *O. lindheimeri forma linguiformis*, or Cow's Tongue, has long, narrow pads shaped like a cow's tongue. *O. bigelovii*, or Teddy Bear Cholla, spines grab you and then take on the mood of a grizzly. Handle these Cacti with heavy gloves to avoid the unpleasant task of digging them out of your hands.

CACTI

Century Plant

Agave species

| Other Names: Agave, Maguey
Height x Width: 6 to 10 feet x
   13 feet
Flowers: Insignificant yellow florets
Bloom Period: Summer, once in
   five to fifty years
Foliage Color: Blue-green
Zones: 8 to 20
Color photograph on page 219. | Light Requirement | Water |

The Century Plant is very striking, especially for the architectural nature of the flower stalk and its spike, or candelabra. It has dramatic rosettes of broad, thick, fleshy leaves with unusual color variations radiating from barbs along their margins. Eventually the flower spike arises to cause a sensational reaction among observers. Of course, we never know when it will arise. That's why they're called Century Plants. We do know that somewhere within five to fifty years the plant will devote all its energy to producing the spike. It grows to about 6 inches in diameter and over 30 feet tall, with a tiered candelabra forming at the top of the stalk. When people see a Century Plant blooming for the first time they become excited. It upsets them to hear the plant will evenually die, but it does leave offshoots for use elsewhere. (LM)

REGIONAL TIPS

Agaves will not tolerate freezing conditions, as is the case outside southern Nevada.

WHEN, WHERE, AND HOW TO PLANT

Plant Agave from containers or offsets in the spring where it will get full to filtered sun. Like other plants, it prefers a well-drained soil so roots can grow unencumbered. Loosen the soil to three times wider than and as deep as the rootball. Mix some organic matter in with the backfill soil and plant. Create a slope away from the base of the plant and build a water basin to keep the crown dry and avoid crown rot. Water young plants three to five times a week until established.

CARE AND MAINTENANCE

Water established Agaves monthly throughout the summer but keep them dry during winter. (Expect damage when temperatures drop below 20 degrees for long periods of time.) Allow plants to grow naturally except for a once-a-year "clean-up" by removing all dead and untidy leaves. In nature, the cup-shaped leaves form channels to capture rain and funnel it to the roots. A happy plant will have full, plump leaves, but if Century Plant is stressed for water, the shrinking roots create openings or cracks to trap even more water. Water it weekly using an emitter that runs for a couple of hours, and be sure to locate emitters about a foot away from the plant to prevent root rot. Agave weevils can kill a Century Plant unless found early; the plant wilts despite attempts to revive it with water. If it is infested, it will topple easily if pushed. Moist conditions at the base of the plant prove ideal for weevils, which like to feed on it at the soil line. If you suspect an infestation, spray the base with a product called Cygon.

LANDSCAPE MERIT

Agaves are excellent where you want boldness, form, and contrast—especially against structures. Situate other plants around it, but remove them as Century Plant matures in size; it is outstanding where other plants fail and does well in containers. Because of the sharp leaf tips, keep it away from high foot-traffic areas and swimming pools.

ADDITIONAL SPECIES, CULTIVARS, OR VARIETIES

Century Plant is only one of some 100 species that are available in sizes from very small to very large.

Desert Spoon

Dasylirion wheeleri

Other Name: Sotol	**Light Requirement**	**Water**
Height x Width: 6 feet x 3 feet		
Flower Color: Creamy white		
Foliage Color: Silvery green		
Bloom Period: Summer	**Beneficial Characteristics**	
Zones: 8 to 11		
Color photograph on page 219.		

From the *Agave* family come several plants used in landscapes. *D. wheeleri*, or Desert Spoon, is one of the most commonly used in southern Nevada. It has narrow, 1-inch-wide silvery-green leaves with toothed margins up to 3 feet long; the tips are bushlike; and leaves radiate from a bulbous trunk to about 3 feet high at maturity. Occasionally, side trunks, or "pups," come from the older plant. Older specimens develop a short, stout trunk to 3 feet tall, and the lower leaves dry and lie against the trunk and form a tan-colored skirt. You'll find the leaves spoon-shaped where they attach to the plant, which explains why the Native Americans used them as eating utensils. Occasionally a bloom stalk emerges from the center of the plant between May and July, reaching a height of 10 feet and lasting for more than a season. Creamy-white flowers open on the erect stem and tan seeds follow. From a distance, it appears to be an oversized head of wheat. (LM)

REGIONAL TIPS

Desert Spoon is only adapted to southern Nevada's weather conditions.

WHEN, WHERE, AND HOW TO PLANT

The Desert Spoon does best when planted during hot weather and in full sun but will tolerate some shade. It prefers loose, rocky, gravelly, and sandy soil with good drainage. Use heavy gloves to handle the plants when planting because the leaves have sharp teeth. Loosen soil to a width of 3 feet prior to planting and tuck the plant into its bed, firming the soil around the roots. Water weekly, with emitters on for an hour at a time, until it becomes established.

CARE AND MAINTENANCE

After becoming established Desert Spoons get by on twice-monthly waterings (let emitters run for 2 hours); hold off on the water after Halloween to enhance winter hardiness. Desert Spoons do not require much fertilizer, but give them half a cup of ammonium sulfate in the early spring prior to irrigation. The only pruning they need is to remove the dead leaves and the flowering stalk. Desert Spoons do not have any pest problems.

LANDSCAPE MERIT

Desert Spoons fit in with other silver-green plants such as Brittlebush, Texas Ranger, and Dusty Miller, if you want to have a silvery landscape. They make dramatic accent plants. Because of the sharp teeth along the leaf margins, these plants create formidable barriers.

ADDITIONAL SPECIES, CULTIVARS, OR VARIETIES

Another plant in the *Dasylirion* genus is *D. longissimum*, or Toothless Sotol. It is very graceful in the landscape, creating a lush plant with its long, narrow green leaves up to 4 feet long and rounded leaves that look like teeth. It does not bloom until it reaches mature size, and then blooms annually. I like the way the old leaves cascade down and eventually turn brown to create a dry thatch. It is an excellent clump plant. *D. texanum*, or Texas Sotol, has stiff green leaves with sawtoothed margins that create a rounded head. In the spring, a single, erect flower stalk rises as tall as 15 feet, bearing small, creamy-white flowers on a slender, densely packed column high on the stem. It also creates its own mulch as the older leaves die. *D. acrotriche*, or Green Desert Spoon, brings a bright green to the landscape and a rather tropical effect. It produces a Yuccalike whorl of leaves 3 feet wide and long; a bloom stalk will reach 10 feet high.

Fishhook Barrel Cactus

Ferocactus wislizenii

Height x Width: 4 feet x 2 feet
Flower Color: Orange to red
Foliage Color: Yellow to red edged
with yellow
Bloom Period: Summer
Zones: 8 to 10
Color photograph on page 219.

Light Requirement

Water

Beneficial Characteristic

From the *Ferocactus* genus comes *F. wislizenii*, or Fishhook Barrel Cactus, and *F. acanthodes*, or Compass or Fire Barrel Cactus. Fishhook Barrel Cactus's shape develops from ball-shaped to columnar as it ages. It can grow as high as 10 feet with a trunk diameter of 2 feet. The ribs are heavily armed with spines. Some of the spines in each cluster are red-brown with the longest up to 4 inches long with a rather pronounced hook on the end—the Native Americans used the hooks to catch fish. Numerous yellow to red-edged-with-yellow flowers 2½ inches long are grouped at the top of the barrel, opening during the summer. Rounded, fleshy yellow fruit persists on the plant for some time, extending seasonal interest. The Compass Cactus was known to pioneer travelers as a life-saving Cactus for thirsty palates. The pulp contained within the barrel could be crushed to release moisture for the traveler. It wasn't exactly a cold glass of water, but it was certainly thirst-quenching in the hot desert. (LM)

REGIONAL TIPS

The Fishhook Barrel Cactus will only grow in southern Nevada, as it cannot tolerate the harsh winters of northern Nevada. If the south experiences a severe freeze, it will also freeze down, though it is hardy to 0 degrees Fahrenheit.

WHEN, WHERE, AND HOW TO PLANT

Fishhook Barrel Cactus does best planted in hot weather and needs full sun but can take some shade. (It flourishes under full sun, but you will need to provide protection by covering it with cheesecloth until it becomes adapted to the climate if you plant during extremely hot weather.) Fishhook Barrel Cactus prefers loose, rocky, gravelly, or sandy soil and must have good drainage. Use heavy gloves when handling pads as they do bite back. Blend some organic matter in the soil prior to planting and tuck the plants into bed, firming the soil around the roots. Water weekly until the Cacti become established.

CARE AND MAINTENANCE

This Cactus has a very low thirst for water. After becoming established it gets by on monthly soakings—let 1-gallon-per-hour drip emitters run for 2 hours. Learn to "read" the ribs of the barrel: If you can't get your fingers between the ribs, water; as the plant takes up water, the ribs expand again. Refrain from watering after Halloween to enhance winter hardiness. If we go over a month without rain, it will be necessary to irrigate in the winter. These Cacti don't have a great need for fertilizer, but it is okay to work a cup of ammonium sulfate around the plants prior to irrigation. This species does not bring any pests to the garden; the defense mechanisms of the plant keep everything from attacking it.

LANDSCAPE MERIT

It makes a great accent or specimen plant with both flowers and fruit having great ornamental value. Out in the desert, Fishhooks are very conspicuous as they characteristically lean to the southwest.

ADDITIONAL SPECIES, CULTIVARS, OR VARIETIES

F. acanthodes, or Compass Barrel Cactus, has a unique characteristic. The Native Americans used it as a direction-finder, as the Cactus always tilts to the southwest—hence the name "Compass." When in bloom, you'll find it becomes very attractive, with yellow- to orange-cupped flowers with a touch of red thrown in.

Golden Barrel Cactus

Echinocactus grusonii

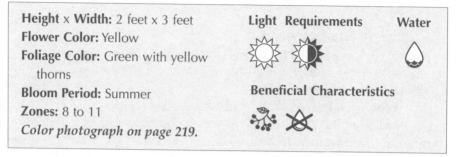

Height x **Width:** 2 feet x 3 feet
Flower Color: Yellow
Foliage Color: Green with yellow thorns
Bloom Period: Summer
Zones: 8 to 11
Color photograph on page 219.

Light Requirements

Water

Beneficial Characteristics

From the *Echinocactus* family come the popular barrel cacti with names such as Golden Barrel, Candy Cactus, Devil's Head, Horse Crippler, and Cotton Top. Golden Barrel Cactus is my favorite. No one but the architect in the sky could put together a Golden Barrel Cactus. A closer look at its top reveals a dense swirl of ribs, spines, and the feltlike covering of the plant's growing point. Yellow straw-type flowers appear from the growing point in the summer. (They remind me of the Strawflowers my mother loved to use in her dried arrangements.) Like all Cacti, Golden Barrel does best in full sun with some afternoon shade. If the barrels pale while becoming acclimatized, it is getting too much shade. Out in the wild, you'll find Golden Barrels perched under other plants, synergistically coping with the many days between rainstorms. Take a page out of their book and do the same in your landscape. Golden Barrel Cactus is very slow growing, to the ultimate height of 2 to 3 feet and as wide. (LM)

REGIONAL TIPS

The *Enchinocactus* genus has trouble coping with cold winter, so this is a plant for southern Nevada only.

WHEN, WHERE, AND HOW TO PLANT

Golden Barrel Cactus does best when planted in spring, especially if you start with a younger plant. It will take full sun, but park it where it will get some afternoon shade to nurse it along. It will grow in any soil providing it has good drainage, which you can ensure by blending in some organic matter prior to planting. Use heavy gloves when handling Cacti, as they do bite back. Tuck the Cactus into its permanent location, firming the soil next to roots. Water weekly the first year.

CARE AND MAINTENANCE

Golden Barrel Cactus has a very low thirst for water. After it's established, water it monthly; let 2-gallon emitters run for 2 hours. When it's very hot (100 degrees), go to twice-monthly waterings. Keep an eye on the weather, and if it has been a long time since rain, irrigate. Or watch the Cactus ribs. When they shrink closer together, much like an accordion, or when you can't get your finger between the ribs, water. As the plant takes up water, the ribs will spread out. Hold off on watering after Halloween to initiate winter hardiness. If a Cactus is stressing for water when it freezes, the outcome can be devastating. Golden Barrel Cactus doesn't have any fertilizer or pruning needs. The agave weevil burrows in at the base of the plant and feeds inside; if you suspect this problem, apply a systemic insecticide. The defense mechanisms of the plant will keep many bugs from attacking it.

LANDSCAPE MERIT

It is the most garden-friendly of many Cacti and not very "desert-ish." A solo Golden Barrel Cactus makes a bold statement, but when combined with a few others it also creates a striking appearance in the landscape.

ADDITIONAL SPECIES, CULTIVARS, OR VARIETIES

The following are some of *E. grusonii*, or Golden Barrel's, cousins used often in our landscapes: *E. polycephalus*, or Cottontop Barrel, is a native clumping Cactus sometimes composed of fifteen to a clump. Its fruit has dense, hairlike wool, giving it the cottontop appearance. *E. horizonthalonius*, or Turk's Head, Blue Barrel, or Eagle's Claw, has pink, funnel-shaped flowers that open to about 3 inches wide. And *E. texensis*, or Candy Cactus, Devil's Head, or Horse Crippler, comes covered with spines—daring anyone to reach in to pluck its candy.

Joshua Tree

Yucca species

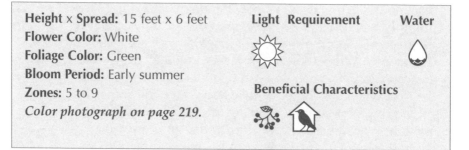

Height x Spread: 15 feet x 6 feet	Light Requirement	Water
Flower Color: White		
Foliage Color: Green		
Bloom Period: Early summer		
Zones: 5 to 9	Beneficial Characteristics	
Color photograph on page 219.		

As I travel through the Mojave Desert, I find Joshua Trees growing naturally around the 3000- to 5000-foot elevation level. They are among the oldest creatures in the desert. They have become the symbol of the Mojave and are the most recognized of the species. Many states have laws to protect them and require special tags, or they may be confiscated. A Joshua Tree needs to be propped up after transplanting, and needs supplemental irrigation until established. It develops many side branches with some arms longer than others, and grayish or dull-green leaves cover the arms. The real beauty comes when it blooms: Clusters of white blossoms appear at the end of each branch. If you bring the plant to the lower valleys, you will find we do not get enough cold weather to cause it to fork. As a result, many of the arms will reach upwards for 30 feet and never fork. (LM)

REGIONAL TIPS
Most Yucca species will take temperatures down to 0 degrees and lower. That means these fine plants will grow across the state. Most Yuccas are from the southwest deserts and therefore can play a greater role in desert landscaping.

WHEN, WHERE, AND HOW TO PLANT
Plant from March through June. They need plenty of warmth to establish themselves, good drainage, and full sun. Transplant container-grown specimens into an open hole at least three times the width and as deep as the rootball. Plant it at the same depth at which it was growing in the container to keep the trunk dry—this will force the new roots out into the surrounding soil faster. Mulch to maintain moisture in the soil, and give the tree a good soaking once a week until established.

CARE AND MAINTENANCE

Water to a depth of 2 feet twice a month from May through August the first year, and then once a month throughout the summer thereafter. There is no need to water Yuccas through the winter (November to February), and excessive water at the base of the plant can lead to root rot. Most desert plants get by without any fertilizer, but to put more luster into the greenery, add nitrogen in the early spring, and if the leaves still don't attain the desired luster, add iron. As beautiful as the flowers are, after they fade they are unsightly to some gardeners; if this is so for you, remove them.

LANDSCAPE MERIT

Joshua Trees are excellent where you want boldness, form, and contrast, such as in Xeriscape settings. They even look nice in containers.

ADDITIONAL SPECIES, CULTIVARS, OR VARIETIES

Y. recurvifolia, or the Curved Yucca, has fast-growing, dark green leaves that are very soft and relaxing. Flowers rise 5 feet above the foliage in the spring and are fast becoming a regular in garden settings. *Y. elata*, or Soaptree Yucca, gets to about 10 feet tall. Leaves are grasslike but hang down with age, creating an attractive thatch. Top leaves are light green with white edges, giving plants a grayish cast. Flower spikes rise above to display fragrant, snowy-white blooms. *Y. aloifolia*, or Spanish Bayonet, grows slowly to 10 feet with stiff, deep green leaves closely set along the stalk. Later, lilylike flowers rise out of the plant on stalks. Spanish Dagger (*Y. gloriosa*) looks at home as an accent plant, with its fleshy, stiff, yellowish-green leaves. If you remove the older foliage it looks like a miniature palm. It too grows slow to 8 feet, developing several trunks, and large, creamy flowers appear above the plant.

CHAPTER FOUR

Ground Covers

GROUND COVERS ARE PLANTS USED TO COVER the soil and form a continuous, low mass of foliage. They are often used as a durable, undemanding substitute for turf grass because these plants need little upkeep and can thrive where traditional turf grass struggles. Loosely gathered under the umbrella term "ground cover," these include, but are not limited to, low-growing, creeping, or spreading shrubs, vines, perennials, and some annuals. Long a staple of parks, highway verges, and other public landscapes, ground covers are finding an important place in home landscapes. In addition to handling problem spots and cutting down on lawn maintenance, ground covers provide an exciting design element; their wide range of foliage and flowers can add splashes of color or texture to the garden.

It's worth examining for a moment why we "cover" the ground in the first place. In Nevada, ground covers can reduce the amount of dust coming into the house. If you don't plant ground covers, nature will provide them in the form of weeds. Therefore, a leafy cover of your choosing will inhibit weeds, keep the soil cooler, and break the force of a drenching rain. Beneath the surface, roots of ground cover will hold the soil against erosion and also provide for better water penetration.

Trees can cause two problems for lawns: shade and competition for roots. One or the other can make growing grass difficult; the two together permit a skimpy lawn at best. There are a number of tough ground covers that perform better than a lawn under trees. Also, steep slopes in a lawn area can make it difficult to establish and maintain a lawn, where a ground cover will do fine. Some home landscapes have areas that are just not large enough for a lawn. For instance, if an area is too small for a lawn mower, think of a patch of ground cover as a throw rug. Some ground covers can also easily flow around boulders and between steppingstones.

The narrow strips of soil between a curb and a fence, a fence and a wall, or a driveway and sidewalk are well suited to restrained ground covers. In large areas not subject to foot traffic, you might also consider masses of shrubs as a ground cover.

The wide range of color and texture found in the foliage and flowers of ground covers can be deployed in the landscape—much as a painter uses color on a canvas—to create bands, drifts, or large pools of color. Foliage color, because it can persist through much or all of the year, creates permanent effects.

As attractive as ground covers can be, there is also a strong economic consideration: the saving in resources and labor. Nowhere is this saving more visible than in the use of water. The lawn is by far the thirstiest customer in the home landscape, the greediest in its use of fertilizers, and the most demanding of attention. The dry West, which has for decades faced the problem of a rapidly growing population and a scanty water supply, can appreciate how water-conserving ground cover plants offer a unique alternative to turf grass. Ground covers certainly require much less labor than lawns. A good start is the key to minimal costs down the line for ground cover. Select plants adapted to your site and to your growing conditions; once they're established, they will usually take care of themselves, with perhaps an annual grooming and occasional damage repair.

Carpet Bugle Ajuga

Ajuga reptans

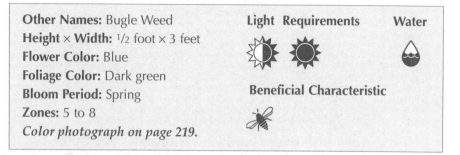

Other Names: Bugle Weed	**Light Requirements**	**Water**
Height × Width: 1/2 foot × 3 feet		
Flower Color: Blue		
Foliage Color: Dark green		
Bloom Period: Spring	**Beneficial Characteristic**	
Zones: 5 to 8		
Color photograph on page 219.		

Carpet Bugle Ajuga is a low-growing and very colorful ground cover; it's one of the best ground covers for shaded areas. It comes dressed with dark green, spoon-shaped leaves that take on a purplish-blue effect as the weather cools. In the spring, spikes arise from the mat to about 6 inches high, and tiny blue flowers cover the spikes from spring to early summer. Ajuga makes an ideal plant to fill open spaces where you need something to cover the ground. I love it in front of taller shrubs because its colorful foliage will bring out their virtues. It is especially good to fill in along walkways or around the edges of patios. I recall one growing in a container: this ground cover spilled over its walls, covering the container, spread out into the neighboring garden soil, and took off from there. It obviously will take some foot traffic, as I have seen it used between steppingstones. (LM)

REGIONAL TIPS

The hot summer sun in the south may prevent it from performing at its maximum level when planted in full sun.

WHEN, WHERE, AND HOW TO PLANT

Ajuga is available in the nurseries in the spring. In the north, plant it as soon as the frost is gone from the ground; in the south, plant it anytime it is available. (You'll find it most often sold in flats.) Ajuga does its best in a partially shaded location with some relief from Nevada's afternoon sun. Because Ajuga propagates itself by above-ground runners, it is important to prepare the entire bed. Add copious amounts of organic matter to the soil to accommodate the new roots as they emerge from the stem nodes to thicken the mat. Space the plants 6 to 12 inches apart at the same depth at which they were growing in the flats to avoid crown rot. Follow with a good soaking of the bed at least three times a week until established.

CARE AND MAINTENANCE

Keep the soil moist under the plant to aid rooting. Water the area at least three times a week throughout the heat and at least monthly through the winter. Ajuga only needs a complete fertilizer in early spring and fall (it's also safe for lawns and plants adjacent to the ground cover). It will break your heart to prune Ajuga with a mower, but lift the blade to the highest height and mow off the flower spikes after each blooming cycle. You can expect fungus diseases if the plant has to struggle to stay alive. It also has trouble competing with tree roots and the tree usually wins—the roots affect the matting habit of the Ajuga, leaving it with spotty growth. Insects are not a problem.

LANDSCAPE MERIT

Carpet Bugle Ajuga is a true low-growing ground cover that works well in planters, under shrubs, and in rock gardens and flower beds.

ADDITIONAL SPECIES, CULTIVARS, OR VARIETIES

'Bronze' Ajuga comes dressed with bronzy-green leaves with wavy margins and tiny blue flowers on 4- to 5-inch spikes; 'Burgundy Glow' comes with reddish foliage marbled green-and-white and very showy; 'Silver Beauty' comes fully clad with green and marbled white leaves; *A. crispa*, or Giant Ajuga, has a metallic quality and larger leaves than *A. reptans*, which is more vigorous and has blue flowers on spikes (it will take some foot traffic).

Centennial Broom

Baccharis × 'Centennial'

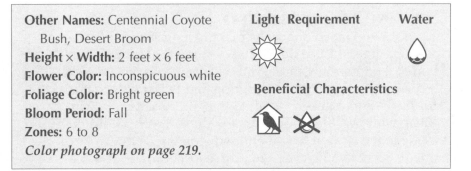

Other Names: Centennial Coyote Bush, Desert Broom
Height × Width: 2 feet × 6 feet
Flower Color: Inconspicuous white
Foliage Color: Bright green
Bloom Period: Fall
Zones: 6 to 8
Color photograph on page 219.

Light Requirement

Water

Beneficial Characteristics

You've heard the phrase "He certainly is an improvement on the old stock." That's what my dad said to others about me. Well 'Centennial' Broom definitely is an improvement on its parents. Researchers took the best of the Coyote Bush *B. pilularis* and the best of Desert Broom *B. sarothroides,* and we now have 'Centennial'. It is larger and more vigorous, with attractive mounding and spreading qualities that are greater than those of Coyote Bush. 'Centennial' left the fluffy flower heads with desert bloom behind and brought along more heat tolerance. 'Centennial' Broom has become the mainstay in desert landscapes, providing a durable, long-lived, bright green ground cover over large areas where you want an undulating, mounding effect. It is prized for its year-round, striking, pale-green, glossy foliage on slender, vibrant stems that form dense mounds of greenery 2 feet high and 6 feet wide. (LM)

REGIONAL TIPS
'Centennial' is not hardy in northern Nevada.

WHEN, WHERE, AND HOW TO PLANT
Plant Centennial Broom from October to March but not during the summer. Know the dimensions of this beauty when planting, because if it competes with other plants for light, it becomes woody underneath. (Planting farther apart keeps the foliage dense.) It will take partial shade but does best planted in sunny situations. You need to keep it away from sidewalks because it is a fast-growing evergreen, and because it is such a fast grower, purchase smaller plants. Open up a hole three times wider than and as deep as the container. It will tolerate a wide range of soils but needs good

drainage, so mix organic matter into the onsite soil and plant. After making a reservoir around the plant, give it a good soaking three times a week until established.

CARE AND MAINTENANCE

It can get by on a low water budget, but 'Centennial' takes on a fresher appearance if watered more. Water it weekly throughout the heat, remembering that too much water will cause root rot. To keep it happy, feed it a balanced fertilizer around Valentine's Day and Labor Day. Each winter, remove the older stems and thin out the plant to keep it looking fresh. If you are pruning it often, either cut back on the water or fertilizer or be content to prune often. Red spider mites cause a dusty look on the lower parts of the plant. If they become a problem, direct a strong force of water weekly to keep them in check. A small caterpillar may also be troublesome during the spring and summer. A biological control known as *Bacillus thuringiensis* will easily conquer this pest.

LANDSCAPE MERIT

Centennial Broom produces an oriental or tropical effect in the landscape and works well with water features and rocks. Its color and texture provide a strong contrast for silver-leafed plants such as Dusty Miller.

ADDITIONAL SPECIES, CULTIVARS, OR VARIETIES

B. pilularis 'Twin Peaks', also known as Dwarf Coyote Bush, is a low-growing ground cover with a tight, compact appearance. *B. sarothroides*, or Desert Broom, gets about 10 feet tall and makes an excellent screening plant. *Baccharis* hybrid 'Starn Thompson' is new and has all the traits of 'Centennial' without the chance of female flowers and their unwanted fluff, along with other significant improvements. The reason for its popularity is in its maleness—it doesn't make messy whiffs of seedhead litter, produced in abundance by the female 'Centennial'. As a male plant, 'Starn Thompson' also eliminates the production of unwanted seedlings that often grow up through stands of 'Centennial' shrubs, causing them to mass together over a large area.

Creeping Dalea

Dalea greggii

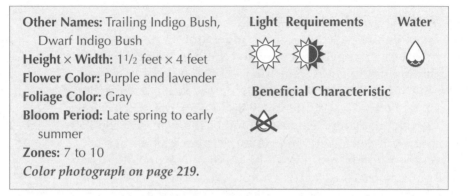

Other Names: Trailing Indigo Bush,
Dwarf Indigo Bush
Height × Width: 1¹/₂ feet × 4 feet
Flower Color: Purple and lavender
Foliage Color: Gray
Bloom Period: Late spring to early
summer
Zones: 7 to 10
Color photograph on page 219.

Light Requirements

Water

Beneficial Characteristic

Creeping Dalea sneaks up on you! It goes almost unnoticed covering the ground, but when it blooms, Wow! It is as if someone painted the garden with hues of lavender and purple. Creeping Dalea brings peace and tranquility to the garden—and it covers the ground so fast! Tiny gray leaves attached to reddish stems curve and bend into a twisted mass of cover. Then clusters of tiny lavender to purple pea-type flowers bloom from spring to early summer and small pods follow. Creeping Dalea creates a low-mounding, billowing appearance for an undulating effect across the yard. (LM)

REGIONAL TIPS

Recommended for the southern region because it loves the additional heat.

WHEN, WHERE, AND HOW TO PLANT

Plant it anytime from containers (because it is fast spreading, purchase 1- or 5-gallon containers). Research finds smaller plants will equal larger container plants within 5 years; in fact, a gallon-size Creeping Dalea plant will cover up to 10 square feet in its first season. For best results, plant it in full sun to partial shade. The more open your soil is, the better it performs, but the soil must drain to avoid root rot. Because Creeping Dalea stems root at nodes, prepare the entire bed by adding copious amounts of organic matter at least to 6 inches; then, remove enough soil to place the plant. As Creeping Dalea sends out its stems, the new growth will take off much sooner. (Observation tells me if the roots are happy your plant will perform much better.) Use water to help settle the soil for better root-to-soil contact and thoroughly soak the rooted area and surrounding soil. Repeat these irrigations three times a week until established. Because it's a ground cover, you don't need to mulch, as most ground covers create their own soil coverings.

CARE AND MAINTENANCE

Water it once a week throughout the heat—water is the key to good-looking Creeping Daleas. If a Creeping Dalea runs shy of water, it goes dormant and some injury may result. Because it has seedpods, it is a member of the legume family and makes its own nitrogen; so you can forget feeding this species. The best time to contain Creeping Daleas is at planting time, by locating them back from your walks and curbs. This will significantly reduce time spent cutting them back. Otherwise you will be shearing them often to fit the space. As they begin to lose the mounding look, it's time to cut back into the old wood to about ankle-high. Then your Creeping Daleas will take on a fresh new look. Pests are not a problem with this ground cover.

LANDSCAPE MERIT

Creeping Dalea is one of our best drought-resistant ground covers and is rabbit resistant as well. It tolerates some foot traffic but recovers slowly. Creeping Dalea is a fast-growing, dependable performer that blends well in Xeriscapes as well as in traditional landscapes, and it is hardy.

ADDITIONAL SPECIES, CULTIVARS, OR VARIETIES

D. capitata, or Golden Dalea, is an excellent ground cover with abundant golden blooms in spring and fall. 'Sierra Gold' and 'Sierra Negra' are becoming very popular in Las Vegas. *D. pulchra*, or Bush Dalea, is a rugged, upright evergreen shrub with small, hairy, silver-gray leaves; numerous small rose-purple flowers come along in the late winter. *D. frutescens*, or Black Dalea, makes the garden shine with its clusters of purplish flowers in the fall.

 Did You Know?

Creeping Dalea repels rabbits.

Germander

Teucrium chamaedrys 'Prostratum'

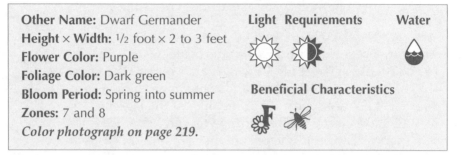

Other Name: Dwarf Germander	**Light Requirements Water**
Height × Width: 1/2 foot × 2 to 3 feet	
Flower Color: Purple	
Foliage Color: Dark green	
Bloom Period: Spring into summer	**Beneficial Characteristics**
Zones: 7 and 8	
Color photograph on page 219.	

Germander is much like Santa and his Elves. They work hard all the year and, come time for the festive season, they really make people happy. Germander is the same: Little plants ankle-high spread slowly over a 3-foot-circle area so thickly that weeds can't start. It goes unnoticed, keeping itself looking fresh and green, but then commands attention when it starts blooming. The individual flowers are so small; you need to get up close to feel the full impact of this ground-hugger. You'll find numerous upright branches with egg-shaped, small, dark green leaves covering the stems. In the late spring, clusters of small purple sweet-pea flowers only 1/2 inch in diameter plaster themselves along those many stems. The flowers attract bees. In the meantime, the lower stems trail along the ground and root where they touch soft soil, eventually creating more of a mounding carpet. This little plant fits so well toward the front of a sunny border, mixed in with coarse-leafed plants. And if you crush the foliage, an aromatic fragrance will fill the air. (LM)

REGIONAL TIPS

Germander is another plant you northerners miss out on; it just won't withstand your harsh winters. But it is a great ground-hugger for the south.

WHEN, WHERE, AND HOW TO PLANT

Plant anytime through the year, but it prefers being planted in the fall. Although it grows in partial shade, it becomes even denser when grown in full sun. Germander has a great tolerance for poor soil, heat, wind, and drought; and here's another virtue: You don't have to mulch it. The stems that go out horizontally, covered with leaves, do their own self-shading. Because Germander does root down at stem nodes, improve the entire bed by mixing in a generous amount of organic matter at least 6 inches deep. Purchase 1-gallon plants and place them at the same depth they were growing in the container. Thoroughly soak the area at least three times a week until established.

CARE AND MAINTENANCE

Keep the soil moist with thrice-weekly waterings once the temperature climbs into the 90s. Water monthly throughout the winter. Fertilizer is not a real issue with Germanders, but you could add the contents of a 1-pound coffee can filled with an all-purpose fertilizer containing 10 to 16 percent nitrogen. This will cover an area of 100 square feet. Work the fertilizer into the soil in the early spring and again after flowering. Germanders often freeze down during the winter—do not remove the foliage until new growth emerges; then remove all growth to the ground. The plant will come back with a vengeance. Spider mites sometimes work on the lower leaves and cause them to look dry. If there is a problem, direct a strong jet of water at the plant to wash off the pests.

LANDSCAPE MERIT

Use Germander as edging for dwarf hedges or massed in among rocks. They fit in herb and cottage gardens and thrive in southern Nevada heat.

ADDITIONAL SPECIES, CULTIVARS, OR VARIETIES

T. majoricum grows ankle-high and 2 feet wide with silvery gray foliage and a show of rosy purple, honey-scented flowers in the spring. *T. marum*, or Cat Thyme, gets a foot high and wide with gray-green dense foliage and pink to purplish flowers.

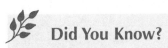 **Did You Know?**

I find cats love this beauty, and from a distance, it does have a Catnip look.

Japanese Spurge

Pachysandra terminalis

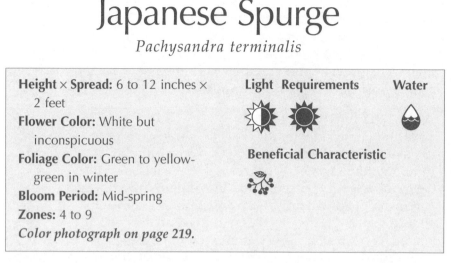

Height × Spread: 6 to 12 inches × 2 feet	Light Requirements	Water
Flower Color: White but inconspicuous		
Foliage Color: Green to yellow-green in winter	**Beneficial Characteristic**	
Bloom Period: Mid-spring		
Zones: 4 to 9		
Color photograph on page 219.		

Well, it's almost true that Japanese Spurge will grow in the dark. It is one of the few plants that will grow well in deep shade and form a loose but dense ground cover. It forms a low-growing mat that will get to 12 inches high at the very most and spread out to at least 2 feet. Because it has rhizomatous stems it will root as it creeps along, so it can spread farther—you're just not sure where the old plant ends and the new plant from the rhizome begins. It does have white flowers developing on terminal spikes, but the flowers are very tiny and not really showy. In the late summer, the fruit forms: a white three-horned drupe. The evergreen foliage is a bright, shiny green and each leaf is oblong and the upper half toothed. In the spring the leaves are often tinged with a little purple, and in the fall and winter they turn a yellow-green. (DP)

REGIONAL TIPS

Japanese Spurge grows in all the regions of the state. In the hot region, be sure it's in the shade. In the coldest of the mountainous regions, it might come through the winter better if covered with mulch and uncovered in the spring.

WHEN, WHERE, AND HOW TO PLANT

Plant Japanese Spurge anytime during the growing season. As with all nursery plants, you will have the best selection in the spring. This is a very useful ground cover that can be planted in the dense shade of trees and still look good. As the trees start to shade the yard, the lawn under them fades away, leaving bare soil behind, and Japanese Spurge will rapidly cover the ground with a carpet of leaves. In the cooler regions it will grow in full sun. Japanese Spurge tolerates almost any soil but will grow best in a soil with lots of organic matter in it. When you prepare the soil, add a 4-inch layer of organic mulch to the surface and mix it thoroughly into the top 6 inches; you can also add a complete fertilizer at the same time. For an area that is 100 square feet (10 feet by 10 feet), fill a 1-pound coffee can with a fertilizer containing about 10 to 16 percent nitrogen and about the same amount of phosphorous and potassium. Japanese Spurge is usually sold in 1-gallon cans, so when you plant, dig the hole only as deep as the rootball and about twice as wide, spacing the plants about 18 inches apart.

CARE AND MAINTENANCE
Japanese Spurge is very easy to care for and not messy. If you are tempted to shear the plants to shape them up—Don't. They don't tolerate pruning. They will do fine on 1 inch of water twice a week, and I fertilize mine with a water-soluble fertilizer once in the spring. They don't have any pest problems.

LANDSCAPE MERIT
Japanese Spurges are good plants for the rock garden or as a ground cover for that shady spot in the flower bed or shrub border (but they aren't adapted for growing between steppingstones). They mix nicely with Hostas, another shade-loving plant.

ADDITIONAL SPECIES, CULTIVARS, OR VARIETIES
There are a few cultivars to try, and one is 'Green Sheen', which has extremely glossy leaves. Another is 'Green Carpet', with dark green leaves. It will yellow in full sun.

Kinnikinnick

Arctostaphylos uva-ursi

Other Name: Bearberry

Height × Spread: 12 to 18 inches × 2 to 4 feet

Flower Color: Pink

Foliage Color: Reddish green, reddish purple in winter

Bloom Period: Mid-spring, followed by red berries in fall

Zones: 2 to 8

Color photograph on page 219.

Light Requirement

Water

Beneficial Characteristic

The first time I can remember seeing Kinnikinnick is when we went Christmas tree hunting in Montana when I was six or seven. After finding a tree our next job was to gather materials for the wreath, and Kinnikinnick was one of the things Mom wanted. We found it on the south sides of the mountain where the snow had melted, and we'd cut off a bunch of twigs with their roundish leaves and red berries. It was very hard to propagate, so it was hard to find for many years. Now that the propagation mystery has been solved (leading to better survival), it is used quite a bit. Kinnikinnick is a great, slow-growing, evergreen ground cover that can get to 18 inches high. The cultivars that have been bred rarely get above 12 inches and spread to 4 feet at the most. The leaves are oval, thick, and leathery, and pink flowers grow at the ends of the twigs and hang in clusters that bloom in mid-spring. The fruit ripens in early fall and is a bright, shiny, red berry that looks good enough to eat; it is actually mealy and tastes lousy. But birds love it. (DP)

REGIONAL TIPS

Kinnikinnick is best adapted for the high desert and mountainous regions of the state. It does not do well in hot, dry heat, but it will survive if it's pampered.

WHEN, WHERE, AND HOW TO PLANT

Kinnikinnick is grown sometimes in balled-and-burlapped form but it's grown mainly as container plants. If it is balled and burlapped, it needs to be planted in the spring; as a container plant it can be planted anytime during the growing season. It grows best in full sun and doesn't do well in shady areas of the garden. Kinnikinnick doesn't require any special soil mixes, but it prefers sandy or well-drained soil. If the bed has been prepared for other plants, it will work just fine. Plant Kinnikinnick about 18 inches apart in the garden. Dig the hole just as deep as the rootball and about twice as wide. If the plant is balled and burlapped, remove the burlap and all the twine and wire so the plant will not be girdled or rootbound. After planting, give it a good soaking.

CARE AND MAINTENANCE

Kinnikinnicks are very tidy plants, easy to care for, and pests don't bother them. Just let them grow. They don't tolerate pruning, so the only pruning needed is to remove dead or damaged twigs. They don't require much water either, and they grow best when you allow the soil to dry out first. Use a water-soluble fertilizer in the spring according to directions.

LANDSCAPE MERIT

Kinnikinnick is a very attractive, low-growing evergreen plant that is colorful in the fall with its bright red berries. Kinnikinnick makes a great ground cover for hillsides and other places with sandy or dry soils. It is particularly nice in alpine and rock gardens. I see it used sometimes in narrow planters because of its slow growth.

ADDITIONAL SPECIES, CULTIVARS, OR VARIETIES

'Radiant' has large, bright-red fruit that lasts throughout the fall and into the winter. 'Big Bear' is fast growing, with shiny, dark green leaves. And 'Emerald Carpet', which also has deep green leaves, will grow in the shade better than the others.

Lamb's Ear

Stachys byzantina

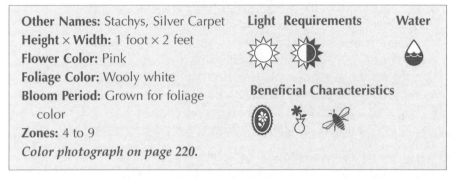

Other Names: Stachys, Silver Carpet
Height × Width: 1 foot × 2 feet
Flower Color: Pink
Foliage Color: Wooly white
Bloom Period: Grown for foliage
    color
Zones: 4 to 9
Color photograph on page 220.

Light Requirements

Water

Beneficial Characteristics

You need something old and something new in the garden. Lamb's Ear is one of those oldies that still commands attention, especially with children. As the name suggests, the silvery foliage is not only attractive but also soft as a lamb's ear or as a new baby's skin. Children love to feel these ears. Lamb's Ear grows a foot high and 2 feet wide to eventually form clumps to make a prostrate spreading mat so dense that weeds can't grow through it. Leaves grow thick on spreading stems and soon fuzzy spikes (*Stachys*, the genus name, means spike) of tiny pink flowers and small tubular scarlet flowers appear in the summer. They are not showy and are best removed, as they detract from the beauty of the leaves. (Some florists use the flowers in fresh bouquets.) The foliage is covered with fine hairs that insulate the leaves during the heat of the summer. Herbalists use the fresh or dried leaves to make a tea. The plant could have been listed as a perennial, but because it covers the ground I have it here—it complements so many of the ground covers and shrubs. (LM)

Regional Tips

Lamb's Ear does great in southern Nevada, but it is a marginal plant for the northern part of the state.

When, Where, and How to Plant

Plant new Lamb's Ear in spring when new plants become available. Lamb's Ear is not too fussy about the soil, providing it has good drainage. It needs full sun to keep the grayish and compact leaves intact but will tolerate some filtered shade. Plant it near walkways or rock gardens or mixed in a flower bed. Dig a hole three times wider than the plant and place it at the same depth it was in its previous home. Backfill the soil and water in well. Give Lamb's Ear a thorough soaking three times a week until established.

CARE AND MAINTENANCE

Keep water off the plant; direct watering smashes leaves down to make them mushy, so use drip emitters below the plants. Because of the lushness of this plant, it will need water up to three times a week as the temperatures climb into the 90s. Fertilize in the spring around Valentine's Day, as well as Labor Day, with a balanced shrub fertilizer. Cut off flower stems as they appear, and cut back in the late winter to renew growth; transplant this ground cover when new growth begins appearing in the early spring. You usually divide them every three to four years; but if your plants start dying from the center, it's time to divide them. Dig up the clump, discard the center, divide the remainder into 6-inch-diameter clumps, and replant. If we have a frosty winter, expect some damage to the leaves. No bugs or diseases bother Lamb's Ear.

LANDSCAPE MERIT

The silvery foliage brings out colors of plants such as Lavender, Candytuft, Veronica, and Roses. Lamb's Ear is good in borders and for color contrast. It is a gorgeous, unusual ground cover known more for its beautiful gray foliage than for its flowers.

ADDITIONAL SPECIES, CULTIVARS, OR VARIETIES

S. byzantina 'Silver Carpet' is similar but a little larger. 'Big Ears' has larger leaves and is larger overall.

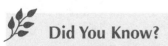 **Did You Know?**

Lamb's Ear doesn't require mulch, as it makes its own with its dense foliage.

Lily Turf

Liriope muscari

Height × Spread: 15 inches × 12 inches

Flower Color: White, lavender, and blue

Foliage Color: Deep green

Bloom Period: Summer to fall

Zones: 6 to 8

Color photograph on page 220.

Light Requirements

Water

Lily Turf forms nice, neat clumps in the garden and doesn't spread. The long, grasslike dark-green leaves get as long as 15 inches and about 1/2 inch wide. Lily Turf flowers on spikes that extend above the foliage, and it comes in shades of blue, lavender, and white. After flowering, the fruit is a shiny black berry. I have 'Variegata' in my garden, and the interesting thing is that the leaves are edged with gold. They are normally evergreen, but with the cold, open winters of the high desert, the tips of the leaves die back and are not too attractive. The drawback is that when we do have a harsh winter it takes them until midsummer to look good again. (DP)

REGIONAL TIPS

They need some protection from the sun and hot, dry winds in southern Nevada. They are not hardy in the mountainous regions.

WHEN, WHERE, AND HOW TO PLANT

You can plant Lily Turf anytime, but you will have much better establishment if you do it in the spring. Our dry open winters often make late fall and winter planting a little risky in the north. You can only get them as container plants, so purchase one-gallon cans. They aren't fussy about the soil but they do better if planted in a well-drained soil; add about 3 inches of organic mulch to the surface of the soil and till it in to a depth of 6 inches. They have a low demand for feeding, but you could add the contents of a 1-pound coffee can filled with an all-purpose fertilizer containing 10 to 16 percent nitrogen. This will cover about 100 square feet. Work the fertilizer into the soil at the same time that you mulch. Space the plants about

12 inches apart and dig the hole as deep as the rootball and a little wider; place the rootball in the hole, and backfill. After planting, give it a good soaking.

CARE AND MAINTENANCE

Lily Turf is very easy to maintain. When any of the leaves start to look yellow or brown, cut them off; this makes the plant look tidier. When the temperatures are in the 90s and above, water three times a week. After the plants have been in the garden for a few years, divide them (you will have the best results if you divide them in the early spring before the plants start to grow). They are relatively pest-free.

LANDSCAPE MERIT

Lily Turf makes a very good ground cover, particularly for those hard-to-plant shady areas under trees. The texture of the leaves adds interest to rock gardens, and they are great for edging plants too. The mounding habit adds character to flower beds.

ADDITIONAL SPECIES, CULTIVARS, OR VARIETIES

'Monroe White' has white flowers instead of blue. 'Majestic' has rich lavender flowers. 'Variegata' is one of the lower-growing Lily Turfs (at only 1 to 15 inches high), and it has the added interest of green leaves edged with gold. *Liriope spicata* is the creeping Lily Turf, and it only gets to 9 inches high, with leaves that are only 1/4 inch wide. It is also a little hardier then the *L. muscari*.

Mother-of-Thyme

Thymus serpyllum

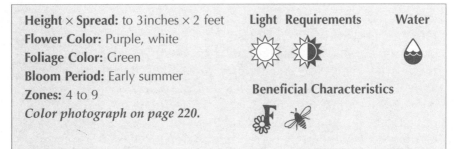

Height × Spread: to 3inches × 2 feet
Flower Color: Purple, white
Foliage Color: Green
Bloom Period: Early summer
Zones: 4 to 9
Color photograph on page 220.

Light Requirements

Water

Beneficial Characteristics

Mother-of-Thyme is a perennial herb that is way more than a ground cover. The foliage is very aromatic, and when used around steppingstones you get a good whiff every time you crush the leaves. The leaves are small and somewhat rounded. Mother-of-Thyme loves full sun and will grow very rapidly to form a dense mat in the garden. It will tolerate some light shade. (I have one growing in full shade, but it's leggy and flowering is very limited.) Another benefit of this plant is the flowers. The blooms are generally purple, though some varieties may be white or even rose. The flowers form in clusters at the end of the stems and bloom in early summer. Mother-of-Thyme is not the herb used for cooking; if that's what you need, plant English Thyme, *Thymus vulgaris*. This is a taller and more shrublike plant that also has fragrant leaves and lilac to white flowers. English Thyme is great for enhancing the flavor of meat. (DP)

REGIONAL TIPS

Mother-of-Thyme will grow in all regions of the state. It will tolerate the heat even in the hot region, but more frequent irrigation may be needed.

WHEN, WHERE AND HOW TO PLANT

Plant Mother-of-Thyme anytime during the growing season—in the hot region of the state plant it in the winter. Generally you will have a better selection during the spring. It grows best in full sun to part shade. You can plant Mother-Of-Thyme as a container plant or from seed. If you are going to start from seed, start it in the house. It will take about seven weeks to get a good, sturdy transplant. In the high desert and mountainous regions, sow the seed by the middle of March; in the hot region you can sow the seed in December. It is not fussy about the soil, but it will grow better in a well-drained soil: add 3 inches of organic mulch to the surface and mix it in to a depth of 6 inches. You can also mix in a complete fertilizer containing between 10 and 16 percent nitrogen at the same time. I use a 1-pound coffee can filled with the fertilizer for every 100 square feet of garden. Space the plants 10 to 16 inches apart, and give them a good soaking once planted.

CARE AND MAINTENANCE

Mother-of-Thyme is easy to care for. Older plants can get a little leggy, so shear back to make them bushier. They need 1 inch of water twice a week at the most.

LANDSCAPE MERIT

Many think Mother-of-Thyme was invented for use around steppingstones, and while that's not quite true, it is certainly the best suited for the purpose. It can also be used as a ground cover to cover paths that are used infrequently, because it will withstand some foot traffic, but not tromping by the whole clan on a daily basis. It is also ideal for those sunny rock outcroppings in the rock garden, where it will drape gracefully down over the rocks.

ADDITIONAL SPECIES, CULTIVARS, OR VARIETIES

T. citriodorus is the Lemon Scented Thyme. It grows to 12 inches tall and has lavender to pink flowers.

Did You Know?

Mother-of-Thyme is an excellent plant if you live in an area that has rabbits, squirrels, or deer—they won't eat it.

Periwinkle

Vinca species

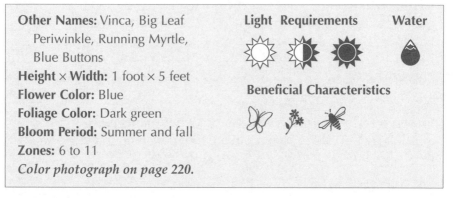

Other Names: Vinca, Big Leaf Periwinkle, Running Myrtle, Blue Buttons
Height × Width: 1 foot × 5 feet
Flower Color: Blue
Foliage Color: Dark green
Bloom Period: Summer and fall
Zones: 6 to 11
Color photograph on page 220.

Light Requirements

Water

Beneficial Characteristics

Vinca takes me back to my mother's patch of Vincas that were visible out her kitchen window. I guess it was the evergreen leaves that brought her a feeling of eternity, or was it the deep blue starlike flowers that emerged each morning to remind her of a fresh day ahead? Whatever it was, that patch is still there to remind me of the greatness of this enduring plant—you can use it in so many ways. My mother's Periwinkle wanders out into the lawn and into her Irises. It trails over planter beds and climbs fences and a host of other places, to give you that jungle feeling. There is just something about the glossy green leaves and the cooling effect the blue flowers bring to any landscape. The single blooms, 2 inches in diameter, look like spinning cartwheels and appear among the foliage in the spring. (LM)

REGIONAL TIPS

Plant these beauties after the last frost (March 15 in the south and May 22 in the north).

WHEN, WHERE, AND HOW TO PLANT

Vincas come in flats and containers, so plant anytime in the south; plant in spring in the north. Vincas tolerate a wide range of soil conditions as long as drainage is good, but they can't take wet feet. Vinca loves full sun but will take partial shade in the north; in the south it needs relief with afternoon shade. It likes the east side of a house if it has its choice. Because Vincas have the ability to put down roots wherever nodes touch the ground, it is best to prepare the entire bed rather than planting in holes. (As a side note: this habit makes them easy to propagate.) Thoroughly mix some organic matter into the top 6 to 8 inches of soil. Space the *V. major* plants about 18 inches apart and *V. minor* plants 12 inches apart. When planting, make sure you plant them at the same depth you found them growing in the container. Follow with a good soaking.

CARE AND MAINTENANCE

Vinca has a quick way of telling when it needs water: The lushness in leaves disappears and glossy leaves go limp and lackluster. Learn to watch your plants; they are the best indicators of when to water. Water will quickly revive them. Vinca is a high water user in the south and moderate drinker in the north, and enjoys a good feed in the early spring and fall. Add the contents of a 1-pound coffee can filled with an all-purpose fertilizer containing 10 to 16 percent nitrogen. This will cover about 100 square feet. Work the fertilizer into the soil prior to irrigation. Prune as needed to keep within bounds, and shear or mow plants to within a few inches of the ground in the late winter. Aphids, snails, and slugs bother Vincas. Wash off the aphids and use snail bait for snails and slugs.

LANDSCAPE MERIT

It is a slow grower but in time it is invasive. The thickness of the mat suppresses weeds. When planted below other shrubs, the glossy foliage and the bluish flowers bring out the best in both plants.

ADDITIONAL SPECIES, CULTIVARS, OR VARIETIES

There are two Vincas: *V. major* and *V. minor*. *Vinca major* has much larger leaves and flowers; *Vinca minor* has smaller, darker green leaves and is slower growing.

Did You Know?

Vincas are often confused with Catharanthus roseus. *Both go by "Vinca" and "Periwinkle."* C. roseus *is an annual and Vincas are perennials, but the flowers are similar.*

Prostrate Myoporum

Myoporum parvifolium

Other Names: Trailing Myoporum, Australian Racer
Height × Width: 1/2 foot × 6 feet
Flower Color: White
Foliage Color: Bright green
Bloom Period: Spring
Zones: 8 to 10
Color photograph on page 220.

Light Requirements

Water

Prostrate Myoporum spreads across the ground like prairie fire, growing runners in a 360-degree circle. As it spreads, dense foliage follows. Bright green, fleshy, lance-shaped leaves store moisture to enhance the spread. And get this: the water-filled leaves make it fire retardant. In the spring, white star-shaped blossoms cover the foliage like snow. After flowering, small, insignificant purple berries splatter themselves across the foliage. Where it really shines is planted along the side of a dry creek with runners reaching down into the creek bed for moisture—it makes it seem as if water is there and it gives a cooling effect to the mind. A lady whom I know planted Prostrate Myoporum to the side of her real creek. The long stems reached down into the passing water to take a dip, and gentle breezes caused them to bounce up and down. Prostrate Myoporum is a low-maintenance or forget-me plant, my kind of plant. This ground cover damages quickly if people persistently walk across it. (LM)

REGIONAL TIPS
Prostrate Myoporum is not hardy enough for northern Nevada. In the south, during the heat of summer, the foliage becomes yellow even if there is enough water.

WHEN, WHERE, AND HOW TO PLANT
Prostrate Myoporum is best planted in the fall to give it time to establish. Because of its aggressiveness, use only 1-gallon containers. It needs a good, rich soil to accommodate the new roots as they emerge from the stem nodes. Here is another feature often over-looked: stem nodes drop roots as they spread across the ground to form a tight, dense carpet. This is why it is so important to prepare

all the ground under the plants so nodes can root and create a more appealing plant. Prepare the entire bed down to 6 inches for future rooting. Simply remove enough soil to place the rootball in the ground. The plant does need good drainage and performs best in full sun to partial shade. Follow planting with a deep soaking and then twice weekly (but do not keep the soil too soggy) until established.

Care and Maintenance

Keep the soil moist under the plant for rooting, but keep moisture off foliage or the water will cause dieback. Because the root system is small and shallow, it needs water three times a week as the temperatures climb into the 90s. Fertilizer is not a real issue with Prostrate Myoporum. If the plants are around lawns or other plants, add some to Prostrate Myoporum when you fertilize the rest. It may require occasional edging if you get it too close to paving; otherwise, remove the older growth in the early spring to improve appearance. It can't tolerate foot traffic and suffers from root rot if overwatered, but it does not have any pest problems.

Landscape Merit

Prostrate Myoporum is ideal for use on mounds, producing a dense, lush cover to become a refreshing island of green in a desert landscape.

Additional Species, Cultivars, or Varieties

'Dwarf Pink' is a miniature version of the species and does great in small areas. 'Burgundy Carpet' has purple new growth hanging on red stems. 'Pink', as you might have guessed, bears pink flowers. 'Putah Creek' is taller than the species and not quite as wide spreading

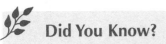

Did You Know?

In Las Vegas, it is known as the Australian Racer because of its rapid, spreading habit.

Prostrate Rosemary

Rosmarinus officinalis 'Prostratus'

Other Names: Dwarf Rosemary, Rosemary
Height × Width: 2 feet × 4 feet
Flower Color: Blue
Foliage Color: Dark green
Bloom Period: About all year
Zones: 6 to 10
Color photograph on page 220.

Light Requirements

Water

Beneficial Characteristics

Prostrate Rosemary is one of the best ground covers in Nevada, especially in southern Nevada. Everyone, including casinos, uses it throughout the landscape. It is valued for its durability and fast growth. It has dark, gray-green, almost needlelike foliage, and a picturesque form up to 4- to 6-feet high. Our heat does take some starch out of the green during the summer. Branching, stiff stems are lined with resinous, aromatic needlelike leaves and the many pale-blue flowers cover the branches from winter into fall. Whether it is grown as a ground cover, shrub, or in pots, you can use the leaves fresh, dried, or in cooking. When you crush the foliage, it is extremely aromatic and lemon scented. Birds and bees love Rosemary. As the plant matures, its compact, mounded form becomes more irregular, with branches spreading as wide as the plant is tall. *Rosmarinus* means "dew of the sea," reflecting the plant's native habitat on seaside cliffs in the Mediterranean region. (LM)

REGIONAL TIPS

Apologetically I'll say to northern Nevadans, Prostrate Rosemary cannot take your tough winters. But it is a wonderful ground cover and a very useful herb for the southern part of the state.

WHEN, WHERE, AND HOW TO PLANT

Plant anytime from containers but preferably in the fall. It is tolerant of a wide range of soils but needs good drainage. It loves full sun but will tolerate some shade. Dig the planting hole 3 times wider and as deep as the rootball. Mix compost with the soil removed from the hole, and fill it in around the rootball. Use water to further settle the soil; build a water basin and water three times a week until established.

CARE AND MAINTENANCE

It will tolerate a great deal of heat and may yellow slightly if kept too dry, but err on the side of dryness—overwatering plants makes them unattractive, rank, and haphazard in their development. Control it by pruning to remove the overgrown branches, or just cut back on the water. If it is placed in tight quarters, it will need to be pruned more often. Prostrate Rosemary does have a tendency to build up dead wood and may need to be replaced. It has a low demand for feeding, but it's a good idea to add the contents of a 1-pound coffee can filled with an all-purpose fertilizer containing 10 to 16 percent nitrogen. Work the fertilizer into the soil while mulching around Valentine's Day, and again Memorial Day. Pinch tips of branches to encourage fullness and bushiness and to prevent the branches from becoming woody, and use the clippings in your cooking. Rosemary mainly stays pest-free, but Bermuda Grass can become a real problem if the two become entwined. Spittlebugs are occasionally found but they are not a problem.

LANDSCAPE MERIT

Prostrate Rosemary is an aromatic plant and good in tough situations. It creates a very exciting site when it spills over a wall by branches covered with blooms. It is prized as a culinary herb.

ADDITIONAL SPECIES, CULTIVARS, OR VARIETIES

'Lockwood de Forest' is a low-growing plant similar to 'Prostratus' but has bluer flowers and lighter-colored foliage. 'Collingwood Ingram' is low-growing and has gracefully curving branches, blue-violet flowers, and spreads 4 feet wide. 'Tuscan Blue' is an upright, large-growing type to 5 feet with rigid branches, rich green foliage, and blue-violet flowers. 'Arps' is the most hardy of the genus that will reach 6 feet tall.

Did You Know?

The flowers on Rosemary are edible; add them to salads or use as a garnish. Use the leaves as seasoning in all seasons.

Trailing Lantana

Lantana montevidensis

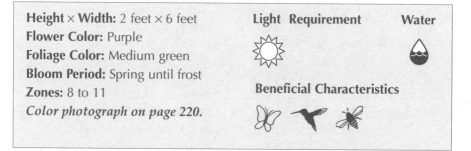

Height × Width: 2 feet × 6 feet
Flower Color: Purple
Foliage Color: Medium green
Bloom Period: Spring until frost
Zones: 8 to 11
Color photograph on page 220.

Light Requirement

Water

Beneficial Characteristics

I love Trailing Lantana. It works from sunup to sundown, week in and week out even during cool winters, producing masses of blooms for us. In the winter when production cuts back, this trailing vine turns its lightly frosted foliage a deep purple, almost hiding the flowers still on the vine. It is hardiest of the Lantanas and fast in covering its territory; in fact, it may crowd out other plants. It has become a valued addition to our gardens because it produces abundant clusters of lavender flowers that cover the plant continually from spring until frost. Tiny black berries follow and they are poisonous; if you have children, prune the berries off. It is useful as a ground cover in hot areas, and hardly any effort on your part is needed. It is one of my lazy-man plants—why, it even cleans off its own spent flowers! Trailing Lantana often goes through the winter unhurt by the cold weather if planted on the southwest side of a home. The lower stems root along the ground, causing it to spread for great lengths. (LM)

REGIONAL TIPS

Sorry, northern Nevadans, Trailing Lantana will not withstand your harsh winters although you could treat it as an annual. But it is a wonderful ground cover for the southern part of the state as long as you don't have a cold winter.

WHEN, WHERE, AND HOW TO PLANT

Because it can be frost-tender, plant it in the spring. It loves sun, so plant it in full sun. It isn't fussy about soil conditions as long as it has good drainage. Since Trailing Lantana roots down as the lower stems spread across the ground, improve the soil of the entire bed. Mix in generous amount of organic matter at least 6 inches deep. Purchase flats or 4-inch pots and place them at the same depth they were growing in the container. Thoroughly soak the area at least three times a week until established. Trailing Lantana covers the ground quickly, so no mulch is necessary.

CARE AND MAINTENANCE

Water weekly throughout the summer and then gradually wean the plants to once-monthly watering through the winter. Trailing Lantana thrives on very little fertilizer, but feed it if you are feeding other plants in the area. If flower production slows, you are most likely overfeeding or overwatering. By the same token, underwatering and underfeeding will slow flower production significantly. Do not remove the frozen foliage until danger of frost passes. Although this is unsightly, it does protect the roots. As the season warms up, cut back the older foliage to the ground to renew growth and future flowering. It does not have any pest issues.

LANDSCAPE MERIT

Trailing Lantana shows well in natural gardens, tucked in among boulders, as a foreground for perennials, or draped over walls or containers—always happily blooming! The undulating, mounding growth habit complements taller plants.

ADDITIONAL SPECIES, CULTIVARS, OR VARIETIES

Other Lantanas include the shrub-type: *L. horrida*, or Desert Lantana, which comes with yellow-orange flowers that cover the bush. It closely resembles its cousin *L. camara*, which has the same flowers but throws red into the scene. It is perhaps the most popular Lantana in southern Nevada. 'Spreading Sunset' and 'Spreading Sunshine', both of which have yellow flowers, are more prostrate and combine well with tall background shrubs.

Ornamental Grasses

G RASSES HAVE PLAYED A MAJOR ROLE in the ecology of plant life and in the development of human society. Many basic crops—wheat, rice, and corn—are grasses. Today, grasses are playing an increasingly important role in the garden landscape. The versatility, adaptability, and exquisite beauty of ornamental grasses make them the perfect companion and counterpoint plants to flowering perennials and woody ornamentals. Some grasses work well as ground covers, others serve better as accent pieces or focal points. With their vast array of colors—from cold blue to fiery red—and their varied shapes and sizes—from dense ground-level clumps to towering 20-foot-tall reeds—ornamental grasses are valued for their beauty and durability in landscape borders, beds, and gardens.

Unlike lawn grasses, ornamental grasses are left to flourish in their natural states. Lawn grasses are frequently cut and are, in fact, invigorated by the process. Ornamental grasses, on the other hand, are weakened and eventually perish through frequent low cuttings. Unlike lawns, whose beauty lies in the form and texture of a carpeted expanse, ornamental grasses are valued for their individual aesthetic properties, even when planted in masses. Some are pendulous; some stand erect. They form mounds or have vertical culms (stems), are single-colored or variegated, grow singularly from one clump or from spreading rhizomes (a horizontal underground stem that sends up a succession of stems or leaves at the nodes).

In these ways, ornamental grasses give a sense of texture, form, and color. Taller-growing species cast dominant silhouettes that act as accent points, while lower-growing species act as contrasting ground covers. Indeed, there are limitless possibilities when designing with ornamental grasses. One can build an interesting and aesthetically pleasing picture that contains both horizontal and vertical elements, distinctness and mass, regular and irregular textures and colors, natural forms and calculated design concepts. In addition to being aesthetically appealing, ornamental grasses require very little maintenance. They usually do not require staking or spraying, and most grasses grow in a variety of environmental conditions, appearing throughout the year.

Despite the adaptability and versatility of ornamental grasses, many people do not think of using them in their landscaping concepts. (In fact, most nonexperts don't know what an ornamental grass is and what it is not.) But whether used as specimens, ground covers, borders, or accents, ornamental grasses offer a wide range of possibilities to enhance the beauty of a garden.

Sometimes we need to make a transition in the landscape and don't know what to use. What better way to go from a manicured lawn to a more informal landscape than with ornamental grasses— and they grow so quickly with such little fanfare. They'll take full sun or partial shade and seem just as happy with each. There really is an ornamental grass for every nook and cranny.

Ornamental grasses have really risen to the occasion in Nevada. We are finding them used more and more in landscapes, and as water conservation becomes a more pressing issue, the golf courses are using them as accent plants. Ornamental grasses give the impression that water is near even though they are low water users. This offers a certain "coolness" as well. No matter how you use them, the soft, delicate foliage becomes their strength. Even on the hottest day, they will acknowledge the slightest breezes, suggesting a cooling effect is on its way. What wonderful additions ornamental grasses make to our landscapes.

Bigelow's Bear Grass

Nolina bigelovii

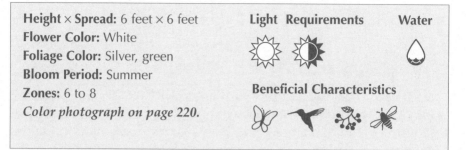

Height × Spread: 6 feet × 6 feet	**Light Requirements**	**Water**
Flower Color: White		
Foliage Color: Silver, green		
Bloom Period: Summer		
Zones: 6 to 8	**Beneficial Characteristics**	
Color photograph on page 220.		

B igelow's Bear Grass is part of the *Agave* family but looks like an ornamental grass. It is a toughie with stiff, coarse, grasslike leaves that are stemless, a yard long, and an inch wide. They are medium to dark green, thick and scabrous on the margins (but without offensive spines). The leaves are blunted and, as they age, hang like thatch on Palm trunks. Along with its cousins, Bigelow's Bear Grass make excellent landscape plants. They have the soft visual texture of grass, but they are lower maintenance because they're evergreen and more drought resistant. Sometimes leaves at the bottom turn tan, but these can be trimmed out. Bigelow's Bear Grass has the capability of developing trunks in its old age, as high as 6 feet; other varieties are a handy size for patio and courtyard gardens. Once established, roots of *Nolina* are massive and deep. When they are used as accents, give them a lot of space so the ends of their leaves don't become cramped. Rocks, flowers, other succulents, and true grasses look good around them. Flowers are small, creamy-white developing panicles, blooming in early summer. You can expect huge clusters of flowers on spikes that get about 10 feet tall. The flowers aren't that colorful but they add silhouette interest. (LM)

REGIONAL TIPS

Bigelow's Bear Grass is a very durable grass adapted to southern Nevada weather conditions. It will not take the harsh climate of the north.

WHEN, WHERE, AND HOW TO PLANT

Plant Bigelow's Bear Grass in the spring, in full sun to get the most out its greenery. And for it to really function properly, plant it in a well-drained soil. Since it is a clump grass, purchase in 5-gallon containers. Make a hole three times as wide and as deep as the rootball. Work some organic matter in with the on-site soil and nestle the backfill soil in around the roots. Make a water basin to hold water to soak the rooted area twice weekly until established.

CARE AND MAINTENANCE

During summers, water weekly, and in the winter, monthly. If you use a 2-gallon-per-hour drip emitter, let it run an hour with each irrigation. Bigelow's Bear Grass really doesn't need much fertilizer; it won't hurt to mix in a cup of ammonium sulfate in the early spring to keep it lush and green. If the lower leaves die, remove them. In the summer, a flowering stalk will shoot up to about 10 feet, looking like an overgrown barley-head of grain. After flower stalks die down, reach down in the plant and cut them off. Don't panic—it doesn't die like Century Plants do after blooming. And you'll love this part: It is pest-free.

LANDSCAPE MERIT

It makes a dramatic accent plant in a rock garden, near water features and it brings out interesting textural changes of other plants. And it makes a good plant for poolside provided there is ample room.

ADDITIONAL SPECIES, CULTIVARS, OR VARIETIES

N. longifolia, or Mexican Grass Tree, is an upright mound of grasslike leaves that may reach 10 feet high and 6 feet wide; its flowers are similar to *N. bigelovii*. *N. matapensis*, or Tree Bear Grass, gets about 10 to 25 feet tall and spreads out 10 feet, while *N. microcarpa* is more upright. *N. nelsoni* has blue leaves without teeth (but razor sharp!), growing 3 to 12 feet tall and spreading out 6 feet. *N. parryi* is a fairly small *Nolina* with 3- to 6-foot flower spikes rising 6 to 12 feet.

Deer Grass

Muhlenbergia rigens

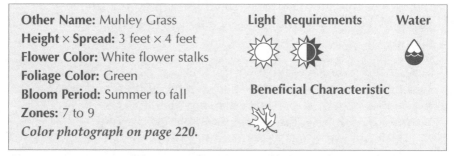

Other Name: Muhley Grass
Height × Spread: 3 feet × 4 feet
Flower Color: White flower stalks
Foliage Color: Green
Bloom Period: Summer to fall
Zones: 7 to 9
Color photograph on page 220.

Light Requirements

Water

Beneficial Characteristic

The graceful foliage and airy flowers of Deer Grass bear soft-colored seedheads in the fall which remain through winter. This rapid grower produces a lush head of grass that billows out like a flowing spring, with the grass tips falling back to the ground, sweeping under its bush as the winds swish the blades back and forth. It is at home in dry creeks with grass spilling over the rocks along the streambed, as a gentle breeze causes it to dust the rocks. Grass, to me, connotes moisture and gives the impression of a natural cooling effect. Deer Grass, in its unusual beauty, holds its color through the summer even without additional summer water. Flowers are slender, whiplike spikes, 2 to 3 feet tall, that emerge grayish in early summer and mature to buff later in the season. Even when dormant, Deer Grass remains upright, well shaped, and a handsomely colored buff with faint undertones of green. It's rugged for a grass, and even in desert gardens it needs only a little irrigation. When planted as a ground cover, it looks formal with its separate clumps, but for a less formal look, you can use one or more as an accent. There are many Muhleys that are pretty. (LM)

REGIONAL TIPS

Deer Grass only tolerates temperatures down to the teens and thus is only suitable for the southern climate.

WHEN, WHERE, AND HOW TO PLANT

Plant Deer Grass when you find it at the nursery in spring. Because it is a clumping grass, purchase it in 1-gallon containers. (You won't get excited with what you see because ornamental grasses are in the dormant state in spring.) Deer Grass loves full sun, but it will tolerate light shade. To get the most out of seedheads in the fall, plant in full sun. In order for Deer Grass to thrive, plant it in a well-drained soil. Make a hole 3 feet wide and a foot deep. Work some organic matter in with the onsite soil and nestle it in around the roots. Make a water basin to help soak the rooted area at least twice a week until established or when you see new growth emerging.

CARE AND MAINTENANCE

It does require once-a-week waterings in the summer and monthly watering throughout the winter. Deer Grass needs a balanced fertilizer around Valentine's, Memorial, and Labor Days to keep it lush. To renew Deer Grass, cut the foliage back in February to 5 inches above the ground. About every five years, divide the mature clumps in the early spring, making four divisions from one clump, and transplant elsewhere. Keep the soil moist until you see new growth emerging from the clump. Deer Grass has no pest problems.

LANDSCAPE MERIT

It is a fine choice as a specimen and an accent in the garden. Its handsome foliage and showy flowers complement native gardens. It makes an excellent border plant when used in masses or groupings, works well around water features or along dry creeks, and in rock gardens or as an accent plant. It brings an oasis alive, especially in the fall.

ADDITIONAL SPECIES, CULTIVARS, OR VARIETIES

M. lindheimeri is larger and bolder than Deer Grass, with blades folded lengthwise down the middle. Flowers are narrow, upright silver plumes to 5 feet tall, and it is very drought tolerant once established.

Fountain Grass

Pennisetum setaceum

Height × Spread: 5 feet × 3 feet
Flower Color: White tinged with pink
Foliage Color: Medium green
Bloom Period: Fall
Zones: 5 to 8
Color photograph on page 220.

Light Requirement

Water

Beneficial Characteristics

Pampas Grass was my first love affair with ornamental grasses, but it gets so big and cumbersome. My next romance came with Fountain Grass, an eye-catcher I find to be very decorative planted among rocks and boulders and along dry creeks. I especially like it near creeks; I find ornamental grasses in general suggest nearby water, and that suggests coolness. Fountain Grasses are easily recognized as a group by their plush flowers and seedheads in the fall. This grass has a dual purpose. During the summer it brings a grassy green to the scene in clump form and later turns the color of straw in the late summer. It forms tufts or clumps of narrow, grasslike leaves 2 to 3 feet long, in a medium green that turns golden brown when going dormant in winter. The blades are stiffer and arch somewhat—but not as dramatically as other ornamental grasses. Leaves form a dense mound that produces many thin stems rising above the foliage and developing 4- to 6-inch-long plumes that are generally white and tinged to pink or purple. Late summer and autumn are the height of the season for the showy grasses, when the foliage fades to blush tan and the silken texture of the flowers becomes fluffier. Light reflecting off the leaves and seed-heads makes Fountain Grass glow, and gentle breezes make the stems dance. (LM)

REGIONAL TIPS

Apologetically I'll tell northern Nevadans: Fountain Grass will not grow as a perennial because of your harsh winters. But it makes a wonderful ornamental grass for the southern part of the state.

WHEN, WHERE, AND HOW TO PLANT

Plant Fountain Grass when the nurseries have it for sale in the spring, and as it is a clumping grass, purchase it in 1-gallon containers.

People have a tendency to crowd plantings of ornamental grasses; if you crowd Fountain Grass, it quickly fills in and loses its gracefulness. Fountain Grass loves full sun but will tolerate light shade and also likes a well-drained soil. Make a hole 3 feet as wide and as deep as the clump, working in some organic matter with the on-site soil and snuggling it all back around the roots. Make a water basin and fill it to thoroughly soak the rooted area twice a week until you see new growth emerging.

CARE AND MAINTENANCE

Fountain Grass requires weekly watering until temperatures rise over 90 degrees Fahrenheit; then go to thrice-weekly waterings and monthly irrigations in winter. Work a cup full of ammonium sulfate around each clump on Valentine's, Memorial, and Labor Days, and follow with good irrigation. If leaves turn an off-green shade, you need to add some iron fertilizer. To renew Fountain Grass, cut back to 5 inches above the ground at the time of the first spring feeding. And remember that ornamental grasses do have an ugly side to them, in the spring after you have removed the top growth from last year. No pests bother Fountain Grass.

LANDSCAPE MERIT

Use it along borders, in masses, near water features, in rock beds, and as filler. It makes a good contribution to any landscape. Remember *P. setaceum* is a heavy seed-producer; it may escape cultivation where water is present. You may want to consider the sterile cultivars.

ADDITIONAL SPECIES, CULTIVARS, OR VARIETIES

P. setaceum 'Rubrum' is a smaller, neat, round clump of grasslike foliage, with reddish-brown blades and attractive rose-red flower spikes on 4-foot stalks in the fall. *P. cupreum* 'Cupreum' has deep-reddish foliage, wider leaves, and coppery plumes. 'Atrosanguineum' is purple with purple seed spikes. All are sterile.

Leather Leaf Sedge

Carex buchananii

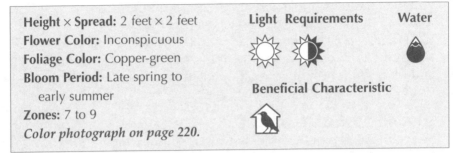

Height × Spread: 2 feet × 2 feet
Flower Color: Inconspicuous
Foliage Color: Copper-green
Bloom Period: Late spring to
  early summer
Zones: 7 to 9
Color photograph on page 220.

Light Requirements

Water

Beneficial Characteristic

Grasses add an interesting texture to the landscape because of their fine foliage, and Leather Leaf Sedge is no exception. It is an evergreen grass that grows in tall clumps to over 2 feet high. The leaves are typical of all *Carex* and are three-sided, starting out very stiff and upright, and having a tendency to spread and tip to the ground as they mature. The leaves are a reddish-brown color that makes it one of those plants that you either love or hate, because it looks brown and dormant year around. I like the winter effect. The flowers are small and look more like tiny tufts that grow out of the sides of the axils of the triangular leaves. When planted with other green grasses it makes a good accent. Being in the Sedge family, it grows best in moist soils but will tolerate some drought once it is established. (DP)

REGIONAL TIPS

Leather Leaf Sedge needs protection from the direct sun in the hot regions of the state and even in the high desert it would do better if protected from the afternoon sun. It needs to be mulched in the cold mountainous regions of Nevada during the winter; rake off the mulch in the spring.

WHEN, WHERE, AND HOW TO PLANT

Plant Leather Leaf Sedge anytime during the growing season, but you will find the best selection in the spring. In the hot regions it can be planted most anytime of the year. It will grow in either full sun or part shade. Leather Leaf Sedge is sold as a container plant but it can be divided in the spring to give you an everlasting supply of new plants, and it can also be started from seed. Start it inside in pots, and transplant it into the garden when you have clumps of grass that tightly fill a 4-inch pot. It will take about six to seven weeks from the time you sow the seed until you have a transplant. It will grow in almost any soil, but it grows best in a well-drained one. Space the plants about 12 inches apart in the garden, and give them a good soaking after planting.

CARE AND MAINTENANCE
Leather Leaf Sedge is considered a short-lived perennial that persists in the garden only for three or four years. By dividing them every couple of years you will rejuvenate the plants. Because they need to be divided, many gardeners don't use them as the center of their gardens. If they are under continued drought stress, they will become weak and are then attacked by aphids. So it's important to use this plant where it can stay moist, even though it will tolerate some drought.

LANDSCAPE MERIT
This is a plant ideally suited not only for dry streambeds but also actual streams and ponds. Sedges love the water. With the interest in water gardens, this plant is a natural. If you have a meadow garden, plant Leather Leaf Sedge in low areas where all the irrigation water drains—it loves that, too. And yet it is also adapted to the rock garden.

ADDITIONAL SPECIES, CULTIVARS, OR VARIETIES
There are a number of Sedges used in the landscape. *Carex comans* 'Frosty Curls' is one with almost white leaves that look like someone curled the tips like a ribbon for gift-wrap. Or try *C. elata* 'Bowles Golden' with its wide yellow leaves.

Maiden Grass

Miscanthus sinensis

Other Names: Silver Grass, Japanese Eulalie
Height × Spread: 5 feet × 4 feet
Flower Color: Reddish bronze
Foliage Color: Dark green
Bloom Period: Fall
Zones: 5 to 8
Color photograph on page 220.

Light Requirements **Water**

Beneficial Characteristics

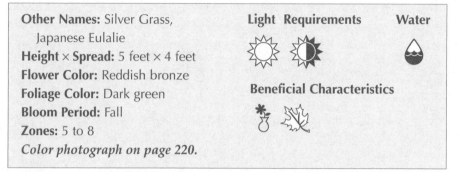

Maiden Grass, like other ornamental grasses, is a filler, a screen, and a hedge throughout the year; but when the weather cools, it moves onto center stage. Its long, arching leaves moved by gentle breezes conjure up images of ballerinas dancing in the breeze as the entire clump moves in unison, each stem leaning on the others for direction. When you couple ornamental grasses with gentle winds, it is poetry in motion. Maiden Grass is one of the showiest and liveliest plants in the garden. From a distance, fine-textured leaves appear silvery and give the plant an almost ghostly luminosity. It is sometimes referred to as Silver Grass because the blades and plumes have a silvery cast. Maiden Grass is a short-lived perennial of about four years but don't let this distract you, as you can divide the clumps and replant. (LM)

REGIONAL TIPS

Maiden Grass is not hardy enough for northern Nevada.

WHEN, WHERE, AND HOW TO PLANT

Plant Maiden Grass when it shows up in containers at the nursery, usually in the spring. Because it is a clumping grass, purchase it in 1-gallon containers. Yes, it is a blah-looking plant at the time, but keep the expected fall show in mind. All plants have a downside, and for the ornamental grasses, it is their spring appearance. People have a tendency to crowd plantings of grasses; if you do so with Maiden Grass, it quickly fills in and loses its gracefulness. Maiden Grass loves full sun but will tolerate light shade and likes an open, well-drained soil. Make a hole 3 feet wider and a foot deeper than the clump, working in some organic matter with the on-site soil and snuggling it all back around the roots. Make a water basin and fill it to thoroughly soak the rooted area twice a week until established.

CARE AND MAINTENANCE

It requires once-a-week watering in the summer and monthly watering throughout the winter. Maiden Grass doesn't need much fertilizer, but a light application of a fertilizer high in nitrogen around Valentine's Day and Labor Day will make a bushier plant. To renew Maiden Grass from year to year, cut the foliage back to 5 inches aboveground at the time of the spring feeding. After five years, divide the mature clumps in the early spring into four divisions and transplant elsewhere, keeping the soil moist until you see new growth emerging from the clumps. There are no pest problems.

LANDSCAPE MERIT

Use Maiden Grass as a background plant, hedge, or screen, but expect it to take center court with its show of fall colors. It is a plant that will really make a statement in any landscape.

ADDITIONAL SPECIES, CULTIVARS, OR VARIETIES

'Variegated Maiden Grass' has a creamy-white stripe along its dark-green blades. 'Morning Light' has variegated green-and-white blades that grow in clumps, with reddish-bronze plumes in late summer. 'Cabaret' leaf blades are silvery with milky white–striped centers that make a bold accent in the garden. 'Purpurascens', or Flame Grass, has brilliant orange-red fall foliage. *M. sinensis* 'Strictus', or Porcupine Grass, has bright-yellow variegated horizontal bands on stiff leaves resembling porcupine quills. It is also called Zebra Grass. *M. giganteus*, or Giant Chinese Silver Grass, has silver grass and is prized for its huge, vigorous foliage and silvery plumes.

Mexican Feather Grass

Nassella tenuissima

Height × Spread: 18 inches × 18 inches
Flower Color: Yellowish
Foliage Color: Bright green
Bloom Period: Summer
Zones: 7 to 10
Color photograph on page 221.

Light Requirements

Water

Beneficial Characteristics

Have you ever wondered what landscapes will look like in Heaven? As I ponder the thought, I can see meadows filled with Mexican Feather Grass. It is a very fine-stemmed clumping grass with upright and arching habits. Needle-thin, flexible leaves form dense clumps 18 inches tall and as wide. The bright green foliage is almost iridescent, especially when backlit by the evening sun. The numerous flower heads are a silky green in summer and turn golden as they mature, revealing the way the wind blows the grass by the way they lie. There is a slow change of colors from spring to fall. Bright green foliage mixed with some pale brown will shift to pale brown with less green. It becomes very casual with its windswept look. And as the plant matures, it becomes gnarled. (LM)

Regional Tips

This finely textured ornamental grass makes an excellent contribution as a perennial in southern Nevada landscapes and suffers in the harsher climates.

When, Where, and How to Plant

Plant Mexican Feather Grass in the spring. I must caution you that it is not all that pretty sitting on the nursery shelf. You must keep the summer in mind, when this grass will be out in all its beauty. This is one plant that looks good if you crowd it some, as the awns twist together as they mix in the wind. Mexican Feather Grass loves full sun but will tolerate light shade. Like other plants, it needs a well-drained soil or it will develop a disease called root rot. Since it is a clumping grass and it will spread, purchase it in 1-gallon containers. Make a hole 3 feet wider and a foot deeper than the clump, working in some organic matter with the on-site soil and snuggling it back around the roots. Make a water basin and fill it to thoroughly soak the rooted area twice a week until established. If you use a 2-gallon-per-hour drip emitter, let it run for an hour each time.

CARE AND MAINTENANCE

Mexican Feather Grass requires once-a-week watering in the summer and monthly watering throughout the winter. It doesn't need much fertilizer, but a cup of ammonium sulfate around Valentine's Day and Labor Day will create a more lush plant for its showoff time. To renew Feather Grass from year to year, clip off the grass close to the ground at the time of the spring feeding. After three years, divide the mature clumps in the early spring into four divisions and transplant elsewhere, keeping it moist until established. It doesn't have any pest problems, but it can be invasive, as it reseeds freely.

LANDSCAPE MERIT

Mexican Feather Grass is striking planted alone or in large masses or drifts. It is also attractive in rock gardens. Bunches of this grass make spectacular flower arrangements.

ADDITIONAL SPECIES, CULTIVARS, OR VARIETIES

N. gigantean, or Giant Feather Grass, grows about 4 feet high. The attractive seedheads are very striking, appearing on 5-foot-high spikes; these make a graceful, billowy, cut flower throughout the summer. *N. comata*, or Thread Grass, grows 3 to 4 feet tall. *N. pennata*, or European Feather Grass, shows pennantlike flowers distinguished by long, silky awns 8 to 10 inches above the foliage. *N. pulcherrima*, or Magnificent Feather Grass, is prized for its silky awns.

Did You Know?

An awn is a thin attachment that is found on the secondary spikes (spikelets) of many grasses.

Regal Mist

Muhlenbergia capillaris 'Regal Mist'

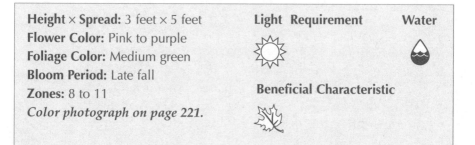

Height × Spread: 3 feet × 5 feet	**Light Requirement**	**Water**
Flower Color: Pink to purple		
Foliage Color: Medium green		
Bloom Period: Late fall		
Zones: 8 to 11	**Beneficial Characteristic**	
Color photograph on page 221.		

Beautiful, graceful, colorful, soft, feminine, billowing, feathery, gentle, and cooling are words I use to I describe 'Regal Mist'. Yes, I used to tout the virtues of Pampas Grass each fall, but after planting 'Regal Mist', it now dominates my conversations in the fall, when it is in the height of its glory. You have to see 'Regal Mist' in full bloom to believe it. This plant transforms my yard into a glowing work of art. Its incredible blooms appear like clouds of purple gas coming off the plumes when backlit by the evening sun. At other times, the blooms look like fluffy cotton candy on stems. About all you need to know is: Plant it, divide it, and cut it back each spring. After that, bright green, gracefully thin leaf-blades emerge, and by October the grass is back to a full-sized mound—this is when the plumes reach a foot or so above the foliage to put on their spectacular show. It is a great plant among boulders or in clusters in perennial gardens. It is a real traffic-stopper wherever you find it planted, and it becomes even more striking when backlit by the fall sun. (LM)

REGIONAL TIPS
This magnificent specimen is grown as a perennial in southern Nevada and as an annual in northern Nevada.

WHEN, WHERE, AND HOW TO PLANT
Plant 'Regal Mist' anytime you find plants available at the nurseries, with spring being the best time. 'Regal Mist' may be dormant at the time, but visualize what it will look like in the fall. It grows best in full sun for the best show of plumes but will tolerate light shade, and it requires an open, well-drained, organic soil for the grass to put on its best show. Since it is a clumping grass that will spread, purchase it in 1- or 5-gallon containers. Loosen up the soil at least three times

as wide, and as deep as the rootball. Work some organic matter into the on-site soil and nestle it in around the ball. Make a water basin around the plant, and thoroughly soak the rooted area at least twice a week until it establishes itself later in the early summer.

Care and Maintenance

It is a drought-tolerant plant but it prefers deep, weekly irrigations through the summer and monthly irrigation in the winter to ensure a good display in the fall. Renew 'Regal Mist' in February by cutting the brown foliage back to about 5 inches above ground level. Because it is a grass, you need to fertilize it with a balanced fertilizer high in nitrogen around Valentine's Day, Memorial Day, and Labor Day to develop a lush, bushy clump. To keep the clump looking its best, divide it every three to five years in the early spring. Divide the clump into three to four divisions and plant, keeping the soil moist with frequent irrigations until it establishes itself. It does not have any pest problems.

Landscape Merit

This ornamental grass is striking in any garden. It fits well in rock gardens, around boulders, along borders, and any-where you want to create a strong accent in the fall.

Additional Species, Cultivars, or Varieties

M. emersleyi, Bull Grass, has bright green foliage and creamy-white flower clusters that grow above the foliage clumps and bloom about the same time as 'Regal Mist', but it is certainly not as dramatic.

Ribbon Grass

Phalaris arundinacea 'Picta'

Height × Spread: To 3 feet spreading

Flower Color: White to pinkish spikes

Foliage Color: Green with white stripes

Bloom Period: June with seedheads persisting through winter

Zones: 4 to 9

Color photograph on page 221.

Light Requirements

Water

Beneficial Characteristic

Ornamental grasses have become an interesting way to landscape and add a new dimension, with many of the grasses as interesting in the winter as they are in the summer. This is true of the Ribbon Grass. In the summer, the long, narrow leaves add a fine texture to the garden with long, slender blades—dark green with white stripes—waving gracefully in the slightest breeze. In the winter, the leaves turn tan and add a different look. The flower spikes are white to pinkish and grow to about 15 inches long. Ribbon Grass grows to about 3 feet high and spreads by rhizomes. The spreading nature of this plant is something that needs to be taken into consideration; it can be a nuisance if it is not contained, so grow it in containers. (DP)

REGIONAL TIPS

Ribbon Grass will grow in all the regions of Nevada, growing actively throughout the year in the hot region. In the high desert and mountainous regions, it will go dormant in the wintertime.

WHEN, WHERE, AND HOW TO PLANT

Ribbon Grass is purchased as a container plant and can be transplanted anytime during the growing season. In the high desert and mountainous regions, it is best to plant it in the spring and summer before it goes dormant so that it will become established before winter. It prefers full sun but will tolerate a little shade. Ribbon Grass will grow in any soil, and no special care is needed to get it established. If you are planting it from a container directly into the garden, dig the hole just as deep as the rootball and slightly wider.

Place the rootball in the hole, fill in around it with soil, and give it a good soaking.

CARE AND MAINTENANCE

Ribbon Grass doesn't have any pest problems and is easy to take care of. You can mow it down periodically just to get some new growth. Mow it down in the fall when it goes dormant. If you want the leaves to add contrast to the winter garden, then mow it down in the spring before the new growth comes out. Don't use any herbicides that will kill grass or you'll kill this, too. Give it an inch of water twice a week, and as it is very aggressive, there's no need to fertilize it.

LANDSCAPE MERIT

Ribbon Grass makes a nice addition to the shrub beds or it is great as an accent in flower borders. I have seen Ribbon Grass and other grasses used to accent dry streambeds. It looks very natural when planted among the rocks and other plants; it's great for creating a meadow as well. Because it can spread very rapidly, you do have to be careful where you plant it. If left unconfined in flower beds, it will take over very soon. My solution is to plant it in plastic bowls like the ones used as color bowls. They are 14 inches in diameter and 6 inches deep with drainage in the bottom. After planting in the bowl, I bury the bowl right up to its lip. My Ribbon Grass has been there for four years and hasn't spread at all.

ADDITIONAL SPECIES, CULTIVARS, OR VARIETIES

An interesting variety is *P. arundinacea* 'Dwarf Garters'. The white-striped leaves of this plant grow to about 8 inches long and the flower plumes rise as high as 12 inches. It is considered less invasive.

Weeping Love Grass

Eragrostis curvula

Other Name: African Love Grass
Height × Spread: 3 feet × 3 feet
Flower Color: Bronze-red
Foliage Color: Dark green to
  bluish-bronze
Bloom Period: Fall
Zones: 7 to 10
Color photograph on page 221.

Light Requirement

Water

Beneficial Characteristics

This ornamental grass is called Weeping Love Grass because the fine grass blades become totally entwined with each other. Weeping Love Grass comes up in the spring with dark green, finely textured, almost hairlike foliage to form dense tufts of grass. Its thin leaves grow up to 3 feet and taller and remain that way until fall. The foliage turns a bluish-bronze-red as the frost settles in, and then 2- to 3-foot-long, fine flower clusters emerge on arching, weeping stems, changing in color from purple to gray as they mature. The flowers are very airy to allow the delicate seedheads to move easily with the slightest breezes. This weeper shows off equally well as a single, finely textured accent or when it is grown in groups. Later in the fall, Weeping Love Grass begins to decline, losing some of its glamour. Enjoy the fall colors, then prune during the winter to rejuvenate the plants. (LM)

REGIONAL TIPS
Weeping Love Grass will die down to the ground in southern Nevada and will frost out in northern Nevada.

WHEN, WHERE, AND HOW TO PLANT
Weeping Love Grass is best planted from a container anytime throughout the year, but it does best when planted in October and November. This ornamental grass, like others, generates its best fall color when exposed to full sun to partial shade. It must have good drainage or you can expect diseases like root rot to settle in. Because our soils are so compacted, make a hole 3 feet wider and as deep as the rootball, mixing in organic matter with the on-site soil when you plant. Also, build a water basin around the plant to keep it soaked until established.

Care and Maintenance

This plant will survive on a very limited water diet, but to keep it lush and attractive, supplement with weekly watering throughout the summer. It's a plant you must vigorously prune right back to within 5 inches of the ground in February, because after the plant dies down in the winter, the entwined grass becomes a distraction. From February to April is what you might call its downtime, but as temperatures warm, the foliage comes back. After pruning, apply a balanced shrub fertilizer high in nitrogen. Repeat again Memorial Day and Labor Day to keep the lush growth coming. Throughout the summer, prune back the long extending branches—it can get out of bounds— to keep it more attractive. A sticky substance on the leaf blades is a sign of an aphid problem. Spray the leaves with a strong jet of water, or use insecticidal soap.

Landscape Merit

Weeping Love Grass makes an interesting flowering accent. Its tough rooting habits make it an excellent plant to stabilize soil on banks for erosion control.

Additional Species, Cultivars, or Varieties

There are not many varieties of Weeping Love Grass. Here are a few: *E. spectabilis*, or Purple Love Grass, is a showy grass with colorful reddish-purple flowers and a compact height that make it a worthy and versatile player in the garden. *E. trichoides* 'Bend' is a clumping, bending Love Grass that can be used in northern Nevada. It grows vigorously until the flowers emerge in the late summer. They are pinkish on large, nodding panicles which almost obscure the foliage.

CHAPTER SIX

Palms

THERE ARE MORE THAN 3,000 SPECIES and over 200 genera in the palm family. These fascinating plants grow in shady, tropical rain forests and also under intense sun. You'll find them in the deserts and along seashores. Southern Nevada, with its hot summers and mild winters, creates a climate suitable for growing palms, and the palm is one of the most distinctive plants of the Southwest. Exceedingly decorative leaves are the palm's hallmark. We divide them into feather-leaved and fan-leaved palms according to the way they look. Fan-leaved palms offer larger leaf surfaces and that means more transpiration; therefore, they must be watered more.

Palm trees can be a potentially beautiful part of a desert landscape. Unfortunately, people who mistake them for desert plants and don't water them, or who are overenthusiastic tree trimmers, may abuse them. The unusual development features of this plant also make conventional methods of propagation (as for other trees and shrubs) inapplicable. Thus, the palm grower, whether a professional growing for profit or a homeowner growing for pleasure, needs detailed information about the management of these striking and valuable plants.

All palms are frost-tender to one degree or another, but they grow vigorously in hot weather if they are cared for with an adequate watering program. (That is why you always find them growing naturally around springs. There is a classic example found in Moapa, Nevada, about sixty miles east of Las Vegas.) When watering, you must keep the "heart" of the palm dry. You'll find the heart located just below where new leaves emerge from the trunk. When the heart rots, the palm is finished. Standing water or cold temperatures in the root region can be just as lethal.

Palms can be great for landscaping around a swimming pool. They don't drop their leaves unless you leave the dead fronds on as a "skirt." Insects are not attracted to palms and they don't harbor

Chapter Six

birds that drop "things." Also, palms do not have extensive root systems that could damage a swimming pool or sidewalks, unless they are planted too close to them. Give palms ample room to grow.

Palms are unique in their morphology and, not surprisingly, in their cultural requirements. They are perhaps the most susceptible of all ornamental plants to nutritional disorders. They therefore differ greatly from broadleaf trees and plants. Because of their unique root systems, large specimen palms are easy to transplant in comparison with large broadleaf trees.

Palms are among the younger plants in the history of the evolution of the botanical system. Palms, despite their ability to reach treelike heights, have more in common with lawn grasses, corn, and rice than with Ash or Olive Trees. They belong to the division of plants known as monocotyledons. This group includes grass, corn, Lilies, and Orchids. Very few other species of monocots attain the size that palms attain.

There is one difference between monocots and dicots. The dicots have a layer of specialized cells called the *vascular cambium* (between the water-conducting tissues called *xylem* and the food-conduction tissues called *phloem*) that wraps around the branch. For most monocots, including palms, these same vascular tissues occur in bundles scattered throughout the internal tissues of the stem, with little or no regenerative ability. The bundles of these conducting tissues within the palm last the entire life of the palm.

The palms mentioned in this book are the best adapted for southern Nevada. Some are very common, while others need to be used more on the smaller lots that are now becoming more prevalent.

Canary Island Palm

Phoenix canariensis

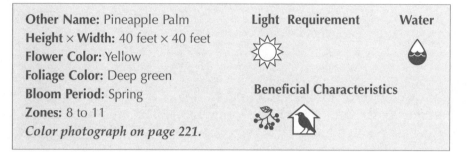

Other Name: Pineapple Palm
Height × Width: 40 feet × 40 feet
Flower Color: Yellow
Foliage Color: Deep green
Bloom Period: Spring
Zones: 8 to 11
Color photograph on page 221.

Light Requirement

Water

Beneficial Characteristics

The Canary Island Palm has large, lush, feathery leaves resting on a woody trunk, developing slowly at first into a pineapple-shaped palm. The long, gracefully-arching branches with deep-green, glistening fronds grow upward in their youth but spread out more than 20 feet as they mature, giving it a distinct, fountainlike outline and form—I call it the "lollipop look." The lowermost leaflets on each leaf are reduced to long, stiff, hazardous, sharp thorns that line the bases of the leaves. Fortunately, the palm eventually grows tall, putting the thorny problem out of reach. Seed stalks arise among the leaves and bear unisexual flowers, meaning that male and female trees need to be planted together for date production. The flowers are small and yellowish in large, hanging sprays; they precede clusters of non-edible fruit. That is not the purpose for planting Canary Island Palm in southern Nevada; we plant it for its ornamental value and the tropical feel it brings to the landscape. It loves our summer heat and will survive winter cold down into the upper teens. (LM)

REGIONAL TIPS

Because it comes from the warm deserts, the palm is very frost tender and will not tolerate long-term freezing conditions; young trees are even sensitive to severe frosts in southern Nevada. If a frost does kill the leaves, do not remove them until the next spring, as the leaves insulate the heart of the palm from further damage.

WHEN, WHERE, AND HOW TO PLANT

Plant it any time from a container, but it does best planted from spring into midsummer. Canary Island Palm will grow in poor soils but it must have good drainage and get full sun. To plant, make the hole three to five times wider than the rootball for better root development in compacted soils. Plant the rootball at the same level in the ground as it was found in the container or the roots will suffocate. Build a water basin beyond the rootball and fill thoroughly with water three times a week, using 2-gallon-per-hour emitters for two hours the first month. As a bonus, mulch with humus or compost; it is the best way to cool our soils in the summer for more root development.

CARE AND MAINTENANCE

Water weekly until temperatures get in the 90s, and then water twice a week. Canary Island Palms like nitrogen, so work 2 cups of a balanced fertilizer containing 10 to 16 percent nitrogen around the palm in the early spring and again on Memorial Day. If fronds turn a pale green, add iron. Remove dead fronds and seed stems as they occur, but because of the sharp and stiff thorns, bring in an arborist to do the pruning. However, if you insist, remove only the fronds that hang down below the three o'clock and nine o'clock positions. If the emerging fronds die, the plant has bud rot—a major concern during the raining season. Treat with Bordeaux mixture. There are no other pests.

LANDSCAPE MERIT

The Canary Island Palm, if pruned properly, gives the impression of a spring of water billowing out of the trunk. While it is young, grow it in a tub, as it is a slow grower— but you'll eventually have to transplant it in the landscape. These palms may become quite large, and they are best suited to large lots. Avoid planting under power lines or roof eaves. Allow plenty of space between the trunk and sidewalks or driveways.

ADDITIONAL SPECIES, CULTIVARS, OR VARIETIES

Phoenix dactylifera, or the commercial Date Palm, is more open with 20-foot-long, gray-green fronds arching outward and downward to make a graceful crown. *P. roebelenii*, or Pygmy Date Palm, does well in containers, bringing a lush tropical effect with bold foliage to a desert oasis. It only grows to 6 to 10 feet.

Guadalupe Fan Palm

Brahea edulis

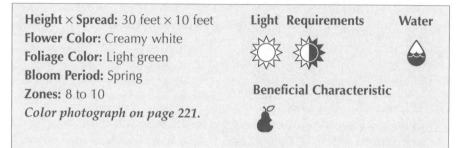

Height × Spread: 30 feet × 10 feet
Flower Color: Creamy white
Foliage Color: Light green
Bloom Period: Spring
Zones: 8 to 10
Color photograph on page 221.

Light Requirements

Water

Beneficial Characteristic

The rather tropical-looking Guadalupe Fan Palm has an ornamental large crown of light-green fronds atop its stout trunk. They contrast beautifully with the blue fronds of its cousin, the Mexican Blue Palm. It grows a little faster—much to the liking of most people—reaching 30 feet, with a spread of 10 feet or more. It does not dominate landscapes like other palms, but brings to the yard a stout, corky trunk that is very attractive, especially as it matures. And the fronds stay green until hit by a severe frost. This lazy man's plant cleanly sheds its own fronds, leaving no shaggy stragglers hanging from the tree. These fronds come without all the barbs (knives) or spines. Why can't we breed this trait into the other palms? When finished shedding, the trunk has the look of a naked elephant hide ringed with scars. We need to use this palm more in southern Nevada. Flowers appear on 4- to 5-foot-long garlands to produce heavy clusters of small, black, edible fruit. It shows off well as a single specimen or planted in clusters or lining your sidewalk. And don't overlook it as a container plant while it's still young. (LM)

Regional Tips

Guadalupe Fan Palms hail from the warm island off Baja, California, making it very tender at temperatures below 20 degrees Fahrenheit. It will not tolerate long-term freezing conditions in northern Nevada.

When, Where, and How to Plant

Plant it any time from a container, but it does best planted in spring and early summer. If you must transplant it, do it in the spring or early summer to give it a chance to initiate more roots. Young plants, which are generally slow starting, tolerate exposure to full sun, but it needs well-drained soils to be a winner in the landscape. Purchase

5- to 15-gallon specimens and make the hole three to five times wider than the rootball to open up the soil for good root development and drainage. Build a water basin beyond the rootball and fill with water thoroughly, three times a week for the first month. As a bonus, mulch with humus or compost; it is the best way to cool our soils in the summer for more root development.

CARE AND MAINTENANCE

Water weekly using 2-gallon-per-hour emitters running for 2 hours. When it gets above 90 degrees Fahrenheit, water twice a week. Because palms come from the grass family, they like nitrogen fertilizer—work in a cupful of a balanced fertilizer that has from 10 to 16 percent nitrogen in the early spring and again around Memorial Day. We are finding that palms need more potassium, iron, and manganese; if you see blotchy or yellowing leaves, add these supplements. The palm does not require pruning, as it sheds itself, making it very popular in many landscapes. This palm does not bring any pests to the yard.

LANDSCAPE MERIT

Guadalupe Fan Palm comes with a large crown of handsome fronds, making it an excellent palm for oasis landscapes. It is good for yards with limited space and is small enough to consider as a container plant. Finally, it brings quite a tropical effect to the landscape.

ADDITIONAL SPECIES, CULTIVARS, OR VARIETIES

B. nitida, or Hesper Palm, is another small palm, making it desirable for smaller landscapes. *B. prominans*, or Canyon Palm, is even shorter and slower growing.

Mediterranean Fan Palm

Chamaerops humilis

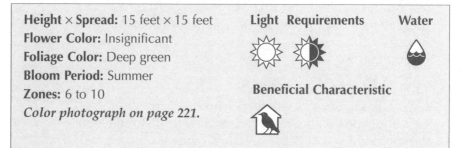

Height × Spread: 15 feet × 15 feet
Flower Color: Insignificant
Foliage Color: Deep green
Bloom Period: Summer
Zones: 6 to 10
Color photograph on page 221.

Light Requirements

Water

Beneficial Characteristic

If you ever go to the Mediterranean area, you will feel right at home with all the Mediterranean Fan Palms in the landscape. It is probably the best palm for the small landscape here in Nevada, since it grows only 6 inches a year. It has the potential to get 15 or more feet high and does spread out 15 feet, but it is extremely variable in growth habit. Plants may have one or many trunks, depending on your taste. It suckers to form clumps of several heads at the base of trunks, which lean outward—a desirable characteristic in the landscape. If you desire a single head, remove the suckers and plant them elsewhere. This palm always looks great around swimming pools or in containers and makes a striking accent plant with other architectural features. Fronds vary in color from deep green to yellowish-green on top with a whitish bloom underneath, adding interest when the summer winds toss fronds back and forth. The stems (petioles) that hold the fronds have unfriendly spines spread along them. Flowers are creamy to yellowish, followed by a date-shaped brown fruit. (LM)

REGIONAL TIPS

The Mediterranean Fan Palm is probably one of the hardiest palms, surviving to 10 degrees Fahrenheit, and it remains unaffected by heavy frosts.

WHEN, WHERE, AND HOW TO PLANT

Plant the Mediterranean Fan Palm any time from a container, but it does best planted from spring to early summer. It loves full sun but does equally well in shaded conditions. It requires a rich, well-drained soil but will tolerate other soils, even accepting alkaline conditions. When planting, make the hole three to five times wider than the rootball to open up the soil. Work some organic matter in the backfill soil to enrich it. After planting, build a water basin around the palm; fill with water three times for the first month and then only once a week. Or let 2-gallon-per-hour drip emitters run for 2 hours at a time. As a bonus, mulch with humus or compost to cool soils and conserve water.

CARE AND MAINTENANCE

As the temperature gets above 90 degrees Fahrenheit, go to twice-a-week waterings. Mediterranean Fan Palms like nitrogen so work 2 cups of a balanced fertilizer containing 10 to 16 percent nitrogen around each palm in early spring and around Memorial Day. If fronds turn a pale green, add iron. This slow-growing palm takes many years to reach a respectable size. Remove the dead and oldest fronds to expose the trunk structure, which is beautiful, and to maintain a tidy appearance. Be cautious when handling the fronds because they are armed with very sharp straight or hooked spines along the stems. If you don't like the side shoots, cut them off close to the main trunk and replant them elsewhere. If left alone, plants develop multiple-stem growth. This palm occasionally suffers from a fungus called leaf spot; use Bordeaux mixture for control. Spider mites will work on the older leaves, causing them to appear dry and dusty; control them with Neem oil.

LANDSCAPE MERIT

The Mediterranean Fan Palm is a very appealing, shrubby palm when used either as an accent or in clusters. It is very reliable and durable. It is an excellent container plant for the patio, and it blends well in desert landscapes. As it matures, the palm with many trunks becomes fascinating, leading to many conversations with your visitors.

ADDITIONAL SPECIES, CULTIVARS, OR VARIETIES

There are none.

Mexican Blue Palm

Brahea armata

Height × Spread: 30 feet × 15 feet
Flower Color: Creamy white
Foliage Color: Blue-green,
   waxy fronds
Bloom Period: Spring
Zones: 8 to 10
Color photograph on page 221.

Light Requirement

Water

Beneficial Characteristics

You haven't lived until you've seen the Mexican Blue Palm in bloom. In the spring, fragrant creamy-white flowers form along long strands (flower stalks) called "garlands" that extend well below the arching fronds. You can walk right up to them to enjoy their beauty and fragrance. Much to its credit, the Blue Palm is a slow-growing palm, ultimately reaching 30 or more feet, with a crown spreading out 10 to 15 feet. The next thing that grabs your eye are its blue-green, waxy, fan-shaped fronds. They arch out from the trunk to form a wide-spreading crown, and they retain their color until they bend down to form a hanging brown skirt. What a pleasant contrast it brings to traditional green landscapes. It is very much at home in a desert garden setting, but this versatile palm is also excellent in containers while yet small. The species is native to northern Baja, California, and northwestern Mexico, where it grows in rocky canyons—that explains why it does well in poor soils. (LM)

REGIONAL TIPS

The Mexican Blue Palm tolerates a wide range of growing conditions as well as the summer desert heat, and it will take winter temperatures down to 20 degrees Fahrenheit. It can withstand severe frosts without permanent damage in the south. Because of its low threshold for cold temperatures, though, it will not survive in northern Nevada.

WHEN, WHERE, AND HOW TO PLANT

Plant it any time from a container, but it does best planted in spring and into early summer. If you must transplant, do it in the spring or early summer to initiate new root development. (I find it difficult to move larger plants.) The Mexican Blue Palm requires full sun to get the best color in the fronds. To plant, make a hole three to five times wider than the rootball. Drainage is critical with this palm; check the hole for drainage by filling it with water. If the water drains away in 8 hours, plant. To open up the soil, add some organic matter to the backfill and plant the palm. Build a water basin around the rootball and fill with water three times a week, or if you use 2-gallon-per-hour emitters, let them run for 2 hours each time. To diminish this palm's water demands, add mulch—this will also cool the soil and allow for more root development.

CARE AND MAINTENANCE
As the temperature heats up above 90 degrees Fahrenheit, begin watering twice a week. Mexican Blue Palms don't need much nitrogen, but to put more lushness into the plant, work 2 cups of a balanced fertilizer containing 10 to 16 percent nitrogen around the palm in early spring and again on Memorial Day. If fronds turn a pale green, add iron. Remove dead fronds and those showing signs of aging, but because the fronds are so vicious, always approach them with tough gloves and sharp shears and saws. After pollination, reddish-brown, hard, berrylike fruits develop. Remove the stalks as they finish blooming. This durable palm does not bring any pests to the garden.

LANDSCAPE MERIT
The Mexican Blue Palm is a very reliable plant. Its attractive foliage inspires landscape architects to use it in their designs, it shows off well when grown in containers, and it fits well in small landscapes. The bluish leaves bring a cooling effect to the yard. I find it a handsome plant when grown as a specimen plant, something I can't say of other palms. It is a fine specimen for home landscapes due to its relatively small size and slow growth.

ADDITIONAL SPECIES, CULTIVARS, OR VARIETIES
There are none.

Mexican Fan Palm

Washingtonia robusta

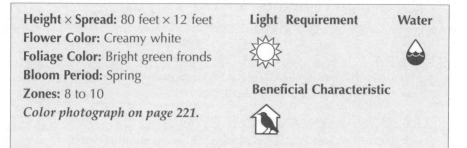

Height × Spread: 80 feet × 12 feet
Flower Color: Creamy white
Foliage Color: Bright green fronds
Bloom Period: Spring
Zones: 8 to 10
Color photograph on page 221.

Light Requirement

Water

Beneficial Characteristic

The Mexican Fan Palm is, to me, the standard. When people think of palms, it is the Mexican Fan Palm that runs through their minds, and why not? It is so easy to grow. It is a lazy man's plant; you can plant it and forget about it. That becomes even truer if you let the dead brown fronds form a "hula skirt" on the tree. (They don't do any harm to the tree, and if they fit your landscape theme, leave them.) This native of the Southwest may ultimately reach 80 or more feet, with glistening, bright-green fronds forming a luxuriant, compact head with a spread of foliage to about 12 feet—it grows a new crown of foliage before the middle of each summer. Interesting curvatures develop in the trunks. I have never seen a straight-trunked palm; there is always a bend or two. I most appreciate palm trees at night. Looking up through the canopy and to the moon, you see fronds dancing to the gentle desert summer breezes. It is a rewarding scene that goes unnoticed by most gardeners. (LM)

REGIONAL TIPS

This slender-trunked palm adapts well to desert heat and low humidity but may suffer if temperatures plunge below 20 degrees Fahrenheit.

WHEN, WHERE, AND HOW TO PLANT

Late spring to early summer is the best time to plant this specimen, allowing the plant time to initiate new roots. (I kid people, telling them to plant on the hottest day of the year.) Mexican Fan Palms require full sun in a well-drained soil. Dig a hole as deep as and at least three to five times wider than the rootball, and check the drainage: Fill the hole with water; plant if the water is gone within 8 hours. It's important to plant at the same depth it was growing in the original site. Mix some organic material with the onsite soil to open it up for greater root growth. As you fill in around the rootball, add water to further settle the soil. Build a water basin to contain the water so it will penetrate.

CARE AND MAINTENANCE

Keep the soil moist, never letting the rootball dry out. Water weekly while cool, but as temperatures heat up, go to twice-a-week waterings. If you use 2-gallon-an-hour drip emitters, let them run 2 hours each time. This palm uses nitrogen, so work 2 cups of a balanced fertilizer containing 10 to 16 percent nitrogen around the base before an irrigation in March, May, and September. It is best to remove fronds in the summer after the flowering stalks emerge. Fronds and flower stalks can be dangerous as they freely drop, and they might hit someone. There aren't any pests that bother this noble palm.

LANDSCAPE MERIT

Mexican Fan Palms look better planted in clusters. It adds even more to the effect to use plants of various heights. Single trees have a telephone-pole effect as the tree extends to new heights. These fast-growing palms become rather large, often outgrowing their space. They are best suited for large lots. Avoid planting under power lines.

ADDITIONAL SPECIES, CULTIVARS, OR VARIETIES

W. robusta, or California Fan Palm, is a close cousin and is almost as popular. The California Palm has a much wider trunk than its cousin, and the fronds produce noticeable cottony threads on the undersides. I find the California hula skirt more formal and attractive, and it fits well in a Southwest landscape theme. Clusters of these noble palms seem to say, "You are in the Southwest!"

Pindo Palm

Butia capitata

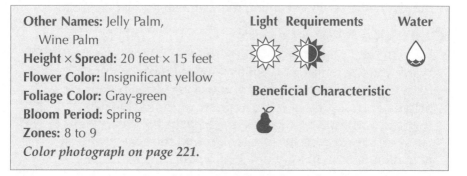

Other Names: Jelly Palm, Wine Palm

Height × Spread: 20 feet × 15 feet

Flower Color: Insignificant yellow

Foliage Color: Gray-green

Bloom Period: Spring

Zones: 8 to 9

Color photograph on page 221.

Light Requirements

Water

Beneficial Characteristic

The Pindo Palm, also called Wine or Jelly Palm, is a graceful, small-scale, feathery palm. It has gray-green fronds that are narrow-leafed or feathery and flutter with the slightest breezes. They curve deeply, bending downward to create a cascading effect that makes the plant readily recognizable and eye-catching. They also have no spines, making the palm very user-friendly. Fronds form a dense crown that spreads out about 15 feet. The plant itself grows slowly to 20 feet, making it excellent for the typical home landscapes, especially as home lots become smaller. The trunk, when trimmed properly of old fronds, has an attractive texture to make an excellent accent plant. Young plants make very decorative and hardy container specimens. Female Pindos bear large clusters of edible fruits with a pineapple-like flavor. Because of the Pindo's gray foliage, it combines well with desert plants and contrasts well with tropical plants. This palm is not used enough in southern Nevada landscapes. (LM)

REGIONAL TIPS

The Pindo Palm tolerates the desert summer heat yet will take winter temperatures down to 15 degrees Fahrenheit. It has withstood severe frosts in the south without permanent damage.

WHEN, WHERE, AND HOW TO PLANT

Plant any time from a container, but it does best when planted from early spring into midsummer. If you must move palms, do it in the spring or early summer to give them a chance to initiate more roots. The Pindo Palm prefers full sun but will tolerate light shade, and it really turns on the charm when you plant clusters of the same kind. It's tolerant of most soils but requires good drainage. To prepare the hole, make it three times wider than and as deep as the rootball to open up the soil for good root development. Enrich the soil by mixing in some organic matter, plant the palm, then build a water basin beyond the rootball and fill it with water twice a week until you see new fronds emerging from the top of the tree. If you use 2-gallon-per-hour drip emitters, let them run for 2 hours each time. To make better use of your water, mulch the area to cool down soils in the summer for more root growth.

CARE AND MAINTENANCE

After establishment, water weekly, but as it heats up, go to twice-a-week waterings. The palm is not a heavy feeder, but 2 cups of a balanced fertilizer containing 10 to 16 percent nitrogen worked into the soil prior to irrigation will add lushness to the plant in the early spring. Keep an eye on the fronds—if they turn pale in color, add iron. Remove old, drooping, or dried fronds and fruiting stalks. To keep Pindos looking tidy in appearance, the palms need careful grooming in the early spring. If the top growth suddenly dies, bud rot could be the problem. The best control for bud rot is to avoid wetting the crown. Treat with Bordeaux mixture. Pindos don't have any bug problems.

LANDSCAPE MERIT

The grayish foliage makes a nice contrast with traditional greens and fits well into a desert oasis. Its small size should be extremely inviting for new homeowners with small lots.

ADDITIONAL SPECIES, CULTIVARS, OR VARIETIES

There are none.

Sago Palm

Cycas revoluta

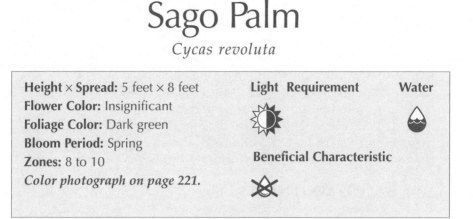

Height × Spread: 5 feet × 8 feet	Light Requirement	Water
Flower Color: Insignificant		
Foliage Color: Dark green		
Bloom Period: Spring		
Zones: 8 to 10	Beneficial Characteristic	
Color photograph on page 221.		

The Sago Palm is a very handsome plant that resembles a palm. Its leaves sit closely together and come off the trunk looking like a miniature palm. *Cycas* means "palmlike." So although it isn't a true palm, it's a palm in my book. Notice the conversations it stimulates whenever you are around one. Because of its miniature features, it is excellent for small gardens. It will tolerate low light and humidity and grows slowly, which means it rarely needs repotting or transplanting. You get a new flush of growth each spring, and it slows through the summer, with no growth through the winter. This amazing palm may develop more than one head; leave them on to form a multiple-trunked specimen or transplant them elsewhere. It is a prized garden plant and we need to use it more in southern Nevada. (LM)

REGIONAL TIPS

The Sago Palm will tolerate a wide range of hot and cold conditions, hardy to 15 degrees Fahrenheit. If the leaves frost out, new leaves emerge quickly. But the leaves must go from one season to the next to replenish the food reserves within the plant. If they are continually frozen back each year, it depletes nourishment to a point that the plant weakens and dies.

WHEN, WHERE, AND HOW TO PLANT

Plant in spring after the last frost or any time in protected areas before its annual flush of leaves emerges. This pseudo-palm tolerates full sun but loves filtered shade. It must have excellent drainage or the roots will rot. Treat it like a palm, making a wide hole, but dig only to the depth of the rootball. Next, check the drainage by filling the hole with water. After 8 hours, if the water has drained away, plant the palm. Enrich the backfill soil with organic matter, and firm the amended soil around the rootball as you refill the hole. Soak the soil using 2-gallon-per-hour drip emitters for 2 hours, three times a week, until established.

CARE AND MAINTENANCE

Water the plant using the emitters weekly until it gets above 90 degrees Fahrenheit, and then water twice a week. It doesn't require any water through the winter unless it is dry and windy. The Sago Palm does not require much maintenance; just trim away the old leaves as they die. This is a plant that requires an all-purpose fertilizer with micronutrients mixed in at monthly intervals throughout the growing season. Any time you see blotches showing up on the leaves, reach for the potassium, iron, and manganese (all-purpose fertilizers carry these elements)—make sure they are part of your continuous feeding program. Scales and mealybugs are both very visible insects. When you see them, spray the plant with insecticidal soap or Neem oil.

LANDSCAPE MERIT

Use Sago Palm indoors and outdoors, in atriums, and in rock gardens. Use the tiny plants in Bonsai. It will survive many years in the small pots. It has a very refined, elegant form and texture that brings an oriental and tropical effect to the landscape. Or use this specimen as a regal guardian of the entryway or as an accent in containers. It is very tough for such a lush-looking plant. You can even miss an irrigation or two without much foliage loss, which is what makes it so popular in the warmer climates.

ADDITIONAL SPECIES, CULTIVARS, OR VARIETIES

There are none.

Windmill Palm

Trachycarpus fortunei

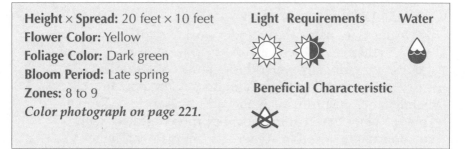

Height × Spread: 20 feet × 10 feet	Light Requirements	Water
Flower Color: Yellow		
Foliage Color: Dark green		
Bloom Period: Late spring		
Zones: 8 to 9	**Beneficial Characteristic**	
Color photograph on page 221.		

If you want a plant that looks top-heavy, plant a Windmill Palm. I find myself wondering when mine will topple. But to this day, it stands tall and strong in the most severe winds. I understand why when I look at the small, stiff, windmill-shaped fronds. They truly twist like a windmill when the southerly breezes pass through. Let's go to the trunk: It is covered with loosely arranged, dark brown, fibrous material that makes it look thicker than it really is. (The Chinese strip the fiber from the trunk and use it as a lining material for hanging baskets and to make fine waterproof cloaks, brooms, brushes, and doormats.) It is a slow-growing palm, reaching about 20 feet high with a 10-foot crown. Here is another wonderful palm to plant in our now smaller landscapes, and it won't dwarf the home. With a spread 10 feet wide and 20 feet in the air, it will create more shade than you might think. I also like it because of its symmetrical, radiating crown of fan-shaped leaves. Some older fronds often persist and clothe the upper part of the trunk as a skirt. The flowers and fruit are not ornamentally important, but if you want to have fruit, you will need male and female trees. The flower stalks bear yellow flowers, which are quite showy. It responds to regular watering and feeding, but it isn't a demanding palm. (LM)

REGIONAL TIPS

This palm loves southern Nevada heat and is hardy down to 10 degrees Fahrenheit, making it one of the hardiest palms for southern Nevada.

WHEN, WHERE, AND HOW TO PLANT

Early spring into midsummer is the best time to plant the Windmill Palm. It prefers full sun but will tolerate light shade. This palm really turns on the charm when you plant clusters of the same

kind together and then comes a mild summer breeze—
I just know the windmill will be "pumping water." It is
tolerant of most soils, but they must be open and have
good drainage. Make a hole three times wider than and as
deep as the rootball. Improve the soil by blending in some
organic material and plant the rootball. Build a water basin
beyond the rootball and fill with water twice a week until
new fronds emerge. If you use 2-gallon-per-hour drip emitters, run them 2 hours each time. To make better use of
your water, mulch the area; it also cools the soil and the
plant can develop more roots.

CARE AND MAINTENANCE
After establishment, water weekly, but as it heats up, water
twice a week. The palm is not a big feeder but work 2 cups
of a balanced fertilizer containing 10 to 16 percent nitrogen
into the soil prior to irrigation to add lushness to the plant.
It is a very low-maintenance plant and will tolerate neglect
once established, but it becomes less attractive if you leave
the fronds on the tree; remove dead fronds and seed stems
as they occur. Do not "skin" trunks, as the fibers protect
the plant in our blistering heat. Windmill Palm doesn't
bring any pests to the garden.

LANDSCAPE MERIT
This handsome, semi-dwarf, compact palm is well adapted
for planting as a solitary specimen, or in clumps for screen
plantings. It makes a beautiful accent plant, lending a tropical flavor to formal or tropical home landscapes.

ADDITIONAL SPECIES, CULTIVARS, OR VARIETIES
There are none.

CHAPTER SEVEN

Perennials

PERENNIALS MAY BE THE MOST aesthetically rewarding of all landscape projects; in fact, perennials have become the backbone of color in gardens. That's why we like to call them "The Fashionable Plants." They are permanent and winter hardy, and it is not necessary to plant them each spring as you do annuals. A perennial is defined as a plant having a life cycle lasting more than two years. They may be evergreen or deciduous, with the visible parts of the plant dying each winter and growing new plant parts each spring. Perennials can be shrubs and trees as well as tender plants such as Geraniums and African Violets.

The first settlers brought along their favorite plants, many of which we use now. Some imported plants felt so much at home here in America that they became weeds. The common Daisy, Dandelion, Devil's Paintbrush, Tansy, and others arrived as garden flowers or medicinal herbs, but spread rapidly. The walled garden probably got its start when a colonist built a wall around his wife's flower garden to keep the flowers from spreading into his fields.

But not all perennials are immigrants. Some are native to North America's fields and woods—wildflowers such as Lady's Slipper, Bee Balm, and Mountain Bluebell were admired by early settlers and planted into their yards and gardens. But a great many of today's popular perennials bear little resemblance to those our ancestors grew, due to the efforts of amateur and professional horticulturists. Dedicated hybridizers have created literally *thousands* of varieties.

Because of their ability to last for long periods of time, it is wise to plan carefully before you install perennial plants. And though perennials are more expensive than most annuals, when you consider that they represent a long-term investment, the cost amortized over the years makes them very reasonable. With thousands of

Chapter Seven

varieties available, you'll find a perennial suitable for every possible location and growing condition in your garden.

With some exceptions, most perennials are difficult to grow from seed. They often require special conditions to get them started. Translation: We recommend you purchase plants rather than waste time trying to start them from seed. In addition to the nurseries and garden centers that have a large supply available, there are vast numbers of mail-order garden supply centers that offer an almost unlimited supply of perennial plants.

When planting perennials, it is wise to consult zone designations regarding the climate. Some perennials are not appropriate for all areas. If you try to grow a perennial that is not suited for your area, it may produce nothing but long-term problems in a garden or land-scape. Also, perennials that are designed for full sun need a location with no shade at all, or at least eight hours each day with no shade—reflective light bouncing off buildings doesn't do any good.

There has been a continuing and expanding interest in perennials. The craze isn't so surprising when you consider the great diversity these plants offer gardeners. They are fascinating in part because most bloom for only short periods of time and seldom look the same for two days in a row, or for two years in succession. Perennial gardening has a facet to suit every interest or need, and perennials generally require less care than annuals. This is a major reason for having perennials in the landscape design. Easy-care plants are an important consideration when planning a garden—and that's what we've considered in the writing of this chapter on perennials.

Asparagus Fern

Asparagus densiflorus 'Sprengeri'

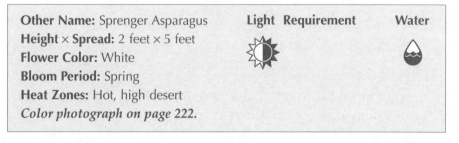

Other Name: Sprenger Asparagus	Light Requirement	Water
Height × Spread: 2 feet × 5 feet		
Flower Color: White		
Bloom Period: Spring		
Heat Zones: Hot, high desert		
Color photograph on page 222.		

The Asparagus Fern could fit a multitude of situations—as a shrub, a vine, a perennial, in containers, and even (stretching it a bit) as an evergreen. It was all these things for my mother, taking a spot in her house during the winter and in her yard through the summer. Here in Nevada, if Asparagus Fern had its choice of locations, you'd find it on the east side of the house. If you do move it around outside of the home, you have to add some shade. And as you increase the shade, expect the foliage to decrease as it stretches for light. The inch-long, needlelike leaves are lime green in a cluster of two to eight located at each node. Plants spread by long stems up to 4 feet in length which contain small sharp spines to help it climb. White-pink blooms locate themselves along stems in clusters in the early spring and in fall, and then you'll find bright red berries showing up. Neither flowers nor fruit are anything to brag about, but the lacy vine is what stands out in people's minds. (LM)

REGIONAL TIPS

The Asparagus Fern will grow in all hardy zones but needs protection, such as moving it indoors through the winters. After sixty years, my mother's plant is still going strong in northern Utah.

WHEN, WHERE, AND HOW TO PLANT

Plant the Asparagus Fern anytime, but plan to bring it indoors through the winter in the colder climes. It loves partial shade and even tolerates dappled shade, but it is a plant that must have a well-drained soil or it quickly dies. Enrich the soil with copious amounts of organic mater before planting. Make a large hole to open up the compacted soil so the roots are able to reach out and mine for nutrients. Thoroughly water the plant often until you start to see new growth emerging.

CARE AND MAINTENANCE

Asparagus Fern demands a moderate amount of water.
Water it once a week throughout the spring and fall; it
needs more water when in bloom, and even more through
the summer when it's hot. It is a plant that doesn't require
much fertilizer to keep it happy, but once a year in spring,
work a cupful of ammonium sulfate under the plant before
watering. Plants may show a yellowing of the leaves; if so,
apply iron fertilizer to put lushness back into the foliage. If
your plant gets a little untidy, prune it back, removing the
longest trailers and dead stems first, and if you want to
rejuvenate the plant, cut it back to the ground. Asparagus
Fern doesn't have any insects that pester it.

LANDSCAPE MERIT

You'll find these plants lining borders, filling planters
and containers both in and out of the home, covering the
ground, cascading over walls, and bringing that tropical
effect to the garden.

ADDITIONAL SPECIES, CULTIVARS, OR VARIETIES

A. setaceus, more often grown indoors, has branching,
woody, climbing vines and tiny, threadlike leaves forming
feathery dark-green sprays that resemble fern fronds. Tiny
white flowers come along (and then purple-black berries)
in the spring and eventually in the fall. The dense, fine-
textured foliage mass is useful as a screen, attaching to
walls and fences. Florists use the foliage as filler in bouquets;
it holds up better than delicate ferns. *A. densiflorus* 'Myers'
is also quite popular.

Basket-of-Gold

Aurinia saxatilis

Height × Spread: 9 to 12 inches ×
12 inches
Flower Color: Yellow
Bloom Period: Late winter to spring
Heat Zones: Hot, high desert,
mountainous
Color photograph on page 222.

Light Requirements

Water

Beneficial Characteristic

B asket-of-Gold produces golden yellow flowers in your garden for many years. Originally the plant was classified as being *Alyssum saxatile,* so you will often find it listed under both names or as one or the other. The flowers are very small, yellow blooms, 1/2 inch in diameter. When in bloom the entire plant is covered with so many flowers that you cannot see the foliage. Once the plant has finished flowering, you can see the compact habit and the gray-green foliage that make an attractive background plant even when not in bloom. Plan ahead, so you can leave some room around the plants to fill in with annuals. They will contribute color to the garden after Basket-of-Gold finishes flowering. (DP)

REGIONAL TIPS

Basket-of-Gold flowers in late winter in the hot regions, while in the high desert and mountainous regions it flowers in the spring.

WHEN, WHERE, AND HOW TO PLANT

Basket-of-Gold can be planted in the late winter, or in early spring indoors if you want to start your own from seed. When purchased as a bedding plant, as long as it has been acclimated to your climate, it can be planted any time the ground isn't frozen—though in zones 4 to 6 it is still better to plant either in the fall or spring. It flowers best when planted in full sun but will tolerate part shade. Because it is a perennial, you need to plant it in a spot where it can grow undisturbed for a few years. If you want to start your own from seed it will take about six to seven weeks from the time you sow the seed till it is ready to transplant into the garden. Often perennials aren't mature enough to flower the first season when started from seed the same spring. Basket-of-Gold grows best in sandy soil but has done very well for me when I have amended the soil with organic mulch. Adding about 3 inches of organic mulch on top of the soil and tilling it in to a depth of 6 inches will help to loosen the soil so that it drains better. When planting, dig the hole as deep as the depth of the rootball and a little wider (space plants about 9 to 10 inches apart), put the plant in the hole, and cover the roots with soil; then give it a good soaking.

CARE AND MAINTENANCE

Basket-of-Gold is very easy to take care of, isn't bothered by insect and disease pests, and is a low water user and can be allowed to dry out between waterings. After it has finished flowering, give the plant a light shearing but don't trim back more than half of its growth. This removes the dried-up flowers and also encourages the plant to branch out more.

LANDSCAPE MERIT

Basket-of-Gold is ideal for planting in rock gardens or as an early-flowering edging plant. The plants can also be planted in containers and along with other spring-flowering plants. Plant them on a ledge so they can cascade over the side.

ADDITIONAL SPECIES, CULTIVARS, OR VARIETIES

A few varieties that are available include 'Plena', a double-flowered type, 'Silver Queen', which is very compact, and 'Citrina', with pale yellow flowers.

Beach Wormwood

Artemisia stellerana

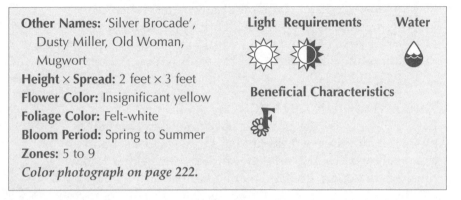

Other Names: 'Silver Brocade', Dusty Miller, Old Woman, Mugwort
Height × Spread: 2 feet × 3 feet
Flower Color: Insignificant yellow
Foliage Color: Felt-white
Bloom Period: Spring to Summer
Zones: 5 to 9
Color photograph on page 222.

Light Requirements

Water

Beneficial Characteristics

If you want a plant with unusual colors and leaf shapes, consider planting Beach Wormwood for its interesting leaf texture and aromatic, feathery silvery-gray to white foliage. It always enhances the surroundings, providing an admirable foil for vivid flower colors, blending subtly with soft blues, lavenders, and pinks. You'll find the foliage finely divided or dissected, adding a lacelike delicacy to the shimmering lightness. Flowers are insignificant, tiny daises found in little clusters. It grows 2 feet high. (LM)

REGIONAL TIPS

Beach Wormwood does poorly in hot, humid situations. Therefore, southern Nevadans must keep water off the plant when it's really hot. It will struggle with the harsh winters of northern Nevada.

WHEN, WHERE, AND HOW TO PLANT

Beach Wormwood thrives in full sun but will tolerate some shade. It will grow okay in poor soils with good drainage, but if you enhance the soil with some organic matter, an added lushness come over the plant. To plant Beach Wormwood, make an extra-large hole only as deep as its rootball, firm the soil around the rootball as you replace it, also adding water to settle the soil even more. Build a water basin around the plant and fill it with water. Soak the soil twice a week until you are confident the shrub is established.

CARE AND MAINTENANCE

Keep the rooted area moist by watering weekly, but when it gets hot (90 degrees Fahrenheit), water twice a week. If you use emitters, let

them run for 2 hours each time. Since you are growing
Beach Wormwood for foliage, nitrogen becomes the key
element; work a cup of ammonium sulfate in the soil
under the bush's canopy around Presidents' Day, and
again Memorial Day and Labor Day. If the plant becomes
unkempt, you may be watering and fertilizing too much.
Cut the shrubs fairly heavily in January before the first
flush of spring growth to keep growth compact, and be
brave and cut it back to the ground. That's what I do, and
it comes back with a vengeance. Beach Wormwood does
not bring any pests to the yard.

LANDSCAPE MERIT

The feathery silvery-gray to white foliage contributes a
welcome change to an otherwise green landscape, as it
seems to make all appear an even more lush green.
Wormwood always enhances the surroundings when
used as a border or edging or mixed in with perennials
and annuals. Since the grayish foliage has a cooling effect
upon the viewer, it takes the heat out of hot-colored plants
such as red, yellow, and orange blooms. It will work as a
ground cover and fill in between those plants waiting to
mature, it fits well nestled in among boulders and rocks,
and it is at home in a desert or a lush landscape.

ADDITIONAL CULTIVARS, SPECIES, OR VARIETIES

A. absinthium, or Common Wormwood, brings silver-gray
foliage to the yard. *A. ludoviciana albula*, or Silver King,
has a graceful, upright habit with very light gray foliage
that is absolutely stunning against dark green backgrounds.
A. schmidtiana, or 'Silver Mound', is a showy little plant
with extremely fine feathery foliage. *A. caucasica*, or Silver
Spread, has silky, silvery green foliage, with small yellow
flowers that will take our heat.

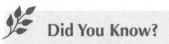

Did You Know?

Artemesia 'Powis Castle' was the grayish plant UNLV
Arboretum used to make the block-letter "UNLV" sign
on campus.

Bearded Iris

Iris germanica

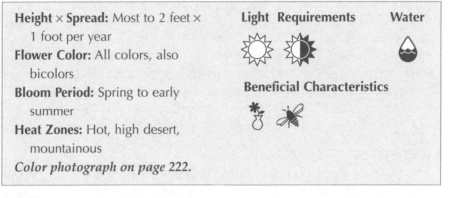

Height × Spread: Most to 2 feet ×
  1 foot per year
Flower Color: All colors, also
  bicolors
Bloom Period: Spring to early
  summer
Heat Zones: Hot, high desert,
  mountainous
Color photograph on page 222.

Light Requirements

Water

Beneficial Characteristics

Bearded Iris gets its name from the beard that resembles a woolly caterpillar, lying on each of the fall petals. Iris flowers are made up of two types of petals: fall petals and standard petals. The fall petals are the true petals and are the parts of the flower that flop over and hang down. They come in a full range of colors including red, yellow, white to purple, and everything in between; they come in bicolors as well. The standard petals can be a different color than the fall petals. Irises flower for about three weeks in the late spring through early summer and are extremely showy, so don't hide them. The sword-shaped leaves add an interesting texture to the garden, even when the plant is not in bloom. (DP)

REGIONAL TIPS

Bearded Iris grows all over the state. In the hot regions, give the plants part shade such as morning light with protection from the hot afternoon sun. In the high desert and mountainous regions they should get full sun.

WHEN, WHERE, AND HOW TO PLANT

Bearded Iris can be planted from containers anytime during the growing season, and the most common method is to plant rhizomes. When they are planted as rhizomes, they should be divided and transplanted about three to six weeks after they bloom. This is the correct timing for the north, but wait until Labor Day to plant in the south. Because they do spread, plant them where they can be left undisturbed for a few years. Bearded Iris thrives in soil that is slightly alkaline, well-drained, and rich in humus (it will get rot if planted in wet, poorly drained soil). To divide, carefully dig under the plants with a spading fork and lift the rhizomes, plant and all, out of the ground. Cut each rhizome into 6-inch sections with a fan of leaves attached to each one. The divisions need to be left out in the shade for a few days to heal over the cut ends—this prevents rot when it is planted. Plant them like ducks in the water, half in the soil and half out. I make two furrows about 3 inches deep in the soil with a ridge between them, place the rhizome on the ridge and let the roots dangle into the furrows, and then fill in the furrows with soil. Dig holes for container-grown plants that are as deep as the container and a little wider, filling in around the rootball with soil after planting; then give them a good soaking.

CARE AND MAINTENANCE

Bearded Iris is carefree, easy to grow, and doesn't have any pest problems. Fertilize with a water-soluble fertilizer about once a month during the growing season, and water once or twice a week with one inch of water. For the best flowering, the plants should be divided about every two to three years.

LANDSCAPE MERIT

Bearded Irises are great in a bed by themselves or as accent plants in flower beds. I like to plant them in groupings of five, on up to nine or ten.

Did You Know?

Many new varieties of Iris bloom more than once during the season, much to the delight of Iris lovers.

PERENNIALS

Black-Eyed Susan

Rudbeckia hirta

Height × Spread: 3 to 4 feet × 15 inches

Flower Color: Yellow, orange, mahogany, and bicolor

Bloom Period: Summer to early fall

Heat Zones: Hot, high desert, mountainous

Color photograph on page 222.

Light Requirement

Water

Beneficial Characteristics

Black-eyed Susan is a great plant for large areas in the garden. It is considered a short-lived perennial because it usually persists in the garden for only a few years. The plants get up to 4 feet tall and have upright branching, with flowers that are large and single with dark brown to black centers, and blooms that grow to 3 to 7 inches in diameter. Though most are yellow, they come in shades of orange, russet, and mahogany as well. The 'Pinwheel' variety is an interesting bicolor that has mahogany-and-gold flowers, and some of the other flowers have zonal bands of differing colors—and while most of them have single flowers, there are also some double-flowered varieties. They flower from early summer to fall and keep well as cut flowers in floral arrangements. The seedheads are very interesting in the winter garden, rustling in the wind, so don't cut them down in the fall. (DP)

REGIONAL TIPS

Black-eyed Susans will grow in all regions, and in the high desert and mountainous regions they reseed themselves. Because of the heat of the hot region, it is not adapted for a meadow landscape there.

WHEN, WHERE, AND HOW TO PLANT

Plant Black-eyed Susans in the spring, and because they are short-lived perennials, consider placing them where they will not be disturbed for a few years. They are easy to grow from seed or transplants, with transplants providing flowers much sooner; if they are started from seed they will flower the first year, and they will also reseed themselves. Black-eyed Susans do best in full sun and love the summer heat, growing in almost any kind of soil—but the better the soil, the larger the plants and the more they flower. Add 3 inches of organic mulch and work it in to a depth of 6 inches. As with most plants, Black-eyed Susans will get off to a much better start if you work some fertilizer into the soil at the same time you till in the mulch. Add the contents of a 1-pound coffee can full of fertilizer containing 10 to 16 percent nitrogen to 100 square feet of garden. Dig the hole as deep as the rootball and a little wider, spacing plants about 15 inches apart, then giving them a good soaking after planting.

CARE AND MAINTENANCE

Black-eyed Susans are very carefree and don't require any special attention. While they tolerate poor, dry soil, they should be watered with 1 inch of water about twice a week for best appearance. As with all plants in the garden, they will perform better all summer long if they are fertilized with a water-soluble fertilizer used according to directions.

LANDSCAPE MERIT

They can be used anywhere in the garden, but because of their size, they are best as background plants. Mix them with some of the ornamental grasses, along with some blue-flowered Larkspur, and you'll have a great mountain-meadow effect.

ADDITIONAL SPECIES, CULTIVARS, OR VARIETIES

'Gloriosa Daisy' has single flowers in various color combinations, and there is also a double 'Gloriosa Daisy'. 'Goldilocks' is a low-growing variety, growing to only 10 inches high. One of the more interesting ones is *R. hirta* 'Kelvedon Star'. It is a single yellow flower with a mahogany-brown center, with the mahogany color extending towards the tip of the petals from the center.

Blanket Flower

Gaillardia × grandiflora

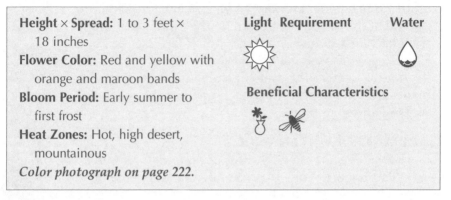

Height × Spread: 1 to 3 feet × 18 inches

Flower Color: Red and yellow with orange and maroon bands

Bloom Period: Early summer to first frost

Heat Zones: Hot, high desert, mountainous

Color photograph on page 222.

Light Requirement

Water

Beneficial Characteristics

Blanket Flower is a very hardy perennial that has brightly colored, daisylike flowers of red and yellow. Some have combinations of red or yellow with bands of orange or maroon on the petals. The flowers get to be between 3 and 4 inches in diameter and are extremely showy in the garden. 'Goblin', for example, has red petals tipped with yellow, and 'Red Plume' is a red double-flowered variety. Plants range in height from 12 inches to over 3 feet, flowers bloom from early summer until the first frost, and foliage is a gray-green color and somewhat hairy. They aren't just good for looking at in the garden; they also make long-lasting cut flowers. (DP)

REGIONAL TIPS

The native habitat of the Blanket Flower is closer to the high desert and mountainous regions, meaning better growth in these areas.

WHEN, WHERE, AND HOW TO PLANT

Plant Blanket Flower in the late winter to early spring in hot regions, and after the last frost in the other regions. Remember that they will be in the garden for a long time, so be sure to plant them in a spot where they will not be disturbed for a few years. You can plant Blanket Flowers from seed, or as bedding plants. Seed can be planted directly into the soil, and though it takes longer to get the plants to the bloom stage, they will flower the first year. If you are going to plant them from seed, scatter the seed and cover it with a thin mixture of half peat moss and half sand. In the colder, higher parts of the high desert and mountainous regions, my own preference is to transplant them to the garden rather than from seed. If transplanting, dig the hole as deep as the rootball and a little wider. Space them about 15 inches apart and give them a good soak after planting. They are not fussy about the soil and in fact don't do very well in rich, moist soils. This is why they work so well as meadow plants. Even so, if you are preparing a bed for them, add about 3 inches of organic mulch and till it in—this will help the soil drain better. There's no need to apply any fertilizer during seedbed preparation.

CARE AND MAINTENANCE

Blanket Flowers are pretty much carefree. They tolerate drought and don't appear to have any specific insect or disease problems. The plant clumps should be divided at least every other year in order to maintain vigor. In the spring you might even have to thin out the seedlings as they emerge, for they often reseed themselves. Fertilize monthly during the summer using a water-soluble fertilizer mixed according to directions.

LANDSCAPE MERIT

Use them in border plantings along with other tall flowers. They are also great for creating a meadow garden, especially effective when planted with some of the ornamental grasses. You can mix them with Black-eyed Susans, Larkspur, and Forget-me-not, as well as Cosmos, for a meadow extravaganza.

ADDITIONAL SPECIES, CULTIVARS, OR VARIETIES

Try 'Burgundy', with deep-red flowers, 'Goblin', a dwarf growing to only 12 inches high, and 'Yellow Queen', which has yellow petals with an orange center. 'Tokajer' grows to 30 inches high and featured gold flowers with a red ring circling the petals. Another species includes one with double flowers, *G. pulchella* 'Double Mix'.

Bush Morning Glory

Convolvulus cneorm

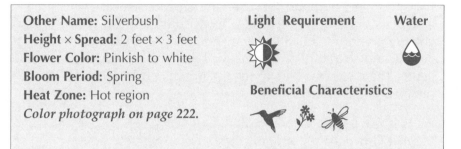

Other Name: Silverbush
Height × Spread: 2 feet × 3 feet
Flower Color: Pinkish to white
Bloom Period: Spring
Heat Zone: Hot region
Color photograph on page 222.

Light Requirement

Water

Beneficial Characteristics

Unlike its weedy relative Morning Glory Vine, Bush Morning Glory is an asset to any garden. It is a fast-growing, low-mounding evergreen that doesn't spread. It stays in its territory and is beautiful and blessed with distinctive soft foliage. The foliage and its form blend well with other plants in the garden as a foreground for taller Cassias and Texas Rangers. It fits so well in natural garden settings, particularly if boulders are a primary part of the scene. Then when it comes into full bloom, the large white trumpet- or funnel-shaped flowers call for closer inspection. At closer range, white blooms take on a pinkish tint, focusing your attention even more to their bright yellow throats. I find that most plants hailing from dry climates have yellow flowers (a color to beckon bees to come and share their nectar). These blooms cover the bush with soft, silvery foliage to accentuate their beauty, and are most profuse during the early spring, then spasmodically through the summer into fall. (LM)

REGIONAL TIPS

Bush Morning Glory is a wonderful ground cover for the southern part of the state, with its soft grayish foliage and charming blossoms. I am sorry, northern Nevadans, but it will not withstand your harsh winters.

WHEN, WHERE, AND HOW TO PLANT

Plant in cool weather, preferably in October and November, to give the roots time to spread out. I find plants have less leaf scorch and less dieback when planted in the fall. As you prepare the planting hole, make it at least three times as wide and as deep as the rootball. Although Bush Morning Glory will grow well in desert soils, it prefers a rich organic soil with good drainage. Check the drainage by filling the hole with water; if it has all drained away within 8 hours, drainage is good. Mix a generous supply of organic matter into the on-site soil and tuck the bush into the hole. Build a water basin around the plant and give it a good soaking. Because of its mounding effect as it spreads across the soil, it doesn't require mulch.

CARE AND MAINTENANCE

The plant desires weekly waterings into the summer, but as it gets above 90 degrees Fahrenheit, go to twice-a-week waterings, and monthly through the winter. If using emitters, run them 2 hours each time. Bush Morning Glory has low fertilizer demands, so work a cupful of ammonium sulfate under the bush prior to irrigation around Valentine's Day, and again Labor Day. Severe pruning in December or January will keep plants vigorous, bushier, and producing more flowers. If you see dry, dusty leaves at the base of the plant, spider mites are the culprit. Force them off with a strong jet of water or use insecticidal soap.

LANDSCAPE MERIT

Bush Morning Glory is a very showy plant. Its silvery foliage seems to lighten up a landscape dominated by dark green plants. It becomes a very effective foreground plant for other shrubs and shines in mass plantings, planters, containers, hanging baskets, and rock gardens.

ADDITIONAL SPECIES, CULTIVARS, OR VARIETIES

C. mauritanicdus is better as a foreground plant; it has lavender-blue flowers combined with gray-green foliage and it blooms longer.

Candytuft

Iberis sempervirens

Height × Spread: 6 to 12 inches × 18 inches
Flower Color: White
Bloom Period: Spring
Heat Zones: Hot, high desert, mountainous
Color photograph on page 222.

Light Requirements

Water

Beneficial Characteristic

Candytuft makes a good ground cover that will grow in all regions of Nevada. The plant is very compact, growing to only 12 inches, but it spreads up to 18 inches wide. Candytuft flowers from early spring to June, but in the milder climates it will start blooming in November. The flowers are white and arranged on dome-shaped tufts that completely cover the plant when it is in bloom, and stems are long enough to allow them to be used as cut flowers. The leaves are about an inch long, narrow, and a shiny, dark green. If you are looking for something very low growing and compact you might want to try 'Little Gem'. It only grows to about 4 inches tall. 'Snowflake' grows to 12 inches tall but will spread to over 3 feet. (DP)

REGIONAL TIPS

Candytuft will stay evergreen all year in the hot region and semi-evergreen in the rest of the state.

WHEN, WHERE, AND HOW TO PLANT

Candytuft can be planted in either the spring or the fall and can withstand part shade, but the plants do best in full sun. They are perennial, so remember to plant them where you can leave them undisturbed for a few years. They can be planted from seed if you start them inside in flats and then transplant them out into the garden. Planting time is the same for transplants and bedding plants. Candytuft prefers a well-drained soil, so add about 3 inches of organic mulch to the soil surface and also add the contents of a 1-pound coffee can filled with a fertilizer containing between 10 and 16 percent nitrogen. This is enough to fertilize a space 10 feet square. Till both the organic matter and the fertilizer into the soil to a depth of 6 inches. Space the plants 8 inches apart, digging the holes as deep as the rootballs and slightly wider, and place the rootballs in the holes and cover with soil. After they have been planted, give them a good soaking.

CARE AND MAINTENANCE

Candytuft is very easy to care for. The plants need to be watered with 1 inch of water once or twice a week, and the fertilizer applied to the soil at the time of planting will last them throughout the growing season—if they are overfertilized, they will become leggy. After they finish flowering, prune them back hard or they will lose that nice, compact look. Candytuft doesn't have any pests.

LANDSCAPE MERIT

Candytuft can be planted in the rock garden, border plantings, and it may be used as an edging plant. It is great in planters and containers and, as mentioned, some varieties make excellent ground covers.

ADDITIONAL SPECIES, CULTIVARS, OR VARIETIES

'Snow White' is a low-growing plant to 6 inches that will spread to form a nice mat of white flowers in the spring. Like all Candytuft, it needs to be sheared after it flowers. There are also some annual varieties that are worthy of mention, even though you have to plant them year after year. One is *I. unbellata* 'Brilliant Mix', growing to 10 inches high and forming a carpet of flowers ranging from red, purple, lilac, pink and rose to white—and they flower all summer long.

Canna Lily

Canna × generalis

Other Name: Canna
Height × Spread: 5 feet × 3 feet
Flower Color: Yellow, orange, ivory,
white, pink, salmon, apricot,
coral, red, and many bicolors
Bloom Period: Midsummer to fall
Heat Zones: Hot, high desert
Color photograph on page 222.

Light Requirements

Water

Beneficial Characteristics

Canna Lilies definitely bring the tropics to your yard. They produce a continuous show of bold flowers in strong colors from summer through frost that really is a sight to see. Flowers are densely set along spikes that rise a foot or so above the foliage and catch even a child's attention. Cannas come in yellow, orange, ivory, white, pink, salmon, apricot, coral, red, and many bicolors. The leaves are large and rich-green to bronzy-red to emphasize the tropical look, and they provide a dramatic backdrop for the flowers. Hybridizing among the species has given us such bold plants, with a couple of hybrids that have become the hallmarks of the changing world of Cannas. They have multicolored leaves of purple-red dramatically striped with green and yellow veins, commanding enough to cause a second and even third look. Place the rich-red bloomers alongside deep-green foliage plants and you'll never forget the view. (LM)

REGIONAL TIPS

Canna Lilies make a great perennial for southern Nevada gardens. They struggle with the harsh winter weather in northern Nevada (but they can be grown as annuals there).

WHEN, WHERE, AND HOW TO PLANT

Plant Cannas as they become available at the nursery. Cannas prefer a rich soil with good drainage and respond best to an eastern exposure or filtered sun. Make the planting hole at least three times wider than and as deep as the rootball, mixing organic matter into the on-site soil so roots can gather the needed nutrients and water to produce the blooms. Build a water basin around the plant and give it a good soaking. Because of Canna's clumping effect, cover the soil with mulch.

CARE AND MAINTENANCE

Cannas need ample moisture and humidity to keep their lushness, so water twice a week until it gets above 85 degrees Fahrenheit and dry, then water three times a week. If you are using emitters, let them run for two hours at a time. Cannas can remain in the ground year round, but you need to mulch them. Use a balanced fertilizer often to keep them lush and vigorous, even to the point of feeding them monthly. Remove the dead and faded flowers and cut plants to the ground in late fall as growth declines. Divide Cannas every three to five years to keep the flowers coming. Snails and slugs bother Cannas and should be treated with a snail and slug bait. If leaves take on a dusty appearance, suspect spider mites. Spray with insecticidal soap or Malathion.

LANDSCAPE MERIT

Cannas show off best when planted in masses. They add to water features, and the tropical effect they bring with giant leaves and showy flowers is without equal.

ADDITIONAL SPECIES, CULTIVARS, OR VARIETIES

The best known of the hybrids includes 'Minerva', with yellow-striped green leaves and yellow flowers. 'Pretoria' has similarly variegated leaves with orange blossoms; 'Tropicanna' has hot orange blooms over purple foliage that becomes striped green. 'Red King Humbert' has reddish-bronze leaves and orange to red flowers; 'Wyoming' has bronzy purple foliage and bright orange blooms. *Canna* 'Durban' has fierce, fiery orange-red blooms atop its spikes, and *Canna* 'Phaison' produces clear, brilliant orange flowers.

Did You Know?

In 1992 the All-American Selections was awarded to 'Tropical Rose'. The selection came true from seed. Until that time, rhizomes were used to propagate Cannas. The flowers of this one are self-cleaning—meaning one less chore for you.

Coral Bells

Heuchera sanguinea

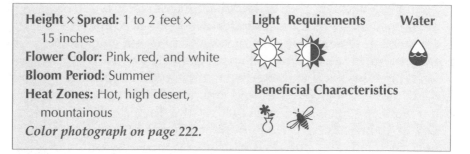

Height × Spread: 1 to 2 feet × 15 inches
Flower Color: Pink, red, and white
Bloom Period: Summer
Heat Zones: Hot, high desert, mountainous
Color photograph on page 222.

Light Requirements

Water

Beneficial Characteristics

Coral Bells are great, long-lasting perennials that will persist in the garden forever. The bell-shaped flowers develop in clusters at the top of wiry stems that grow from about 12 to 24 inches high, and they are available in red, pink, or white. The flowers are very good in arrangements and last for a long time as cut flowers. The plants are compact, low growing, only getting to 8 to 12 inches high, and leaves are rounded, 2 to 3 inches in size, with ruffled edges making the plants attractive even when not in bloom. They bloom throughout the summer, but the heaviest bloom is in early summer. (DP)

REGIONAL TIPS
In the hot regions they will stay green most of the year, while in the high desert and mountainous regions they will get a reddish tinge in the leaves in the fall and then turn brown.

WHEN, WHERE, AND HOW TO PLANT
Plant Coral Bells almost any time of the year, but in the high desert and mountainous regions, spring is best. They can be planted from seeds, but the best way is to purchase them as container plants. Remember they are perennial plants, so plant them in a spot where they will not have to be disturbed for a few years. While they like full sun, they will bloom even in part shade. Coral Bells grow best in a soil that has lots of humus (organic matter) in it. For best results, add a 6-inch layer of organic mulch over the top of the soil and mix it thoroughly to a depth of 6 to 8 inches. This loosens up our tight, clayey soil and provides better drainage for the plants. They don't require much fertilizer, but if you fill a 1-pound coffee can half full of a complete fertilizer that contains between 10 and 16 percent nitrogen, spread it evenly over 100 square feet, and till it in with the

mulch, you will have sturdier plants as a result. Dig the hole only as deep as the rootball and a little wider, and place the plant in the hole and fill in around the rootball with soil; then give the plant a good soaking.

CARE AND MAINTENANCE
Coral Bells are pretty much pest-free. Once they have been planted they don't need any special applications of fertilizers. They produce more flowers if you divide them about every three to four years, so divide them in the spring in the high desert and mountainous regions, and in the hot region they can be divided in the fall. Give them 1 inch of water twice a week during the growing season.

LANDSCAPE MERIT
If you are looking for a great edging plant, Coral Bells will be one of the best. I have them in my rock garden where they spread out and flow over the rocks. They can be used as a ground cover, and when planted in a mass they form a colorful mat; another effective use is as an edging for shrub beds.

ADDITIONAL SPECIES, CULTIVARS, OR VARIETIES
There is one other species that is available, and it is *Heuchera micrantha* 'Palace Purple'. It has large, maplelike, purplish-red leaves and grows to 18 inches high and about as wide, with flowers that are white to pinkish. I like this one for the foliage color and the coarse texture it adds to the garden.

Coreopsis

Coreopsis verticillata

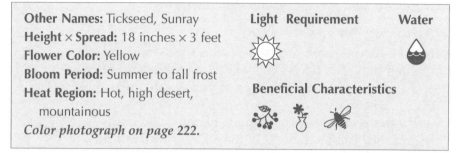

Other Names: Tickseed, Sunray	**Light Requirement**	**Water**
Height × Spread: 18 inches × 3 feet		
Flower Color: Yellow		
Bloom Period: Summer to fall frost		
Heat Region: Hot, high desert,	**Beneficial Characteristics**	
mountainous		
Color photograph on page 222.		

I f you are looking for something that will give your garden a bright
yellow glow, you need Coreopsis. They flower all summer long and
all you can see are the blossoms, in either single or double blooms
that get to 2 inches in diameter. The foliage of *C. verticillata* has a lacy,
threadlike appearance, and is green to gray-green depending on the
variety. 'Golden Showers', for example, has bright yellow flowers that
bloom throughout July and August, growing to 2 feet high and as wide.
'Moonbeam' also has wiry, fernlike foliage, but with pale yellow flowers that cover the plant from June through September. (DP)

REGIONAL TIPS
Coreopsis likes the heat but will perform anywhere in Nevada,
including some of the coldest areas in the mountainous regions.

WHEN, WHERE, AND HOW TO PLANT
It can be planted from containers throughout the growing season,
but availability is always best in the spring. If you are planting seed,
sow the seed indoors in the spring and transplant the started plants
out to the garden after the last frost. By the way, they have a tendency to reseed themselves. While they will grow in part shade, they
bloom best in full sun. Coreopsis does best in a well-drained, sandy
soil. If you are preparing a flower bed to be filled with other flowers,
there is no need to prepare it any differently for Coreopsis. I add 3 to
4 inches of organic mulch and mix it into the upper 6 inches of soil.
This goes a long way toward keeping the soil loose for better aeration and better drainage. Coreopsis plants are light feeders, so
fertilizer is not needed at planting. When transplanting, dig the hole
as deep as the rootball, toss the plant in the hole, fill in around the
rootball with soil, and then give it a good soaking.

CARE AND MAINTENANCE

Coreopsis is a very easy plant to maintain. While it doesn't require much plant food, it won't hurt it if you feed it along with the other plants in the flower bed. The easiest way is to use a water-soluble fertilizer about once a month throughout the growing season, according to directions. To keep Coreopsis blooming, remove the faded blossoms. It tolerates drought very well, but it will look better if you give it an inch of water twice a week in the high desert and mountainous regions, and twice that amount in the hot regions. About every two to three years, divide the plants to maintain vigor.

LANDSCAPE MERIT

Coreopsis is a utilitarian plant for the garden and can be used anywhere. Its bright flowers make this plant stand out in any setting. While it is usually a plant for the border or flower bed, it can also be part of a meadow scene— mix it with other flowers like Blanket Flower and some of the ornamental grasses. Coreopsis plants are also used effectively in planters and containers. 'Moonbeam', with its very light, ferny appearance, is adapted for use in hanging baskets.

ADDITIONAL SPECIES, CULTIVARS, OR VARIETIES

Other species of Coreopsis to try are *C. grandiflora* 'Early Sunrise', which grows to 2 feet high by 1 foot wide and has orange to yellow flowers through midsummer. *C. lanceolata* is also 2 feet high and 1 foot wide, with yellow flowers and a longer blooming period.

Daylily

Hemerocallis × hybrids

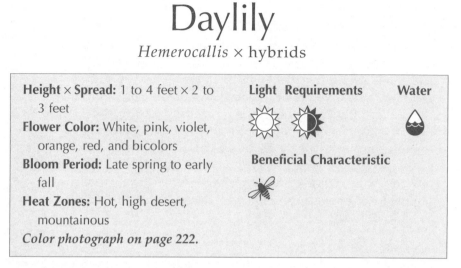

Height × Spread: 1 to 4 feet × 2 to 3 feet

Flower Color: White, pink, violet, orange, red, and bicolors

Bloom Period: Late spring to early fall

Heat Zones: Hot, high desert, mountainous

Color photograph on page 222.

Light Requirements

Water

Beneficial Characteristic

Daylilies add a very interesting texture and flower to the garden, with leaves that are long, straplike, and arching and grow in large clumps. The leaves are usually an inch wide and up to 2 feet long. The lilylike flowers are produced on branched stems and get to be from 3 to 8 inches across, in shades of pink, rust-red, orange, yellow, violet, white, and cream, with many combinations as well. They are mostly single flowered, but 'Siloam Double Classic' has a very attractive, peach-colored double flower. 'Todd Monroe' is an interesting bicolor, with the center of the flower a deep rose, the outer half white, and the throat yellow. One of the interesting things about Daylilies is that the red ones need heat to develop the best color. Daylilies are also very good as cut flowers; cut the flower stocks with the buds after they have developed, and bring them inside to watch as each bud opens on the stems. (DP)

REGIONAL TIPS

While Daylilies do very well almost anywhere, they might be a little slow getting started in the colder areas of the mountainous regions.

WHEN, WHERE, AND HOW TO PLANT

Plant Daylilies any time of the year if they are obtained as container plants; however, you will have a much better choice of varieties in the spring. Daylilies are planted as transplants and divisions. Plant them in a sunny spot or one with part shade. They grow in any kind of soil, but if you are planting a new bed, add organic matter to improve the drainage. Add a 3-inch layer of organic mulch to the soil surface and till in to a depth of 6 inches, at the same time adding the contents of a 1-pound coffee can filled with a complete fertilizer that contains between 10 and 16 percent nitrogen for every 100 square feet of garden. Plant Daylilies about 2 feet apart and only as deep as the rootball, and give them a good soaking.

CARE AND MAINTENANCE

Daylilies are very tough plants, so no pests bother them. They require 1 inch of water a week when they are in the foliage stage, but when they are in bloom, give them 1 inch twice a week so they don't wilt. Remove the faded flowers for continued flowering and a tidier looking plant. If you fertilized when you planted, then give them another application around midsummer. When the plants start to get crowded, divide them, preferably in the early spring or the late fall.

LANDSCAPE MERIT

These are versatile plants that have many uses in the garden. They work very well in large flower beds and in border plantings, particularly when used with other plants. Because of the long, straplike leaves, they add a tropical look to the garden and are particularly attractive when planted next to a pond or stream where the leaves can drape over the water. They are excellent for mass plantings in areas such as banks or under tall trees where shade is minimal. The dwarf varieties are very well adapted for use in rock gardens.

ADDITIONAL SPECIES, CULTIVARS, OR VARIETIES

There are plenty of varieties to choose from. 'Pink Tangerine' is a combination of pink and tangerine and has flowers that are 6 inches across. Or try 'Stella de Oro', with 2-inch gold blooms that never stop. How about 'Shortee', with 1-inch yellow flowers on 9-inch-high plants?

Dianthus

Dianthus species

Height × Spread: 6 inches to 2 feet × 2 feet	**Light Requirement**	**Water**
Flower Color: Pink, white, purple, yellow, orange, and red		
Bloom Period: Late spring to fall	**Beneficial Characteristics**	
Heat Zones: Hot, high desert, mountainous		
Color photograph on page 223.		

Dianthus encompasses very large groups of hardy annuals and perennials. All flower during the summer, and a few of them have a very spicy fragrance. The one that everyone is most familiar with is the florists' Carnation. The plants are weak and gangly in the garden and have to be tied up, so they're not an appealing choice for me. One of the garden types that is excellent in Nevada's gardens is Sweet William, *D. barbatus*, a biennial with 3-inch-long leaves and growing to 20 inches tall. It has clusters of pink, white, rose-red, purple, and bicolored blooms that get to 4 inches in diameter. Another that blooms well is the Maiden Pink, *D. deltoides*, which has small leaves and only gets 12 inches tall and develops a loose mat, with flowers up to 1 inch blooming in the summer and often again in the fall. Though they are called Pinks, they come in white, rose, and purple. The Cottage Pink, *D. plumarius*, is another excellent selection. Flowers are produced on 10- to 18-inch stems above the foliage. They are available in shades of rose, pink, and white, with dark centers. Cottage Pinks have a very pleasant, spicy fragrance. The flowers are either single or double, and they bloom from early summer to fall. All have a mounded shape, and the foliage is narrow and either blue-green or green. (DP)

REGIONAL TIPS

Sweet Williams are great for the mountainous regions of Nevada; I have even found them in some of the old mining camps. In the hot regions, plant them in part shade.

WHEN, WHERE, AND HOW TO PLANT

Plant Dianthus in the spring—they are available in garden centers throughout most of the spring and summer. They grow best in full sun, but in the hottest region of the state they will benefit from light shade in the afternoon. They are not fussy about the soil conditions and do well in Nevada's alkaline soils; in fact, they prefer alkaline soil to acid. Soil preparation is important for the best growth after planting. Because they all grow best in a soil with good drainage, the addition of organic matter will help, as will a preplant application of fertilizer, although they don't require much once they are established. Dianthus are usually planted as bedding plants and transplanted into the garden. Space them about 12 inches apart and plant only as deep as the rootball, giving them a good soaking after planting.

CARE AND MAINTENANCE

Dianthus is fairly easy to care for. The plants should not be overwatered. They are susceptible to fusarium wilt, a soil-borne fungus disease that also attacks many other garden plants; wilted plants should be removed immediately and destroyed. They can be propagated by taking cuttings from the tips of the growing shoots, or by division. After blooming, remove the spent blossoms.

LANDSCAPE MERIT

Dianthus can be used anywhere in the garden, from border plantings to beds. The low-growing mat types are an excellent choice for rock gardens. They are wonderful for containers as well. Sweet William looks best when mixed with other flowers and when used in color bowls, which show up in the garden centers in the spring.

ADDITIONAL SPECIES, CULTIVARS, OR VARIETIES

A few of the Sweet William varieties are 'Messenger', 'Indian Carpet', and 'Summer Beauty'. If you are interested in Maiden Pinks, try 'Vampire' or 'Arctic Fire'. Some Cottage Pinks to try are 'Highland' and 'Sonata'.

Dusty Miller

Centaurea cineraria

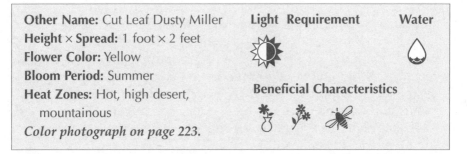

Other Name: Cut Leaf Dusty Miller
Height × Spread: 1 foot × 2 feet
Flower Color: Yellow
Bloom Period: Summer
Heat Zones: Hot, high desert,
  mountainous
Color photograph on page 223.

Light Requirement

Water

Beneficial Characteristics

If you want to cool off and lighten up your landscape, plant clusters of Dusty Miller. Most of the plants discussed in this book feature cheerful blossoms, and they are great, but let's focus on the foliage here. The large and heavily lobed leaves are painted chalky white with a pale green in the background. As the breeze blows, the leaves glisten differently. When I see this color in landscape, the temperature seems to drop 10 degrees. (I continue to gaze, hoping it will drop some more.) Dusty Miller gets about a foot high and spreads out twice as much. Yellow and sometimes purple flowers occur in single, thistlelike heads, 1 inch in diameter, throughout the summer. It needs full sun to thrive and bring out the cool color in the leaves, and it does this all on a "water-miser's" diet. You'll find these flowers at the florist, too, in many arrangements. If you plant *Centaurea*, plan to use as cut flowers. (LM)

REGIONAL TIPS

Dusty Miller is the most widely used species of *Centaurea* in southern Nevada landscapes because it loves heat. Use it in the north as an annual.

WHEN, WHERE, AND HOW TO PLANT

Plant it during the cool months or when it's on sale at the nursery. Dusty Miller does well in desert soils but needs good drainage. It will grow in partial shade but does best in full sun, and constant winds don't seem to affect it. This durable plant tolerates various soil and moisture conditions, making it a good choice in the categories of low water and low maintenance. It needs a hole at least three times wider than and as deep as the rootball. Mix a generous supply of organic matter to open up southern Nevada's tight soils so the roots can gather nutrients and water to produce the blooms you dream of.

After planting, build a water basin around the plant and give it a good soaking.

CARE AND MAINTENANCE

Start this plant off in the spring with weekly waterings. The plant is prone to root rot if overwatered, though. As the temperatures climb into the 70s, change to deep, infrequent, weekly irrigations throughout the summer, and monthly when it's cold. Its fertilizer demands are low, but an application of nitrogen will make prettier blooms. *Centaurea* plants self-seed easily, so remove the spent flowers. The beauty of this task is that it rejuvenates the plant and keeps it from becoming leggy, causing more blooms the following season.

LANDSCAPE MERIT

Dusty Miller emphasizes its foliage more than its flowers. It fits well in rock gardens and along borders and makes an excellent container plant. Its grayish foliage really brings out the colors of other plants such as Petunias and those with rich-green color.

ADDITIONAL SPECIES, CULTIVARS, OR VARIETIES

Here are some species recommended for southern Nevada: *C. hypoleuca* flowers are deep rose, blooming throughout the summer on smaller plants; 'John Couts' has brilliant, rosy flowers throughout the summer; *C. macrocephala* has large, yellow, thistlelike flowers on 4-foot-high plants. *C. montana* flowers are one of the darkest blues in the garden. The plant gets about 3 feet high with the leaf undersides often covered with fine white hairs. Flowers 2 to 4 inches across come in white, yellow, and shades of blue and purple. This desert plant thrives in our heat.

Hardy Chrysanthemum

Chrysanthemum hybrids

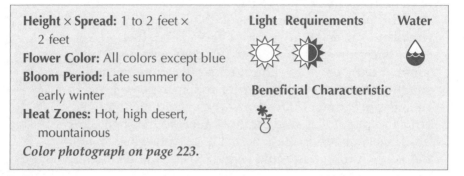

Height × Spread: 1 to 2 feet × 2 feet

Flower Color: All colors except blue

Bloom Period: Late summer to early winter

Heat Zones: Hot, high desert, mountainous

Color photograph on page 223.

Light Requirements

Water

Beneficial Characteristic

Hardy Chrysanthemums are the best fall-flowering plants we have, creating a solid mass of color with no foliage in sight. You can get yellow, dark red, purple, pink, rust, white, orange, and even a few combinations. There are different flower types, such as spiders, spoons, quills, anemones, doubles, and even a few semi-doubles. The flowers range in size from 2 inches to well over 6 inches and make some of the best flowers for cutting you can find, lasting for weeks in arrangements indoors. The only difference from the florist's Mum is the size of the flower, and you can get larger flowers if you pinch off all but the terminal bud on each stem. This is truly a great flower for any garden. (DP)

REGIONAL TIPS

Chrysanthemums are really great flowers for all of the state, but they grow a little better in the high desert and mountainous regions. In the mountainous regions, the white-flowered ones may get brown petals from the first frost in the fall. In the south, pinch the terminal bud growth monthly until August to keep plants compact.

WHEN, WHERE, AND HOW TO PLANT

Hardy Chrysanthemums are generally planted in the spring, but if you buy them in full bloom in the late summer and fall, you will have instant fall color. Remember to plant them in a place where they can be left undisturbed for a few years. Chrysanthemums do best in a good soil with lots of organic matter, but they will also do very well in most soils. When the bed is first prepared, you will get best growth and best flowering if you add about 3 inches of organic mulch to the soil and till it in. Because Chrysanthemums are considered heavy feeders, incorporate a complete fertilizer into the soil at the same time. The contents of a 1-pound coffee can filled with a fertilizer containing between 10 and 16 percent nitrogen are just right when applied to 100 square feet of garden. Dig the planting hole as deep as the rootball and a little wider, place the plant in the hole, cover the rootball with soil, and give it a good soaking. Space the plants about 2 feet apart in the garden.

CARE AND MAINTENANCE

Hardy Chrysanthemums are pretty carefree. They will tolerate some drought but do best if given 1 inch of water twice a week; also use a water-soluble fertilizer according to directions once a month during the growing season. Though Chrysanthemums are perennial, they need to be divided about every two to three years in the spring while they are still dormant; get the divisions from the edges of the plant, where the growth is more active. Aphids often attack them, so wash them off with a good stiff spray of water at first sighting.

LANDSCAPE MERIT

Each spring Chrysanthemums develop into nice, compact green bushes, which make a great background for annual flowers when planted around them. They are at home in border plantings and massed in large beds, and are equally at home in planters and large flower pots placed around a patio or deck. Some are even trained to trail gracefully as they spill over the edges of hanging baskets.

ADDITIONAL SPECIES, CULTIVARS, OR VARIETIES

Try 'Purple Pirate', 'Snowdrift', 'Martian', and 'Ravioli', just to name a few. There are some really special ones out there, but you might have to hunt for the unusual ones.

Lily-of-the-Valley

Convallaria majalis

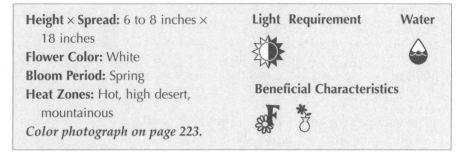

Height × Spread: 6 to 8 inches × 18 inches **Flower Color:** White **Bloom Period:** Spring **Heat Zones:** Hot, high desert, mountainous *Color photograph on page 223.*	**Light Requirement**	**Water**
	Beneficial Characteristics	

L ily-of-the-Valley is considered by some an old-fashioned flower, with waxy-looking white blooms that resemble bells, drooping down from 6- to 8-inch stems that look like shepherd's hooks. The flowers have a delicate appearance, are popular in arrangements as a cut flower, and have a very sweet fragrance that permeates the air on still nights. One of the interesting points about this plant is its flowering pattern. The first year a single leaf comes up, but no flower. In the spring of the second year, two broad leaves appear and the flower stem emerges from the center of them. These plants bloom in the spring but can be forced into blooming indoors. As beautiful as they are, there is a need for caution—all parts of the plants are considered poisonous. (DP)

REGIONAL TIPS

In the high desert and mountainous regions, give them about 1 inch to 1½ inches of water twice a week, and in the hot regions they will need about twice that amount.

WHEN, WHERE, AND HOW TO PLANT

In the hot regions of the state, plant Lily-of-the-Valley in November and December, but in the high desert and mountainous regions, plant in September and October. This plant spreads by rhizomes, so if you plant one you will have a garden-full in a few years. Lily-of-the-Valley is planted by using pips: short, upright rootstocks. They are planted both as clumps and single pips; when you purchase dormant plants you generally get the single pip. They make a good ground cover in areas where they will get only partial shade. Lily-of-the-Valley will do best in a soil that is high in organic matter, so when you prepare the soil, be sure to add at least 4 to 6 inches of organic mulch and till it in to a depth of 6 inches. At the same time, incorporate the contents of a 1-pound coffee can full of a complete fertilizer that contains between 10 and 16 percent nitrogen over 100 square feet. If you are planting clumps, space them about 1 to 2 feet apart so they will have room to grow; if planting pips, space them 4 to 5 inches apart. You can force pips to bloom indoors. Obtain them around the first of November and place them in a plastic bag. Keep them in the vegetable crisper of your refrigerator until January so they will get their winter dormancy requirement. When you take them out of the refrigerator, plant them in a pot and keep them moist— they will soon flower indoors. Once they have finished flowering, they can be transplanted out to a permanent spot in the garden.

CARE AND MAINTENANCE

Lily-of-the-Valley is generally pretty carefree. The plants need a medium amount of water, so they should be watered deeply at least twice a week. You can also apply a water-soluble fertilizer according to directions sometime in midsummer. They will do even better if you cover them with a blanket of organic mulch in the fall. I have noticed they have a little problem with slugs, but not enough to worry about.

LANDSCAPE MERIT

Even when not in bloom, they make a very nice, green ground cover until frost. Mine grow on the north side of the house and under the Apple tree (they will grow under trees and large shrubs that don't produce heavy shade).

Moss Pink

Phlox subulata

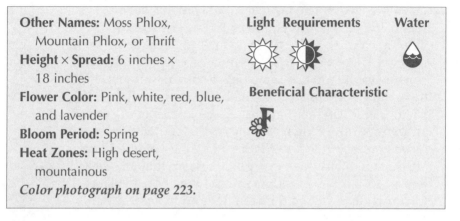

Other Names: Moss Phlox, Mountain Phlox, or Thrift

Height × Spread: 6 inches × 18 inches

Flower Color: Pink, white, red, blue, and lavender

Bloom Period: Spring

Heat Zones: High desert, mountainous

Color photograph on page 223.

Light Requirements

Water

Beneficial Characteristic

One of the brightest flowers you can get for your garden is the Moss Pink. It often starts blooming in April or May in flowers 3/4 to 1 inch in diameter, and you can't see the foliage for all the flowers. Moss Pinks really put on a show when in bloom; imagine dense mats of blue, white, red, and lavender flowers growing in drifts. Moss Pink flowers mainly in the spring and the show lasts for about three weeks at the very longest. The plants grow to a maximum of 6 inches high, and flower stems are about as long as the foliage stems. The leaves of this plant are needlelike and remain evergreen in the hot regions of the state and semievergreen in the other regions. (DP)

Regional Tips

They grow best in the high desert and mountainous regions of the state. They are sort of Nevada's answer to the colorful Ice Plant growing in the valleys of California.

When, Where, and How to Plant

When purchased as container plants, they can be planted at any time of the year, but there is a better selection in the spring. (You can start them from seed, but bedding plants are the best way to go.) One of the added benefits of transplanting in the spring is that those in 1-gallon containers are usually in bloom, providing color for the garden the minute they're planted. Moss Pinks do best in full sun but will tolerate part shade. They are very tolerant of Nevada's alkaline, clayey soils, yet will grow much better in soil that is well-drained. To prepare the soil, add 3 inches of organic mulch. For every 100 square feet of garden, add a pound of a fertilizer containing between 10 and 16 percent nitrogen and thoroughly mix it into the top 6 inches of soil along with the mulch. Space the plants 8 to 10 inches apart, planting them as deep as the rootball and filling in around the rootball after planting. You can take cuttings from established plants, root them, and transplant them into the garden. After planting, cut the foliage back about halfway on the new transplants—it makes them bushier from the start. You can also divide established plants after the flowers fade. Keep them moist for the first week after planting.

CARE AND MAINTENANCE

Allow the upper 2 inches of soil to dry out between waterings; Moss Pinks don't like soggy soils. After the flowers fade, shear them back halfway to force them to form new leaves and achieve more vigorous growth. This practice generally results in a light flowering in the fall.

LANDSCAPE MERIT

Moss Pinks are a natural anywhere you need a ground cover, and an added benefit is that they provide good ground stabilization on slopes. They are very effective as a colorful cover for banks; imagine a rock garden with the colorful blooms cascading over the rocks. I use them for edging the flower beds, but they are also great if you are looking for a low border plant.

ADDITIONAL SPECIES, CULTIVARS, OR VARIETIES

A few varieties you might want to try include 'Red Wing', a crimson-flowered cultivar with a dark burgundy center, and 'White Delight', a pure white-flowered cultivar.

Penstemon

Penstemon species

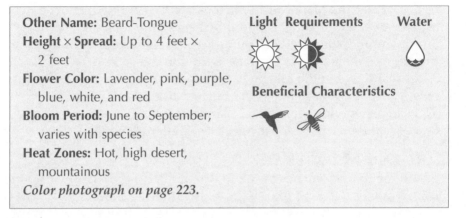

Other Name: Beard-Tongue

Height × Spread: Up to 4 feet × 2 feet

Flower Color: Lavender, pink, purple, blue, white, and red

Bloom Period: June to September; varies with species

Heat Zones: Hot, high desert, mountainous

Color photograph on page 223.

Light Requirements

Water

Beneficial Characteristics

This is one plant that stands out in the garden when in bloom. Because of its upright habit, it makes a very fine accent. The flowers of Penstemon are tubular in shape and about 1 inch long, varying in color from deep pink, blue, lavender and purple and red, and they are very showy from June through September. The foliage is also variable, but most have narrow, leathery leaves that get to be around 1 1/2 to 3 inches long; they all tend to develop woody stems over time. Some of the more popular cultivars are *P. spectabilis* Beard-Tongue that gets to 4 feet high and about 2 feet wide, with red-lavender flowers; and *P. eatonii* Firecracker, with bright red flowers. In many cases, the native Penstemons of the Sierra Nevada Range have been selected from the wild to end up in the nursery. (DP)

REGIONAL TIPS

Though most of the Penstemons are native to the mountainous areas, I have successfully grown *P. palmeri* along the freeway just east of Las Vegas.

WHEN, WHERE, AND HOW TO PLANT

Plant Penstemon any time of the year if it is container-grown, but availability is much better in the spring. It can be planted either by seed or as transplants; you can also root cuttings from your own plants and transplant them to the garden after they have rooted. Penstemons like full sun but will tolerate partial shade and are best adapted to rocky, sandy soils; many gardeners will add gravel or sand to the soil for better drainage. (You have to remember, though, that when you have clayey soils, the addition of sand and gravel ends up making concrete.) I have Penstemons growing in my garden soil with no problems so far—minimum soil preparation is all that is needed. If you are planting them from cultivar seed, plant them in the early spring. Native seed (the label will tell you if it's native) is usually planted in the fall for better germination. It often takes about two years to get flowers from seed. When planting from a container, dig the hole as deep as the rootball and a little wider. Fill in around the rootball with soil after planting and give it a good soaking.

CARE AND MAINTENANCE

Penstemons are very easy to maintain. The only problem you might have with them is overwatering; twice-a-week waterings providing 1 inch of water each time will be sufficient. Once the plants have been established for a few years they can go for days without any water. Fertilize once in the spring with a water-soluble fertilizer used according to directions.

LANDSCAPE MERIT

Penstemons are very useful in all parts of the garden. If you have a rock garden, they fit in very well, and they can be used for accents in the garden and mixed with other plants. Some, like the *P. mewberry* Mountain-Pride Penstemon, will grow very nicely on a hot, rocky knoll. They are also planted on slopes for bank stabilization.

ADDITIONAL SPECIES, CULTIVARS, OR VARIETIES

Prairie Penstemon, *P. ambiguus,* grows to 2 feet and has white or pink flowers from June to September. *Penstemon strictus* is the Rocky Mountain Penstemon and is also 2 feet high but with purple flowers, and the Crested Tongue Penstemon, *P. eriantherus*, is only 1 foot high with lilac-colored flowers.

Did You Know?

Penstemons have the name "Beard-Tongue" because some species have outward-projecting stamens that don't fit inside the flower tubes.

PERENNIALS

Peony

Paeonia hybrids

Height × Spread: 2 to 4 feet × 3 to 5 feet	**Light Requirement** **Water**
Flower Color: Red, yellow, pink, and white	
Bloom Period: Late spring to early summer	**Beneficial Characteristics**
Heat Zones: High desert, mountainous	
Color photograph on page 223.	

Imagine blooms that are up to 8 inches in diameter in shades of pinks, brilliant reds, yellow, and white. While most Peonies are double-flowered, there are some singles as well. One of the singles is 'Silver Dawn', in pastel shades contrasted by the golden-yellow stamens in the centers of the flowers. The plants are nicely shaped bushes that are a little wider than they are tall, and they have dark-green leaves with large lobes. There is one called Double Fern Leaf Peony, which, as the name implies, has fernlike foliage. To add even more interest at a different level, try the Tree Peony, *Paeonia suffruticosa*. It is trained to a single stem and considered a shrub, but the flowers are definitely those of a Peony. They bloom for a few weeks, although different varieties make it possible to have one of them in bloom for over a month; but they won't bloom without full sun. (DP)

REGIONAL TIPS

Peonies grow best in the cooler parts of the state; they need winter cold to develop the best blooms.

WHEN, WHERE, AND HOW TO PLANT

The best time to plant Peonies is in the fall, but they are more readily available as container plants in the spring. Because they are large plants that take up a lot of room, don't plant them where they will have to compete with other plants. Plant them where they will get full sun. If they are shaded, they just don't bloom. Peonies are one of the touchiest plants to transplant. Generally, you purchase a tuberous root with at least three to four eyes, or buds. The tricky part is the depth of planting: too deep and they won't bloom. The eye

should be no deeper than 2 inches. If planting from containers, plant them at the same depth they were growing in the containers. This is one plant that is sensitive to nitrogen, so don't let nitrogen fertilizers or fresh manure come into contact with the roots. Peonies like a rich organic soil. Apply an organic mulch to a depth of 6 inches and till it into the upper 8 to 10 inches of soil. You can apply a phosphorous fertilizer according to directions, and incorporate it into the soil at the same time you till in the mulch. After planting, give it a good soaking

CARE AND MAINTENANCE

Peonies can get top-heavy when they are in full bloom, so it is usually necessary to give them support. When I was growing up, Dad placed heavy wire ring-stands over the plants as they were starting to grow in the spring and trained the plants through them. Give Peonies 1 inch of water about twice a week. After they have established, fertilize them the same as other plants in the garden, using a water-soluble fertilizer according to directions every month. If you must divide them, do it in the fall; but it is best to leave them alone. In our dry air, fungus problems encountered in other parts of the country are not a problem.

LANDSCAPE MERIT

Nothing compares to the flowers of a Peony. Their massive blooms will stand out in any garden.

Did You Know?

People always call up and want to know why their Peony plants are full of ants. If you look closely at the buds you can see drops of sap oozing out between the folds of the buds. The sap is candy to the ants; they don't eat the buds.

Russell Lupines

Lupinus 'Russell' hybrids

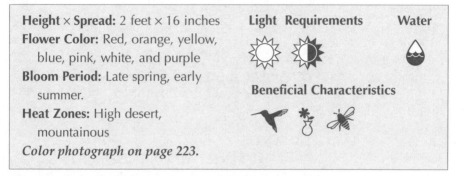

Height × Spread: 2 feet × 16 inches

Flower Color: Red, orange, yellow, blue, pink, white, and purple

Bloom Period: Late spring, early summer.

Heat Zones: High desert, mountainous

Color photograph on page 223.

Light Requirements

Water

Beneficial Characteristics

Russell Lupines are among the most attractive plants in the garden. Their flower spikes are up to 2 feet high and stand above the height of the plant itself. They come in a variety of colors ranging from rich blues and purple to white, cream, and yellow, and also pink, red, and orange. It is the bicolor blooms of Russell Lupines that really make them stand out—imagine the standard (upper petal) in a bright yellow and the keel (lower petals) in blue; or how about red on the bottom and orange on top? There are as many combinations as there are colors. Each flower measures up to an inch across and they are packed tightly together up the stem, opening from the bottom to the top. The flowers resemble typical pea-family flowers that will open if you pinch the throat of the flower. (DP)

REGIONAL TIPS

This plant is limited to the high desert and mountainous regions, where early summers are cool. It is not adapted to the hot region.

WHEN, WHERE, AND HOW TO PLANT

The best time to plant Russell Lupines is in the spring, especially if you are planting from seed. Plant them in full sun or light shade; a good spot is where they will get only morning sun. Russell Lupines are usually transplanted into the garden from 1-gallon containers, but occasionally you might find them in 4-inch pots. You can start them from seed in the early spring. Because they are hard to germinate, scratch the seed coats and soak them in hot water for a few hours. (A legume aid that contains nitrogen-fixing bacteria also helps in germination.) Plant the seed according to the directions on the packet. Lupines are not too fussy about the soil, and they don't respond to nitrogen fertilizer, being a legume. If you have prepared the soil for other plants, it will be fine for the Russell Lupines. Space them about 15 inches apart and dig the holes as deep as the rootballs and a little wider; after planting, give the bed a good soaking.

CARE AND MAINTENANCE

Russell Lupines need the soil to be kept moist, particularly during the hottest part of the day, so water every other day with about 1/2 inch of water. They will also do better if a breeze can move around them, and you can extend the flowering period a little longer by mulching over the roots to keep them cooler. Check young plants for aphids. When the temperatures start to get hot, they will start to go dormant, and powdery mildew often attacks them. (The mildew will attack even sooner if they are water stressed.)

LANDSCAPE MERIT

Lupines are great as accents in the garden. Use them in flower beds to frame lower-growing plants, and as great border plants as well. One thing to take under consideration is that these plants don't flower all summer long, so when selecting a site, plan on something else to fill in for the rest of the summer and fall.

Did You Know?

Native Lupines can be found all over northern Nevada. You often find dwarf Lupines when you visit the desert in the spring. The Sierra Nevada Range is home to the Brewer Lupine, the Sierra Lupine, and the Gray's Lupine, at elevations ranging from 3,000 feet to over 10,000 feet. It is against the law to harvest seeds from any Federal lands. Just visit to look.

Sea Pink

Armeria maritima

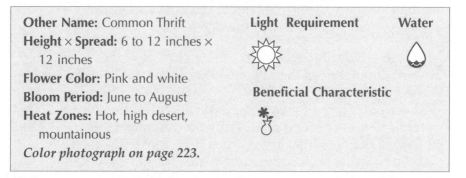

Other Name: Common Thrift
Height × Spread: 6 to 12 inches × 12 inches
Flower Color: Pink and white
Bloom Period: June to August
Heat Zones: Hot, high desert, mountainous
Color photograph on page 223.

Light Requirement

Water

Beneficial Characteristic

Sea Pink is a tidy-looking plant that forms a clump resembling grass that has been trimmed into a nice little mound. The flowers form very compact, round balls—about an inch in diameter—at the top of wirelike stalks that extend above the foliage. The most popular color is the deep rose, but they also come in white and pink. When the wind blows you get an interesting effect of all these little pink globes weaving back and forth. The flowers can be used as cut flowers and the foliage has a nice dark-green color that makes this plant attractive even when not in bloom. The leaves look like the blades of a fine-textured grass. (DP)

REGIONAL TIPS

It will remain green all year even in the high desert regions of the state. You might experience some winterkill in the mountainous regions of Nevada.

WHEN, WHERE, AND HOW TO PLANT

Container plants can be planted throughout the year, with the exception of the coldest parts of winter. The best time to plant is in the spring when you have the best selection of plants to choose from. Plant them in full sun if you want them to flower. They prefer a well-drained soil and do best in somewhat sandy soils; because our soils tend to be on the clayey side, add organic mulch to loosen the soil for better drainage. Till to a depth of 6 inches and till in about 3 inches of organic mulch at the same time. Sea Pink is usually planted from 1-gallon containers, but you can find them in 4-inch pots. Seed is available, but you need a spot indoors with lots of sunlight to get them going—plan on about seven weeks from the time you plant the seed to having a transplant ready for the garden. Space the plants about 6 to 8 inches apart, dig the holes as deep as the rootballs and a little wider, and place the plants in the holes and backfill with soil; then give them a good soaking.

CARE AND MAINTENANCE

Sea Pink doesn't require a lot of care and isn't bothered by insects or disease pests. In the mountainous regions of Nevada, you might want to trim off the dead tips of the leaves in the spring. Sea Pink has a medium-to-low water need, so twice-a-week waterings are all that is necessary (that amounts to about 1 to 2 inches of water per week). They are light feeders, so if you use a slow-release fertilizer once in the spring, that will take care of their needs for the whole season.

LANDSCAPE MERIT

Because of their growth habit, they have many uses in the garden. I have them in my rock garden because they produce the "Alpine garden" effect. Sea Pinks are also great for edging around flower beds. Place them on the edge of a planter if you want a cascading look; they could even be used as a ground cover.

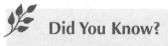

Did You Know?

One thing that is important: if you live in an area where rabbits, squirrels, and deer are a problem, this is a plant for you, because these critters won't bother it.

Sedum

Sedum hybrids

Other Name: Stonecrop **Height × Spread:** To 2 feet × 2 feet **Flower Color:** Pink **Bloom Period:** Late summer **Heat Zones:** Hot, high desert, mountainous *Color photograph on page 223.*	**Light Requirements** **Water** **Beneficial Characteristics**

The flowers of Sedum form flat, tight clusters that get to 6 inches in diameter and become more dramatic as the season progresses. The blooms of Sedum range from a deep pink to almost white. 'Autumn Joy', for example, has a light pink color in the summer and develops into shades of deep pink in the fall. This succulent adds a lot of interest to the garden, even when it isn't in bloom, with its large, thick leaves growing to 3 inches long (succulents are plants with thick, fleshy leaves that are full of moisture). The plants get up to 2 feet tall and wide, and in the late summer, flower buds form at the ends of the stems. Because of their height and their very showy flowers, Sedums become a focal point in the garden. (DP)

WHEN, WHERE, AND HOW TO PLANT

Plant Sedums anytime during the growing season, but the best selection is in the spring. They are vailable in 1-gallon containers and as small as 4-inch pots. Sedums prefer a sandy soil but don't appear to be fussy—they did very well in one of my demonstration gardens that had been compacted to road-grade specifications. As with any plant, if you are preparing the flower bed, add a layer of at least 3 inches of organic mulch to the soil along with the contents of a 1-pound coffee can filled with a complete fertilizer containing between 10 and 16 percent nitrogen; mix the fertilizer and the mulch into the soil to a depth of 6 inches. Space Sedums from 12 to 20 inches apart, at the same depth they were growing in the containers. After planting give them a thorough soaking.

CARE AND MAINTENANCE

Sedums have a low water requirement and will do best when they are given only 1 inch of water once a week in the high desert and mountainous regions of the state. In the hot regions of Nevada around Las Vegas, where temperatures exceed 100 degrees Fahrenheit, water three times a week. Sedums will do fine if fertilized every other year. They are not bothered by insects or diseases, which makes them very easy to care for. To maintain active, healthy plants, divide them every three years in the fall.

LANDSCAPE MERIT

They are a great addition to flower beds and border plantings, and are often planted in water conservation gardens. I have also seen them used in rock gardens and on slopes. Because of their height they make excellent accents in any garden.

ADDITIONAL SPECIES, CULTIVARS, OR VARIETIES

Sedum 'Autumn Joy' is the most popular and has pink flowers starting in July. *Sedum* 'Rosy Glow' grows to only 12 inches high with a spread of about the same, with pink flowers in August and September. *S. spectabile* grows to 18 inches high and as wide and also flowers in August and September. *Sedum album* has small, 1/4-inch-long tubular leaves and small white flowers, and only grows to 6 inches high; but each leaf will start a new plant, so watch out.

Did You Know?

The flowers of 'Autumn Joy' Sedum are particularly interesting as dried flowers in the garden throughout the winter; you can also use them in dried arrangements. I use them as miniature trees for my model railroad.

Snow-in-Summer

Cerastium tomentosum

Height × Spread: To 6 inches × 3 feet **Flower Color:** White **Bloom Period:** Summer **Heat Zones:** High desert, mountainous *Color photograph on page 223.*	**Light Requirements** ☀ ◐ **Beneficial Characteristic** 🐝	**Water** 💧

Snow-in-Summer is one of the most dependable ground covers we have in the high desert and mountainous regions of Nevada. It forms a mat so thick that grass will not grow through it. It grows only to 6 inches high but spreads to 3 feet. The flowers are about 1/2 to 1 inch in diameter and single, but when they are in bloom, you can't see the foliage for the flowers. The blooms are white and, as their name implies, they really do look like snow in the middle of summer. They start flowering in the late spring and continue through much of the summer; and even when they are not in bloom they are still interesting. The foliage is a gray-green with medium texture that adds a wonderful contrast with other plants in the garden. (DP)

REGIONAL TIPS

Snow-in-Summer does well in the high desert and mountainous regions, but give it part shade in the hot regions.

WHEN, WHERE, AND HOW TO PLANT

Plant Snow-in-Summer throughout the growing season if purchased as a container plant, with best selection of plants available in the spring. It can also be started from seed. If you want to start plants from seed, start them inside (it should take about six or seven weeks) and transplant out to the garden; but the best way is to purchase them as bedding or container plants. While Snow-in-Summer grows best in a soil with good drainage, it does very well in our clayey Nevada soils. Applying at least 3 inches of organic mulch to the surface of the soil and tilling it into a depth of 6 inches can increase the drainage and aeration. Because Snow-in-Summer forms a thick mat faster if it is not lacking in nutrients, it is beneficial to add a complete fertilizer that contains 10 to 16 percent nitrogen and work it in at the same time you till in the mulch. Use the amount you can put in a 1-pound coffee can, for 100 square feet of garden. Space plants about 10 inches apart for a more instant effect, even though they will spread to 3 feet. Dig the planting holes as deep as the rootballs and a little wider, and give them a good soaking after planting.

Care and Maintenance

Snow-in-Summer is very easy to maintain, is not bothered by any pests, and doesn't require much water. While it will do best on 1 inch of water twice a week, it is also tolerant of drought. After a few years it may start to fade out in the center of the plant; this can be avoided by mowing the plant lightly after it blooms.

Landscape Merit

Snow-in-Summer is an excellent plant for any area where you need good, solid coverage, and it does a good job of holding the soil on banks. It is used as a hanging-basket plant because of its trailing habit and makes a great edging plant as well (it does have to be in a sunny location). It works very well for filling in the narrow islands between walks and fences, or driveways that are usually planted with grass but which are hard to mow.

Soapwort

Saponaria ocymoides

Height × **Spread:** 6 inches × 18 inches **Flower Color:** Pink **Bloom Period:** Early summer **Heat Zones:** Hot, high desert, mountainous *Color photograph on page 223.*	**Light Requirement**	**Water**
	Beneficial Characteristics	

Soapwort is a great little plant that adds an amazing amount of color to the garden for its size—it grows to a height of only 6 inches and spreads out to 18 inches. The flowers are star-shaped and develop to 1/2 inch in diameter, with bright-pink blooms completely covering the plant when in bloom. The leaves are oval shaped and have a nice dark-green color. It is semievergreen during the winter in the northern part of Nevada and stays green at the warmer, lower elevations. The overall appearance of Soapwort is light and airy. (DP)

REGIONAL TIPS

As delicate as it looks, it thrives in the hottest spots in the garden. Soapwort is a very hardy plant for any region of the state.

WHEN, WHERE, AND HOW TO PLANT

Plant Soapwort in the spring. While it could be planted from containers anytime during the growing season, you get the best selection during the spring and early summer. If you purchase them in late May or June they will already be in bloom, adding instant color. Soapwort seed is hard to find, so planting from containers is the only way to go, from either 1-gallon cans or 4-inch pots. They will do best in a well-drained soil; when you are preparing the soil, add at least 3 inches of organic mulch and till it to a depth of 6 inches. Fill a 1-pound coffee can full of a complete fertilizer that contains between 10 and 16 percent nitrogen, and spread it over 100 square feet of garden. Space plants about 12 inches apart, digging the holes the depth of the rootballs and wide enough so they have a few inches of space around them. Cover the rootballs with soil and give them a good soaking after planting.

CARE AND MAINTENANCE

Soapwort is an easy plant maintain, disease- and insect-free for the most part. To keep the plant vigorous for many years, give it a light pruning after it flowers; this also keeps the plant from becoming leggy. While Soapwort generally needs a medium amount of water (about 2 inches per week), it can withstand some drying out between waterings. (By drying out, I mean the soil is dry to an inch deep.) Fertilize monthly using a water-soluble fertilizer mixed according to directions

LANDSCAPE MERIT

Soapwort is a good plant for flower borders or even as a mass in larger beds. Because of its trailing nature, it works very well for covering walls, and it looks good in rock gardens as it softens the hard angles of the rock. I've also seen it used along both dry and active streams. If you have a niche where nothing ever seems to grow because of the heat, Soapwort is the plant to try.

ADDITIONAL SPECIES, CULTIVARS, OR VARIETIES

A close relative of Soapwort is Bouncing Bet, *S. officianalis.* Bouncing Bet is a much taller plant, growing to a height of 2 feet, and 2 feet wide. It has light-green leaves and the flowers are pale pink, blooming from June to September. In my experience it can become a little weedy.

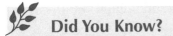 **Did You Know?**

Soapwort is an excellent plant for those areas that might be plagued by rabbits, squirrels, and deer—they won't eat it.

Speedwell

Veronica species

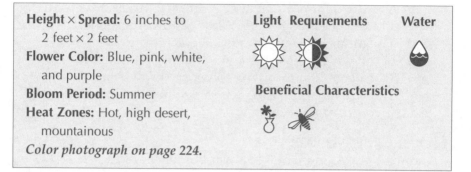

Height × Spread: 6 inches to
  2 feet × 2 feet
Flower Color: Blue, pink, white,
  and purple
Bloom Period: Summer
Heat Zones: Hot, high desert,
  mountainous
Color photograph on page 224.

Light Requirements

Water

Beneficial Characteristics

There are a number of Speedwells that perform very well in Nevada gardens. They flower on spikes that extend above the foliage, with flowers from 1/4 to 1/2 inch in diameter, and they bloom all summer long in shades of pink, white, rose, or a rich blue. Speedwell is one of those plants that looks attractive whether it is in bloom or not. It can also be enjoyed in floral arrangements indoors, making excellent cut flowers. Speedwells have various growth habits depending on the species or variety. All are very free-branching, forming bushy, dense plants. Some, like *Veronica grandis* 'Holophyla', grow to a height of 2 feet and have long spikes of rich-blue flowers. *Veronica prostrata* hugs the ground, with the flower spike rising above to a height of 6 inches. If you choose *Veronica* hybrids there is everything from upright types that grow to 18 inches tall to spreading types growing to only 10 inches. The hybrids offer the best color selection. (DP)

REGIONAL TIPS

Speedwells are very hardy and can be planted in even the coldest places in the state. In the high desert and mountainous regions, they winter better if they are mulched.

WHEN, WHERE, AND HOW TO PLANT

As with most perennials that are purchased in containers, they can be planted almost anytime, but the best selection is going to be in the spring. The easiest way to plant is to use bedding plants, which flower the first year. They can be planted from seed, but it might be the following year before they bloom. Speedwells bloom best in full sun but tolerate light shade; because they are perennial, plant them where they can grow undisturbed for a few years. They are not particular about the soil they grow in but they prefer well-drained soil. With our Nevada soils, we need to add organic matter to loosen the soil and also to improve the drainage. One way to do this is to apply a 3- to 4-inch layer of organic mulch to the soil and till to a depth of 6 inches. Speedwell benefits from the addition of a complete fertilizer containing between 10 to 16 percent nitrogen. Space the plants about 18 inches apart when transplanting them into the garden.

CARE AND MAINTENANCE

Speedwell is very easy to maintain, as it doesn't seem to have any problems specific to it. Because of our dry climate, Nevada gardeners don't experience things like bacterial leaf spots and other diseases that are often a problem in more humid areas of the country. Speedwells require a medium amount of water, so 1 inch of water about twice a week will supply their needs (mat-forming types appear to be more drought tolerant). Fertilize about every three weeks during the growing season using a water-soluble fertilizer according to directions.

LANDSCAPE MERIT

Speedwells are rather versatile plants in the garden because of the various growth habits. The taller ones are welcome additions to flower beds and border plantings; the lower-growing ones are perfect for rock gardens or as ground covers.

ADDITIONAL SPECIES, CULTIVARS, OR VARIETIES

V. austriaca 'Royal Blue' is a large plant that grows to 36 inches high and 24 inches wide, with sky-blue flowers; *V. spicata* 'Pink Goblin' is a very attractive plant that grows to 18 inches with dark-green leaves and 10-inch spikes of rosy-pink flowers.

Winter-Flowering Bergenia

Bergenia crassifolia

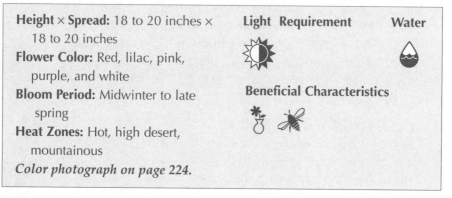

Height × Spread: 18 to 20 inches × 18 to 20 inches
Flower Color: Red, lilac, pink, purple, and white
Bloom Period: Midwinter to late spring
Heat Zones: Hot, high desert, mountainous
Color photograph on page 224.

Light Requirement

Water

Beneficial Characteristics

Winter-flowering Bergenia has hanging clusters of 1-inch flowers that can be red, lilac, pink, purple, and white. The flowers are bell-shaped and develop on long stems extending 10 inches above the foliage, flowering from January to February in the hot regions of Nevada and late spring to early summer in the rest of the state. While the flowers are bright and attractive, it's the foliage that is important— that's what's used in floral arrangements. The leaves are dark green and up to 8 inches long and almost as wide, finely toothed with wavy edges. This plant has the appearance of a low-growing mound and is evergreen in the hot regions, but it will look a little ragged during the coldest part of the winter in the other regions. (DP)

REGIONAL TIPS

Winter-flowering Bergenia needs part shade in the hot and high desert regions of the state. In the mountainous regions, where it is cool, plant it in full sun.

WHEN, WHERE, AND HOW TO PLANT

Plant it in the fall in the hot region and in the spring in the rest of Nevada. The plants need to be in a place where they will get part shade and be out of the wind. So if you have a shady garden like mine, the plants are a welcome addition. In the high desert and mountainous regions, they do great when planted with an eastern exposure. Because it is a perennial, plant it in a spot where you can leave it undisturbed for a few years. Winter-flowering Bergenia can be planted from seed, but it is easiesr to purchase bedding plants in 1-gallon containers. While these plants will grow in almost any soil, they will do much better in a good soil. Because our soils tend to be on the clayey side and don't drain well, it is always a good idea to incorporate about 3 inches of organic mulch into the soil prior to planting. I like to spread the contents of a 1-pound coffee can, filled to the brim with a complete fertilizer that contains between 10 and 16 percent nitrogen, over 100 square feet of garden and till it in with the mulch. When planting, dig the hole the same depth as the rootball and a little wider, cover the roots with soil, and give it a good soaking.

CARE AND MAINTENANCE

Winter-flowering Bergenias are generally pretty carefree. Once the plants are established, fertilize them about once a month using a water-soluble fertilizer, following the directions. Prune back annually, as they tend to become leggy if you don't, and divide the clumps when they become too crowded. Give Bergenias an inch of water twice a week. Those large leaves are an attraction to slugs and snails, so you need to put out bait as soon as you notice their presence. Both of these critters are active at night—look for trails of slime across the leaves—if they are feeding, you will see a series of holes stretch along the slimy path.

LANDSCAPE MERIT

Winter-flowering Bergenia is a landscape plant that is useful not only for its flowers but also as a contrast in texture, with its large leaves. Plant in flower borders or under trees. If you have an area where you might want an interesting ground cover, it will be ideal for that spot as well.

Roses

NO MATTER WHAT CENTURY OR CULTURE IT IS, people have always celebrated the rose. From ancient times until today, in poetry and song, during wars and festivities, people from all walks of life have honored this "Queen of Flowers." The United States Congress has selected the rose as this country's national flower.

According to paleontologists, the rose appeared on earth well before man and was distributed throughout the temperate regions of the northern hemisphere. At the time of the Egyptians and then the Greeks, the rose had been developed for medicinal properties, although modern research has not authenticated this use. We are aware that the ripe rose hip is a valuable source of Vitamin C. The Egyptians grew large numbers of roses in the Nile delta to use in religious ceremonies.

The Roman Empire provided a tremendous boost to the cultivation of the rose. A Roman banquet was not complete without decorations of rose blooms and rose petals. There is some evidence that the Egyptians created a very lucrative practice of exporting rose blooms to Rome. There are also references to roses in the works of various Roman authors who wrote on agriculture, especially in the writings of Pliny the Elder, who devoted much of the thirty-seven volumes of *Historia Naturalis* to roses.

The advance of Islam into western Europe helped to spread the rose along the caravan routes. There is no doubt that the distribution of the roses benefited greatly from this colonial expansion from the East. And with the decline of the Roman Empire, the expanding Christian church adopted the rose in many forms as a symbol in architecture, heraldry, and nationalism. Rose windows in ecclesiastical buildings were but one part of an expanding art form, and the establishment of rosarian collections became fashionable. The rose as a symbol and an art form received especially high recognition in the

Chapter Eight

courts of Versailles. Madame de Pompadour and her successor, Madame du Barry, were so enamored of the rose that it became a fetish. However, it was the wife of Napoleon, Empress Josephine, who some one hundred years later assembled an extraordinary collection of rose varieties at the palace of Malmaison. Pierre-Joseph Redonte was known as a painter of roses, with his works enjoying popularity at the end of the eighteenth century and the beginning of the nineteenth century. It is important to note that although historians are meticulous in charting the development of the rose in Europe and the Near East, it must not be forgotten that the rose was cultivated in China some 2,000 years before the Christian era.

The rose family is a vast collection of plants, many of which are common in gardens today. They include such diverse members as Blackberries, Quince, Pears, Plums, and herbaceous plants including Spirea, Potentilla, and Strawberry. Botanically, roses are described as *Dicotyledons* or a family of ninety genera including about 2,000 species of herbs, shrubs, and trees found in most parts of the world. Rose-petal wine is a favorite in old country recipe books and will make a dry or sweet wine according to taste.

The ancestors of all rose hybrids are the wild roses. Wild roses have developed their simple beauty and unpretentiousness freely in nature without human interference. This distinguishes the wild rose from the cultivated, hybridized rose. In the future, we will need to preserve the wild rose in order to perpetuate the hybrids we value so highly.

Climbing Rose

Rosa species and hybrids

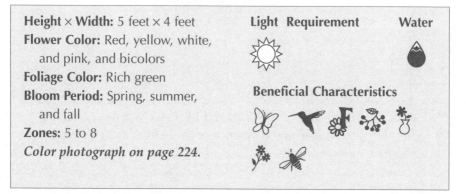

Height × Width: 5 feet × 4 feet
Flower Color: Red, yellow, white, and pink, and bicolors
Foliage Color: Rich green
Bloom Period: Spring, summer, and fall
Zones: 5 to 8
Color photograph on page 224.

Light Requirement

Water

Beneficial Characteristics

It seems we all have something to hide, and there isn't a better plant for the task than a climbing rose. My mother used climbing roses to hide an old, dilapidated garage, and the sight was awesome when the roses were in bloom. That is just what climbing roses are supposed to do—cover problems. And they don't take long to do their work, as most climbers are quick in covering an area. Decorate with a split-rail fence or other structures, and when the blooms come along they provide the icing on the cake. Many gardeners like a climbing rose growing at their entrances as an accent feature. And let us not forget the many limbs climbers have. From each limb comes a giant bouquet of roses. (LM)

REGIONAL TIPS

Rose care is about the same across the state. In the north, the vine will experience more winter injury and require more pruning after a severe winter. In the south, reduce but do not stop watering and fertilizing during winter.

WHEN, WHERE, AND HOW TO PLANT

Plant climbers before Valentine's Day in southern Nevada and before Mother's Day in northern Nevada. It's important to get climbers planted before heat sets in. Climbers like sunny locations; if you choose a shady environment, they need at least 6 hours of direct sunlight per day. Make sure the roots have room to expand. If roots struggle, so does the rest of the plant. Dig a hole three times wider than and as deep as the rootball. Improve the on-site soil with organic matter so roots can find the needed nutrients. To water climbers, build a basin around the plant base and thoroughly soak it twice weekly until established. Use mulch to cool the rooted area and to conserve water.

CARE AND MAINTENANCE

Climbers require a lot of water and excellent drainage or you can expect root rot, iron chlorosis, and dieback. Water deeply twice a week. As temperatures climb into the 90s, water three times a week. Each month through the season, add a rose fertilizer to the bushes. Cut the rates in half through the hottest part of the heat. You do not prune climbers like other roses. Let the plant go through its blooming cycle and then heavily prune. Allow the long canes to develop many laterals, as they bear the blooms. After two to three years of growth, thin out the weak shoots, and prune laterals back to the main stems, saving two to three buds. This encourages new shoots and more flowers from the older part of the plant. Because climbing roses don't twine or develop any tendrils or suction roots, provide a trellis for climbing and support. Use twist-ties or non-adhesive tape to tie vines to a trellis. As far as pests go, aphids feed on the leaves and buds, leaving a sticky substance called honeydew; thrips cause stained spots on the petals; mites make the lower foliage appear dry and dusty. Use the organic product Neem to control these pests.

LANDSCAPE MERIT

Climbing roses cover eyesores, bring "blah" walls to life, or delicately weave along a picket or rail fence.

ADDITIONAL SPECIES, CULTIVARS, OR VARIETIES

'Joseph's Coat' changes colors from the time the blooms open until they wither. 'Don Juan' has dark, velvet-red petals. 'Berries and Cream' has blooms of strawberry red and whipped-cream white.

🌿 Did You Know?

Wild rose hips contain twenty-four times more Vitamin C than orange juice.

Floribunda Rose

Rosa species and hybrids

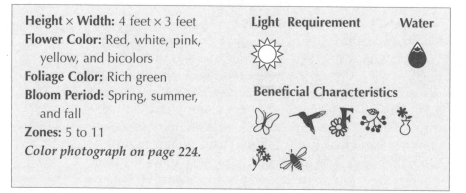

Height × Width: 4 feet × 3 feet
Flower Color: Red, white, pink,
  yellow, and bicolors
Foliage Color: Rich green
Bloom Period: Spring, summer,
  and fall
Zones: 5 to 11
Color photograph on page 224.

Light Requirement

Water

Beneficial Characteristics

As the name implies, floribundas produce an abundance of flowers in clusters in late spring and throughout the season. They have a wide array of colors, and now breeders have learned how to create striped blooms, so expect to see more of them. The fragrance of floribunda roses is usually light, but they make a wonderful addition to a bouquet of flowers. Use floribundas successfully in mass plantings or as a short hedge; I love them near the patio, along a walkway, or in containers for close viewing. (LM)

REGIONAL TIPS

Rose care is about the same across the state. In the north, roses experience more winter injury. Because of the warm temperatures in the south, you need to strip leaves off the bushes to force them into dormancy.

WHEN, WHERE, AND HOW TO PLANT

In the south, plant container-grown floribundas anytime and plant bare-root roses before Valentine's Day. In the colder regions, plant both kinds before Mother's Day. Dig a hole 2 feet by 2 feet by 2 feet, in a place where they will get 6 hours of sunlight to produce those beautiful blooms. Mix copious amounts of organic matter in the on-site soil along with a cup each of soil sulfur and bone meal—floribundas do best planted in a highly organic soil with good drainage. For bare-root planting, refill the hole, but build a pyramid of soil within the hole to peak at the soil surface. Clip off any damaged roots and place the plant on the soil pyramid, distributing the healthy roots over it. Finish refilling the hole, and firm the soil around the roots. For container plants, dig a hole three times wider than and as deep as the rootball. Build a water basin around the plant and water twice weekly until established. (Add mulch to cool the rooted area and to conserve water.) Wait until after the first flush of flowers to fertilize.

CARE AND MAINTENANCE

Water deeply twice a week. As temperatures climb into the 90s, water three times a week. Feed floribundas monthly with a balanced rose fertilizer. After each blooming cycle, remove spent blooms. From this will come your next cycle of blooms. Pruning can be intimidating. To take the fear out of it, get rid of the top third of the bush. Eliminate all crisscrossing canes, remove all but three to five new canes at the crown, and strip off all the remaining leaves. Make the final cut on the saved canes about 2 feet above the ground at an outside bud and seal the wounds to thwart rose cane borer. As for pests, you'll recognize aphids by the sticky honeydew they leave; thrips thrive in the bud and stain the petals as it unfolds; and mites suck the sap out the lower leaves, leaving them dry. You can use a strong jet of water to remove the aphids and mites, but it will require a systemic insecticide to get the thrips.

LANDSCAPE MERIT

Floribundas, because they produce many flowers, are an excellent choice for smaller landscapes. Plant them near your patio to enjoy their light fragrance in the evening.

ADDITIONAL SPECIES, CULTIVARS, OR VARIETIES

'Iceberg' is one of the best white roses; 'Scentimental' brings fragrance and vivid red-and-white striping together for a lasting memory; 'Fragrant Apricot' brings a strong musk scent and hybrid flower form to make an excellent Floribunda; 'Brass Band' got its name for the brassy color within the blooms—the coloration changes with time and weather conditions.

Grandiflora Rose

Rosa species and hybrids

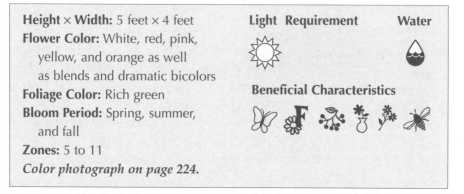

Height × Width: 5 feet × 4 feet
Flower Color: White, red, pink,
yellow, and orange as well
as blends and dramatic bicolors
Foliage Color: Rich green
Bloom Period: Spring, summer,
and fall
Zones: 5 to 11
Color photograph on page 224.

Light Requirement

Water

Beneficial Characteristics

It's amazing what hybridizers do once they are turned loose with a
pool of rose genes. Gardeners wanted roses taller than hybrid teas,
but they liked the clusters of floribundas. Walter Lammerts did just
that, crossing his hybrid tea 'Charlotte Armstrong' with his floribunda
'Floradora' to create the first grandiflora. He named it 'Queen Elizabeth'
in honor of Elizabeth, soon to be crowned Queen of England at the
time. Grandifloras are similar to hybrid teas, with two major exceptions: they are bushier and taller and produce blooms in clusters. The
blooms are similar to the hybrid teas in shades of white, red, pink,
yellow, and orange as well as blends and dramatic bicolors. Because
of their size, grandifloras need sufficient space, so locate them behind
other lower-growing varieties. (LM)

REGIONAL TIPS
In southern Nevada, plant bare-root grandifloras before Valentine's
Day or anytime from containers. In the north, plant after the last
frost, which is May 22.

WHEN, WHERE, AND HOW TO PLANT
Plant so they receive 6 hours of sunlight in a highly organic soil
with ideal drainage. Dig a hole two cubic feet. Mix copious amounts
of organic matter in with the on-site soil along with a cup each of
soil sulfur and bone meal, and refill the hole. For bare-root planting,
build a soil pyramid, or inverted cone, within the hole so that it
peaks at the soil surface. Clip off any damaged roots and distribute
the healthy ones evenly over the pyramid. In the north, place the
bud union (or crown) an inch below the soil surface. In the south,

leave it above the soil level. Refill the hole, firming the soil around the roots. Build a water basin around the plant and water three times a week until established. (Add mulch to cool the rooted area and to conserve water.) Wait until after the first flush of flowers to fertilize.

CARE AND MAINTENANCE

Grandifloras demand a lot of water, especially when blooming. Water them deeply twice weekly, but as temperatures climb into the 90s, water three times a week. During the growing season, feed them monthly with a balanced rose fertilizer. After blooming, remove spent blooms, making the cut down where the cane is thicker than a pencil, at a 45-degree angle. From this will come more blooms. Pruning roses can be complicated; here's a simpler way. Walk up to the bush and indiscriminately remove the top third. Next, remove all crisscrossing canes to open up the bush. Select three to five of the strongest canes and remove all others at the crown. Make the final cut on your selected canes about 2 feet above the ground at an outside bud. Seal the wounds with pruning paint to prevent rose cane borer. Honeydew on the leaves tells you aphids are present and dusty, dry leaves signal mites. Wash both off with a strong blast of water or use Neem. Since thrips work inside the rosebud, use a systemic insecticide.

LANDSCAPE MERIT

Grandifloras fit in anywhere in the landscape, especially if you want to liven up a spot or distract visitors' attention from an ugly site.

ADDITIONAL SPECIES, CULTIVARS, OR VARIETIES

There are scores of grandifloras from which to choose. Get to the nursery early to make the best choices. Here are a few of my favorites: 'Tournament of Roses', 'Arizona', 'Love', 'Sundowner', 'Cherry Vanilla', and 'Gold Medal'.

Did You Know?

Over twenty million mothers receive roses on Mother's Day.

Hybrid Tea Rose

Rosa species and hybrids

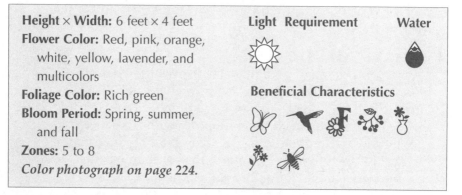

Height × Width: 6 feet × 4 feet

Flower Color: Red, pink, orange, white, yellow, lavender, and multicolors

Foliage Color: Rich green

Bloom Period: Spring, summer, and fall

Zones: 5 to 8

Color photograph on page 224.

Light Requirement

Water

Beneficial Characteristics

Say the word "rose" and images of long-stemmed hybrid tea roses flood my mind. One bloom per stem makes hybrid teas the choice for viewing, cutting, and arranging. The initial bloom is referred to as the "Queen" or "King" bloom. To encourage maximum size, you must remove (disbud) the smaller roses that form at the base of the larger bloom. Hybrid teas are upright growers to 6 feet, making them well suited for planting anywhere in the garden, and they come in a brilliant variety of colors. Hybrid tea roses were first bred in 1867, and we now have thousands to choose from. There isn't a plant that requires more time, fertilizer, or pruning, but when blooms come, it's like living in the Garden of Eden. When asked for my favorite rose, I quickly state that every one has grown a place in my heart. (LM)

REGIONAL TIPS

Plant bare-root roses before Valentine's Day in southern Nevada and before May Day in the colder regions. The earlier you get them in, the better chance they will have of coping with the summer heat.

WHEN, WHERE AND HOW TO PLANT

In southern Nevada, plant bare-root roses before Valentine's Day, or plant container roses anytime. In northern Nevada, plant them around Mother's Day. Give them 6 or more hours of sunlight in a highly organic soil with ideal drainage. Dig a hole at least two cubic feet and check drainage. Mix copious amounts of organic matter, and a cup each of soil sulfur and bone meal, in with the on-site soil. When planting bare rootstock, build a soil pyramid within the hole so it peaks at the soil surface. Clip off any damaged roots and evenly distribute healthy ones over the pyramid. Finish refilling the hole and use water to settle soil around roots. Build a water basin and irrigate three times a week until established—adding mulch is a wise way to conserve water. Do not add any more fertilizer until after the first blooms.

CARE AND MAINTENANCE

Hybrid tea roses demand a lot of water, especially when blooming. Water deeply twice a week. As temperatures climb into the 90s, water three times a week. Each month throughout the season, add a rose fertilizer to the bushes. Remove spent blooms to stimulate repeat blooming. In the spring, chop off the top third of the bush to evaluate what to remove; next, remove all crisscrossing canes; then, select three to five strong new canes and remove all others at the crown. Make the final cut on a selected cane above an outside-facing bud and seal the wound to guard against rose cane borer. As for pests, a sticky substance (honeydew) on leaves indicates an aphid infestation; wash them off or use insecticidal soap. Thrips work within the bud, causing stains on the petals. Be proactive and use a systemic insecticide for protection.

LANDSCAPE MERIT

Hybrid tea roses fit in with other plants, along borders, in masses, and in containers and hanging baskets, cascading over the sides.

ADDITIONAL SPECIES, CULTIVARS, OR VARIETIES

People can't look at the 'Peace' rose and not have peace in their hearts; the fragrance and dark red color of 'Mister Lincoln' has become an enduring favorite; and the blooms of 'Double Delight' are a delight for their double color and double fragrance.

Miniature Rose

Rosa species and hybrids

Height × Width: 12 inches ×
12 inches

Flower Color: Red, pink, yellow,
white, and bicolors

Foliage Color: Rich green

Bloom Period: Spring, summer,
and fall

Zones: 5 to 11

Color photograph on page 224.

Light Requirement

Water

Beneficial Characteristics

Everyone loves miniature roses. They are the cutest flowers on the planet! That might be going a little too far, but when I see a bed of them, I find each one is cuter than the next. They are so dainty, almost to the point that I'm afraid to touch them. Miniature roses range in size from those the size of the head of a hatpin to the newest class of minis, the larger mini-flora. Their color range is wide, from the purest white to almost black-red, with many blends and striped patterns mixed in. Flower forms run the gamut from single (five-petaled) blooms to high-centered beauties that look like tiny hybrid teas. There are minis that grow upright, minis with pliable canes to bring a hanging basket alive, and even climbing minis to train on a trellis or fence. The plants of some miniatures are very short and compact, while others get quite tall—emphasizing that the term "Miniature" refers to bloom size. The bush-size miniatures make ideal container plants, and many are surprisingly hardy. These little beauties never get much above a foot high. It's hard to imagine, but you don't treat these delicacies any different from the way you treat normal roses. (LM)

REGIONAL TIPS

Because of the warm winters, continue to water miniature roses through the winter in the south. They may require more pruning after a severe winter in the north.

WHEN, WHERE AND HOW TO PLANT

Plant container roses anytime during the growing season in the state. You'll find them in the spring after the big roses are in the nurseries. If you plant bare-root roses, plant them by Valentine's Day in the south, and by Mother's Day in the north. Give them 6 hours of sunlight per day and a highly organic soil with good drainage for best growth. If you choose to plant these toughies in the ground, dig a hole as deep and twice as wide as the root clump. Loosen any roots wrapped around the clump. Backfill the amended soil around the rootball, build a water basin, and thoroughly soak the ball and surrounding soil with twice-weekly waterings. Because water is such a precious commodity, mulch around the base of the plant—it not only conserves water but also suppresses weeds.

CARE AND MAINTENANCE

Miniature roses are like big roses: They still need water on a twice-weekly schedule and a balanced rose fertilizer monthly, but only one-fourth the amount recommended for big roses. Pruning miniatures does become tedious. You can shear them, but it's best to thin out twiggy growth and remove older canes as they become unproductive. Mites, thrips, and aphids seem to be the worst pests. Go after them with a strong jet of water or Neem, an organic pest control.

LANDSCAPE MERIT

You have winners when using miniature roses in containers. They fit in any windowsill, hanging basket, or out in the garden; or use them in front of larger plants to show off the miniature blooms.

ADDITIONAL SPECIES, CULTIVARS, OR VARIETIES

Note their names and you'll know what they're like: 'Dazzler' blooms have red edges on yellow petals; 'Little Jackie' has touches of cream in the throat, turning to bright red blooms; 'Lipstick 'N Lace' has creamy-white petals with red lipstick dressing the edges; 'Minnie Pearl' blooms open the show in delicate, soft-pink petals; 'Roller Coaster' has splashes of red on some white petals and red-white rolling onto other red petals.

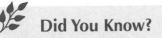 **Did You Know?**

The rose is the world's number one flower.

ROSES

The gardener who
plans reaps the greatest
reward . . .

Ageratum
Ageratum houstonianum

Calendula
Calendula officinalis

Flowering Kale and Cabbage
Brassica oleracea acephala

Gazania
Gazania species

Geranium
Pelargonium hortorum

Lobelia
Lobelia erinus

Marigold
Tagetes erecta

Moss Rose
Portulaca grandiflora

Pansy
Viola × wittrockiana

Petunia
Petunia × hybrida

Phlox
Phlox drummondii

Scarlet Sage
Salvia splendens

Snapdragon
Antirrhinum majus

Stock
Matthiola incana

Sunflower
Helianthus annuus

Sweet Alyssum
Lobularia maritima

Sweet Pea
Lathyrus odoratus

Verbena
Verbena × hybrida

Zinnia
Zinnia elegans

Crocus
Crocus species

Daffodil
Narcissus × hybrids

Gladiolus
Gladiolus hybridus

Grape Hyacinth
Muscari species

Tulip
Tulipa species

Beavertail Cactus
Opuntia basilaris

Century Plant
Agave species

Desert Spoon
Dasylirion wheeleri

Fishhook Barrel Cactus
Ferocactus wislizenii

Golden Barrel Cactus
Echinocactus grusonii

Joshua Tree
Yucca species

Carpet Bugle Ajuga
Ajuga reptans

Centennial Broom
Baccharis × 'Centennial'

Creeping Dalea
Dalea greggii

Germander
Teucrium chamaedrys 'Prostratum'

Japanese Spurge
Pachysandra terminalis

Kinnikinnick
Arctostaphylos uva-ursi

Lamb's Ear
Stachys byzantina

Lily Turf
Liriope muscari

Mother-of-Thyme
Thymus serpyllum

Periwinkle
Vinca species

Prostrate Myoporum
Myoporum parvifolium

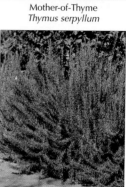

Prostrate Rosemary
Rosmarinus officinalis 'Prostratus'

Trailing Lantana
Lantana montevidensis

Bigelow's Bear Grass
Nolina bigelovii

Deer Grass
Muhlenbergia rigens

Fountain Grass
Pennisetum setaceum

Leather Leaf Sedge
Carex buchananii

Maiden Grass
Miscanthus sinensis

Mexican Feather Grass
Nassella tenuissima

Regal Mist
Muhlenbergia capillaris 'Regal Mist'

Ribbon Grass
Phalaris arundinacea 'Picta'

Weeping Love Grass
Eragrostis curvula

Canary Island Palm
Phoenix canariensis

Guadalupe Fan Palm
Brahea edulis

Mediterranean Fan Palm
Chamaerops humilis

Mexican Blue Palm
Brahea armata

Mexican Fan Palm
Washingtonia robusta

Pindo Palm
Butia capitata

Sago Palm
Cycas revoluta

Windmill Palm
Trachycarpus fortunei

Asparagus Fern
Asparagus densiflorus 'Sprengeri'

Basket-of-Gold
Aurinia saxatilis

Beach Wormwood
Artemisia stellerana

Bearded Iris
Iris germanica

Black-Eyed Susan
Rudbeckia hirta

Blanket Flower
Gaillardia × grandiflora

Bush Morning Glory
Convolvulus cneorm

Candytuft
Iberis sempervirens

Canna Lily
Canna × generalis

Coral Bells
Heuchera sanguinea

Coreopsis
Coreopsis verticillata

Daylily
Hemerocallis × hybrids

Dianthus
Dianthus species

Dusty Miller
Centaurea cineraria

Hardy Chrysanthemum
Chrysanthemum hybrids

Lily-of-the-Valley
Convallaria majalis

Moss Pink
Phlox subulata

Penstemon
Penstemon species

Peony
Paeonia hybrids

Russell Lupines
Lupinus 'Russell' hybrids

Sea Pink
Armeria maritima

Sedum
Sedum hybrids

Snow-in-Summer
Cerastium tomentosum

Soapwort
Saponaria ocymoides

Speedwell
Veronica species

Winter-Flowering Bergenia
Bergenia crassifolia

Climbing Rose
Rosa species and hybrids

Floribunda Rose
Rosa species and hybrids

Grandiflora Rose
Rosa species and hybrids

Hybrid Tea Rose
Rosa species and hybrids

Miniature Rose
Rosa species and hybrids

Alpine Currant
Ribes alpinum

Arizona Rosewood
Vauquelinia californica

Autumn Sage
Salvia greggii

Baja Red Fairy Duster
Calliandra californica

Barberry
Berberis species

Butterfly Bush
Buddleia davidii

Creosote Bush
Larrea tridentata

Dwarf Myrtle
Myrtus communis 'Compacta'

Ebbing's Silverberry
Elaeagnus × ebbingei

Euonymus
Euonymus species

Feathery Cassia
Cassia artemisioides

Flowering Quince
Chaenomeles speciosa

Forsythia
Forsythia × intermedia

Glossy Abelia
Abelia × grandiflora

Heavenly Bamboo
Nandina domestica

Indian Hawthorn
Rhaphiolepis indica

Japanese Yew
Taxus cuspidata

Junipers
Juniperus species

Lilac
Syringa vulgaris

Mock Orange
Pittosporum tobira

'New Gold' Lantana
Lantana × 'New Gold'

Oleander
Nerium oleander

Oregon Grape
Mahonia aquifolium

Pomegranate
Punica granatum

Primrose Jasmine
Jasminum mesnyi

Pyracantha
Pyracantha coccinea

Red Clusterberry Cotoneaster
Cotoneaster lacteus

Red-Osier Dogwood
Cornus sericea

Red Yucca
Hesperaloe parviflora

St. Johnswort
Hypericum calycinum

Scotch Broom
Cytisus scoparius

Shiny Xylosma
Xylosma congestum

Snowberry
Symphoricarpos albus

Spirea
Spiraea species

Strawberry Bush
Arbutus unedo 'Compacta'

Sugar Bush
Rhus ovata

Texas Sage
Leucophyllum frutescens

Viburnum
Viburnum tinus

Waxleaf Privet
Ligustrum japonicum 'Texanum'

Weigela
Weigela florida

Ash
Fraxinus species

Birch
Betula species

Blue Atlas Cedar
Cedrus atlantica 'Glauca'

Blue Palo Verde
Cercidium floridum

Chaste Tree
Vitex agnus-castus

Chinese Elm
Ulmus parvifolia

Common Hackberry
Celtis occidentalis

Crabapple
Malus species

Desert Willow
Chilopsis linearis

False Cypress
Chamaecyparis species

Flowering Plum
Prunus cerasifera 'Atropurpurea'

Goldenrain Tree
Koelreuteria paniculata

Holly Oak
Quercus ilex

Horse Chestnut
Aesculus hippocastanum

Incense Cedar
Calocedrus decurrens

Maples
Acer species

Mexican Palo Verde
Parkinsonia aculeata

Mountain Ash
Sorbus scopulina

Northern Catalpa
Catalpa speciosa

Pine
Pinus species

Spruce
Picea species

'Swan Hill' Olive
Olea europaea 'Swan Hill'

Sweet Acacia
Acacia smallii

Texas Honey Mesquite
Prosopis glandulosa

Thornless Honey Locust
Gleditsia triacanthos 'Inermis'

Washington Hawthorn
Crataegus phaenopyrum

White Fir
Abies concolor

Boston Ivy
Parthenocissus tricuspidata

Cat's Claw Vine
Macfadyena unguis-cati

Chinese Wisteria
Wisteria sinensis

Coral Vine
Antigonon leptopus

Creeping Fig
Ficus pumila

Grape
Vitis vinifera

Hall's Honeysuckle
Lonicera japonica 'Halliana'

Lady Bank's Rose
Rosa banksiae

Lilac Vine
Hardenbergia violacea

Silver Lace Vine
Fallopia baldschuanica

Trumpet Vine
Campsis radicans

HEAT ZONE MAP

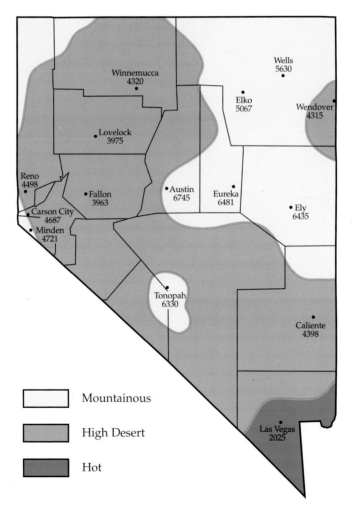

Wells
5630

Winnemucca
4320

Elko
5067

Wendover
4315

Lovelock
3975

Reno
4498

Austin
6745

Eureka
6481

Fallon
3963

Ely
6435

Carson City
4687

Minden
4721

Tonopah
6330

Caliente
4398

Mountainous

High Desert

Hot

Las Vegas
2025

231

USDA HARDINESS ZONE MAP

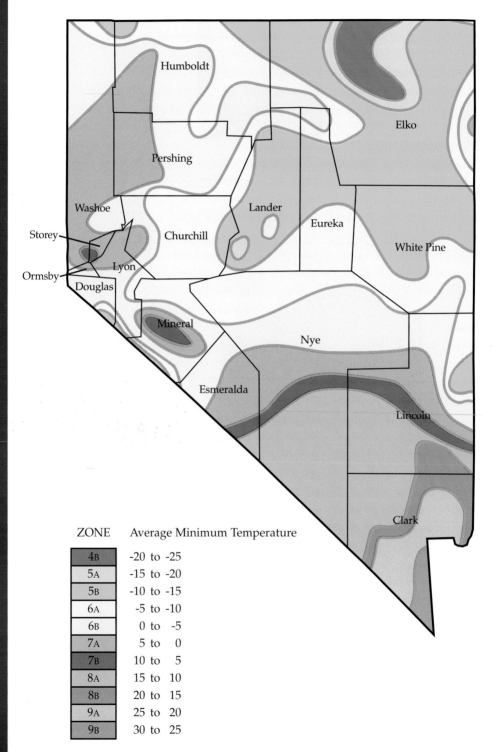

ZONE	Average Minimum Temperature
4B	-20 to -25
5A	-15 to -20
5B	-10 to -15
6A	-5 to -10
6B	0 to -5
7A	5 to 0
7B	10 to 5
8A	15 to 10
8B	20 to 15
9A	25 to 20
9B	30 to 25

Gardening

is a journey, not a

destination . . .

CHAPTER NINE

Shrubs

A SHRUB IS OFTEN A MULTITRUNKED WOODY PLANT placed in a landscape among trees, flowers, and lawns. But this keystone of a landscape design can also be grouped in borders and hedges, interplanted in flower beds, highlighted as specimens, and clustered in foundation plantings. In a desert environment, it is important not to commingle drought-tolerant shrubs with those that require substantial water for ultimate plant health. It's also important not to mix shade-lovers with those that seek the sun. But the right shrubs in the right places can create a primary focus or a secondary focus for a garden or landscape design. Regardless of how they are used, shrubs are an important aspect of any landscape.

Shrubs can bring varied leaf shapes, textures, sizes, and colors to provide contrasts in gardens and landscaping. Shrub colors can cover the spectrum from gold to blue-gray to all shades of green as well as red, burgundy, and variegated splashes or stripes. In winter, many deciduous shrubs have colorful bark patterns to compensate for their leafless state.

Every gardener—whether starting from scratch on newly cleared ground, revamping an existing garden, or just incorporating a new specimen or two—eventually faces the question of design. Shrubs, because of their relatively large sizes and permanence in the landscape, dictate an especially careful design. Perennials and annuals can be moved with relative ease, but an ill-placed shrub on its way to maturity is a great deal harder to move and to ignore. The best way to approach this design factor and to avoid mistakes is first to put a plan on paper.

A shrub design can be arranged by flowering seasons to include all four seasons of the year. The design can make use of these plants beneath trees, as a shrub border, as a mixed border with other plants,

Chapter Nine

as a hedge, or as ground cover. Use shrubs as specimens in lawns and planted in pots.

Shrubs can also be used for a transition zone between trees and lawn or grassland. Many benefit from the shelter of trees and tolerate partial shade. If trees have been cut or trimmed and have bare trunks without side branches, use shrubs to soften the unnatural edges of the trees.

Some shrubs also make effective visual screens. If there is an electrical or mechanical box in a front yard, plant a shrub to screen it off. In this type of situation, avoid a deciduous shrub because it's important to maintain the "screening" effect all year long.

Shrubs may also be used as living fences or hedges. The branches and foliage will screen views, and will tactfully reinforce boundaries with neighbors. It is a great misconception to assume that a hedge has to be formal and neatly clipped with plants in a rigid row, needing shearings often in order to maintain their shape. Practical and beautiful solutions can be found in this chapter to demonstrate creative and unexpected uses of shrubs. An informal, unshaped hedge of shrubs planted in a single or staggered double row may feel more natural, and will definitely be easier to maintain.

Alpine Currant

Ribes alpinum

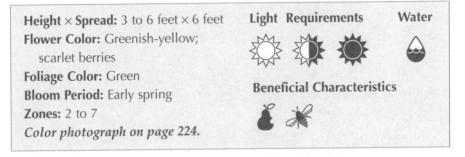

Height × Spread: 3 to 6 feet × 6 feet	**Light Requirements**	**Water**
Flower Color: Greenish-yellow; scarlet berries		
Foliage Color: Green		
Bloom Period: Early spring	**Beneficial Characteristics**	
Zones: 2 to 7		
Color photograph on page 224.		

The Alpine Currant is a great shrub for much of northern Nevada because of its hardiness. It will grow almost anywhere, and it is a good plant for shade gardens. This is a "dioecious" plant, which means plants are either male or female. The flowers are not very showy but the fruit on the female plant turns scarlet and is good to eat. The leaves are of three to five lobes, hairy on top, and the plant develops a nice, rounded, bushy shape. The Alpine Currant is one of the first shrubs to leaf out in the spring, which is a welcome sight after a winter of dull brown. It can be sheared and makes a great formal hedge plant. (DP)

Regional Tips

Its exceptional hardiness is important in areas like Austin and Eureka where it can freeze anytime during the summer.

When, Where, and How to Plant

Plant Alpine Currant as a bare-root plant in the early spring; containerized plants can be planted any time of the year as long as the ground isn't frozen. It grows very well in full sun, but it is particularly good for planting in more mature gardens because it grows just as well in shady areas. The Alpine Currant is tolerant of any soil and is not adversely affected by slightly alkaline soils. Because much of the soil in the high desert environment of Nevada is poorly drained, the ideal method of planting is to dig the hole about three to four times the diameter of the rootball but no deeper than the rootball's depth. Don't amend the backfill soil—that could slow down drainage and result in a planting hole that won't drain at all, and the roots could become waterlogged and die. After planting, give it a good soaking.

CARE AND MAINTENANCE

Alpine Currants don't require any special care. Because of their bushy, dense habit, they can be pruned to encourage new growth. They can be pruned anytime. I don't like to shear these plants unless they are to be used as a formal hedge. (When I look around some neighborhoods I see everything sheared to the same shape, resulting in a boring landscape filled with green bowling balls rather than an expanse of interesting colors, shapes, and textures.) Water twice a week, applying 1 inch of water at each application. In areas where the humidity is high, this plant can be plagued with leaf spots and a variety of insects. In our dry climate, leaf diseases are not a problem, and insects don't appear to be a problem either.

LANDSCAPE MERIT

It can be used as a border planting or for the mass effect. It also works very well as a low hedge and makes a good contrast in color and texture when planted with other shrubs.

ADDITIONAL SPECIES, CULTIVARS, OR VARIETIES

The Golden Currant, *A. aureum*, is a good choice. It grows to 6 feet tall and up to 8 feet wide, with yellow flowers of a spicy fragrance.

Arizona Rosewood

Vauquelinia californica

Height × Spread: 15 feet × 10 feet
Flower Color: White
Foliage Color: Dark green
Bloom Period: Spring and early
  summer
Zones: 8 to 10
Color photograph on page 224.

Light Requirements

Water

Beneficial Characteristics

Arizona Rosewood is a vigorous, dense, upright, evergreen shrub that is fast becoming an excellent alternative to the Oleander in landscape designs; it also doubles as a small tree. Arizona Rosewood gets its common name from the heartwood of its branches, ranging from red to shades of brown. It has lance-shaped and leathery dark-green leaves about 3 inches long and 1/2 inch wide—from a distance the untrained eye may even mistake it for an Oleander. In the fall and winter the leaves become a bronzy color, and it bears clusters of tiny snow-white flowers resembling flat-topped cauliflower heads that decorate the plant from late spring to early summer. Woody seed capsules remain attached throughout winter and the reddish bark, if exposed, adds to the winter drama in the landscape. From these upright branches come numerous erect, twisting branches that eventually reach 15 or more feet tall and 10 feet wide. It looks gawky in the nursery but fills out into a globe-shaped shrub when established. Arizona Rosewood loves our heat and is a plant that will surely work its way into the lazy man's heart, being tolerant of adverse conditions, intense sun, poor soil, hot winds, and cold. (LM)

REGIONAL TIPS

This plant originates from the lower deserts of the Southwest, making it an ideal addition to the plant palette of southern Nevada landscapes. It is not hardy enough for the harsh winters of northern Nevada.

WHEN, WHERE, AND HOW TO PLANT

Plant this durable shrub all year from containers, but for best results, plant it in the fall. It grows well in either partial or full sun but does not establish easily, so open the soil with the addition of organic matter to start it off right. Make the hole three to five times as wide and as deep as the rootball. Also make sure the soil has good drainage: that is, you can fill the hole with water and it drains away within 8 hours. After planting, build a water basin around the plant and soak the rootball.

CARE AND MAINTENANCE

You can stress this plant for water but it does best watered weekly throughout the summer. Its appetite for fertilizer is small, but working a cup of ammonium sulfate under each bush in the early spring and fall will enhance the luster. To develop dense growth, prune only to control size, and to keep it more appealing, remove some of the inner, older canes to stimulate new growth from within. If you want it to be a tree, remove the lower branches and it will eventually grow up to 20 feet high. If you find dry, dusty-looking leaves, you have the telling signs of spider mites; if you find sticky honeydew on the leaves, you have aphids. A jet of water will send them hiking, or use Neem oil or insecticidal soap.

LANDSCAPE MERIT

Use it as a tall informal hedge to serves as an effective privacy screen or noise barrier. Use it as a perimeter plant, hedge, large accent shrub, or in many applications, in place of Oleanders. Its advantages over Oleander include slower growth, ease of maintenance, limited leaf and flower litter, and plant parts that aren't toxic to people or pets.

ADDITIONAL SPECIES, CULTIVARS, OR VARIETIES

V. corymbosa angustifolia is another desirable Rosewood similar to *V. californica* except it has very narrow, serrated leaves, which give the foliage an unusual threadlike effect. It hails from West Texas and northern Mexico and it's typically sold as *V. corymbosa.*

Autumn Sage

Salvia greggii

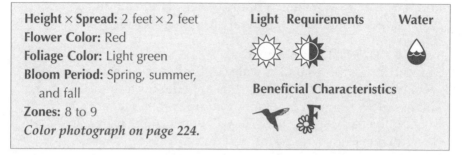

Height × Spread: 2 feet × 2 feet	Light Requirements	Water
Flower Color: Red		
Foliage Color: Light green		
Bloom Period: Spring, summer, and fall	**Beneficial Characteristics**	
Zones: 8 to 9		
Color photograph on page 224.		

For a splash of color just about all year, turn to Autumn Sage. Why, oh why, do we give a plant a name like Autumn Sage when it produces flowers most of the year? My first acquaintance with it was seeing it blooming into the fall. The flowery show is profuse during the spring and tapers off through the season. Flowers are in loose clusters on a short spike, tubular, rosy red, and 1 inch long, with the lower flowers bigger and showier than the upper ones. Autumn Sage is a very dependable flower producer and the plant itself is a small, tough, durable evergreen shrub with many upright stems covered with medium-green leaves that have a minty fragrance when brushed. (LM)

REGIONAL TIPS

Autumn Sage will not survive the harsh winters in the north as a perennial, but you can grow it as an annual shrub there. In the south it becomes a wonderful bush, especially if you want color through the winter.

WHEN, WHERE, AND HOW TO PLANT

Plant this durable bloomer any time in the south and in spring in the north. To get the most out of the blooms, plant in full sun, but it will do fine in filtered to partial shade. Drainage is a key issue, and an improved soil is necessary to get even more out of this workhorse. Since Nevada soils are so hard and deficient in humus, prepare to plant by opening a hole at least three times as wide and as deep as the rootball. Work some organic matter into the backfill soil, and then plant, firming the soil around the ball. Be careful not to plant Autumn Sage too deep or root rot will set in and kill the plant. Build a water basin to contain the water to thoroughly irrigate the entire rootball. Soak the plant three times weekly until established; and to cool the soil and stretch out our most precious natural resource, add a layer of mulch.

CARE AND MAINTENANCE
Autumn Sage performs best with twice-a-week irrigations. If you have drip emitters, let them run for 2 hours each time. I have noticed that when the blooms slow down, it is a signal to water more. Plan on monthly supplemental applications of a cup of ammonium sulfate throughout the summer to encourage more flowering. Shear Autumn Sage after the blooming season to maintain form and keep it compact. It doesn't require much care, but when it begins to look rangy, I cut it back to the ground and it bounces back with more blooms. It doesn't have any pest problems.

LANDSCAPE MERIT
Autumn Sage is useful as a foundation plant or foreground plant and is one of the very best for low water–demand landscapes. It looks fine as an individual specimen, in groups, or as a clipped hedge.

ADDITIONAL SPECIES, CULTIVARS, OR VARIETIES
Here some other good selections: pure-white 'Alba'; hot-pink 'Big Pink', with showier flowers; 'Desert Blaze', with brilliant true-red flowers; and deep-red 'Furman's Red', with shades of orange.

Did You Know?
Salvia is in the same family as Coleus, Ajuga, and Mint. There are over 750 species ranging from annuals to shrubs.

Baja Red Fairy Duster

Calliandra californica

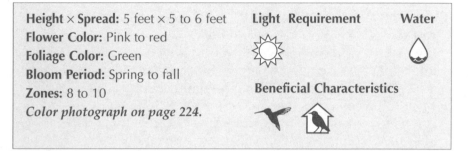

Height × Spread: 5 feet × 5 to 6 feet
Flower Color: Pink to red
Foliage Color: Green
Bloom Period: Spring to fall
Zones: 8 to 10
Color photograph on page 224.

Light Requirement

Water

Beneficial Characteristics

The Baja Red Fairy Duster "has this town a-whirl." Doesn't the name "Fairy Duster" conjure up the thought of fairies dusting your garden each day? It is a small, airy shrub with slender branches and lacy green foliage covered by bright-red fairy duster flowers. It is striking at close range, but the real treat is peering through the blossoms into the evening sunset; that's when I stutter for words to describe their glow. The blooms continue, but not with as much gusto as the season progresses. A severe frost can cause you to lose this shrub—a friend plants hers in pots on her patio and pulls them against the house for the winter. The botanical name *Calliandra* refers to the beautiful stamens that make up the flowers. Use this shrub to lure in wildlife and provide food for hummingbirds. It is also well suited to traditional gardens, where its nearly evergreen foliage and delicate blossoms provide added interest. It is my kind of plant, requiring very little care. (LM)

REGIONAL TIPS

Baja Red Fairy Duster is a great shrub, but only for southern parts of the state. It will not live through the harsh northern Nevada winters. Creosote Bush and Ocotillo are fast becoming indicators of where this plant will thrive.

WHEN, WHERE, AND HOW TO PLANT

Plant this beauty in the spring as a container plant to allow ample root growth before the return of cold weather. It thrives on a well-drained sandy to gravelly soil, under full sun. Loosen the soil so that new roots will have an easy time breaking ground. Dig a hole only as deep as and three times wider than the rootball on 4-foot centers. You don't need to amend the soil to put around the rootball, as this is a very tough plant. It does need water, so build a water basin around the rooted area and give thrice-weekly watering until established.

CARE AND MAINTENANCE

It is one of those lazy man's plants that I included in my yard, as it needs only minimal care. To keep plants leafy and encourage flowering, water established plants weekly; but as the temperature gets above 90 degrees Fahrenheit, go to twice-a-week waterings. If flowers thin out or the plant looks leggy, increase the amount of water. Because it is a legume it doesn't require much fertilizer, but you could work 1/2 cup of ammonium sulfate into the soil in the spring. Just after the spring flush of blooms, prune it to encourage new growth—the result will be more blooms next season. This desert beauty doesn't bring any pests to the yard.

LANDSCAPE MERIT

It's a flowering accent in the landscape that combines well with just about any plants in the garden. Give it a close-up spot to enjoy the blooms. I use it as an accent along my dried creek and between boulders. It seems to add stability to my garden. But it shows off best when planted with defining plants such as Prickly Pear, Yuccas, and Century Plants.

ADDITIONAL SPECIES, CULTIVARS, OR VARIETIES

The native Fairy Duster or False Mesquite, *C. eriophylla*, is very compact, with tiny pink, wispy flowers occurring in spring and fall. Although it is an indispensable flowering shrub for the water-wise garden, it does not show off like the Baja.

Barberry

Berberis species

Height × Spread: 3 to 6 feet × 4 to 7 feet

Flower Color: Small, yellow; bright red berries in fall

Foliage Color: Green, red, and deciduous

Bloom Period: Spring

Zones: 4 to 8

Color photograph on page 224.

Light Requirements

Water

Beneficial Characteristic

Barberries have a dense, rounded form that is broader than it is tall. The leaves are quite varied in their sizes and shapes, depending on the species. Barberries have small yellow flowers that appear in the spring at the same time as the leaves. Its fruits are teardrop-shaped, small red berries that last well into the winter. Barberries also have thorns, making them a good barrier plant. In Nevada, the most popular of the Barberries is the Japanese Barberry, which has purplish-red twigs and deep-green leaves. The leaves are small, giving the plant a fine texture, and turn orange to scarlet in the fall. Equally popular is the Red Leaf Japanese Barberry, which has reddish foliage from the time the leaves emerge in the spring till they drop off in the fall. When I want a dwarf shrub for defining a pathway, I choose the Crimson Pygmy Japanese Barberry. This dwarf never gets over 1½ feet tall and about as wide. (DP)

Regional Tips

While Barberries are hardy throughout the state, they don't grow as well in the south because of the heat. They should be provided with afternoon shade. They are not very hardy in Ely, Eureka, and Austin, because of short growing seasons and extreme winter temperatures.

When, Where, and How to Plant

Plant container-grown Barberries any time during the growing season. If they are planted bare root, plant in the late winter, or early spring before they start to leaf out. Barberries do very well in full sun or part shade, and are tolerant of our alkaline Nevada soils. They are also very tolerant of dry conditions. Dig the hole only as deep as the rootball, about three times the diameter of the rootball, and slope the sides of the hole so it's narrower at the bottom than at the top. Rake the sides of the hole to avoid glazed sides that become impervious to water. In our hard, poorly drained soils it is not necessary to use soil amendments in the backfill—this can slow down drainage and the roots might get waterlogged. After planting, give it a good soaking.

CARE AND MAINTENANCE

Barberries are susceptible to a number of leaf spots, rots, and insects, but with the dry, hot summers of Nevada, they are generally pest-free. They will sometimes suffer winterkill, resulting in dead twigs that need to be pruned out each spring; they withstand pruning and can be pruned any time of year. Water once a week with 1 inch of water, but in southern Nevada, use twice as much water.

LANDSCAPE MERIT

Barberry is a small shrub that is equally useful in the garden as a foundation plant to set off the house or as a barrier plant to keep the neighborhood dogs from cutting across your yard. Because of its texture and shape, it is a useful plant in shrub beds.

ADDITIONAL SPECIES, CULTIVARS, OR VARIETIES

Japanese Barberry (*Berberis thunbergii*) grows to 4 feet and has solitary spines at the nodes, and the leaves are small and oblong. The variety 'Atropurpurea' has red leaves, and the variety *B. thunbergii* 'Atropurpurea Nana' has red foliage but grows only to 2 feet high. Mentor Barberry (*B. x mentorensis*) is only hardy to zone 5 and can be evergreen in the warmer parts of the state. It has three spines at the leaf nodes.

Butterfly Bush

Buddleia davidii

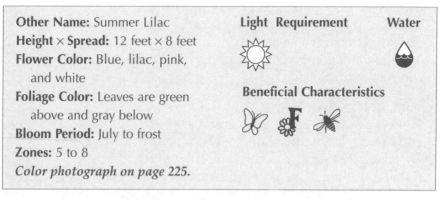

Other Name: Summer Lilac
Height × Spread: 12 feet × 8 feet
Flower Color: Blue, lilac, pink, and white
Foliage Color: Leaves are green above and gray below
Bloom Period: July to frost
Zones: 5 to 8
Color photograph on page 225.

Light Requirement

Water

Beneficial Characteristics

Butterfly Bush is an outstanding shrub when it is in bloom. The fragrant flowers form on spikes that are 6 to 12 inches long, starting in July and continuing until the first killing frost in the fall, in shades of pink, purple, blue, white, and lilac. The flowers look very much like those of Lilacs (thus the name Summer Lilac), and they attract butterflies (thus the name Butterfly Bush), and bees are attracted to them as well. The plant is not the most attractive choice to plant in the garden because of its ragged appearance, but if it is cut back each spring it forms a much fuller bush. It is taller than it is wide. Its foliage is green on the upper surface and gray-green on the lower, covered with fine hairs described by some as feeling like felt, and very coarse in texture. (DP)

REGIONAL TIPS

In the high elevations and mountainous regions of Nevada they can be grown as perennials rather than as shrubs. They are quite tender under extremely cold conditions. It is best to plant them in the spring after the danger of frost in the coldest regions of the state—Ely, for example. Foliage emerges from roots each spring.

WHEN, WHERE, AND HOW TO PLANT

Butterfly Bush is sold in containers, so you can plant it any time of the year if the ground isn't frozen. Plant in full sun for best flowering. It grows best in a well-drained soil but seem to do fine in any soil. Before planting, dig a hole that is as deep as the rootball and about three times as wide. Scrape the sides of the hole, particularly if the soil looks shiny after digging; the shininess indicates the soil has been sealed off and drainage will be slowed. Plant Butterfly Bush at the same depth it was growing in the container. There isn't a need to mix soil amendments with the soil you are going to use for filling in around the rootball— research has shown that when you have a soil with organic matter in it and put it into a hole dug in clayey soil, you end up with a giant teacup that won't drain. After planting, give it a good soaking to settle the soil around the roots.

CARE AND MAINTENANCE

Butterfly Bush doesn't need much care when it is growing. If you feed the plants when you are fertilizing the other plants, that will take care of their nutrient needs. They require only a medium amount of water, so give them about 2 inches once or twice a week. Because of their ragged appearance, they should be cut down to about 6-inch-high canes. Do this after they have finished blooming in the fall after frost. They grow very rapidly and flower on this new growth. The result is lots of flowers and a better-looking plant.

LANDSCAPE MERIT

Because of its rank, unruly growth, it is best used in the back of the garden. It can be very effective when massed with other shrubs; it is not a specimen shrub.

ADDITIONAL SPECIES, CULTIVARS, OR VARIETIES

Other species are the Alternate Leaf Butterfly Bush (*B. alternifolia*), which gets to 12 feet tall and 8 feet wide. It has fragrant, lilac-colored flowers on a deciduous shrub. *B. marrubiifolia*, or Woolly Butterfly Bush, is a desert native with silvery, fuzzy foliage and clusters of orange flowers. It is hardy in southern Nevada.

 Did You Know?

The seedpods can be used in dry arrangements.

Creosote Bush

Larrea tridentata

<table>
<tr><td>

Other Names: Chaparral Bush, Greasewood

Height × Spread: 8 feet × 6 feet

Flower Color: Yellow

Foliage Color: Green

Bloom Period: Spring

Zones: 5 to 8

Color photograph on page 225.

</td><td>

Light Requirement

Water

Beneficial Characteristics

</td></tr>
</table>

The Creosote Bush as a landscape plant is one of the best-kept secrets in southern Nevada. It is the most common shrub in the Mojave Desert, where it grows in large, often pure, stands in all directions from Las Vegas. After a good rainstorm, this plant emits a very distinctive fragrance. Let it do the same in your yard! Tiny, resinous, bright-green leaves are the source of the fragrance; it's not a real Creosote, as the name suggests. Twisted gray stems rising from a central base are sparsely foliated with shiny green leaves, giving it an open, airy appearance. As the plant becomes stressed with heat the leaves turn yellow-green, but under favorable moisture conditions it will keep its luster. Creosote Bush may reach 10 feet high, but a more typical size is 8 feet high and 6 feet wide. In the spring, bright yellow flowers sprinkle the foliage and fuzzy pea-sized fruits follow, covered with silvery hairs. It will bloom again in the fall if we have rains. Its extensive root system has the reputation of mopping up any water that falls under its canopy. (LM)

REGIONAL TIPS

It only grows in the southern part of the state. In fact, it is indigenous to the Mojave, Sonoran, and Chihuahuan deserts.

WHEN, WHERE, AND HOW TO PLANT

Creosote Bush may be hard to find as it is difficult to propagate and raise in containers—nurseries will order it for you if it's not available. Plant it from containers anytime, but it establishes best when planted in the spring. It's a plant that loves the sun. It prefers sandy soils but tolerates other soils, especially those underlaid with caliche. To plant, make a hole three times as wide and as deep as the rootball. To increase the lushness of the plant, incorporate organic matter into on-site soil and fold it in around the rootball, then build a water basin and fill with water. Water twice a week until it is established. Water becomes extremely important with Creosote Bush. If you consistently overwater it, root rot will quickly kill the plant. To determine this, dig down and smell the soil around the roots; if it is putrid, cut back the water.

CARE AND MAINTENANCE

Creosote Bush is extremely drought tolerant once established. Keep the plant moist the first summer with weekly waterings as the temperature climbs into the 90s. After the first year, work a cup of ammonium sulfate in soil in the early spring and summer prior to watering to increase plant density. Forget regular prunings; let it develop naturally, but expect to remove dead wood. There are no major pest problems—the foliage odor is objectionable to pests but the flowers attract bees.

LANDSCAPE MERIT

Creosote Bush combines well in informal groupings with other desert plants and makes an excellent screen. The twisted, ascending, and spreading trunks and branches create a unique background for other colorful plants. Its ease in maintenance makes it effective as an accent or in mass plantings where it will get limited care. The delicate foliage is a good contrast to bold cacti and succulents such as Agaves.

Did You Know?

Creosote Bushes produce a toxin that limits other plants from growing under their canopies. Indians used the seed balls as a medicine, and the resin found on branches mended arrow points and pottery. Traditionally we use it in antiseptic dressings to treat wounds and rheumatism, and it has been used to treat tuberculosis and intestinal disorders.

Dwarf Myrtle

Myrtus communis 'Compacta'

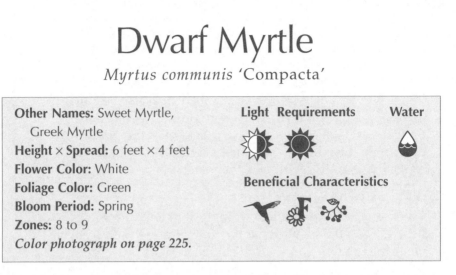

Other Names: Sweet Myrtle, Greek Myrtle
Height × Spread: 6 feet × 4 feet
Flower Color: White
Foliage Color: Green
Bloom Period: Spring
Zones: 8 to 9
Color photograph on page 225.

Light Requirements   **Water**

Beneficial Characteristics

If you want a formal hedge in your yard that will take shearing without evidence of leaves being damaged, then plant Dwarf Myrtle. You can use it in an informal setting, but it becomes mounded if left unpruned. It is a compact shrub with lustrous, glossy, pointed, bright evergreen leaves and it always looks attractive whether it's been clipped or not. You can expect long service from this shrub with very little care. As new leaves unfold, they have the same color as iceberg lettuce, and as we move into summer they take on a forest green color and give off a fragrance when bruised. Tiny fuzzy white flowers with puffs of golden stamens emitting a spicy orange scent emerge from the tips of twigs in June. Blue-black berries follow but don't show until fall, when they become food for birds. (LM)

Regional Tips

Sorry, northern Nevadans, Dwarf Myrtle is another bush that will not withstand your harsh winters. But it is a wonderful bush for southern Nevada.

When, Where, and How to Plant

Plant it any time throughout the year from containers. Dwarf Myrtle takes any soil, but good drainage is essential; it loves full sun but will tolerate partial shade. For best results, plant it where it is protected from our drying winds. The added wind draws more water than the plant can take up and leaves it with scorched leaves. To plant this shrub, make the hole three times wider but no deeper than the rootball, and work copious amounts of organic matter into the native soils. Place the rootball in the hole and firm the soil around the ball for good soil-to-root contact. Build a water basin around the plant and water twice weekly until you see evidence of new growth.

CARE AND MAINTENANCE

Dwarf Myrtle has some drought tolerance but prefers weekly irrigation throughout the summer. If it experiences leaf scorch as the temperatures rise, switch to twice-a-week waterings, and during the winter cut back to monthly waterings. Expect iron chlorosis in poorly drained soils or if waterings are light or too shallow. To sustain its lush growth, apply a cup of ammonium sulfate per plant in the early spring, summer, and fall, and increase the amount as the plant increases in size. Dwarf Myrtle is of the best for low-trimmed hedges, is often used in formal plantings, and can take shearing year round. Dwarf Myrtle also makes a good informal hedge or screen, requiring little or no pruning, or a good specimen shrub. And this plant comes to your garden without any pest problems.

LANDSCAPE MERIT

It is a very versatile shrub that we need to use more often. Dwarf Myrtle looks good planted in groups or rows as a formal hedge, as a foundation plant, or a topiary subject. It's hardy to about 20 degrees Fahrenheit and tolerates southern Nevada's heat, making it an excellent choice for a mini-oasis or transition zone from a xeriscape to normal landscaping.

ADDITIONAL SPECIES, CULTIVARS, OR VARIETIES

'Boetica' is especially upright, with thick, twisted branches and darker leaves; 'Microphylla' is a dwarf ideal for containers; 'Variegata' has leaves marbled gray-green and cream; 'Buxifolia' has small leaves like those of Boxwood (*Buxus*); and 'Compacta Variegata' is similar but with white-margined foliage.

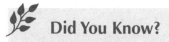 **Did You Know?**

Twisted Myrtle makes an excellent replacement bush for the Hollywood Juniper.

Ebbing's Silverberry

Elaeagnus × ebbingei

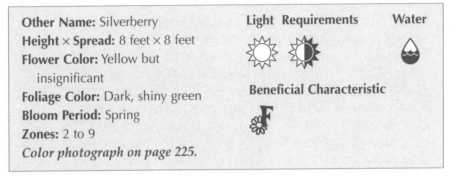

Other Name: Silverberry
Height × Spread: 8 feet × 8 feet
Flower Color: Yellow but
  insignificant
Foliage Color: Dark, shiny green
Bloom Period: Spring
Zones: 2 to 9
Color photograph on page 225.

Light Requirements

Water

Beneficial Characteristic

Ebbing's Silverberry took a while to appeal to me. When I first saw a bush, I sent a sample to an entomologist to identify the specks on the leaves. I was embarrassed to be told it was normal for that bush; scalelike silver dots cover the leaves, shimmering in light or shade to create a sparkling effect. The undersides are all silver with brown spots. (The spots resemble spider mites but don't rub off, as they are part of the plant.) Even now I find myself examining the dots when passing. Another trait you'll find is that it keeps dense without your help, nor does it require much upkeep. Leaves are the most decorative and unique feature of this plant, as they are large and dense and crinkled. You'll love viewing these plants from the far side of the garden or up close. The unique foliage lets you get away from the traditional greens in the landscape. The flowers and berries are insignificant, but some folks make jelly from the fruit. It is a fast-growing shrub that gains a quarter of its size each year until it matures at 8 feet. (LM)

REGIONAL TIPS

This is one shrub that will grow all across Nevada. It will take the northern cold and the southern heat—a combination rare for our plant palette—and still flourish.

WHEN, WHERE, AND HOW TO PLANT

Plant any time of the year, but it is best to plant in October and November. This Silverberry prefers full sun to partial shade and likes a fast-draining, improved soil. Because it grows so fast, purchase only 5-gallon container plants (research finds that smaller container-grown plants catch up to larger plants within five years). Dig a hole three times wider than and as deep as its rootbal. Because Nevada soils are compacted and lack organic content, mix into the on-site soil copious amounts of organic matter and place it around the rootball, adding water at the same time for better soil-to-root contact. Build a water basin around the plant and thoroughly soak the rootball three times a week until established. To improve plant growth, mulch under the plant.

CARE AND MAINTENANCE

This toughie needs weekly waterings until it gets hot (above 90 degrees Fahrenheit), then you need to water twice a week, and as it cools, work toward monthly waterings throughout the winter. Work a cupful of ammonium sulfate in under the bush on Presidents' Day and Labor Day, and follow with a good soaking. Ebbing's Silverberry only requires an occasional pruning to give some direction but don't shear this plant. The large leaves will take on a tattered look if clipped when grown in a formal hedge. Other than that, enjoy the shrub. It is pest-free.

LANDSCAPE MERIT

Use it as a screen, hedge, or buffer for noise abatement. The large leaves deflect sound, light, and wind—something we often overlook in plants. It is a good general-purpose shrub, effective in containers, and it helps to create an Oriental effect. Florists add the silver foliage to their arrangements.

ADDITIONAL SPECIES, CULTIVARS, OR VARIETIES

Don't forget *E. pungens*, or Silverberry, a thorny bush with olive-green leaves that sprawls and grows to 12 feet and as wide if left untrimmed. It too has insignificant flowers that produce edible fall fruit. Russian Olive, *E. angustifolius*, is a cousin of *E. × ebbingii*, but it's a bit weedy. *E. × ebbingei* 'Gilt Edge' is a wonderful variegated form with interesting gold-colored leaf margins.

Euonymus

Euonymus species

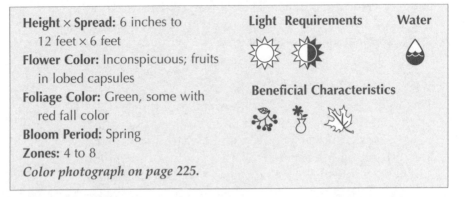

Height × Spread: 6 inches to
 12 feet × 6 feet
Flower Color: Inconspicuous; fruits
 in lobed capsules
Foliage Color: Green, some with
 red fall color
Bloom Period: Spring
Zones: 4 to 8
Color photograph on page 225.

Light Requirements

Water

Beneficial Characteristics

There are two Euonymus shrubs that are used extensively in
Nevada: Burning Bush, *Euonymus alatus*, and Japanese Euonymus,
E. japonica. A third one that is used to a lesser degree is Wintercreeper
Euonymus, *E. fortunei*. They are important for their foliage, which is a
rich, deep green. Japanese Euonymus has oval-shaped leaves that are
dark green or variegated and the plant is evergreen, as is Wintercreeper.
The stems and twigs of Burning Bush have corky wings on them; thus
the alternate name for it is Winged Spindle Tree. Euonymus flowers
are not the reason you'd select these plants, but the seed capsules of
Wintercreeper and Japanese Euonymus have some color, and this is
particularly true of Wintercreeper, with its scarlet fruit. Burning Bush
is by far my favorite because in the fall, no matter what the weather
conditions are, this plant turns the most glowing scarlet you've ever
seen. In the south, Wintercreeper's fall color persists through the
winter. (DP)

Regional Tips
Japanese Euonymus is best adapted to Las Vegas and Burning Bush
is better for the rest of the state; it needs protection from the sun in
Las Vegas or the leaves will burn.

When, Where, and How to Plant
All Euonymus are container grown and can be planted any time of
year. The light requirement differs somewhat for each. Burning Bush
grows in full sun or part shade (where it is hot); Wintercreeper will
grow in deep shade; and the Japanese Euonymus grows in full sun
and part shade. They all prefer well-drained soil but do very well in

Nevada's clayey soils without adverse effects. To plant, dig the hole as deep as the rootball and about three times as wide. There is no need to add any soil amendment to the backfill soil; in fact, they will establish better if you don't use amendments. Be sure to plant them at the same level they were growing in the containers, and after planting, give each plant a good soaking to settle the soil around the roots and eliminate air pockets.

CARE AND MAINTENANCE

Euonymus are easy to maintain. They can be pruned, but they look much better if you let them grow according to their natural forms—sheared plants all start to look the same no matter what they are. Japanese Euonymus is susceptible to powdery mildew and may need some control measures during the growing season. Water about once a week with about 2 inches of water. Growth will also be improved if you fertilize with a complete water-soluble fertilizer in the spring.

LANDSCAPE MERIT

Their main use in the landscape is background greenery. If you are looking for a hedging plant, Burning Bush and Japanese Euonymus are good candidates. They both can be sheared lightly to form a formal hedge or left alone to make an informal one. They are also used as foundation plantings. Burning Bush makes a great accent that will really knock your socks off.

ADDITIONAL SPECIES, CULTIVARS, OR VARIETIES

An interesting cultivar you may want to try is *E. alatus* 'Compacta'. It is a more compact form than the standard Burning Bush but still has great fall color. Variegated Wintercreeper, *E. fortunei* 'Emerald 'n Gold', is 2 feet tall, spreads to 6 feet, and has green leaves with white edges.

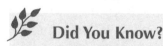 **Did You Know?**

Deer, rabbits, and squirrels do not bother Euonymus.

Feathery Cassia

Cassia artemisioides

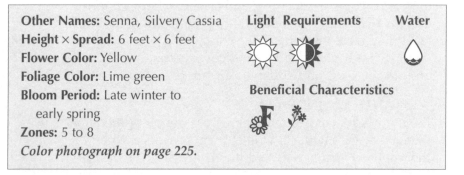

Other Names: Senna, Silvery Cassia
Height × Spread: 6 feet × 6 feet
Flower Color: Yellow
Foliage Color: Lime green
Bloom Period: Late winter to
early spring
Zones: 5 to 8
Color photograph on page 225.

Light Requirements

Water

Beneficial Characteristics

When I lived in the North, Forsythia in bloom indicated it was time to plant tomatoes. Cassia tells me the same thing and also tells me spring is around the corner. When in bloom, the bush covers itself with fragrant yellow flowers that show off for a long time, then three-inch-long flat pods follow and turn brown. The plant will naturalize the area if you leave the pods to mature and spread its seeds. These pods indicate this is a legume that produces its own nitrogen, so you don't have to feed it. Cassia does great in small lots, never trying to overpower the scene with its feathery foliage but providing an airy attraction year-round. It is a shrub that grows fast up to 6 feet high. It can become open and leggy and needs to be cut back to keep it compact and lush looking. It makes an excellent background for perennials, as its feathery foliage blends well with any other plant. (LM)

REGIONAL TIPS

Feathery Cassia is sensitive to frost damage and is adaptable only to the southern part of Nevada.

WHEN, WHERE, AND HOW TO PLANT

Plant from containers any time, but Feathery Cassia prefers establishment in the spring. If you plant in the summer, it is extremely important to give it extra water. It needs a soil that rapidly drains or you can expect root rot. In order to get all those blooms it needs full sun, but it will also do well in partial shade. To plant, make a hole three times as wide and as deep as the rootball. Mix in copious amounts of organic matter with the on-site soil and fold in around the rootball; add water as you refill for better soil-to-rootball contact.

Build a basin around the rooted area and thoroughly soak the rootball each watering until established.

CARE AND MAINTENANCE

Give the plant twice-weekly waterings until established, then weekly irrigations throughout the summer and monthly waterings in winter. If you stress this plant for water, it sheds leaves and continues to take on a woody appearance. This self-fertilizing legume doesn't need any fertilizer. While it is still young, develop a strong framework for the plant to build from. When the pods turn brown, that's a signal to give them a light pruning; if you prune then, it increases plant density and flowering production for next year. If older plants get rangy, severely cut back stems to the base to renew more flowering wood. If the foliage begins to bleach out, it is a good indication you need to give it some iron chelates. Frost may damage Feathery Cassia just before bloom, but it has no problems with heat.

LANDSCAPE MERIT

This deciduous shrub is native to the Southwest. It is great as a filler plant, a screener, background plant, and foundation plant. I love it in a desert garden setting because there is so little maintenance involved.

ADDITIONAL SPECIES, CULTIVARS, OR VARIETIES

Some of the many Cassias are: *C. nemophila* or Desert Cassia, which blooms early, covering its needled foliage, which is greener than the foliage of *C. artemisioides*. *C. phyllodenia*, or Silver-leaf Cassia, blooms even earlier, covering its bladelike leaves and shimmering with the summer breezes. *C. wislizenii* or *Senna wislizenii*, or Shrubby Cassia, generates much larger flowers later in the spring and summer, covering its finely textured foliage. It may be hard to find, but it's a real winner. Botanists place many of the species in the genus *Senna*, but the shrubs are most commonly sold as Cassia.

Flowering Quince

Chaenomeles speciosa

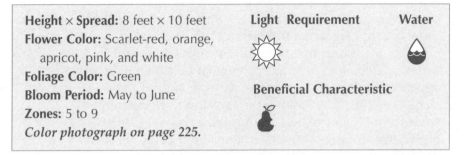

Height × Spread: 8 feet × 10 feet
Flower Color: Scarlet-red, orange, apricot, pink, and white
Foliage Color: Green
Bloom Period: May to June
Zones: 5 to 9
Color photograph on page 225.

Light Requirement

Water

Beneficial Characteristic

Flowering Quince has 1½-inch-diameter flowers that bloom in late spring to early summer. The most common Flowering Quince has brilliant scarlet-red flowers that bloom on two-year-old or older wood. Some of the cultivars blooms in colors of white, pink, apricot, or orange, but the flowers don't have any fragrance. They produce a fruit that looks somewhat like a pear. It will pucker you up if you try to eat it raw, which I can personally attest to, but cook it and add enough sugar and it makes a pretty good jam. The stems and twigs of Flowering Quince have large spines that make it hard to prune, so be careful not to plant it where you might brush against it. The toothed leaves are oblong, grow to 3 inches, and are dark green on the upper sides. One of the distinctive features of a Flowering Quince leaf is the two small, roundish leaves (stipules) found at the base of each leaf. (DP)

REGIONAL TIPS

Flowering Quince doesn't flower as well in the hot regions of southern Nevada because of warm winters, but it does very well in the high desert and all but the coldest parts of the mountainous regions.

WHEN, WHERE, AND HOW TO PLANT

Plant Flowering Quince at any time of the year when the ground isn't frozen. Fall is the ideal time for most deciduous shrubs, but availability is best in spring. Quince is container grown and should be available in anything from a 1-gallon can to a 15-gallon size, if you prefer to start with a full-grown plant. It flowers best in full sun but will grow in any soil. When you plant, dig the planting hole as deep as the rootball and about three times as wide; rake the sides of the hole after it has been dug to improve the drainage. Place the plant in the hole, being sure that it will be planted at the same depth it was growing in the container, and backfill with the soil that was removed from the hole. If it is amended, drainage may suffer by the mingling of the two soil textures. Once it is planted give it a good soaking.

CARE AND MAINTENANCE

Flowering Quince is easy to maintain and is not bothered by pests. To assure they will continue to bloom their best, they need to be pruned heavily right after they bloom. They tolerate drought very well, but give them 2 inches of water once a week for best growth. Feed them in the spring with a fertilizer that contains 20 percent nitrogen, used according to directions.

LANDSCAPE MERIT

Flowering Quince can stand alone, but it is much more effective when planted in groups as part of a shrub bed. It is also very effective as a background shrub for other plants. It is used as an accent plant and for foundation plantings where a large shrub is desired.

ADDITIONAL SPECIES, CULTIVARS, OR VARIETIES

A few cultivars that are available include 'Cameo', which is one that does not have thorns. It does have very attractive apricot-pink flowers. 'Red Charlot' grows to 8 feet high and has double rose-red flowers. 'Jet Trail' is one of the few with white flowers, and it forms a low, compact plant.

Forsythia

Forsythia × intermedia

Forsythia is one of the first shrubs to bloom in the spring and, as such, is often said to call for the end of winter. It has bright yellow flowers that bloom on last year's (and older) wood, so when it is in bloom there are blossoms from the ground right to the tips of the canes. The form of Forsythia varies somewhat with the cultivar. For example, 'Arnold Dwarf' grows 3 feet high and 6 feet wide, and 'Spring Glory' is as high as it is wide with very nice, arching branches. The leaves are yellow-green in the spring when they come out and change to green during the summer and yellow-green in the fall. (DP)

REGIONAL TIPS

Forsythia grows best in zones 5 to 9. In Ely when the temperatures get to 20 degrees Fahrenheit below zero, the flower buds might not survive. Nor do they develop the dramatic blooms in the south. Forsythia is hardy in most of Nevada.

WHEN, WHERE, AND HOW TO PLANT

Plant Forsythia any time of the year if it is containerized. It is easy to plant bare root and is found in the garden centers in the early spring (when there's the best selection), packaged in plastic bags with some sawdust packed around the roots. By the way, pass up the broken bags because the roots will be dry. Be sure to plant bare root in late winter or early spring before the buds start to grow. Forsythia needs full sun to develop the best flowers but is not picky about soil. To plant, dig the hole as deep as the rootball and about three times as wide, place the rootball in the hole, backfill around the roots, and give it a good soaking.

CARE AND MAINTENANCE

Forsythia plants flower best if they are pruned to about half their height right after they flower. Many gardeners recommend pruning them right to the ground, but I haven't seen that practiced very much. They should be fertilized in the spring; the easiest way is to use a water-soluble fertilizer and follow the directions for once-a-year application. For best growth, they need to be watered with 1 inch of water twice a week. They are easy to care for and aren't bothered by pests.

LANDSCAPE MERIT

Forsythia can be used as a specimen shrub or as a mass planting. On the University of Nevada campus it is used very effectively as a foundation planting. When used as a foundation planting around a house, consider where the windows are and how high they are above the ground— you don't want to block the window with the shrub. It can also be used as a screen or hedge. Because it is not in bloom during the summer, many gardeners like to use it as a backdrop for summer-flowering plants. It also works very well as cover for a bank, or even espaliered.

ADDITIONAL SPECIES, CULTIVARS, OR VARIETIES

F. intermedia 'Lynwood' grows to 6 feet high and 6 feet wide and has light yellow flowers. *F. intermedia* 'Beatrix Farrand', the tallest, gets to 10 feet high and 7 feet wide, with large bright-yellow flowers.

Glossy Abelia

Abelia × grandiflora

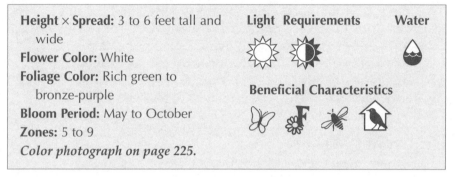

Height × Spread: 3 to 6 feet tall and wide

Flower Color: White

Foliage Color: Rich green to bronze-purple

Bloom Period: May to October

Zones: 5 to 9

Color photograph on page 225.

Light Requirements

Water

Beneficial Characteristics

Here is a lazy man's plant, almost carefree with just the occasional pruning required. This graceful, fountainlike mounding shrub is at home in any garden. Bronzy leaves when it's young turn a rich green through the summer and bronze-purple again in fall. The leaves densely cover branches as they arch upward, outward, and then downward. Bell-shaped flowers in clusters plaster themselves among leaves; they are small but plentiful enough to show off during summer and into the fall to attract bees and butterflies. When blooms drop, they are usually purplish or copper-colored, and sepals remain attached to provide color from early summer to frost. It is a moderate grower to 6 feet, sometimes higher, with a spread of 5 feet or more unless trimmed. (LM)

REGIONAL TIPS

Sorry, northern Nevadans, with your harsh winters, Glossy Abelia is a marginal plant that will require some protection if you attempt to grow it. But it is a wonderful shrub for the south.

WHEN, WHERE, AND HOW TO PLANT

Plant Glossy Abelia from fall to spring from 1- and 5-gallon containers. It requires full sun to partial shade for best flowering, but flowers thin as shade intensifies. Glossy Abelia desires a well-drained soil: Open up a hole three to five times as wide and as deep as the rootball, mix organic matter into the on-site soil and fold in around the plant, then use water to settle the soil as you plant. Build a water basin to contain the water while it soaks through the rootball, and continue to water the plant three times a week until you see emerging growth. Glossy Abelia leaves yellow easily, and this is likely caused by alkaline soils; add some iron chelates.

CARE AND MAINTENANCE

This low-maintenance shrub needs a good irrigation weekly, but as the temperatures rise into the 90s, go to twice-a-week waterings. Because of its lush growth, work a cup of ammonium sulfate into the soil prior to your early spring, summer, and fall feedings. This is one shrub whose new growth can be indiscriminately clipped back because of its blooming habits; flowers quickly return as the plant forms new wood. Thin out the stems periodically to allow more light to reach the plant's center to stimulate new growth. The more stems you remove, the more arching next year's growth will be, keeping Abelia looking graceful. You don't need to remove faded flowers as the petals fall, and the sepals remain attached for a look of miniature dry flowers. You can tell aphids are present by the honeydew covering the leaves. Hit them with a jet of water, but if they persist, use insecticidal soap or Neem oil.

LANDSCAPE MERIT

This shrub has many merits; use it for a background, as a boundary plant, filler, or space divider, to make a visual barrier, as a ground cover, or near a house. It's a neat, clean plant for poolsides or for close-up viewing. It is also a very tough, durable shrub for southern Nevada.

ADDITIONAL SPECIES, CULTIVARS, OR VARIETIES

'Prostrata' is a low, prostrate form featuring white flowers. It grows 18 to 24 inches high and spreads to 4 feet. 'Edward Goucher' is pink-flowering and has bronze-green foliage growing to 4 or 5 feet. 'Sherwoodi' is upright but shorter, at 3 to 4 feet tall. 'Francis Mason' is compact, densely branched, with pink flowers and yellow-variegated leaves. *A. chinensis* has fragrant, pink-tinted white flowers and is deciduous.

Heavenly Bamboo

Nandina domestica

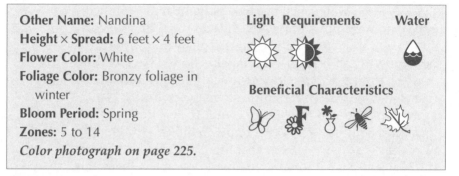

Other Name: Nandina
Height × Spread: 6 feet × 4 feet
Flower Color: White
Foliage Color: Bronzy foliage in
  winter
Bloom Period: Spring
Zones: 5 to 14
Color photograph on page 225.

Light Requirements   **Water**

Beneficial Characteristics

Heavenly Bamboo is not a true bamboo; it just resembles bamboo. It picked up the name Heavenly Bamboo from the Orient, where it is used in temple gardens because of its graceful dainty foliage. The leaves come out pinkish-bronze in the spring, turn a soft, light green through the summer, and reddish-bronze through the winter. This delicate foliage grows outward from each of the bamboolike stems topped by sprays of pinkish-white flower spikes in the spring. Berries follow, turning shiny red in the early fall and becoming food for birds. The autumn leaves and berries make wonderful additions to holiday cut-flower arrangements. It can get up to 8 feet tall, but most keep their slender forms up to 6 feet and seldom get more than 4 feet wide. Yes, it is a plant with grace, but it's tough too—something we need more of in our gardens. (LM)

REGIONAL TIPS

Plantings in the cooler portions of the state are likely to show the best leaf color. Protect plantings in the south from the hot, dry winds.

WHEN, WHERE, AND HOW TO PLANT

Heavenly Bamboo comes in containers from garden centers, so plant any time of the year. Heavenly Bamboo prefers a full-sun to partial-shade location and a highly organic, well-drained soil. Add organic matter at the time of planting to open up the soil for best results. Dig a hole that's much wider than and as deep as the rootball, and position the plant. Fold the prepared soil around it, adding adequate water to make good soil-to-root contact. Form a water basin at the edges of the rootball to move water through the root system and into the surrounding soil.

CARE AND MAINTENANCE

Water your Heavenly Bamboo weekly until the temperature gets into the 90s, and then switch to watering three times a week. Never allow the root zone to dry out; to conserve water, add 2 to 3 inches of mulch. Fertilize Heavenly Bamboo in February and September, using a cup of ammonium sulfate worked into the soil around each bush. Use a chelated iron if foliage turns yellow. Always remove two to three of the oldest canes annually to keep the plant covered with leaves and avoid the exposure of the naked stems. Once berries lose their gloss, remove them. Heavenly Bamboo does not bring any pests into the yard.

LANDSCAPE MERIT

Heavenly Bamboo is an underrated plant, as versatile as any landscape shrub in our plant palette. It is easy to grow, adds interest through the seasons, brings an Oriental look to the garden, and is attractive at close range. Use it as an accent, in narrow spaces, entryways, and atriums, in patios and rock gardens, with perennials, and in containers. It's a striking shrub, especially with night lighting.

ADDITIONAL SPECIES, CULTIVARS, OR VARIETIES

'Compacta' dependably reaches 4 to 5 feet high and about 3 feet wide; 'Nana' is a small mound, 12 to 18 inches high by 15 inches wide; 'Purpurea Dwarf', the same size, is often preferred for its deep-red color; and 'Harbor Dwarf' is a recent introduction that grows to about 2 feet tall and spreads by underground runners.

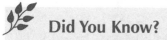 **Did You Know?**

The more you expose the plant to the sun, the brighter the foliage colors will be in the fall.

Indian Hawthorn

Rhaphiolepis indica

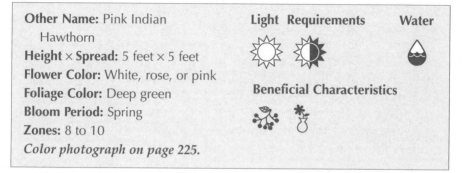

Other Name: Pink Indian Hawthorn

Height × Spread: 5 feet × 5 feet

Flower Color: White, rose, or pink

Foliage Color: Deep green

Bloom Period: Spring

Zones: 8 to 10

Color photograph on page 225.

Light Requirements

Water

Beneficial Characteristics

Indian Hawthorn is a delightful shrub with shiny, dark evergreen foliage that is dense and leathery and forms a cushion or mound. As the new leaves unfold in the spring, they bring a bronzy color to the scene. This makes it a year-round attractive plant. Come spring, a spectacular—even breathtaking—display of white or pink flowers lights up the plant and because of its mounding factor, it looks like a giant bouquet. That is what makes it one of the most widely used shrubs in southern Nevada. Some folks want to use them for cut flowers, although they don't last long; however, they do make lovely filler in arrangements. Purplish-blue-black berries ripen in fall and linger though winter to become food for wildlife. If they become unsightly to you, remove them. Growth is moderate both in height and spread—yet another beauty of this shrub—and it will not outgrow its allotted space. (LM)

REGIONAL TIPS

If you live south of Beatty, you're in luck: Indian Hawthorn will grow in your area. It does not tolerate colder regions of Nevada.

WHEN, WHERE, AND HOW TO PLANT

Plant anytime in southern Nevada from 1- or 5-gallon containers in a fertile soil with good drainage. For optimum growth and bloom production, select a site in full sun, but keep it away from reflective surfaces such as sidewalks or walls to avoid leaf scorch. Make a hole three to five times as wide and as deep as the rootball, and mix in generous amounts of organic matter to open up the soil so the plant does its thing for your landscape. After planting, build a watering basin with a 4- to 6-inch-high wall beyond the rootball.

Water immediately after planting to thoroughly soak the rootball and surrounding soil, and then twice weekly until established.

CARE AND MAINTENANCE

Water twice weekly until the temperature climbs into the 90s, then go to watering three times a week; and remember to water throughout the winter because it is so dry. If you see the leaves yellowing and brown spots developing on the leaves, it is a good indication you are overwatering. To be on the safe side, give the plants some iron chelates. Indian Hawthorn needs regular feedings, so work a cup of ammonium sulfate in the ground around Valentine's, Memorial, and Labor Day weekends. Prune plants regularly to keep them compact; unpruned plants become open and rangy. Always prune after flowering to eliminate seed formation and to increase twig growth for more flowers next spring. Aphids seem to be the only culprit that bothers Hawthorns. They leave behind leaves covered with honeydew. Direct a strong force of water at the critters to wash them off, or apply insecticidal soap, Neem oil, or Malathion.

LANDSCAPE MERIT

This is an all-purpose shrub; use it for formal and informal settings, or as a hedge, or to bring on an Oriental effect. It fits well in a container or as a foreground plant near the patio and can very easily become a large-scale ground cover.

ADDITIONAL SPECIES, CULTIVARS, OR VARIETIES

'Enchantress' has a form that is known as "roundy-moundy" in the nursery trade. This term is given to plants that do not require shearing to maintain their shapes because they grow so evenly and densely. *R. indica* 'Majestic Beauty' may be trained to become a small patio tree.

Japanese Yew

Taxus cuspidata

Height × Spread: To 50 feet × 20 feet	Light Requirements	Water
Flower Color: Inconspicuous; bright red fruit	☀ ☀	💧
Foliage Color: Evergreen, dark green on top and yellowish-green beneath		
Zones: 5 to 7		
Color photograph on page 225.		

Japanese Yew is a very nice-looking plant. If you want to have topiary in the yard, this is the shrub for you. It is tolerant of shearing and pruning, so you can easily trim Japanese Yew into almost any shape you want. The foliage is somewhat feathery in appearance, with the leaves being described as needles. The flowers of Japanese Yew are inconspicuous, but the fruit is bright red and looks like miniature Christmas bulbs scattered around on the shrub. The fruit is not edible and is considered poisonous, as is the foliage. While the native tree can grow to heights of 50 feet, there are many cultivars that are available as manageable spreading shrubs. For example, 'Aurea Low Boy' is a golden yellow cultivar that makes a very attractive ground cover. 'Aurescens' is also a low-spreading shrub with golden yellow on a background of green. (DP)

REGIONAL TIPS

Japanese Yews are best adapted to northern Nevada gardens because they are not tolerant of hot winds.

WHEN, WHERE, AND HOW TO PLANT

Plant Japanese Yew from containers at any time of year. Particularly for northern Nevada gardens, best selection comes in the spring and summer. (Most conifers seem to transplant here better in the spring.) Japanese Yew grows well either in sun or part shade. It is easy to propagate from seed or cuttings, but unless you are adventuresome, purchase it either as a container plant or as a balled-and-burlapped plant in the early spring. It doesn't tolerate soggy soils, so you need to plant it where it will have good drainage. Dig the hole just as deep as the rootball and about three times as wide, take the plant out of the container, and carefully place it in the hole. If it is balled and burlapped, be sure to remove the burlap after placing it in the hole, as well as the wire or twine that holds the burlap in place. Twine or wire left wound around the roots or stem of the plant will kill it in few years, and no matter what anybody says, the burlap will not decompose in our dry climate. Backfill with the same soil you dug out of the hole and give it a good soaking.

CARE AND MAINTENANCE

Japanese Yews are generally free of pests. They will grow better if they are watered three times a week the first year, with about $2^{1}/_{2}$ inches per week. After that, give them 2 inches of water twice a week. Fertilize them the following season after planting; a fertilizer high in nitrogen applied in the spring will encourage the best growth.

LANDSCAPE MERIT

This is a plant that can be used virtually anywhere north of Beatty. You find them sheared into bunnies and ducks and various other shapes. Not many gardeners spend the time to do this, but if you want to exhibit a little whimsy in the garden, try your hand on a Yew. Though not very common any more, I have seen them as hedge plants that have been sheared into a wall, complete with posts. One of the advantages of using this plant as a hedge is that it provides a dense wall that remains green all year long.

ADDITIONAL SPECIES, CULTIVARS, OR VARIETIES

T. cuspidata 'Nana' is a bushy, slow-growing shrub. *T. × media* 'Hatfieldii' is a compact, conical-shaped shrub.

Junipers

Juniperus species

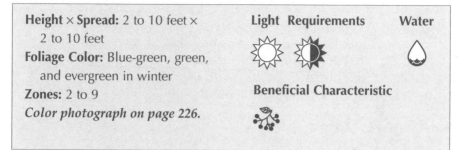

Height × Spread: 2 to 10 feet × 2 to 10 feet	Light Requirements	Water
Foliage Color: Blue-green, green, and evergreen in winter		
Zones: 2 to 9	**Beneficial Characteristic**	
Color photograph on page 226.		

Junipers are the universal garden plants. They provide green foliage all year long, a welcome sight in the middle of winter when everything else in the garden is brown. They are extremely tough, with leaves that are sharp scales. There are a few cultivars that have golden foliage that is particularly attractive during cloudy days. Two varieties that have been overused in the past are the 'Pfitzer' Juniper, a tall-spreading shrub, and 'Tam' Juniper, a low-spreading one. At one time they made up about 90 percent of the evergreens in the gardens of northern Nevada, but there are over two hundred varieties to choose from. The nurseries are getting a much better selection of ground cover types, conical types, and spreaders, so you should find the right one for your garden. (DP)

REGIONAL TIPS

The conical types like Rocky Mountain Juniper are very well adapted to the colder mountainous regions, and are used in Elko and Ely.

WHEN, WHERE, AND HOW TO PLANT

Plant Junipers at any time of the year, but the best selection is in spring, either grown in containers or balled and burlapped. They grow in full sun or part shade but are not fussy about soil. They die out in a few years if they are planted in poorly drained soil and overwatered. Dig the hole as deep as the rootball and about three times as wide. Remove the container, and in the case of a balled-and-burlapped shrub, remove the burlap and any of the wire or twine surrounding the rootball. Backfill with the soil taken from the hole and water it well after planting.

CARE AND MAINTENANCE

Junipers are generally carefree plants. Water once every couple of weeks, or weekly in southern Nevada, with 2 inches of water, and use a complete water-soluble fertilize in the spring according to directions. They can be sheared, but doing so will ruin the natural shapes of the plants forever. Junipers are attacked by spider mites when it gets hot and dry; you can tell by the dull, dusty appearance of the twigs. Use appropriate control measures and be sure to follow the directions on the label. Periodically they also get spittle bugs; these are not really a problem but more of a curiosity, because of the frothy "spit" on the twigs. Just spray the plants with a good, stiff stream of water.

LANDSCAPE MERIT

Junipers are good as foundation plantings, specimen plantings, and even container plants. They are great border plants and make good wind and visual screens. They can be used for topiary, too. An important point: They are very flammable and should not be not be used as foundation plantings in close proximity to the house or near other structures in fire-prone areas.

ADDITIONAL SPECIES, CULTIVARS, OR VARIETIES

If you are looking for a ground cover, try *J. horizontalis* 'Bar Harbor', which grows to 1 foot high and spreads to 10 feet. *J. horizontalis* 'Plumosa' is an interesting low-growing Juniper that is green in the summer and purple in the winter, growing to 18 inches high and 10 feet wide. If you are looking for a very narrow, columnar plant, get *J. scopulatum* 'Skyrocket'.

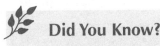 **Did You Know?**

Juniper berries are used as a flavoring for food.

Lilac

Syringa vulgaris

Height × Spread: To 15 feet × 15 feet	Light Requirement	Water
Flower Color: Purple, white, lavender, and magenta		

Height × Spread: To 15 feet × 15 feet

Flower Color: Purple, white, lavender, and magenta

Foliage Color: Green

Bloom Period: Late spring

Zones: 3 to 7

Color photograph on page 226.

Light Requirement

Water

Beneficial Characteristics

There is nothing that surpasses Lilacs when they are in bloom. There are two flower spikes at the end of each twig that grow up to 12 inches long and 3 inches in diameter. When in bloom, they are completely clothed in flowers for about three weeks in the late spring, giving off a very strong fragrance. The flowers are single and in some cases are semi-double. The foliage of the Lilacs is a medium-green and the leaves are 3 to 5 inches long and somewhat heart-shaped. Lilac flowers are excellent for floral arrangements; if you smash the cut ends of the stems with a hammer and plunge them into water, they will last for at least a week indoors. One of the most interesting flowers is on a cultivar called 'Sensation', featuring magenta flowers edged in white; it will be hard to find but well worth the extra effort. If white is what you are looking for, then 'Avalanche' is the one. For a dark purple, look for 'Yankee Doodle'. (DP)

REGIONAL TIPS

Lilac does not grow as well in southern Nevada—it needs cold winters to initiate blooming. Use the Lilac Vine as a substitute.

WHEN, WHERE, AND HOW TO PLANT

Plant any time during the growing season, but the best selection is in the spring. Lilacs are very well adapted to our alkaline Nevada soils as long as they are well drained, and they grow best when the soil pH is between 6 and 8. Dig the hole as deep as the rootball and about three times as wide, but don't amend the soil used to backfill around the roots. Plant them about 10 feet apart if you are planting them as a mass; if they are going to be used for a hedge, plant them about 4 feet apart. After planting, give the shrub a good soaking.

CARE AND MAINTENANCE

Water with 1 inch of water twice a week, and fertilize in the spring with a complete fertilizer used according to directions. Prune after bloom in the spring to remove the seedheads and to shape the plant. If pruned in the late summer or fall, you will cut off all the flower buds that have formed at the tip of the twigs. Lilacs can also be sheared as a more formal hedge. They have two problems, neither of which causes any permanent damage to the shrubs. Strawberry root weevils chew on the edges of the leaves, making them look like they have been snipped with pinking shears. The weevil is about 1/4 inch long with a hooked snout. The other nuisance is the leaf-cutter bee. It likes to use the leaves to line its nest, so it snips out nice circular pieces of leaf, leaving a round hole up to an inch in diameter.

LANDSCAPE MERIT

Lilacs are ideal specimen plants, very good border plantings, and often used as hedges or screens in the garden. If you are really looking for a show, plant a clump of Lilacs together.

ADDITIONAL SPECIES, CULTIVARS, OR VARIETIES

'Al Holden' is a purple-flowered one. If you want white, also try 'Bridle Memories', and for lavender-blue, try 'Wedgewood Blue'. Descanso Hybrids are recommended for areas with mild winters.

Did You Know?

If you live where rabbits and squirrels are a common problem, this is a good plant for you because these critters don't bother Lilacs.

Mock Orange

Pittosporum tobira

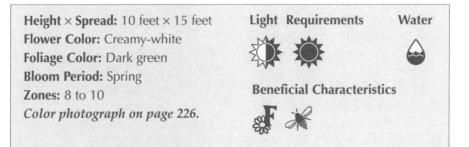

Height × Spread: 10 feet × 15 feet
Flower Color: Creamy-white
Foliage Color: Dark green
Bloom Period: Spring
Zones: 8 to 10
Color photograph on page 226.

Light Requirements

Water

Beneficial Characteristics

I love driving through the Orange groves in California when they are blooming, just to take in the fragrance. I think that's why you find so many Mock Oranges in southern Nevada landscapes. Yellowish, creamy-white flower clusters appear with all that Orange grove fragrance. The clusters consist of many flowers in one bloom, each producing a small green berry in the fall. Mock Orange is best known for its thick, leathery, lustrous, glossy green foliage. You can tell these leaves are shy of water when they turn down along the edges. When picking a home for this plant, remember that it prefers an eastern exposure and needs to be protected in some way from the sun. As exposure to sun increases, growth becomes less vigorous, even the leaf size becomes smaller, and leaves lose their luster. (LM)

REGIONAL TIPS
Mock Orange struggles with the harsh winters of northern Nevada, but it's a wonderful shrub for southern Nevada landscapes.

WHEN, WHERE, AND HOW TO PLANT
Plant Mock Orange any time, but it does best when planted in October and November. I find the roots grow throughout the winter, picking up a year's worth of growth; the following summer, the plant will experience less leaf scorch and twig dieback. Mock Orange is a plant that likes filtered or partial shade. Plant this toughie in any soil as long as the soil drains, though it always responds better if the soil is rich in organic matter. Open up the soil at least three times as wide and as deep as the rootball. Pull the improved soil back in around the plant, with water running to help settle the soil around the plant. Build a water basin around the plant

and water thoroughly twice a week until established. I like to use mulch around the plants to cool the hot soils and to conserve water.

CARE AND MAINTENANCE
Because of Mock Orange's large, fleshy leaves, keep the soil moist. Water twice a week until temperatures climb into the 90s and then switch to three waterings a week, letting emitters run 2 to 3 hours at time. Work a cupful of ammonium sulfate under each plant at Valentine's, Memorial, and Labor Days to keep up the lush growth. Prune only to maintain shape and size. This plant does not adapt well to shearing; selective pruning looks best, so do it just after it blooms. This keeps your plant compact and you will have more blooms next year. Keep pruners handy to clip back the fast-growing twigs. Honeydew on leaves tells you aphids and scales are working the plant. Wash off the aphids with a jet of water or go after both with Neem oil. Control sooty mold by using drip emitters to keep moisture off the plant.

LANDSCAPE MERIT
Use it as a backdrop for shorter plants or as a good screen or informal hedge. I find it very attractive in a container, with annuals around the base. And everybody loves the fragrance.

ADDITIONAL SPECIES, CULTIVARS, OR VARIETIES
P. tobira 'Variegata' and 'Wheeler's Dwarf' are very commonly planted Mock Oranges. 'Wheeler's Dwarf' develops into a dense, compact-spreading mound, ultimately reaching 3 feet in height, excellent as a ground cover or for massing. 'Variegata' grows 5 to 10 feet high and wide and has leaves in gray-green and gray with irregular creamy-white margins.

'New Gold' Lantana

Lantana × 'New Gold'

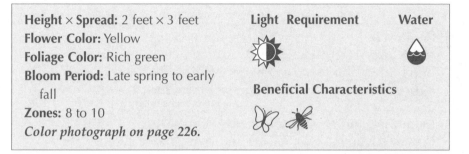

Height × Spread: 2 feet × 3 feet
Flower Color: Yellow
Foliage Color: Rich green
Bloom Period: Late spring to early fall
Zones: 8 to 10
Color photograph on page 226.

Light Requirement

Water

Beneficial Characteristics

The researchers were on their toes when they developed 'New Gold'. This is an eye-catcher that makes people almost drool over it when it is in full bloom. I have ten in my yard and they are always blooming. 'New Gold' is a vigorous, energetic new hybrid introduced by Texas A & M University, a heavier flower producer than its cousins because it does not produce seeds. Oh, the joy that came into this researcher's soul to find a long-blooming plant that sheds its flower petals and doesn't produce any seeds! Each flower is really a cluster of tiny, tubular flowers. All Lantanas and Verbenas have similarly rounded floral heads consisting of smaller, colorful flowers. The plant grows 2 feet high and 3 feet wide and when in bloom is almost totally covered by blooms, with some greenery as a background to show off the flowers even more. There is virtually no maintenance required, with the exception of cleaning out the dead stuff after frosts. Plants do freeze back, but they recover quickly even when temperatures drop to 10 degrees Fahrenheit. (LM)

REGIONAL TIPS:

This is not a perennial shrub for northern Nevada; however, you can use it as an annual planting in a sunny location. It does freeze back to the ground in southern Nevada but comes back as weather warms.

WHEN, WHERE, AND HOW TO PLANT

Plant container-grown plants after March 15 and until midsummer to ensure time for plants to establish themselves. 'New Gold' Lantana prefers well-drained, enriched soil and needs full sun to filtered shade. Dig generous holes, loosening the soil three times wider than and as deep as the rootball. Refill with on-site soil enriched with organic matter, and use water to settle in the plant.

Build a basin around the plant and give it good soakings, three times a week, until established.

CARE AND MAINTENANCE

Water twice weekly during warm weather. Too much or too little water will reduce the blooming potential of this beauty, so let the blooms be your guide for the amount to water. Feed the plant a balanced shrub formula around St. Patrick's Day, and cut it back hard in early spring to remove any frost-damaged branches and to prevent woodiness. If you have sticky honeydew on the leaves, it is a good indication of aphids or whiteflies. If the lower leaves become dusty and dry-looking, suspect spider mites. Direct a strong force of water to that area, or use insecticidal soap and Neem as organic controls, or use Malathion.

LANDSCAPE MERIT

This one makes an excellent show when planted in masses and it does well in containers. Dwarf selections make handsome, flowering ground covers and good focal points for entryways.

ADDITIONAL SPECIES, CULTIVARS, OR VARIETIES

Most Lantana are either *L. camara* or *L. montevidensis*, with hybrids coming from these species. Flower colors of yellow, orange, and red together within a single head—or yellow, peach, and pink combined in one cluster—make these plants quite a sight. *L. camara*, which is the dominant Lantana, comes in pastel yellow, peach, and pink flowers spilling out from the cool bluish foliage. Then there are hybrids such as 'Christine' (with cerise-pink to yellow flowers), 'Dwarf Pink', 'Dwarf Pink Prolific', 'Dwarf White', 'Dwarf Yellow', and many more. I am sure you can tell the colors of the flowers by their names. *L. montevidensis* is the hardier species; it has rosy-colored flowers.

Oleander

Nerium oleander

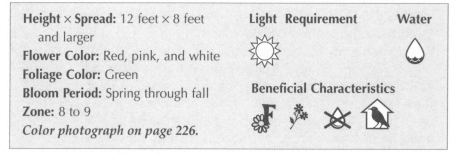

Height × Spread: 12 feet × 8 feet and larger	**Light Requirement** **Water**
Flower Color: Red, pink, and white	
Foliage Color: Green	
Bloom Period: Spring through fall	**Beneficial Characteristics**
Zone: 8 to 9	
Color photograph on page 226.	

Oleander is a love/hate plant, and I happen to love it. Let's be honest—it's taken some pretty good hits by the media, with reports that it is poisonous, but so are Ivy, Boxwood, and Jasmine, and they are in our yards. Others target it as a producer of allergens in massive amounts, and it does produce a heavy pollen that can't disperse as others do; its leaves have rough surfaces that trap other pollens, causing allergic reaction. Oleander comes in all colors, sizes, and shapes, from knee-high to 20 feet tall, with flowers in hot pink, deep-red, or pure-white, in single or double forms showing until frost, with fragrance sweeter than roses. The single-petal blooms shed to always look fresh, while double petals hang on to share their beauty. Oleanders have upright and pendulous branches that form mounds of dense growth in three years, and you can also trim them as trees; they make beautiful bouquets of flowers on a trunk. Leaves are thick, dark green, and leathery, with a prominent vein down the middle that traps pollen from other plants. (LM)

REGIONAL TIPS

Oleander is not hardy in northern Nevada and, at times, suffers from frost damage in the south.

WHEN, WHERE, AND HOW TO PLANT

Plant Oleanders any time of the year from containers. They prefer full sun to light shade—too much shade causes leggy canes and fewer flowers—and they love a well-drained soil. Dig a hole much wider than and as deep as the rootball. Position the Oleander at the same depth it was found in the container and add the prepared soil around the rootball, adding water as you fill the hole. Form a water basin at the edge of the rootball to thoroughly soak the rootball and surrounding soil. Then mulch over the root system with compost to protect the roots from summer and winter temperatures.

CARE AND MAINTENANCE

Oleanders do fine with an occasional deep irrigation, but the more you water them, the more they grow. You need to find a happy medium. They don't require much fertilizer; just feed them when feeding the lawn. They do need periodic pruning, but wear protective clothing because of the poisonous sap. Remove older canes to expose interior parts to sunlight; this will stimulate new wood and make a nicer looking bush. Don't prune Oleander into pompoms; it is unsightly and reduces flowering. And if it's ever damaged by frost, remove the damaged material down to the base. Aphids will leave honeydew on the leaves as a sign of their presence; direct a strong jet of water at them or use insecticidal soap or Neem oil for control. Remove Oleander galls (large growths) by snipping them off, but disinfect pruning shears after each cut.

LANDSCAPE MERIT

Oleander is a showy shrub. Use it as a hedge or space divider, or at the far end of the yard for color. You can plant it alone, but for more color, plant clusters of them; or you can train it into a single-trunked tree—but it requires maintenance forever! Use dwarf types to cover barren walls.

ADDITIONAL SPECIES, CULTIVARS, OR VARIETIES

There are many selections available, but consider these: 'Petite Pink' grows 5 to 6 feet high and as wide with pink flowers; 'Petite Salmon' is smaller, has salmon flowers, and is great as part of plant combinations, in clusters, or as a low hedge; 'Little Red' bears red flowers and grows to 4 feet tall; 'Casablanca' has single white flowers.

Oregon Grape

Mahonia aquifolium

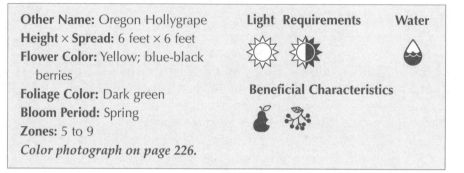

Other Name: Oregon Hollygrape
Height × Spread: 6 feet × 6 feet
Flower Color: Yellow; blue-black berries
Foliage Color: Dark green
Bloom Period: Spring
Zones: 5 to 9
Color photograph on page 226.

Light Requirements

Water

Beneficial Characteristics

If you are looking for a plant that looks something like a Holly and has interesting leaf color changes with the changes of the season, then Oregon Grape is the plant for you. The evergreen leaves are dark green and glossy, each toothed with a spine at the tip. The new leaves that come out in the spring have a dark-reddish hue. When the temperatures start to drop in the fall, the leaves change in color from green to purple. The winter coloration is better in colder regions of the state and also when the plants are in full sun. Oregon Grape has bright-yellow flowers in the spring, extending above the foliage, and flowering lasts for a few weeks. Later on, in August and September, the blue-black berries will have fully developed and you'll notice that birds love them. (DP)

REGIONAL TIPS

In the hot regions of southern Nevada, give Oregon Grape part shade or the leaves will burn. In the coldest regions of the northeastern part of the state, it is severely damaged when winter temperatures drop to 20 degrees below zero Fahrenheit.

WHEN, WHERE, AND HOW TO PLANT

Plant Oregon Grape any time during the growing season as a container-grown plant. You will have the best selection in the spring, however. They grow in full sun but better in part shade, and they thrive in an organic, well-drained, acid soil. But I have seen them doing well even in clayey, alkaline soils. It's best not to amend the soil to backfill around the rootball; the amended soil ends up holding the water and drainage is almost stopped. Dig the hole as deep as the rootball and three times as wide, take the plant from the container, place it in the hole, then backfill with soil and give it a good soaking.

CARE AND MAINTENANCE

Oregon Grape is not bothered by pests. It does get leaf scorch if it has been planted where it is exposed to hot winds. Water it once or twice a week during the summer, which should amount to 2 inches of water, and during dry winters give the soil a good soaking to a depth of 6 inches, once a month. It can be pruned after flowering, but you will remove some of the fruit in the process.

LANDSCAPE MERIT

This is an ideal plant for the north side of the house or for an eastern exposure. I know of a planting of them located on a southwest-facing slope in the Reno area, and they are surviving, but not really thriving, under that exposure. If you want something evergreen as a foundation planting, this is a good plant for the job. It does get to 6 feet tall, so don't plant it in front of windows. A grouping of them repeated in border plantings makes an attractive scene, particularly when they are in bloom, and again when the fruit ripens.

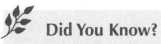

ADDITIONAL SPECIES, CULTIVARS OR VARIETIES

'Compacta' is a good variety when you need a plant 3 feet tall. 'Golden Abundance' has golden-yellow flowers and lots of berries for birds and jelly.

Did You Know?

Rabbits, squirrels, or deer do not bother this plant.

Pomegranate

Punica granatum

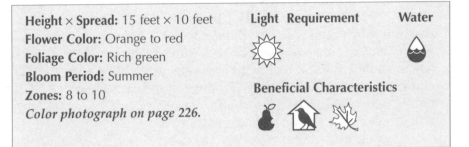

Height × Spread: 15 feet × 10 feet	**Light Requirement**	**Water**
Flower Color: Orange to red		
Foliage Color: Rich green		
Bloom Period: Summer		
Zones: 8 to 10	**Beneficial Characteristics**	
Color photograph on page 226.		

Pomegranate is a winner for your garden. Back in the early days of Las Vegas, everyone had Pomegranates in their yards. And why not? This beautiful shrub is easy to grow, is long-lived, withstands neglect, and most important, produces bushels of Pomegranates to eat fresh or make into jellies and jams. Pomegranate shrubs offer seasonal appeal all year. In the spring, beautiful bronze-colored leaves cover the bush, and later the leaves turn a bright, glossy green. Then bell-shaped red-to-orange carnationlike flowers 2 inches across adorn the shrub. Throughout the summer and into the fall, the 3-inch-diameter fruits glisten while they fill themselves with seeds. The fruit is very sweet and was a favorite of pioneers. As the fruit ripens, the fall leaves take on a bright-golden-yellow tint as the crimson ornaments weigh down the slender branches, creating a weeping effect. Finally, the deciduous plant undresses itself to reveal gnarled branches for the winter. (LM)

REGIONAL TIPS

I am sorry, northern Nevadans miss out on Pomegranates—they can't take the harsh winters. But it is a delightful bush for the south, and it yields bushels of fruit.

WHEN, WHERE, AND HOW TO PLANT

Plant from containers any time, but it's best planted in the fall to early spring. Give it full sun to produce flowers and fruit, and be sure the soil has good drainage. To plant, make the hole as deep as the rootball and three times as wide, working organic matter in with the onsite soil and tucking it around the rootball after placing it in the hole. Build a watering basin and give it a thorough soaking; water twice a week until you see new growth emerging. Mulch the plant to conserve water, control weeds, and cool the soil for better performance.

CARE AND MAINTENANCE

Water weekly until the temperatures get into the 90s, and then water twice a week. Pomegranates easily split as they mature, but gardeners who stop watering after Labor Day significantly reduce splitting fruit. Occasionally a deep freeze kills the plant to the ground. If this happens, clean away the dead material and it will come back. Around Christmas, prune out the interior growth to regenerate the plant, and work a cup of ammonium sulfate under each plant's canopy to increase fruit size. The leaf-footed plant bug is a problem for Pomegranate—the bug's snout makes holes in seeds which allows a fungus to enter. A little fruit beetle enters through these holes and we blame it, but the leaf-footed plant bug (with its leaf-shaped legs) is the one that started the problem. Apply Neem oil as a preventative in the early summer. Internal black rot may cause fruit decay; if this occurs, clean away all the old fruit.

LANDSCAPE MERIT

Little care is its trademark, and fruit is a bonus; we need to use it more. Dwarf varieties make an ornamental effect in the garden, and they do great in containers.

ADDITIONAL SPECIES, CULTIVARS, OR VARIETIES

'Wonderful' and 'Sweet' are the most popular fruiting varieties. 'Sweet' fruit is paler, less acidic, and milder in flavor. Dwarf Pomegranate, *Punica granatum* 'Nana', grows 3 feet high with tiny red fruits. 'Chico' is also a dwarfed compact shrub, generating double orange-red flowers.

Primrose Jasmine

Jasminum mesnyi

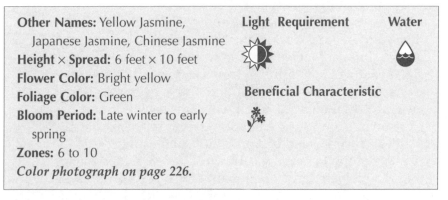

Other Names: Yellow Jasmine, Japanese Jasmine, Chinese Jasmine

Height × Spread: 6 feet × 10 feet

Flower Color: Bright yellow

Foliage Color: Green

Bloom Period: Late winter to early spring

Zones: 6 to 10

Color photograph on page 226.

Light Requirement

Water

Beneficial Characteristic

When I think of Jasmine, Star Jasmine and its super fragrance come to mind, but this isn't a true Jasmine. Primrose Jasmine flowers are unscented but long-lasting, and they bloom in southern Nevada while the rest of the country is buried under snow. This shrub is one of the first to display its blooms in the late winter and continue into spring. It's a sprawling shrub with branches that can reach out at least 10 feet, and if left to go natural, it grows stems as rapidly as water bubbling from a spring. It is easy to train as a wall plant or as a hedge. Not even those who love to shear plants can slow this shrub down, as it blooms profusely either way. The medium-green leaves along the square stems are coarse. Clear yellow single or double flowers are evenly spaced along the stems, resembling popcorn. But the beauty of these flowers is that no seeds follow, and maybe the unscented flowers do not attract the bees. I find it most useful for its cascading branches to cover things. (LM)

REGIONAL TIPS

Primrose Jasmine is not a shrub for northern Nevada because of the harsh winters, but we can enjoy it as a cascading shrub in southern Nevada.

WHEN, WHERE, AND HOW TO PLANT

Plant from containers any time, but it establishes quicker if planted in the fall. Primrose Jasmine does well in most soils but prefers an improved soil with good drainage. You will always have flowers if it's planted in full sun, but it will do fine with some shade. When planting, make the hole at least three times wider than and as deep as the rootball. Mix generous amounts of organic matter into the on-site soil, and because water is so important to establish it properly, let it run in the hole while backfilling, to settle the soil. Next, build a water basin around the plant and fill with water three times a week until you see new growth coming out. Add mulch so you won't have to water as often.

CARE AND MAINTENANCE

Water twice weekly until the temperatures get into the 90s, and then switch to three waterings a week to keep the shrub looking sharp. Fertilize with a cup of ammonium sulfate worked into the soil under each bush around Valentine's, Memorial, and Labor Days, then irrigate to move nutrients to roots. Alkaline soils trigger the yellowing of the leaves, so add iron chelates. If left unpruned it becomes rank, and you can cut it back severely to rejuvenate the plant. Occasionally thin it after bloom to increase flowering next year, or shear anytime following flowering for formal hedging. If you see a sticky honeydew on the leaves, aphids have come. If you see dry, dusty leaves down in the plant, spider mites are present. Wash them off with a strong jet of water or use insecticidal soap, Neem, or Malathion to control.

LANDSCAPE MERIT

Use Primrose Jasmine as a background, foundation, specimen, low formal hedge, soil stabilizer, or cascader over walls or planters, or train it on trellises, walls, or arbors. A bold plant with loads of spring color, it looks good just left alone.

ADDITIONAL SPECIES, CULTIVARS, OR VARIETIES

J. humile is another yellow-flowering Jasmine deserving mention. An evergreen that grows to 6 feet or more, it has single flowers that are smaller but very fragrant. *J. grandiflorum* is also commonly planted, featuring clusters of white, fragrant, tubular flowers.

Pyracantha

Pyracantha coccinea

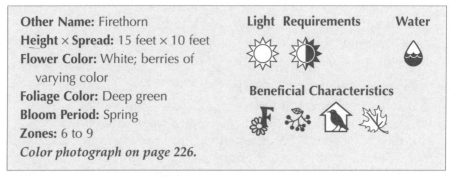

Other Name: Firethorn
Height × Spread: 15 feet × 10 feet
Flower Color: White; berries of
  varying color
Foliage Color: Deep green
Bloom Period: Spring
Zones: 6 to 9
Color photograph on page 226.

Light Requirements

Water

Beneficial Characteristics

Pyracantha flowers delight gardeners in spring and berries thrill the birds in the winter. The flowers are white, but you have your choice of red, orange, or yellow clusters of pea-sized berries. This evergreen has narrow, oval, dark, glossy-green leaves that densely cloak the stiff, thorny, arching stems. The older plants get too large for the small spaces they were planted in, thus they require frequent pruning. To keep them from getting rangy, start the training process when they're young and have flexible branches. If you grow Pyracantha up a wall, attach the wires to the building before planting. Plants can reach over 20 feet tall and are very pretty in the fall. Once established, Pyracantha is remarkably tough, withstanding drought, hot winds, poor soil, and a beating sun. (LM)

REGIONAL TIPS

Cultivars grown in the north may freeze down, but they will rapidly regrow in the spring. But because the flowers bear on last year's growth, there will be no wood for them to bloom on. If the north experiences a warm winter, then flowers will appear.

WHEN, WHERE, AND HOW TO PLANT

Set plants in April and May in the cold zones and anytime in the south. Pyracanthas desire full sun to partial shade, in soils that will drain. Make a hole three to five times the rootball's diameter, but only to the depth of the rootball. Incorporate organic matter in the backfill soil and refill, using water to settle the soil. Build a water basin, and soak the rootball and surrounding area. During establishment, water three times a week, and mulch to conserve water and cool the soil during the heat.

CARE AND MAINTENANCE

After establishment, continue watering twice a week. As the temperatures climb over the 90-degree-Fahrenheit mark, water three times a week. If leaves begin turning yellow, it is an indication you are watering too much; cut the water back and add some iron chelates. Some berries will hang on until birds eat them or until they decay, so to get rid of them, wash off the remaining berries with a jet of water. Wear gloves to prune this thorny plant; if a thorn sticks you, it gives meaning to the name Firethorn. Prune new growth before Pyracantha sets thorns, and prune stems back after flowering to prevent the spread of fireblight, a bacterial disease occurring during wet weather. Woolly aphids attack the base of the plant and often go unnoticed. Wash them off or spray them with Neem oil. If you see brownish leaves down in the lower part of the plant, it's spider mites. Hose them off or use insecticidal soap to control.

LANDSCAPE MERIT

Pyracantha is grown as espaliers on fences or walls, and as hedges. Long, sharp thorns make them good choices for controlling traffic, for security, and for screening.

ADDITIONAL SPECIES, CULTIVARS, OR VARIETIES

'Harlequin' has pinkish-toned leaves and orange-red berries; 'Mohave' produces big orange-red berries, hanging on for a while; 'Orange Glow' covers itself with orange to orange-red berries; 'Red Elf' produces bright-red berries on small plants; 'Ruby Mound' has long, arching branches dressed with bright-red berries; 'Teton' has yellow-orange berries; 'Tiny Tim' has small leaves, few thorns, and red berries; and 'Watereri' is 8 feet tall and wide, with long-lasting bright-red berries.

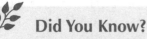 **Did You Know?**

If you have problems with dogs and cats entering your yard, plant a Pyracantha hedge to keep them out.

Red Clusterberry Cotoneaster

Cotoneaster lacteus

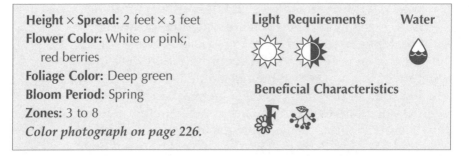

Height × Spread: 2 feet × 3 feet
Flower Color: White or pink;
  red berries
Foliage Color: Deep green
Bloom Period: Spring
Zones: 3 to 8
Color photograph on page 226.

Light Requirements   **Water**

Beneficial Characteristics

Cotoneaster is a strong group of shrubs that includes well over fifty species in all shapes and sizes. They are on my list of carefree plants, with Red Clusterberry being one of my favorites. It fits well as a ground cover, as a medium-to-large shrub, and as a small tree. I was raised around springs and loved to watch water billow out into the stream; Red Clusterberry Cotoneaster reminds me of those billowing springs, continually pushing out new growth from the center of each plant, arching out above the plant's profile and jumping up and down with the summer breezes. Eventually, small white to light pink flowers cluster tightly with a lacy look against the dark-green foliage and cover the branches. Bright-red, fleshy berries color the plant into the fall, weighing the arching limbs down even more. All these qualities add up to a rather elegant plant. (LM)

REGIONAL TIPS

Northern Nevada gardeners will want to plant Cotoneaster in the spring when the soils are warming up. The roots of shrubs planted in the fall in southern Nevada continue to grow throughout the winter, giving the plants a good start well into the next season.

WHEN, WHERE AND HOW TO PLANT

Plant these toughies any time in southern Nevada, but they do better when planted in the fall. (In northern Nevada, plant in the spring.) Red Clusterberry Cotoneaster will tolerate poor soil; it prefers well-drained soil in full sun, but it'll do okay in some shade. Plant it in a hole three to five times wider than and as deep as the rootball, and enrich the on-site soil with copious amounts of organic matter. Cotoneasters have a tendency to become potbound, so cut apart the circling roots before planting. Backfill the hole with an amended soil and add water to settle the soil around the rootball. Make a water basin outside the rooted area and fill it thrice weekly until established.

Care and Maintenance
To sustain Cotoneasters, water twice weekly throughout the summer, and as it cools, spread the waterings out to monthly waterings through winter. Add a layer of mulch to extend the plant's water until the Cotoneaster's canopy shades the ground beneath it. Feed your shrubs on Valentine's, Memorial, and Labor Days with an all-purpose fertilizer. Due to its arching, branching habit, selectively prune to keep the plant within its profile—but never just chop this species back; it takes away from its beauty. Cotoneaster is susceptible to fireblight, especially when it rains and the plant is in bloom. With fireblight, the infected part of the branch looks burnt, so cut back into healthy wood to eliminate the disease. (Disinfect the pruning shears with alcohol to avoid spreading the bacteria.) Planting it in full sun is the best control for this.

Landscape Merit
Use Red Clusterberry Cotoneasters as fillers, to contrast between flowering and deciduous plants, in rock gardens, for erosion control, and to create a cascading effect over rocks and into swimming pools.

Additional Species, Cultivars, or Varieties
Another evergreen Cotoneaster I like is *C. congestus*, or Pyrenees Cotoneaster. *C. lacteus* or *C. parneyi* and *C. microphyllus*, or Rockspray Cotoneaster, are notable for colorful fruit that is long-lasting if the birds don't get it. *C. horizontalis*, or Rock Cotoneaster, is deciduous and is especially attractive in form and branching pattern.

Red-Osier Dogwood

Cornus sericea

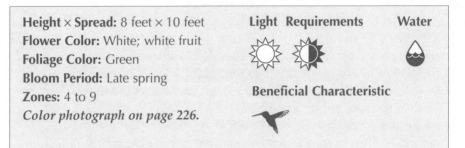

Height × Spread: 8 feet × 10 feet
Flower Color: White; white fruit
Foliage Color: Green
Bloom Period: Late spring
Zones: 4 to 9
Color photograph on page 226.

Light Requirements

Water

Beneficial Characteristic

This is really an interesting plant in the late winter and spring before the leaves emerge, because of its bright red twigs. They are brightest just as they are coming out of winter dormancy. After the leaves come out, the twig color fades, and leaves gain their coarse texture, with very prominent veins. They emerge as yellow-green with a tinge of red and mature to green in the summer, and in the fall they start out yellow, changing to orange and then to dark red. The flowers are white and develop on cymes that look like small, flat plates of flowers, and white fruit ripens in late summer. Red-Osier Dogwood will spread slowly in the garden from rhizomatous roots. Twigs root very easily when they touch the soil. (DP)

REGIONAL TIPS

Red-Osier Dogwood is best adapted to the cooler regions of Nevada and is particularly adapted to the mountainous regions where temperatures often dip to 20 degrees below zero Fahrenheit or lower. It doesn't grow very well in the zone 7 and 8 areas of the state unless it gets daily watering to keep the soil moist.

WHEN, WHERE, AND HOW TO PLANT

A good time to plant Red-Osier Dogwood is in the fall, but the best selection is in the spring. Red-Osier Dogwood is available as a bareroot plant in the late winter and early spring, and as a container plant as well. It grows in full sun or part shade and seems to thrive in the clayey soils of Nevada. If you are planting it as a bare-root plant, dig the hole as deep as the downward length of the roots and three times as wide so the roots can spread out without touching the sides of the hole. Build a cone of soil in the bottom of the hole and spread the roots over the cone. If you lay a shovel handle on the ground across the hole, the crown of the plant (the spot where the stem becomes roots) should be at the handle. If the cone is too low or too high, adjust accordingly. Backfill with unamended soil, and soak with water as you fill the hole. If it is purchased as a container plant, dig the hole the depth of the rootball and three times as wide, remove the container, place the rootball in the hole, and backfill. Don't forget to give it a good soaking.

CARE AND MAINTENANCE

Red-Osier Dogwood is a very carefree plant to have in the garden. It needs 1 inch of water twice a week and annual pruning to keep it in bounds. In order to maintain its natural shape, be careful not to shear it. Fertilize in the spring with a complete fertilizer, according to directions.

LANDSCAPE MERIT

Red-Osier Dogwood is very good for planting in open areas where it will have room to spread. Because of its suckering habit and the ability of the twigs to root easily, it makes an excellent shrub for banks. It's a great plant for border plantings and adds a great contrast in both twig color and leaf texture.

ADDITIONAL SPECIES, CULTIVARS, OR VARIETIES

'Flaviramea' has greenish-yellow twigs; 'Nitida' has green twigs.

Red Yucca

Hesperaloe parviflora

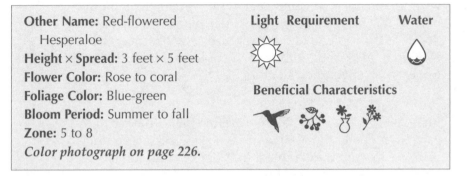

Other Name: Red-flowered
  Hesperaloe
Height × Spread: 3 feet × 5 feet
Flower Color: Rose to coral
Foliage Color: Blue-green
Bloom Period: Summer to fall
Zone: 5 to 8
Color photograph on page 226.

Light Requirement

Water

Beneficial Characteristics

My introduction to Red Yucca was in a plant identification class. The instructor said we were about to meet his favorite desert plant. One look and I said, "Yuk!" But over the years I've grown to love it. Its towering, flowering spikes reach up to 4 feet above the whorl of foliage. This makes it easy to examine the interior of the bell-shaped rose-to-coral flowers, and I find the creamy-white centers go unnoticed if not for the height. Each flower is about an inch long and wide at the face and somewhat egg-shaped and drooping. Red Yucca's show of color generally begins in late April and lasts through August, and the hummingbirds have a heyday fussing in the blooms. Large seedpods follow, but even when it's not in bloom, Red Yucca's narrow, straplike, gray-green fleshy leaves with numerous fibrous threads along the edges (called "old man whiskers") create a feeling of command in gardens, rock gardens, containers, and planters. The leaves are 2 to 4 feet long and rolled and curved, making them distinctly different from the flat leaves of true Yuccas. Plants slowly enlarge outward to form an irregular cluster of foliage 3 to 4 feet wide. You don't see the stem, simply the clustering of leaves whorled around the crown. (LM)

REGIONAL TIPS
This one tolerates temperatures to 15 degrees Fahrenheit. If planted in Zone 5 or lower, treat it as an annual.

WHEN, WHERE, AND HOW TO PLANT
Plant all year from containers, or divide old clumps in late winter to early spring and replant. Plant in full sun; it is not content with shade from any direction, and Red Yucca's flower stalks lean heavily

away from the shaded area. It is content in any soil as long as it has good drainage. Thoroughly loosen the soil at least three times wider than its container to get the most out of this species. Mix some organic matter into the on-site soil, then tuck it around the rootball, and build a water basin around it to contain the water during irrigations. Water this desert beauty weekly until established.

CARE AND MAINTENANCE

Red Yucca is a plant that can get by on very little water, but to put on the show of flowers we expect, it needs weekly waterings until it gets really hot. At this point, go to twice-a-week waterings. It is a tough plant and can get by on very little fertilizer, but to generate more of a show of color, add a cup of ammonium sulfate in the early spring, summer, and fall. After it finishes flowering, remove the old stalks and dead leaves. Plants are easy to divide as clumps spread; dig up the plant and pull it apart, making clean cuts, and allow roots of transplants to dry for a short time in a shaded area to "seal" before replanting.

LANDSCAPE MERIT

Red Yucca brings a desert effect to the landscape and combines well with Palms and Yuccas. It makes a good transitional plant in desert or rock gardens and fits well in containers. Hummingbirds love the flowers.

ADDITIONAL SPECIES, CULTIVARS, OR VARIETIES

H. engelmannii is a hardier form for the northern zones. A light-yellow flowering selection called the Yellow Yucca has recently become available to make an excellent contrast to the Red Yucca.

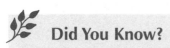 **Did You Know?**

Red Yucca is really a member of the Cactus family, but it has the appearance of a shrub as it matures. It plays an important role in our landscapes as an accent plant.

St. Johnswort

Hypericum calycinum

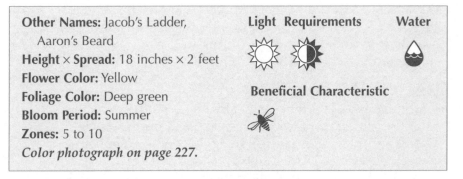

Other Names: Jacob's Ladder, Aaron's Beard	**Light Requirements**	**Water**
Height × Spread: 18 inches × 2 feet		
Flower Color: Yellow		
Foliage Color: Deep green	**Beneficial Characteristic**	
Bloom Period: Summer		
Zones: 5 to 10		
Color photograph on page 227.		

The flowers of St. Johnswort are bright yellow, and I mean really bright. They get to over 3 inches in diameter with five petals and numerous stamens that stick out from the centers of the blooms like pincushions. They bloom in clusters at the end of the new growth, flowering from June through August and even into the fall. The plant becomes a solid yellow mat when in full bloom. St. Johnswort grows to 18 inches high at the most and will spread out to over 2 feet, completely covering the ground. The foliage is dark green and evergreen where winters are mild. It is a spreading plant that should be planted where it has lots of room to grow or can be contained, rapidly growing by underground roots. (DP)

REGIONAL TIPS

St. Johnswort does well in most regions of Nevada with the exception of the coldest. It generally doesn't survive when the temperatures go lower than 20 degrees below zero Fahrenheit.

WHEN, WHERE, AND HOW TO PLANT

Plant St. Johnswort any time during the growing season, but spring is preferable, when nursery selections are best. It grows equally as well in full sun or part shade, is easy to grow, and though it grows best in a well-drained soil, clayey soils don't appear to slow it down. (It grows in poor, sandy soil as well.) St. Johnswort is available in containers, is easy to transplant to the garden, and also roots very easily from cuttings and by transplanting the runners. Plant them about 18 inches apart, dig the holes the depth of the rootballs and two to three times as wide, place the plants in the holes, cover the rootballs with soil, and give them a good soaking.

SHRUBS

CARE AND MAINTENANCE

St. Johnswort doesn't require much fertilizer, but give it some in the spring after pruning. The easiest way is to use a water-soluble fertilizer mixed according to directions. Irrigate twice a week with 1 inch of water. It will usually have at least some winterkill, so the best thing to do in the early spring is to mow it to get rid of all the dead stuff and rejuvenate the plant as well. You don't have to worry about cutting off the flower buds when you mow, because flowers develop on the new growth. St. Johnswort does have one problem: it will spread into the lawn if you don't have a barrier at least 6 inches deep, between the grass and the bed.

LANDSCAPE MERIT

This is one of the few plants that will grow very well under trees and shrubs, making it an excellent ground cover. It is right at home in the rock garden and covers the rocks, making them blend into the landscape.

ADDITIONAL SPECIES, CULTIVARS, OR VARIETIES

There are some other species that have landscape value, one of which is Goldflower, *Hypericum* × 'Moseranum', a small shrub growing to a height of 3 feet by 3 feet.

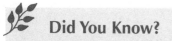

Did You Know?

Yes, this is in the same genus as the herb used for mental health, and no, you should not try to mix up your own concoction.

Scotch Broom

Cytisus scoparius

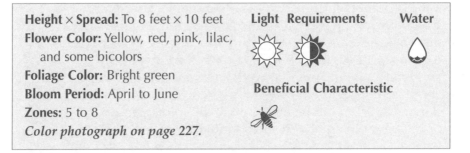

Height × Spread: To 8 feet × 10 feet
Flower Color: Yellow, red, pink, lilac, and some bicolors
Foliage Color: Bright green
Bloom Period: April to June
Zones: 5 to 8
Color photograph on page 227.

Light Requirements

Water

Beneficial Characteristic

Scotch Broom is a very interesting plant because of its leaves and stems. The leaves are sparse, with the leaf shape typical of plants in the pea family. Leaves are trifoliate, meaning they have three lobes. The leaves are bright green, but what is interesting is that the stems are, too—and the stems are what give the plant its name. (By the way, those green stems produce food for the plant just like the leaves.) The shape of the plant is very broad and rounded, and it gets to be a large shrub that grows to 8 feet high, with some dwarf types half that size. The flowers are typical pea flowers, most commonly bright yellow, an inch in diameter, and are produced on stems at least two years old. Some of the varieties have other color combinations that are all bicolor. If you want something with reddish-bronze and yellow flowers, look for the old cultivar called 'Andreanus'. Another more common cultivar is 'Burkwoodii', with a similar-colored bloom. 'Lilac Time' has deep red-purple flowers and it is also a dwarf. The fruit of Scotch Broom is a pea pod that throws its seed when ripe. (DP)

REGIONAL TIPS

Scotch Broom is not very well adapted to the high-elevation areas such as Ely because they are not hardy to 20 degrees below zero Fahrenheit.

WHEN, WHERE, AND HOW TO PLANT

Plant Scotch Broom from containers only; I have not seen any bare root or even balled-and-burlapped. It can be planted any time of year when the ground isn't frozen, but you will have better success and a better selection of plants in the spring. It is a plant that will grow almost anywhere, tolerates poor, dry soils, and thrives in full sun. When planting Scotch Broom, dig the hole as deep as the rootball and about three times as wide. It is best not to use a modified soil for the backfill to cover the roots— if the backfill soil drains better than the native, clayey soil, the roots can become waterlogged and the plant dies. After planting, give it a good soaking.

CARE AND MAINTENANCE

Scotch Broom really thrives on neglect, and it will survive better if it's not overwatered. Give it 1 inch of water weekly, and wait until the shrub has become established before fertilizing. It doesn't have any insect pests, but it does often die out for what seems like no reason; there is a reason, and it's soggy soils. It will tolerate pruning, but keep it to a minimum to maintain its natural shape.

LANDSCAPE MERIT

Use Scotch Broom in shrub beds and on slopes for erosion control. Because of its bright colors it is a very good accent plant. The fine texture of the stems provides a good contrast when planted with medium- and coarse-textured plants.

ADDITIONAL SPECIES, CULTIVARS, OR VARIETIES

An interesting species of *Cytisus* is *C. decumbens*, growing to only 6 inches high and with brilliant yellow flowers. 'Moonlight' is a cultivar of *C. scoparius* that is low growing with pale yellow blooms that completely cover the plant.

🌿 Did You Know?

Scotch Broom has naturalized itself in some of the milder areas of the West and has become a weed and a fire hazard. In wildfire-prone areas it would be best not to plant it next to the house.

Shiny Xylosma

Xylosma congestum

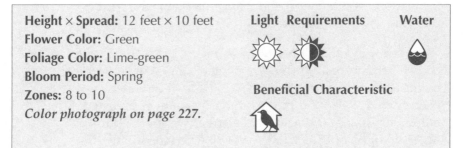

	Light Requirements	Water
Height × Spread: 12 feet × 10 feet		
Flower Color: Green		
Foliage Color: Lime-green		
Bloom Period: Spring		
Zones: 8 to 10	**Beneficial Characteristic**	
Color photograph on page 227.		

It is one of the choice all-purpose landscape plants throughout the Southwest. Southern Nevada needs to use Shiny Xylosma more. It always looks nice, is easy to grow, and requires very little care. I love this evergreen for its new shiny-bronze leaves as they unfold, and throughout the summer the shiny light-green foliage remains fresh-looking. It grows fast, reaching up to about 8 feet high; you can train it into a small tree or espalier it along walls, but it shows off best as a shrub. It is easily trained to screen an ugly situation or tie down the soil of an unsightly slope. It develops characteristic zigzag main stems and side branches that push out to become graceful, arching, even a bit droopy. You'll love it because it tolerates our soils and accepts the heat and wind, but you certainly won't plant it for its flowers; they are green and seldom noticed, making only allergy sufferers happy. I wish nurseries knew how to show it off better—it looks spindly in appearance, but give it a chance and you'll be bragging about it as it matures. (LM)

REGIONAL TIPS

Oh, what you northerners are missing when you can't grow this desert wonder, with its glossy leaves and carefree growth habit. Shiny Xylosma loves southern Nevada's hot climate and has become a real workhorse in our landscapes.

WHEN, WHERE, AND HOW TO PLANT

Plant from containers any time, but it's best in spring. Shiny Xylosma prefers an open, organic soil and tolerates alkaline conditions. It must have good drainage, or expect the plant to suffer from iron chlorosis. To get the most out of this beauty, plant it in full sun; it will take some shade but it becomes leggy. Dig a hole at least three to five times as wide and as deep as the rootball, mix in generous amounts of organic matter with the on-site soil, and add water to settle the soil around the rootball as you plant. Build a basin out beyond the rootball to ensure a thorough soaking of the roots and surrounding soil.

CARE AND MAINTENANCE

Shiny Xylosma tolerates drought but likes twice-weekly deep irrigations when the temperatures jump into the 90s. If you use drip emitters, run them 2 hours each time. It can get by without fertilizer, but a cupful of ammonium sulfate worked under each plant prior to a watering will add some lushness. To put a little more spring green in the leaves, add chelated iron. This carefree shrub can get by with very little care, but to keep it compact and full, clip back any extending branches that reach out. If you see dry, dusty, unthrifty leaves, spider mites have built up on the plant. Direct a jet of water or use insecticidal soap or Neem oil to control them.

LANDSCAPE MERIT

Shiny Xylosma is a first-rate plant as a shrub, small tree, or hedge, and it looks nice up close or at a distance, clipped or unclipped. As a single- or multiple-trunked tree, it develops a lovely canopy for the patio and because of its cleanliness, it fits well around swimming pools. Some plants are spiny, so allow some room if you plant it near pools or walkways.

ADDITIONAL SPECIES, CULTIVARS, OR VARIETIES

A dwarf selection, 'Compacta', grows 4 to 6 feet high and has a tighter branching habit; it's best used for low hedges, borders, or screens.

Snowberry

Symphoricarpos albus

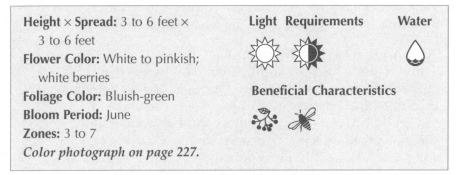

Height × Spread: 3 to 6 feet × 3 to 6 feet	Light Requirements	Water
Flower Color: White to pinkish; white berries		
Foliage Color: Bluish-green	**Beneficial Characteristics**	
Bloom Period: June		
Zones: 3 to 7		
Color photograph on page 227.		

Snowberry is a unique shrub that flowers in June and forms white berries in the fall that last into winter. The elliptic-oblong leaves are opposite and simple, round on the shoots, and bluish-green. It is a bushy shrub with numerous shoots, fine and dense. The flowers are small, white, and tinged with pink but they are not very showy. The fruit, on the other hand, is a large white berry maturing in the fall. Very few shrubs have white fruit, so Snowberry makes quit a contrast in the garden, growing to around 6 feet tall and about as wide. Snowberries are tougher than they look, for they are very tolerant of heat, cold, wind, and drought. They are deciduous, which means they lose their leaves in the fall. (DP)

REGIONAL TIPS

This is a good plant for northern Nevada and will survive the coldest winters Ely ever saw. It will not do well in southern Nevada because of the dry heat.

WHEN, WHERE, AND HOW TO PLANT

Snowberries are often sold as bare-root plants in the late winter and early spring. If you purchase them as bare-root shrubs, transplant them into the garden before they break dormancy. By the way, some stores place their bare-root plants indoors where it is warm, and that's not good for them. Snowberries are also available as container plants; they can be planted any time during the growing season and are easy to transplant. They grow very well under large trees and other shrubs, thriving in part shade as well as full sun, and growing best in a well-drained soil (but they aren't fussy). Dig the hole as deep as the rootball and about three times as wide. Remove the container and place the plant in the hole, backfilling with the same soil to assure better drainage. After planting, give it a good soaking by letting the water run until it forms a puddle. Cuttings are easy to root from softwood taken in June, July, or August.

CARE AND MAINTENANCE

Snowberry only needs to be watered once a week with 2 inches at a time. Fertilize it once in the early spring if you want to encourage faster growth, using a water-soluble fertilizer according to directions. It is a tidy plant, but it can be sheared to thicken it up, and you need to prune out any dead twigs in the spring. It does form suckers, which need to be removed. Snowberries sometimes get aphids; wash them off with water.

LANDSCAPE MERIT

A favored spot for planting Snowberries is near evergreens. They form a nice contrast, with the white berries against the evergreen conifers. They are used for erosion control on banks and as a grouping of plants in shrub borders.

ADDITIONAL SPECIES, CULTIVARS, OR VARIETIES

A tall, broad cultivar is 'Laevigatus', with large and abundant fruit. *S. albus* 'Variegatus' has round leaves edged with white to match the white berries. An interesting relative of Snowberry is Indian Currant, sometimes known as Coralberry. It is *S. orbiculatus* and grows to a little over 2 feet high and 4 feet wide, with magenta-pink fruit instead of white. *S. mollis* is a creeping Snowberry that has low, arching branches that root when they touch the ground.

Spirea

Spiraea species

Height × Spread: 2 to 10 feet × 5 to 12 feet
Flower Color: White, pink, and red
Foliage Color: Green, some maroon-tipped
Bloom Period: Spring, summer, some to fall
Zones: 3 to 9
Color photograph on page 227.

Light Requirements

Water

Beneficial Characteristic

Spireas are a neat group of deciduous shrubs. They are both large and small; they have pink, red, and white flowers, and some have lime foliage while most others are green. *S. japonica* 'Goldflame' has bronze-red young leaves that later turn to bright yellow, then green, and in the fall they are orange, red, and yellow. They grow in the full sun or part shade. The texture of all Spireas is medium to fine, and all have a delicate appearance, with lance-shaped leaves ranging from 1 inch to over 2 inches long. We also have a native Spirea in the Sierra Nevada that is very similar to 'Alpina', a low-growing variety. (DP)

REGIONAL TIPS

Spireas are adapted to all regions of the state. In the mountainous, cooler parts, it is one of the most reliable flowering shrubs.

WHEN, WHERE, AND HOW TO PLANT

Plant Spirea any time during the growing season. In the early spring (when nurseries will have best selection), they are often sold as bare-root plants, and they need to be planted before they start to sprout. Spirea grows best in well-drained soil but seems to tolerate the clayey soil of Nevada fairly well. There is no need to amend the soil when planting this shrub, and to do so could cause drainage problems. Most are purchased as container plants, so remove the container before your put the rootball in a hole dug as deep as the rootball and about three times as wide. Backfill using the soil you removed from the hole. Water it in well by letting the water run until it puddles.

CARE AND MAINTENANCE

Spireas are generally easy to maintain. Water them once or twice a week and during the hottest part of the summer, water at least 2 inches a week. Use a water-soluble fertilizer once in the spring according to directions. Prune Spireas after they flower to maintain their natural shapes. There are not any disease or insect pests that will kill them, but they do get aphids; if you spot them early enough, the aphids can be washed off with repeated stiff sprays of water.

LANDSCAPE MERIT

Use this fast-growing shrub anywhere in the garden. The small ones are excellent as foundation plantings or as part of a shrub border, and taller ones like 'Vanhouttei' Spirea grow to 8 feet tall, so use them at the back of the shrub bed or as a natural hedge. It can also be used as a specimen, for it looks like a cascade of white flowers when it blooms.

ADDITIONAL SPECIES, CULTIVARS, OR VARIETIES

Spiraea japonica is a nice, compact little shrub that grows to 4 feet high by 4 feet wide and has red clusters of flowers. If you really need something small, try 'Little Princess' that only grows to 20 inches high and 3 feet wide, with pink flowers in the summer. Other varieties to try include 'Froeblii' with rose red flowers; 'Shirobana' with white, pink, and red flowers all on the same plant; and 'Crispa', with twisted leaves and pink flowers.

Did You Know?

If you live where squirrels and rabbits are a problem, know that Spirea is not bothered by these critters.

Strawberry Bush

Arbutus unedo 'Compacta'

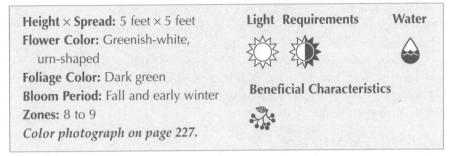

Height × Spread: 5 feet × 5 feet
Flower Color: Greenish-white,
   urn-shaped
Foliage Color: Dark green
Bloom Period: Fall and early winter
Zones: 8 to 9
Color photograph on page 227.

Light Requirements

Water

Beneficial Characteristics

Strawberry Bush makes a good conversation plant, and while you're standing around it talking, let folks eat some berries. They are not exactly strawberries; they're kind of mealy, and lack strawberry's flavor, but I still find myself nibbling on them. (Fruit litter can be a problem if you or the birds don't eat them.) The bush is a dense, slow-growing, broadleaf evergreen that is attractive all year. In the fall and early winter come the greenish-white, upside-down, urn-shaped clusters of flowers, which are often overlooked because they overlap with the strawberry-like fruit. The dark-green leathery leaves, glistening slightly, act as a backdrop for the fruit. If you look closely, you will see the leaves hang on red stems; poke your head deeper into the bush and find bark that peels to expose reddish new bark. As the branches age, they become gnarled and very picturesque. (LM)

REGIONAL TIPS

How sad. Here is a beautiful bush that flowers throughout the winter and produces strawberrylike fruit through the summer, but grows only in southern Nevada. Strawberry Bush will not tolerate northern Nevada's harsh winters.

WHEN, WHERE, AND HOW TO PLANT

Plant this shrub any time from containers, but it's best to establish it in the fall. It performs best when exposed to morning sun and after-noon shade, in a well-drained soil free of alkali. To plant the shrub, open up a hole three times wider than and as deep as the rootball. Mix some organic matter in the on-site soil, place the plant, and refill with the prepared soil along with water to soak the surrounding soil and rootball. Build a water basin over the rooted area and fill with water three times a week until established. To cut back on watering, add mulch under the canopy of the bush.

CARE AND MAINTENANCE

With our hot, dry days of summer, watering is important. Water twice weekly until it gets above 90 degrees Fahrenheit, and then switch to thrice-weekly waterings. It is not a big eater, but place a cupful of ammonium sulfate under the shrub around Valentine's Day, Memorial Day, and again on Labor Day and water in. Because the leathery leaves are part of its appeal, shearing it very much detracts from its beauty, so avoid the urge. Use handpruners to remove interior dead wood as needed in winter. If you find a sticky honeydew substance on your plant, it is a good indication of aphids. Wash them off with a strong jet of water or use insecticidal soap or Neem oil. If you see leaf miners boring into the leaves, use a systemic pesticide for control.

LANDSCAPE MERIT

Strawberry Bush is rich in ornamental character, works well in small gardens, and is easy to control in shape and size. It's suitable for lawn situations, screens, and background plantings, is decorative in the winter, and does well in containers.

ADDITIONAL SPECIES, CULTIVARS, OR VARIETIES

A. unedo, or Strawberry Tree, is a very handsome, small tree. *A. unedo* 'Elfin King', is a compact bush that is more dwarf than the 'Compacta'. New growth on twigs and buds exhibits a reddish cast and produces white flowers in the early spring. *A. unedo* 'Oktoberfest' gets about 8 feet tall with pink flowers.

Did You Know?

Arbutus *is a genus of evergreen shrubs or small trees that is characterized by a many-seeded berry.*

Sugar Bush

Rhus ovata

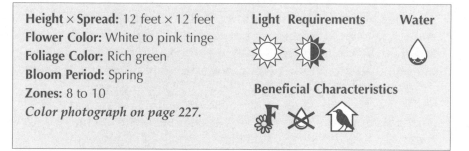

Height × Spread: 12 feet × 12 feet
Flower Color: White to pink tinge
Foliage Color: Rich green
Bloom Period: Spring
Zones: 8 to 10
Color photograph on page 227.

Light Requirements

Water

Beneficial Characteristics

What a shame—here is one of the toughest plants in our arsenal, but nurseries have a difficult time producing it. It is perhaps the most carefree plant in our gallery of plants. Contact your nursery and tell them you want *Rhus ovata,* and they will order it for you. Make sure it has enough space when you plant it and it will become your forget-me-plant. What is so interesting about this plant is that it stays in perfect shape, nary a branch extending out beyond its silhouette. It is a decorative, slow-growing plant with extremely good drought tolerance and still looks well watered with crisp, leathery, bright and deep-green foliage. Leaves get up to 3 inches long and curve upwards, partially folded; they have a vanilla fragrance. They provide a sturdy backdrop to the l-inch clusters of dense spikes of red buds giving rise to white-pinkish flowers and, soon after, red, hairy fruit. As you might guess from the name, the secretion from the fruit is sweet. This dense evergreen shrub rises to 12 feet high with an equal spread. It is well suited as a background or screening plant and really puts on a show when mass planted. (LM)

REGIONAL TIPS

This is a handsome, carefree shrub for southern Nevada. It is sensitive to frost conditions and will not take the harsh winters in the north.

WHEN, WHERE, AND HOW TO PLANT

Plant any time, but the best time is in the spring. It will tolerate poor soils with good drainage. It does best in full sun but will do okay in filtered shade. Open up the soil at least three times wider than and as deep as the rootball. Incorporate some organic matter in with the on-site soil to fold in and around the rootball, and add water as you finish filling the hole. Add a mulch covering to cool the soil for better root development throughout the summer. Give the plant a good, deep soaking weekly until established.

CARE AND MAINTENANCE

Sugar Bush prefers deep irrigations twice monthly in the summer until it gets really hot, and then it needs weekly waterings. Watering it once through the winter will suffice unless it is dry and windy, thus calling for more water. Because of its form, it rarely needs pruning or training—by all means, keep those who like to shear plants away from it or it will lose its natural beauty; only remove dead twigs. It is not a big feeder, but a cup of ammonium sulfate prior to irrigation in the early spring will add luster to the bush. This toughie does not bring any pests to the garden.

LANDSCAPE MERIT

Sugar Bush provides a distinct and refreshing contrast to other species and is very decorative as a specimen or a wide screen, or around a swimming pool.

ADDITIONAL SPECIES, CULTIVARS, OR VARIETIES

Rhus species would not be complete without mentioning *R. microphylla* and *R. virens.* Both of these shrubby Sumacs are native to Southwestern deserts, do well with a little or no supplemental irrigation, and are much like *R. ovata* in character. *R. microphylla* is deciduous and *R. virens* is ever-green. Leaves are green with a rich, waxy appearance, and cultural requirements are about the same as well. At the Desert Demonstration Gardens we grow *R. capallina* (Shining Sumac), *R. glabra* (Smooth Sumac), *R. typhina* (Staghorn Sumac), and the native *R. trilobata* (Squawbush) for fall color. All are deciduous.

Texas Sage

Leucophyllum frutescens

Other Names: Texas Ranger,
   Cenizo, Barometer Plant
Height × Spread: 5 feet × 5 feet
Flower Color: Rose-purple
Foliage Color: Gray-green
Zones: 6 to 9
Color photograph on page 227.

Light Requirement

Water

Beneficial Characteristics

If it's a reliable plant you're looking for, choose Texas Sage. Since the floodgates opened on the demand for low-water-use plants, we now have a wide range of Texas Sages. Researchers at Texas A & M found Sages that didn't require much pruning, had unusual flower and leaf colors—and the list continues to grow. These plants go almost unnoticed in the landscape and are happy with their surroundings, but when it rains they explode with vibrant, bell-shaped flowers. It's a scene hard to forget. The phone lines light up with folks wanting to know about these plants. Each cultivar has a unique color and name: 'Silver Cloud', 'Rain Cloud', 'Thunder Cloud', 'Green Cloud', and 'White Cloud'. A closer look at the leaves reveals dense hairs that channel the air as it moves past the leaf, to cool the plant. When the Xeriscape movement started, Texas Sage was the first plant on our water-conserving palette, and it is still high on the charts. (LM)

REGIONAL TIPS

What comes from our deserts is amazing, and Texas Sage is one of those finds. It's too bad it won't withstand the harsh winters of the north; it sure is a wonderful addition to southern Nevada landscapes.

WHEN, WHERE, AND HOW TO PLANT

Plant from containers anytime, but it roots faster when planted in warm, sandy soils. Death comes quickly if it is planted in soggy soils, so check drainage prior to planting. You certainly want to plant this beauty in full sun to bring out the most color when in bloom. To plant, make a hole three times wider than and as deep as its rootball, mix in some organic matter to open up the soil for good root development, and firm the soil next to the rootball, at the same time adding water to settle the soil. Build a water basin to help soak the rootball and surrounding soil, and irrigate twice weekly until the plant becomes established.

CARE AND MAINTENANCE

For fast growth, continue to irrigate weekly through the summer, but if the plant suddenly wilts and dies, it is a good indication of overwatering or poor drainage. Lightly feed the bush with a cup of ammonium sulfate around Easter. Because it is a lazy man's plant, the degree of maintenance is up to you. If you are meticulous, then nip at the shrub often, but please don't shear the bush; it takes away from its beauty and significantly reduces the number of blooms. Thin it out occasionally to get rid of the older stuff and to renew the flowering wood. There are no pests that bother it.

LANDSCAPE MERIT

Use them as focal points, windscreens, accents, and wildlife habitats. The gray-green foliage suggests coolness in the yard and blends well with other greenery. It is very useful in rock gardens as it causes the rocks to stand out even more.

ADDITIONAL SPECIES, CULTIVARS, OR VARIETIES

L. laevigatum, or Chihuahuan Sage, is also very spectacular. It is a broad-spreading shrub usually as wide as it is tall, with small leaves that are slightly gray but not as silvery as many of *Leucophyllum*. Lavender flowers cover the bush when it's humid. It, too, is very dramatic when blooming.

Did You Know?

It is called Barometer Plant because any time the humidity goes up around Texas Sage, it blooms.

Viburnum

Viburnum tinus

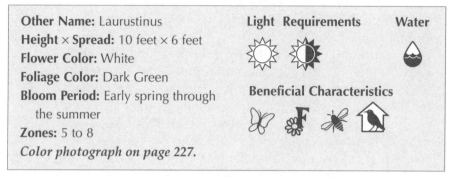

Other Name: Laurustinus
Height × Spread: 10 feet × 6 feet
Flower Color: White
Foliage Color: Dark Green
Bloom Period: Early spring through the summer
Zones: 5 to 8
Color photograph on page 227.

Light Requirements

Water

Beneficial Characteristics

If you are from the Mediterranean area, Viburnum is a must for your yard, as the Mediterranean is where it originated. It grows moderately to 10 feet tall and spreads 5 to 6 feet wide. It is extremely useful as a slender hedge in small narrow landscapes. When given some shade and good care, the blue-green, leathery, dark-green leaves are very attractive as they roll down, hanging from reddish twigs; and the greenery makes a fine contrast with the green of other plants. This is a beauty, but you must train it from day one to keep it compact so that when it gets larger it will create a mass of foliage and flowers. While the buds are still tight, the total cluster reminds me of a head of cauliflower ready to be eaten. As the flower buds unfold, nature paints them a pale pink and then transforms them into delicate and fragrant white flowers. The flowers become food and nectar for birds, bees, and butterflies to feast on until the summer heat sets in. (LM)

Regional Tips

It is a very durable, lush, full shrub for southern Nevada landscapes; it copes well with the heat and does even better when planted in dappled shade. This is not a shrub for northern Nevada because of the cold winters, although there are other great Viburnum for northern Nevada.

When, Where, and How to Plant

Plant this lush-looking shrub any time throughout the year, but for best results, plant in October or November. It requires good soil with good drainage; only avoid alkaline conditions. For best results, plant it in full sun to partial shade to increase in flower production; plant it like the other shrubs. It is paramount to thoroughly soak the rootball during establishment, so build a water basin under its canopy to fill three times a week.

CARE AND MAINTENANCE

Water twice weekly going into the summer, but as it gets above 90 degrees Fahrenheit, water three times a week. If you are using a drip system, allow emitters to run for 2 hours each time. Occasionally during summer, leave the emitters on for an extended time to further flush the rooted area of salts. It isn't a big feeder, so place only a cupful of ammonium sulfate under the bush on President's, Memorial, and Labor Days. Do most of your pruning after blooms fade to increase the density of the plant and, more important, to enhance flower formation the following season. Throughout the summer, occasionally prune away those branches reaching out beyond the silhouette of the bush, to keep it lush and full. Although leaves are large, they will withstand shearing. Control aphids and spider mites with a strong jet of water, or go after them with insecticidal soap and Neem. Use a mild fungicide to control powdery mildew.

LANDSCAPE MERIT

Use this beauty for backgrounds, screens, specimens, a woodsy effect, groupings, formal and informal hedges, espaliers, and cool-season flowering. This is a decorative shrub with handsome form, foliage, and flowers.

ADDITIONAL SPECIES, CULTIVARS, OR VARIETIES

'Spring Bouquet' is more dwarf than other cultivars, and its foliage is a lustrous dark-green; it blooms in the early spring. 'Lucidum' has shiny leaves and is resistant to mildew. 'Dwarf' grows up to 5 feet high to make a good low screen, hedge, or foundation plant. 'Robustum' has coarser, rougher leaves than other cultivars; it grows denser and more erect.

Waxleaf Privet

Ligustrum japonicum 'Texanum'

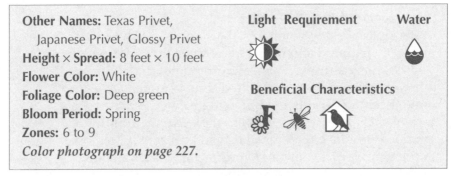

Other Names: Texas Privet,
  Japanese Privet, Glossy Privet
Height × Spread: 8 feet × 10 feet
Flower Color: White
Foliage Color: Deep green
Bloom Period: Spring
Zones: 6 to 9
Color photograph on page 227.

Light Requirement

Water

Beneficial Characteristics

Waxleaf Privet, Texas or Japanese Privet, or whatever you want to call it—this shrub is a real workhorse in southern Nevada. This plant is best known for its long, lustrous, deep-green, glossy, leathery leaves that are densely located along the branches. And if that isn't enough, it doesn't have any pest problems. Large clusters of tiny, creamy white flowers on 6-inch-long spikes are produced from new spring shoots. The flowers tell you when to prune. (You always prune an early-blooming plant after bloom, otherwise you remove most of the flower buds.) The flowers are very pretty, attract bees, and bring fragrance to the landscape. Small blue-black berries follow in the fall and you have a choice: leave them for the birds to eat, or remove them for aesthetic reasons. Remember our birds, because they need something to eat too . . . but it does take them a long time to get to all of the berries. *L. japonicum* 'Texanum' is a third smaller than the species, and denser. (LM)

REGIONAL TIPS

Waxleaf Privet is one of the reliable shrubs, but only for southern parts of the state. It will not live through the harsh northern Nevada winters.

WHEN, WHERE, AND HOW TO PLANT

Plant this beauty any time, with preference for the fall—you will gain a whole year's worth of root growth to face the heat next summer. It must have a good soil with good drainage. Although Waxleaf Privet will tolerate full sun, it loves to set up camp on the north or east side of the home. I find the plant becomes stunted and suffers from sunburn in too much sun when stressed for water. To provide a good home for this plant, make a hole three times wider than and as deep as the rootball, mix in some organic matter with the on-site soil, and fill in around the plant, at the same time, water to settle it in. Add mulch around the plant, and give it a good soaking twice weekly until established.

CARE AND MAINTENANCE

Keep the soil moist by watering twice a week, but as temperatures climb into the 90s, switch to three waterings a week. Fertilize in the late winter with a cup of ammonium sulfate worked into the soil, for more growth and blooms; feed again after bloom and Labor Day. Prune Waxleaf Privets after they bloom to generate more flowering wood for the following year's blooms; pruning before bloomtime eliminates the flower buds. As branches extend, clip them off to keep the proper size and shape. Leaf miners make unattractive holes in the leaves. Use a systemic insecticide to control them.

LANDSCAPE MERIT

Use it as a background for other low-growing plants. It makes an excellent screening plant, shows off well when many are clustered together, and fits well in a container with flowers planted around its base.

ADDITIONAL SPECIES, CULTIVARS, OR VARIETIES

A closely related species, *L. lucidum*, or Glossy Privet, is often confused with Waxleaf Privet, but it grows taller and has larger clusters of flowers. Its leaves are not as glossy and the plant is not as hardy. *L. japonicum* 'Silver Star' has variegated leaves with deep-green centers and creamy-silvery edges. This slow grower is heavily branched and gets about half as high as Waxleaf. Vicary Golden Privet has many erect branches covered with bright golden foliage, and it produces its best color in sunny locations when left untrimmed. It is deciduous.

Weigela

Weigela florida

Height × Spread: 4 to 10 feet × 9 to 12 feet	**Light Requirements**	**Water**
Flower Color: Pink		
Foliage Color: Varies according to season	**Beneficial Characteristic**	
Bloom Period: Late spring to early summer		
Zones: 3 to 8		
Color photograph on page 227.		

One of the most interesting flowering shrubs is Weigela. When it's in bloom, each of the branches is covered with flowers from the base of the branch right out to the tip. The flowers are formed on short, lateral twigs attached to the branches. They are bell-shaped and about 1 inch in diameter. The flowers are generally pink on the outside and paler on the inside, without any fragrance. Weigela flowers in the late spring and early summer, and many continue to flower sporadically even into the fall. Weigela is not described as a beautiful shrub, for it is a very coarse, vase-shaped plant with branches that eventually arch to the ground as the shrub matures. The leaves of this deciduous shrub are green in the summer and get slightly yellow in the fall, but not showy. One of the most interesting cultivars is *Weigela florida* 'Polka', which was developed in Canada. It is a very hardy shrub that will withstand temperatures to minus 40 degrees Fahrenheit. Not only is it hardy, but it has deep-pink flowers that bloom from June to September, and it grows to 6 feet high and wide. (DP)

REGIONAL TIPS
The cultivar 'Polka' is adapted to the coldest regions of the state. Weigela is not used in the hottest regions of southern Nevada.

WHEN, WHERE, AND HOW TO PLANT
Plant Weigela any time of the year, but you will find the best selection of plants in the spring. It is available as either bare root or in containers; if bare root, it needs to be planted in early spring before it leafs out. It withstands part shade, so plant it as colorful filler on the edge of a canopy of trees, and it also grows in full sun. Weigela will grow

in most soils. When transplanting to the garden, take it out of the container after digging a hole as deep as the rootball and three times as wide. Place it in the hole and backfill with the soil that was removed. Once planted, it needs a good soaking until the water starts to puddle.

CARE AND MAINTENANCE

Weigela needs pruning to keep it compact, so prune after it flowers. It should bloom all summer if well pruned. In fact, it seems to grow better if neglected. Water it about twice a week with at least 2 inches, and fertilize in the spring with a water-soluble fertilizer applied according to directions. There are no pests that attack it, making it very easy to care for.

LANDSCAPE MERIT

Because Weigela is very coarse and sort of ragged-looking in the winter, it doesn't fit in with other shrubs, although I think it makes a great specimen plant by itself. I haven't done so yet, but I want to use it as a natural hedge. It is used sometimes as a foundation planting and also looks good when planted as a group of two or three.

ADDITIONAL SPECIES, CULTIVARS, OR VARIETIES

Wine and Roses Weigela, *W. f.* 'Alexandra', has glossy burgundy leaves and large rose-pink flowers. 'White Knight', as its name implies, has white flowers. *W. florida* 'Alba' is another white-flowered one.

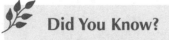

Did You Know?

Weigela is considered to be very tolerant of smog.

Trees

TREES ARE AMONG THE LOVELIEST OF ALL PLANTS. But they are not here as mere cosmetics to make our parks, streets, and gardens look nice. Trees help produce the air we breathe, trap and hold pollutants, offset the buildup of carbon dioxide, control and help stabilize the world's climate, and feed and shelter much of the world's wildlife. An acre of trees can supply enough oxygen each day to support eighteen people.

Trees also help reduce water loss caused by surface runoff, soil erosion by wind and water, and the amount of harmful substances washing into our waterways. In addition to their economic value as lumber and as sources of fuel, they screen unsightly views, soften harsh outlines of buildings, absorb and block noise, and help define spatial arrangements. In Nevada, trees add beauty to homes and shelter us from the harsh desert sun, especially when planted in southern or western exposures.

Trees also produce color. In autumn, trees give an artist's touch to any landscape. Some ornamental trees provide summer and fall fruit not only for us, but for our feathered friends, too. Not only can trees make a home landscape complete, they can enhance the appearance of an entire neighborhood.

A house surrounded by trees is worth more than a house without trees. A house with no trees near it looks hot in summer, appears unbalanced, and suggests, however unjustly, a lack of interest on the part of those who live in it. Old residential areas are usually more inviting and more restful than most new housing developments for one important reason: they are usually well populated by large trees. And on a broader scale, the character of a city is changed by an abundance or a dearth of trees. Cities that spend liberal amounts of money to maintain their old trees and to plant new ones are generally considered nicer places in which to live.

Chapter Ten

The planting of a tree can leave a biological footprint long after we are gone—and some trees, like some people, become famous. Particular trees have figured prominently in the early history of our nation and have become national shrines. Trees can be natural landmarks and memorials because they have more than the allotted years of man, and thus can carry their associations throughout generation upon generation. There are trees living today that were planted by the first president of the United States, and some that are respected as the oldest living things on earth.

Almost everyone likes trees for one reason or another. Some like them for the cool shade they provide during hot summer days. Others like them because they add to the beauty or value of a property. Still others like them for sentimental reasons—perhaps because Grandpa planted the tree when he and Grandma moved into the neighborhood many years ago. Even tourists visit trees; among the trees that are of special interest are the Japanese Cherry Trees, which bloom so magnificently every spring in Washington, D.C. No matter the reason, whether aesthetic, financial, or sentimental, a tree is one of the best investments that can be made to enhance a property or an area.

Ash

Fraxinus species

Height × Spread: 30 to 60 feet × 40 to 60 feet

Flower Color: Green to reddish, inconspicuous

Foliage Color: Green; yellow to reddish in the fall

Bloom Period: Spring, before leaves

Zones: 3 to 8

Color photograph on page 227.

Light Requirement

Water

Beneficial Characteristic

If you are looking for a reliable shade tree that will grow anywhere, Ash is the one. It is somewhat slow-growing but eventually reaches heights of 60 feet and a spread of almost the same, producing a dense shade that helps cool the garden. Ashes have compound leaves made up of three to eleven lance-shaped leaflets that grow to over 5 inches long. Species of Ash grow everywhere in Nevada, with the most common in the high desert and mountainous regions being the Green Ash, *Fraxinus pennsylvanica*. In southern Nevada a common one is *F. velutina*, Arizona Ash. It makes a great shade tree, has good to downright fantastic fall color, and is one of the earliest of the deciduous trees to turn. Cool falls and no frost are needed in order for the arresting, golden-yellow color to develop. Hot temperatures in fall will cause the color to be dull, and frost stops everything dead in its tracks. (DP)

REGIONAL TIPS

The Arizona Ash, *F. velutina*, is used mostly in the hottest regions of the state because it likes it hot and dry, but not cold. There are many others that perform well in northern or southern Nevada.

WHEN, WHERE, AND HOW TO PLANT

The best time to transplant deciduous trees is in the fall, and in spring for container trees, but there is a better selection in the spring. Ashes are available as balled-and-burlapped and bare-root plants, and they need to be planted in early spring before they leaf out. They need full sun and tolerate almost any kind of soil but do best in soils that are well drained. Dig the hole the same depth as the root-ball and three to five times as wide, removing the container and, in the case of balled-and-burlapped, removing the burlap and any wire or twine wrapped around the trunk or roots. If left, wire can girdle the tree and either damage or kill it later on. Don't add any amendments to the backfill soil; left alone, the soil will drain better and the root system will establish more quickly in the native soil. After planting, water it well to establish the roots and to help settle the soil around the roots and eliminate air pockets.

Care and Maintenance

In the north, give the tree a deep watering about every seven to ten days (this means wetting the soil to a depth of 6 to 10 inches). Water weekly in the south. When temperatures exceed 100 degrees Fahrenheit, water twice a week in the south. Prune only to remove dead or broken branches, and if you want to increase the rate of growth, fertilize with high-nitrogen fertilizer in the fall or early spring, following the directions on the label. Ashes are generally pest-free, but the Green Ash does get attacked by leafroller aphids just as the leaves are developing. With this pest, the leaves are folded; when you unfold them, you see an aphid inside. Dormant oil will keep them to a minimum.

Landscape Merit

Because of its size, you need a large yard to host an Ash. They are excellent street trees and great for parks, and because they can withstand high winds, they also make good windbreak trees.

Additional Species, Cultivars, or Varieties

The Autumn Purple Ash, *F. americana* 'Autumn Purple', has deep-green leaves in the summer, turning dark purple in the fall, and it's seedless; Blue Ash, *F. quadrangulata*, has yellow-green leaves in the summer, turning bronze-yellow in the fall. *F. velutina* 'Rio Grande' thrives in the south and tolerates alkaline soils.

🌿 Did You Know?

Green Ash seeds itself very easily. Plant the variety Marshall Seedless Ash, F. pennsylvanica *'Marshall'.*

Birch

Betula species

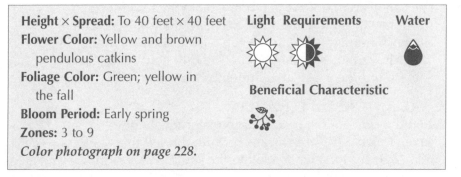

Height × Spread: To 40 feet × 40 feet

Flower Color: Yellow and brown pendulous catkins

Foliage Color: Green; yellow in the fall

Bloom Period: Early spring

Zones: 3 to 9

Color photograph on page 228.

Light Requirements

Water

Beneficial Characteristic

B irch adds something to the landscape that no other tree has: powder-white bark with black markings. The bark sloughs off throughout the year, adding even more interest to the tree. Birch is deciduous, but even in the winter with the leaves gone, it is an attractive tree. The small twigs are a reddish-brown, contrasting with the white bark. Place some evergreens under Birches and you have a great picture in winter. The twigs of the European White Birch are pendulous and hang gracefully to the ground; I guess I'm partial to them, because my small backyard is home to seven of them. The leaves are somewhat heart-shaped, 1¹/₂ inches long, and about as wide. They are light green and turn yellow very late in the fall; its spring flowers are pendulous catkins 1 to 2 inches long. The persistent fruit looks just like the catkin and contains thousands of seeds that attract lots of birds to feed all winter long. (DP)

REGIONAL TIPS

Birch is limited to the high desert and mountainous regions of the state and will not grow in southern Nevada because it won't tolerate the heat.

WHEN, WHERE, AND HOW TO PLANT

Birches grown in containers can be transplanted any time of year, and while the best time is in the fall, the best selection is in the spring. They grow best in a well-drained soil but will survive in most soils. They can be planted as bare-root, balled-and-burlapped, or from containers. If they are balled-and-burlapped or bare-root, transplant them as soon as you get them and before they begin to leaf out. Dig the planting hole just as deep as the rootball and three to five times as wide—this speeds up the time it takes for the tree to become acclimated. After planting, backfill with the soil and give it a good, deep soaking until the water puddles on the surface.

CARE AND MAINTENANCE

I give my Birches 2 inches of water a week, but they don't need any fertilizer once they are established. In the spring, prune out all the twiggy stuff that died over winter; other than that, they don't need any pruning. If a branch has to be removed, it is best to do it in the fall so that the tree won't drip sap; pruning in the spring looks worse than it is, with all that sap running out of the wound. The Cut Leaf Birch will have aphids, so they need to be controlled or you will end up with a sticky mess on anything parked under the tree. In the Reno area, the bronze birch borer (look for 1/8-inch, D-shaped holes in the trunk) is becoming a concern, so River Birch, *Betula nigra*, is becoming a better choice as it is resistant to this pest.

LANDSCAPE MERIT

Birches make a nice shade tree for a large yard, and a group of them works well for a clump effect. I found true multistemmed trees for my yard, and I much prefer them to what you often get, which is three trees planted in one pot.

🌿 Did You Know?

For a tree that is so closely associated with water, you would never think there are Birches native to Nevada. But there are, in the mountains of central Nevada.

Blue Atlas Cedar

Cedrus atlantica 'Glauca'

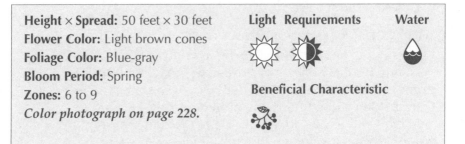

Height × Spread: 50 feet × 30 feet
Flower Color: Light brown cones
Foliage Color: Blue-gray
Bloom Period: Spring
Zones: 6 to 9
Color photograph on page 228.

Light Requirements

Water

Beneficial Characteristic

Blue Atlas Cedar is an evergreen conifer that really stands out because of its blue-gray foliage and the openness and irregularity of its branching. The tree gets to be around 60 feet high in northern Nevada. It has a central trunk with stiff, spreading branches and a pyramidal shape, and it starts getting flat on top as it matures. The needles are really interesting to me because of their arrangement. They are stiff on short spurs extending from the branches about an inch, resembling the ribs of an umbrella as they extend from the center of the spur, and they are a color that really looks blue. Blue Atlas Cedar also has cones that are cylindrical in shape, 2 to 3 inches long, and light brown. The cones grow upward on the branches and will stay on the tree for a long time. (DP)

REGIONAL TIPS

It is hardy in the high desert regions of the state but not in the mountainous areas. It does get some tip burn when winter temperatures dip to minus 15 degrees Fahrenheit.

WHEN, WHERE, AND HOW TO PLANT

Most conifers transplant better in the spring than in fall—the opposite of deciduous trees. If they have been grown in containers, they transplant well any time during the growing season. They grow best in full sun but tolerate partial shade. Blue Atlas Cedars need room to grow, so plant them where they will have at least 30 feet to spread out. A Blue Atlas grows best in a well-drained soil but adapts well to most any soil. Dig the hole as deep as the rootball and three to five times as wide, backfilling with the soil that you take out of the hole and then watering it until it puddles.

CARE AND MAINTENANCE

Blue Atlas Cedar is easy to maintain and is not messy. It needs full sun and deep watering once a week with 2 inches of water. No special fertilizer is required. You can fertilize it along with other plants in the garden. It doesn't need pruning and really should be left alone, but the branches are somewhat susceptible to breaking under a heavy snow load. If the tips of the branches are pruned, the strength of the wood improves. In southern Nevada, it is prone to borer attacks; thus, it tends to be short-lived.

LANDSCAPE MERIT

The cultivar 'Fastigiata' can be used in smaller places because it has a narrow growth habit. It also makes a great specimen tree and is a very interesting tree for public gardens. The cultivar 'Glauca Pendula' doesn't grow very large; it is an interesting weeping tree, growing upward and toppling over. It looks really interesting when placed next to a garden stairway, or cascading over a big rock or waterfall.

ADDITIONAL SPECIES, CULTIVARS, OR VARIETIES

Deodora Cedar is a type that is often used. There are several cultivars available, including *C. deodora* 'Aurea', which has weeping branches and needles of golden-yellow during the summer and yellow-green during the winter. *C. deodora* 'Shalimar' is the hardiest of the Deodora Cedars, with pendulous branches and a blue-green color. (In the high desert region, the tops of Deodara Cedars may die out.)

Blue Palo Verde

Cercidium floridum

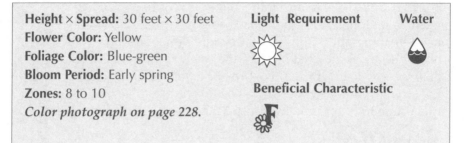

Height × Spread: 30 feet × 30 feet
Flower Color: Yellow
Foliage Color: Blue-green
Bloom Period: Early spring
Zones: 8 to 10
Color photograph on page 228.

Light Requirement

Water

Beneficial Characteristic

Blue Palo Verde might well be the most colorful of all desert trees. It is one of the first trees to bloom in spring, and the entire tree is in bloom for more than a month. Although the subsequent seedpods may be deemed messy, this is a small price to pay for the view of the striking mass of bright yellow flowers that cover the entire canopy. You'll find this lovely deciduous native along washes and flood plains of the Sonoran desert, a visible reminder that it can get by with infrequent irrigations. It is fast-growing to 30 feet, with wide, spreading branches that reach low to the ground. Tiny compound leaves with rounded leaflets shed when stressed for water, making it leafless during the dry season, but this brings out the intricate patterns of the bluish-green trunk and stems. As the tree ages, the bark becomes rough and gray. (LM)

REGIONAL TIPS

This is a tree for southern Nevada, as it will freeze in the rest of the state.

WHEN, WHERE, AND HOW TO PLANT

Plant from containers any time, but the tree does best when planted in the spring, in a site with full sun. It tolerates most soils but prefers sandy soils with good drainage and is one of the few that will tolerate alkaline soil. Because southern Nevada soil tends to be compacted due to its composition, dig a hole up to three times as wide as and as deep as the rootball so the roots can freely move out into their new surroundings. Add some organic matter to the backfill to help keep the porous spaces in the planting hole open, to improve drainage.

CARE AND MAINTENANCE

Blue Palo Verde likes deep waterings at least twice a month in the summer and very little during the winter. Leaves drop during extreme dry spells. This indicates a need to increase the number of waterings. When you prune it, wear gloves to protect yourself from the thorns. Prune branches high on young trees if they are near walks—the added height opens up the tree so you can see the interesting branching structure. The tree's interior growth can become dense, so remove any crisscrossing branches to open up the tree. If you do the job correctly, you can see through the tree when finished. If the seed-pods are unsightly, cut them off as well. Since Blue Palo Verde is from the legume family, it doesn't require fertilizer; however, a pound of ammonium sulfate spread under the tree's canopy in February keeps a more lush appearance. This tree comes to your yard without any pests.

LANDSCAPE MERIT

This tree brings blue-green foliage and bark to the landscape, making it a handsome contrast to traditional plants. Its filtered shade allows for plants beneath it to make a greater visual impact, but it shines most when covered by its bright yellow flowers. The messy seedpods limit its use around pools.

ADDITIONAL SPECIES, CULTIVARS, OR VARIETIES

The *Ceridium* hybrid 'Desert Museum' is quickly becoming very popular. It combines the best qualities of *Parkinsonia aculeata*, *C. floridum*, and *C. microphyllum*. It grows quickly when planted in full sun, is thornless, has larger flowers that last longer, and has fewer seedpods, thus producing very little litter. Provided it has ample water, it is fast-growing.

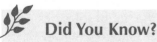 **Did You Know?**

The Indians used the seedpods of this tree as food.

Chaste Tree

Vitex agnus-castus

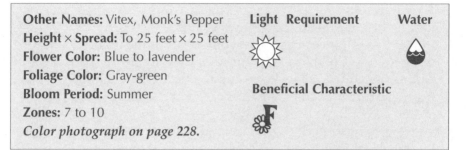

Other Names: Vitex, Monk's Pepper
Height × Spread: To 25 feet × 25 feet
Flower Color: Blue to lavender
Foliage Color: Gray-green
Bloom Period: Summer
Zones: 7 to 10
Color photograph on page 228.

Light Requirement

Water

Beneficial Characteristic

Chaste Tree is a widely adaptable shrub but it has more merit as a multistemmed, small, deciduous tree with wide-spreading branches. It is native to southern Europe, making it a natural for southern Nevada. Without irrigation it remains a shrub, but with moderate amounts of water it grows quickly to 15 to 25 feet high, with an equal spread. The trunk is often picturesque with gray, stringy bark, and foliage is gray-green to dull green, with lower surfaces pale green to almost white. The leaves have a distinct, spicy odor when crushed. Strong branching growth provides support for the 6-inch, fan-shaped leaves. Hot weather is a must to develop the 4- to 10-inch-long flower clusters appearing above the foliage in June, and they may bloom sporadically until fall. Flowers are usually blue to lavender, but there are pink and white selections. Tiny, woody, round, pepperlike seedpods follow bloom and can be mistaken for bugs hanging on the twigs. Chaste Tree adds a most interesting flower color and aroma to the landscape. (LM)

REGIONAL TIPS

It is particularly adaptable to dry, sunny locations and temperatures in the low teens; but it requires hot temperatures to bring the flowers into bloom.

WHEN, WHERE, AND HOW TO PLANT

Plant Vitex from containers any time the soil is warm; I find the best time to plant it in southern Nevada is in the fall. It tolerates a wide range of soils but does best in rich soil with good drainage. Research continues to demonstrate the need to open the soil further out from the main trunk for feeder roots to establish for survival. Dig the hole only as deep as the depth of the rootball but three to five times as wide. Amend the on-site soil with an organic material such as compost or potting soil, place the plant in the hole, and fold the prepared soil back in around the rootball. Build a water basin around the tree and fill with water. Water the tree twice a week until you see new growth emerging. Add mulch to the surrounding soil to conserve water and moderate the soil temperature.

CARE AND MAINTENANCE

Water Chaste Tree at least twice a week the first year, and weekly thereafter. It is a very tough, durable tree and does not require much fertilizer; in fact, too much fertilizer causes the flowers to fade. The tree has a tendency to produce twiggy growth and becomes unsightly, so during the winter do some interior thinning to renew growth and to remove any dead wood. If the tree is located near walkways, raise the lower branches so people can freely walk under it. If you are a really meticulous gardener, you'll want to deadhead the flower stems after they bloom, as they can be distracting and the seeds sprout readily. The brown seeds are small and people may be convinced that the seeds are bugs, but this tree is pest-free.

LANDSCAPE MERIT

It does well around patios or in lawns and quickly becomes the center of interest when in bloom. The fine-textured, lacey foliage makes a pleasant, light pattern against structures. It is also a fast shade-producer, bringing relief in the summer.

ADDITIONAL SPECIES, CULTIVARS, OR VARIETIES

Other Vitex trees have different colors, including 'Alba', which has white flowers, and 'Rosea', which comes with pink flowers.

Chinese Elm

Ulmus parvifolia

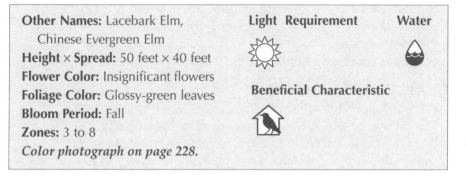

Other Names: Lacebark Elm,
   Chinese Evergreen Elm
Height × Spread: 50 feet × 40 feet
Flower Color: Insignificant flowers
Foliage Color: Glossy-green leaves
Bloom Period: Fall
Zones: 3 to 8
Color photograph on page 228.

Light Requirement

Water

Beneficial Characteristic

Chinese Elm is a wonderful tree but it gets a bad rap because of its cousin Siberian Elm, which is a very undesirable tree. Chinese Elm has dainty, glossy, dark-green leaves that glisten in the sun and dance to the summer breezes as they flip back and forth. Siberian Elm has leaves that are larger, and a deeply furrowed bark, and it brings elm leaf beetle problems to the landscape. The confusion has led to Chinese Elm being condemned as an inferior tree, but nothing could be more wrong. The Chinese Elm is an erect, refined deciduous tree with spreading, arching branches and weeping branchlets that make it a great substitute for those determined to grow Willows in the south. Chinese Elm grows fast to a height of 50 feet, with an even wider spread if grown in deep, moist soil. The trunk is a dappled gray and tan with outer layers flaking off, and thus it is often called Lacebark Elm. In many books this tree is often referred to as Chinese Evergreen Elm because it keeps its leaves in warmer climates, and this does happen at times in southern Nevada. (LM)

REGIONAL TIPS

Chinese Elm will take temperatures down to zero, Fahrenheit. It can be planted in the western and southern regions of Nevada, and will always be a deciduous tree in the north and a semievergreen in the south.

WHEN, WHERE, AND HOW TO PLANT

Plant Chinese Elm anytime from containers, but I prefer fall planting for greater root growth through the winter, which results in less leaf scorch and twig dieback the following summer. Plant this beauty where it receives full sun, in an open, well-drained soil. It will tolerate poor soils, a restricted root system, and soil compaction, but these greatly affect the growth of the tree. To encourage root development, dig a hole at least three to five times as wide and as deep as the rootball, mix some organic matter in the on-site soil, and fold it back in around the rootball. Use water to further settle the soil around the ball and build a water basin. Water two to three times weekly until new growth shows.

Care and Maintenance

Because it is such an extremely tough and durable tree, it does well under most conditions. Throughout the summer, water it twice a week. Reduce the waterings gradually as it cools to once a month throughout the winter (in the south). If you see some burning of the leaf edges, that is an indication to water longer. This tree responds quickly to nitrogen fertilizer, so fertilize it in early spring and again just before it begins to warm up. By nature, Chinese Elm branches reach out and then that season's crop of leaves hang down to give the weeping effect for which they are famous. It doesn't require much pruning, but branches often interfere with people walking under them and need to be removed.

Landscape Merit

It is the perfect tree to replace Weeping Willow and Globe Willow Trees, with its long, weeping branches bringing all the same attributes. It is so pretty for so little effort.

Additional Species, Cultivars, or Varieties

Sometimes you'll find the Chinese Elm listed as *Ulmus sempervirens* 'Drake'. One of the species, *Ulmus parvifolia* 'True Green', has striking bark, a low, rounded crown, and greater retention of foliage during warm winters.

Common Hackberry

Celtis occidentalis

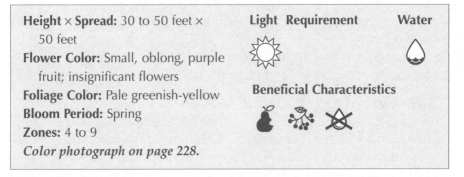

Height × Spread: 30 to 50 feet × 50 feet

Flower Color: Small, oblong, purple fruit; insignificant flowers

Foliage Color: Pale greenish-yellow

Bloom Period: Spring

Zones: 4 to 9

Color photograph on page 228.

Light Requirement

Water

Beneficial Characteristics

Common Hackberry is a deciduous tree that will tolerate just about everything from hot winds to drought. It is a relative of Elm, and the leaves closely resemble those of the Elm. This tree starts out with a slightly pyramidal shape and becomes a more rounded shape as it matures, with branches that are often twisted or zigzagged, giving it an interesting shape. Common Hackberry has a very fine texture in the spring, and as the leaves mature, it takes on a medium texture. The leaves in the spring are a light yellow-green; in the summer they are light green, shiny, and toothed, turning to pale yellow in the fall. The leaves don't linger on the tree in the fall but drop all at once. The fruit is a small, oblong drupe that turns purple when it matures; it tastes a little like a date and is sweet—birds love it. The fruit is edible for people, too. (DP)

REGIONAL TIPS

Common Hackberry is used mainly in the northwestern part of the state, where it became popular during the drought during the late 80s and early 90s due to its drought resistance.

WHEN, WHERE, AND HOW TO PLANT

It can be transplanted most any time but fall is the best, even though best selection is in the spring. It seems to acclimate more quickly if it is planted when young. Plant in full sun in any soil; Hackberries will grow in poor soil, including our alkaline soils. It can be purchased as bare-root in the early spring, but is most commonly seen as a container-grown plant. When digging the hole, don't dig any deeper then the rootball, but widen the hole by at least three times the width—five times is better for faster establishment. Backfill with the same soil that was taken out of the hole to eliminate the drainage problems that occur with an amended soil. After planting, give it a good soaking until water is standing on the surface.

CARE AND MAINTENANCE

Common Hackberry will get along fine with a deep watering of about 2 inches of water every ten to fourteen days. It should only be pruned to remove dead wood or broken branches. In many areas of the country it gets infested with insects, but so far, I haven't had anyone bring any insect or disease problems to my attention.

LANDSCAPE MERIT

Common Hackberry has a deep root system, which allows it to be planted in very narrow parking strips and even close to buildings without raising the foundation or breaking up the concrete. It makes an excellent shade tree and also makes a great street tree because of its high-branching habit, which extends the branches above passing trucks. It's tolerant of air pollution and is useful as a water conservation plant.

ADDITIONAL SPECIES, CULTIVARS, OR VARIETIES

Sugarberry, *Celtis laevigata*, is similar, and it has the same zigzag twigs as Common Hackberry. It has small yellow fruit, which have a sweet, sticky ooze coming out of them, thus the name. Another species is Netleaf Hackberry, sometimes called Western Hackberry, *C. reticulata*, a small tree with small orange fruit. It is one of the few Hackberries that has fall color with its yellow leaves; it is also very drought tolerant.

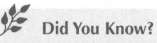 **Did You Know?**

Many other kinds of wildlife besides birds enjoy the fruit of Common Hackberries.

Crabapple

Malus species

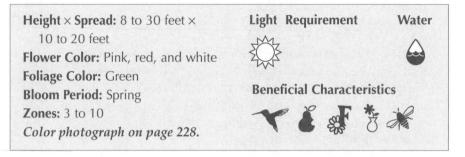

Height × Spread: 8 to 30 feet × 10 to 20 feet Flower Color: Pink, red, and white Foliage Color: Green Bloom Period: Spring Zones: 3 to 10 *Color photograph on page 228.*	Light Requirement	Water
	Beneficial Characteristics	

Crabapple comes as close as anything to a designer tree. There are over four hundred varieties and cultivars to pick from, so no matter what the situation, there's a Crabapple that will fit. One thing they all have in common is beautiful flowers of five petals, although a few, like 'Doubloons', have double flowers. Crabapples are deciduous and come in flower shades from white to pink to dark carmine. Some flower before the foliage and some at the same time. All Crabapples have attractive fruit that range in size from 1/8 inch up to 2 inches in diameter, and the trees range in height from 8 feet to 30 feet. They come in various forms from upright to rounded, and if you want a weeping Crab, plant a 'Candied Apple'. Foliage color varies on Crabapples; most have green leaves that are hairy underneath, but some, like 'Candymint', have purple-green leaves, and 'Red Jade' has bright green leaves. Most Crabapples also have good fall color. (DP)

REGIONAL TIPS

Crabapples are adapted better to the high desert and mountainous regions of the state. Many of them need cold temperatures to develop the best flowers and thus struggle in southern Nevada.

WHEN, WHERE, AND HOW TO PLANT

Plant Crabapples any time during the growing season, though you will have the best selection in the spring when the new stock comes in from the nurseries. It's not a question of where to plant a Crabapple, but of: how many do you have room for? Use them to frame the house or a view, as small shade trees, as specimen plants, or to add lots of color to any streetside planting. Crabapples can be transplanted bare root, balled and burlapped, or from containers. Plant bare-root stock in the late winter and early spring while the tree is still dormant; balled-and-burlapped trees are also available in the spring, and if held properly in the nursery, they can be planted throughout most of the growing season. Container trees can be planted just about any time of year; they prefer full sun and grow best in well-drained soil. Dig the hole only as deep as the rootball, but three to five times as wide to make it easier for the roots to establish in the existing soil. Be sure to remove the container or burlap and any twine or wire from the plant and rootball. After planting, soak around the base until the water puddles.

CARE AND MAINTENANCE

Prune them lightly when they are young just to shape them. Give them a deep watering about once every ten days to two weeks, with 2 inches of water at a time. Some are susceptible to fireblight, a bacterial disease that turns the tips of the branches black, as if they've been scorched—it's best to select resistant varieties. They can also get powdery mildew, but it is generally not a problem.

ADDITIONAL SPECIES, CULTIVARS, OR VARIETIES

'Snowdrift' is a neat tree with white flowers and orange-red fruit; 'Louisa' is a weeping Crabapple with pink flowers and yellow fruit; and *M. baccata* is the very hardy Siberian Crabapple, with white flowers and yellow-to-red fruit. 'Harvest Gold' has golden-yellow fruit, and the fruit on 'Cardinal' is a bright red-purple.

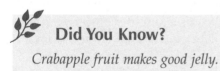

Did You Know?

Crabapple fruit makes good jelly.

Desert Willow

Chilopsis linearis

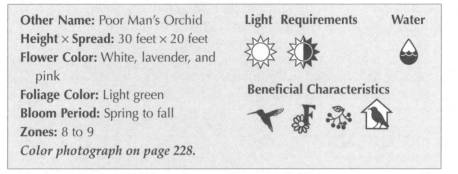

Other Name: Poor Man's Orchid
Height × Spread: 30 feet × 20 feet
Flower Color: White, lavender, and pink
Foliage Color: Light green
Bloom Period: Spring to fall
Zones: 8 to 9
Color photograph on page 228.

Light Requirements

Water

Beneficial Characteristics

Desert Willow is native to the Mojave, Chihuahuan, and Sonoran Deserts, found growing along their dry washes. When left to its natural setting, it grows as a sprawling shrub, as do other native trees and shrubs. It requires removal of the many sprouts that arise from the base of the plant to turn it into a tree. Desert Willow is very colorful throughout the summer, with orchidlike flowers splattered across the deciduous tree—it's often referred to as the "Poor Man's Orchid." I like it because of its constant production of fragrant trumpet-shaped flowers, which appear in April and continue until late summer. If flower production slows, I irrigate the tree more to cause another flush of growth, and more flowers appear. The trumpet-shaped flowers may be 2 to 3 inches long and 1 to 2 inches across, making this tree a welcome addition to an otherwise "blah" landscape. Flowers are shades of white, lavender, and pink, depending on the seedling or cultivar. It is not a true Willow, but its leaves resemble those of Willow. Long, slender pods 4 to 12 inches long follow the blooms and may become a nuisance throughout the winter. (LM)

WHEN, WHERE, AND HOW TO PLANT

Plant Desert Willow from containers anytime, but the preferred time is during the fall for better root establishment. Taking a page from its native habitat, where it grows along the washes, plant it in full sun in a soil that drains well. It is a plant that does not require soil amendments. Simply make a hole three to five times as wide and as deep as the container. Check the drainage by filling the hole with water; if the water is gone within 8 hours, remove the container and place the plant in the hole. Tuck the soil in around the rootball at the same time, using water to further settle it, and build a surrounding water basin, and fill with water. Irrigate the tree twice a week until new growth emerges, and add a mulch to help conserve water.

CARE AND MAINTENANCE

This tree can get by on very little water but if it receives ample water it will grow more, and if it slacks off in flowering, extend the watering time. Water it monthly throughout the winter because of the dry winds. It is a plant that doesn't require nitrogen, but adding a little will add more luster to the greenery. Prune to shape as desired in the dormant season, and for a clean, neat-looking tree, remove seedpods. Desert Willow doesn't have any disease or insect problems.

LANDSCAPE MERIT

It makes an excellent tree to use in a desert oasis. Because a Willow suggests water, it definitely gives the feeling that fresh water is close at hand. It also makes a good transition plant from a luxuriant garden setting to a desert setting.

ADDITIONAL SPECIES, CULTIVARS, OR VARIETIES

'Lucretia Hamilton' brings to the landscape much darker and showier purple flowers. 'Burgundy' and 'Rio Salado' are other selections grown for distinctive flower colors.

Did You Know?

Researchers crossed Desert Willow with Catalpa and we now have the Chitalpa tree. It is a smaller tree, with showy pink or white flowers throughout the summer, and leaves that are larger than those of Desert Willow. It needs to be used more.

False Cypress

Chamaecyparis species

Height × Spread: 2 to 200 feet × 6 to 30 feet	**Light Requirements**	**Water**
Flower Color: Cones		
Foliage Color: Shiny green, some yellow-green	**Beneficial Characteristic**	
Bloom Period: Spring		
Zones: 5 to 8		
Color photograph on page 228.		

It's hard to know where to start when describing False Cypress. There are literally hundreds of them, all with different characteristics, shapes, and sizes. Your choices range from a tree that could reach to over 200 feet high to one that will take ten years to grow 2 feet. The tree is evergreen and foliage varies from leaf scales that are tightly compressed, to twigs, to soft needles. The foliage color also varies from a green color for some, to bright yellow foliage in the summer and bronze in the winter on others. The forms of the species can be pyramidal, columnar, or weeping, to fit any site you might have. They grow best in full sun, but I have a *Chamaecyparis pisifera* 'Squarrosa' that is doing great under a grove of Birches. (DP)

REGIONAL TIPS

False Cypress is better adapted to the high desert and mountainous regions of the state. Even in the community of Ely, where it reached minus 27 degrees Fahrenheit at one point, you can find a False Cypress that will grow there. The hot, dry heat of southern Nevada is hard on them.

WHEN, WHERE, AND HOW TO PLANT

Like all conifers, it is best to plant them in the spring, but in most cases they are grown in containers, so transplant them any time during the growing season. You will find the best selection the spring. Plant False Cypress in full sun or part shade in any soil, but it grows best in one that is well drained. Remove the container before planting—occasionally I see paper pots with instructions to leave the plant in the container and plant the pot too. Don't you dare do it, because the pot won't rot in our dry climate, and the result will be a dead tree. Dig the hole as deep as the rootball and about three to five times as wide, to loosen up that tight, clayey Nevada soil and to allow the tree to acclimate faster. After planting, fill the hole with the native soil and water until it puddles.

CARE AND MAINTENANCE

All False Cypress are easy to maintain. Deeply water them about once a week with 2 inches of water. After the tree has been in the ground for a season, fertilize it with a high-nitrogen fertilizer in the spring. Cold and dry winters can be hard on them, but you can water them once a month to prevent this. We don't seem to have many pests that bother them. A few—like the Sawara Cypress and Hinoki Cypress—need some protection from direct sunlight to prevent brown needles.

LANDSCAPE MERIT

The uses of the tree are as limitless as the varieties. If you need something unusual in the Alpine garden, try *C. obtusa* 'Contorta'. If you are into Bonsai, then try 'Nana Lutea' or 'Ries Dwarf'. How about a shrub for screening the yard from the street? Try Boulevard Cypress. For a tall tree, Lawson's Cypress, *C. lawsoniana*, measuring in at 100 feet, should fit the bill.

ADDITIONAL SPECIES, CULTIVARS, OR VARIETIES

C. nootkatensis 'Pendula' has very graceful branching and is called the Weeping Alaska Cedar. *C. obtusa* 'Lynn's Golden' is a great dwarf, upright-growing tree with golden foliage.

Flowering Plum

Prunus cerasifera 'Atropurpurea'

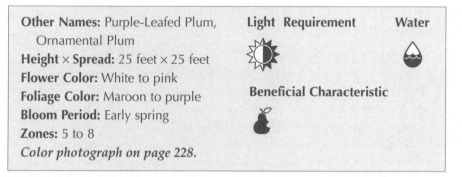

Other Names: Purple-Leafed Plum, Ornamental Plum
Height × Spread: 25 feet × 25 feet
Flower Color: White to pink
Foliage Color: Maroon to purple
Bloom Period: Early spring
Zones: 5 to 8
Color photograph on page 228.

Light Requirement

Water

Beneficial Characteristic

Flowering Plum rarely gets over 25 feet high, making it a welcome addition to smaller landscapes. It is one of the first trees to flower, with a profusion of rosy pink to white flowers in billowy masses in the early spring, before leaf buds unfold to dispel the winter blues. It is among the most beautiful of all deciduous flowering trees. Fruit follows on some varieties, but quality, quantity, and size will vary; the fruit is okay to eat. This tree brings maroon to purple leaves to the landscape, a rarity that lasts all season. In its early life the tree is erect with fairly vertical young branches and is globe-shaped, but it becomes more spreading with age. (LM)

REGIONAL TIPS

In southern Nevada, provide some afternoon relief from the blistering summer sun to help prevent borers.

WHEN, WHERE, AND HOW TO PLANT

Flowering Plums do best when planted in fall and into early spring in southern Nevada and in early spring in the north. It does best when planted in full sun to partial shade. It must have an open, well-drained soil to allow the roots to spread. To accommodate the new plant, dig a hole at least three times as wide and as deep as the container. Check for drainage by filling the hole with water. If the water drains from the hole within 8 hours, plant the tree. Work some organic matter such as compost into the on-site soil, place the tree in the hole, and fold the prepared soil around the rootball. After planting, build a water basin around the tree, fill the basin, and allow the water to soak in. Continue to water three times a week until you see new growth emerging.

CARE AND MAINTENANCE

Young trees need water twice weekly throughout the summer and monthly waterings throughout the winter. Mulching will help conserve water and prolong the life of these beauties. Apply a nitrogen fertilizer in the early spring and again after bloom. Flowering Plums often need iron to prevent chlorosis (or yellowing of leaves). With our highly alkaline soils, it is necessary to use Iron 138—sold in southern Nevada under the trade name of Kerex. Prune only as much as is needed to keep the canopy open to allow dappled light to reach the lower branches. Here's a tip: Prune after bloom to encourage heavy bloom on new wood next year. Flowering Plum Trees are susceptible to borers. Check the trunks periodically for oozing sap. If you find sap, examine under the bark for sawdust—a sure sign of borers. Borers enter the southwest side of a tree, where it is more sunburned. To prevent infestation, paint the trunk with a water-based white latex paint.

LANDSCAPE MERIT

Flowering Plum's purple foliage brings a welcome relief to the greens of the landscape, it's an early spring bloomer, and it makes a great accent plant.

ADDITIONAL SPECIES, CULTIVARS, OR VARIETIES

Flowering Plums can be divided into two groups: some bear edible fruit annually, such as *Prunus cerasifera* 'Atropurpurea'; *P. cerasifera* 'Hollywood', a hybrid between *P. cerasifera* 'Atropurpurea' and the Japanese Plum Duarte; and *P. cerasifera* 'Newport'. Others bear fruit seldom or not at all, and are selected for their foliage and flowers, such as *P. blireiana*, *P. cerasifera* 'Krauter's Vesuvius', and *P. cerasifera* 'Thundercloud'.

Goldenrain Tree

Koelreuteria paniculata

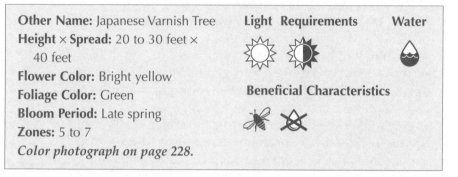

Other Name: Japanese Varnish Tree
Height × Spread: 20 to 30 feet × 40 feet
Flower Color: Bright yellow
Foliage Color: Green
Bloom Period: Late spring
Zones: 5 to 7
Color photograph on page 228.

Light Requirements

Water

Beneficial Characteristics

When Goldenrain Tree is in bloom it is spectacular, with bright-yellow flowers hanging on huge panicles that are 12 inches long and sit above the leaves. The flowers are bell-shaped and about 1/2 inch in diameter, and the tree is completely covered with flowers when in bloom. In the late summer and early fall the fruit develops into three-sided, bladderlike husks—first green and then later yellow—that look a little like miniature Chinese lanterns hanging in the tree. The leaves are compound with between seven to fifteen irregularly lobed leaflets. The fall coloration is yellow but not nearly as spectacular as spring's blooms. The Goldenrain Tree has a rounded outline and seldom grows more then 25 feet high and about as wide; it is a slow-growing tree and develops a flat top with age. This deciduous tree will grow anywhere and is very tolerant of drought and hot wind. (DP)

REGIONAL TIPS

Goldenrain Tree is adapted to all but the coldest regions of the state. I know of at least one on the University of Nevada Las Vegas Campus, and of a number of them on the University of Nevada Reno Campus as well.

WHEN, WHERE, AND HOW TO PLANT

Goldenrain Tree can be transplanted any time of the year, and though fall is the best time to plant deciduous trees, the nurseries have a better selection in the spring. They are easy to plant and are available bare root in the late winter and early spring, and can also be purchased balled and burlapped and as container plants. Goldenrain Tree grows best in full sun but is very well adapted to part shade. It will grow in any soil and is not harmed by alkaline soil. When planting bare root, dig the hole deep enough to accommodate the root system and at least three times as wide. Place a cone of soil in the middle of the hole and arrange the roots over the cone, allowing them to drape down the sides. Use a shovel handle, laid across the hole, to be sure the crown of the tree will be at the same height it grew in the nursery. For both balled-and-burlapped and container plants, dig the hole to the same dimensions, but be sure to remove the burlap and any twine or wire before planting. Backfill around the roots with the same soil that was removed from the hole, then give it a good soaking after planting.

CARE AND MAINTENANCE

Goldenrain Tree is very carefree, needs little maintenance, and pests do not bother it. It thrives with little water and only needs an inch of water once a week, at the very most. There isn't a need to fertilize any more than what it might get when other plants nearby are fertilized. Pruning can do more harm then good, so prune out dead and damaged limbs only.

LANDSCAPE MERIT

It is small enough for the home landscape, thrives in the city, and has deep roots that don't raise sidewalks and driveways.

🌿 Did You Know?

When the Chinese lantern–shaped seedpods open in the late fall, shiny, hard, black seeds about the size of a pea fall to the ground. If they fall on a walkway, walking on it will be like trying to walk on marbles.

Holly Oak

Quercus ilex

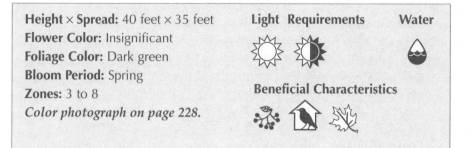

Height × Spread: 40 feet × 35 feet
Flower Color: Insignificant
Foliage Color: Dark green
Bloom Period: Spring
Zones: 3 to 8
Color photograph on page 228.

Light Requirements

Water

Beneficial Characteristics

Oak trees have been slow to catch on in southern Nevada. Back in the early days, people wanted shade Now! and lots of it, and we knew Oaks took millenniums to grow. Then Olives were yanked away because of pollen problems. That set the stage for something new. Holly Oak was the first to show promise, looking like the Olive, and it is evergreen. Holly Oak grows at a moderate rate to 40 feet with a 35-foot spread, and branches have smooth, grayish bark that is fissured on the trunk. The leaves are unique with their irregularly toothed margins similar to Holly leaves—hence the name. Inconspicuous spring flowers produce 1-inch-long, narrow acorns of which the cup may enclose up to one half of the fruit. We are now seeing the use of more Holly Oaks across the state. (LM)

REGIONAL TIPS

In the south Holly Oaks have been, and continue to be, one of the mainstays in the landscape. The Pin Oak is popular in the north.

WHEN, WHERE, AND HOW TO PLANT

Plant Holly Oak anytime, but it prefers going into the ground in the fall; this gives the roots a chance to pick up a year's worth of growth. Plant it in full sun, but it can tolerate partial shade. To speed up the growth, Holly Oak needs a soil enriched with copious amounts of organic matter. Be sure the roots have good drainage. Dig out a hole at least three to five times wider than and as deep as the rootball. Fold the soil around the rootball, firming it to make sure of good root-to-soil contact. Build a water basin under the canopy of the tree and water twice weekly until it becomes established. To further enhance growth, mulch the soil surface under the plant. This will cool the soil for more root growth and will conserve water.

Care and Maintenance

Water the plant weekly through the heat and periodically throughout the winter. Most Oaks will not tolerate water-logged soils or heavy irrigations. Feed with a balanced fertilizer for trees in mid-February and early September for more rapid and dense growth. It doesn't require much pruning to keep this tree in shape. Periodically remove any dead wood, and because it does have a tendency to overproduce twiggy growth, thin it out. (If you can't see through the tree, it is too thick.) Holly Oak is disease- and insect-free.

Landscape Merit

Holly Oak is a handsome tree in any landscape, a moderate grower providing lots of shade, and it does not retard grass growth underneath.

Additional Species, Cultivars, or Varieties

Q. virginiana, or 'Heritage' Oak, grows moderately fast, eventually to 60 feet tall and spreading out twice as wide; *Q. buckleyi* 'Red Rock' Oak develops good shade and poses as a good accent tree, staying around 30 feet high with a 20-foot spread; *Q. emoryi*, or Emory Oak, puts out a full head of shade with a spreading 40-foot span; *Q. fusiformis*, or Escarpment Live Oak, spreads out about 40 feet and reaches 40 feet into the sky; and *Q. lobata*, or Valley Oak, spreads out 30 to 40 feet and reaches up 50 to 60 feet when mature. All are slow to moderate growing.

Horse Chestnut

Aesculus hippocastanum

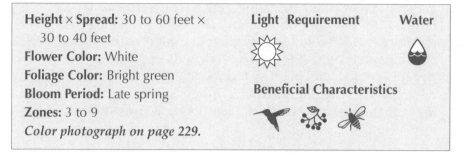

Height × Spread: 30 to 60 feet ×
   30 to 40 feet
Flower Color: White
Foliage Color: Bright green
Bloom Period: Late spring
Zones: 3 to 9
Color photograph on page 229.

Light Requirement

Water

Beneficial Characteristics

I don't know whether to love this tree or hate it. The shape is good and the flowers are beautiful, but the nuts play havoc with lawn mowers and are really hard on bare feet. Horse Chestnuts are in full bloom in April through May in clusters of white flowers that are 12 inches long, pointing upward from the tips of the branches. These flowers are a favorite of hummingbirds. The fruit is a large nut that gets to about 2 inches in diameter and has a rough husk, maturing in the late summer to early fall. The leaves are palmately compound (shaped like a hand) with seven leaflets, each ranging from 7 to 10 inches long. The leaves are dark green and drop rapidly in the fall, with very little color change. This deciduous tree makes lots of shade but is not a deep-rooted tree, so you have to be careful not to plant it too close to sidewalks, driveways, or other paved areas. Deep watering does appear to promote deeper rooting. (DP)

REGIONAL TIPS

Horse Chestnut is best adapted to the high desert and mountainous regions of the state because it is susceptible to leaf scorch from hot, dry winds in other parts of Nevada.

WHEN, WHERE, AND HOW TO PLANT

Plant Horse Chestnuts any time of the year. As with most deciduous trees, fall is the best time to plant, but most of us are tired of gardening in the fall, and besides, you have a better selection in the spring. Plant it in full sun. Although it grows in any soil, it will do better when planted in one that is well-drained. Horse Chestnuts are available balled and burlapped in the early spring and as container plants throughout the growing season. Dig the hole as deep as the rootball and three to five times as wide, being sure to remove the burlap if it is a balled-and-burlapped plant—in the dry desert, the burlap doesn't rot away, and the twine and wire can girdle the trunk and roots and kill the tree. Backfill with the soil you removed from the hole and give it a good soaking.

CARE AND MAINTENANCE

Horse Chestnuts are insect-free and easy to maintain. If they are growing on the lawn and the only water they get is when the lawn is watered, they develop shallow roots. Water them enough to wet the soil to a depth of 18 inches every seven to ten days and they'll develop deeper roots (this usually takes about 3 inches of water). For faster growth, use a high-nitrogen fertilizer in the fall after the leaves drop. Because they have large flowers and nuts, they produce a lot of litter that should be cleaned up periodically. Prune after leaf drop; any dead or broken branches should be removed, as well as weak older branches.

LANDSCAPE MERIT

Horse Chestnuts are large trees, so unless you have an extra-large garden you might not have room. They create a lot of shade in the landscape. You don't want to use them as a street tree; the falling nuts are a road hazard.

ADDITIONAL SPECIES, CULTIVARS, OR VARIETIES

If you want to try something different, try double-flowered 'Brumanni', which is seedless. Another variety is 'Pendula', which has weeping branches; 'Rubicunda' has salmon-red flowers instead of white. The Red Chestnut, *A.* × *carnea*, has 8- to 10-inch pink-to-red flower spikes.

Incense Cedar

Calocedrus decurrens

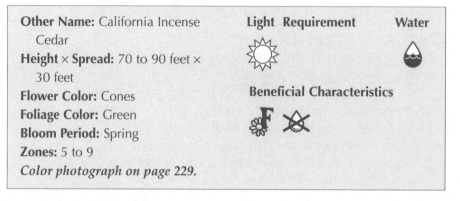

Other Name: California Incense Cedar

Height × Spread: 70 to 90 feet × 30 feet

Flower Color: Cones

Foliage Color: Green

Bloom Period: Spring

Zones: 5 to 9

Color photograph on page 229.

Light Requirement

Water

Beneficial Characteristics

Incense Cedar is a very large evergreen, native to the Sierra Nevada Range, that stands out because of its pyramidal shape. In the wild it grows to over 100 feet high, but in the landscape it is a slow-growing tree that rarely grows over 50 feet. So why plant it in the home landscape? Young Incense Cedars are narrow, compact, upright, slow-growing trees that look a lot like Arborvitae. I like it because of its shape and the texture of the foliage; it's not hard to spot a grove of them in the mountains because of the contrast in foliage to the pines, and also because of their bark. It is deeply furrowed and has a very distinct reddish-brown tint. The foliage is made up of scales rather than needles, and they form flat, fanlike sprays arranged vertically on the branches, in a very attractive, bright, shiny-green color. The scales have glands that emit a woodsy fragrance when crushed, and as summer warms up the aroma intensifies. Incense Cedar is very adaptable and will take summer heat and winter cold. It is also drought tolerant. (DP)

REGIONAL TIPS

Incense Cedar is very well adapted to the high desert, mountainous, and even the hot regions of Nevada. Hot weather or temperatures below zero don't bother it.

WHEN, WHERE, AND HOW TO PLANT

Incense Cedar can be transplanted throughout the growing season if it is container grown, but nurseries generally have the best selection in the spring. They grow in any soil, although a well-drained soil is best. Dig the hole only as deep as the rootball and anywhere from three to five times as wide; in poor, clayey soils, digging out and loosening up the soil helps with establishment. Take the tree from its container and place the rootball in the hole, then backfill around the roots with the soil that was removed. After planting, give it a good soaking until the water starts to puddle on the soil surface.

CARE AND MAINTENANCE

For establishment, give it 2 inches of water a week; you can train it to be more drought tolerant by watering it to a depth of 18 inches (by applying 3 inches of water) about every two weeks after the tree has been established. It doesn't have any special fertilizer requirements and will receive enough as you fertilize other garden plants. Incense Cedar is relatively carefree, is not bothered by pests, and doesn't require any pruning or shearing to maintain its shape.

LANDSCAPE MERIT

It makes a very attractive specimen tree, but it does need some room to grow. I pass one planted in a small yard close to my house and it gives the house that "cabin in the woods" look. Because of other large trees in the neighborhood, it stands out but doesn't dominate the overall appearance of the area. Because it is a very symmetrical tree it has a rather formal appearance. It makes a very good screening plant, and when planted close together with others, will form a solid wall. If you have a windy site, Incense Cedar makes a great windbreak tree. Because of its fragrance and growth habit it should be used more often.

Maples

Acer species

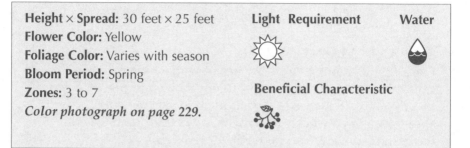

Height × Spread: 30 feet × 25 feet
Flower Color: Yellow
Foliage Color: Varies with season
Bloom Period: Spring
Zones: 3 to 7
Color photograph on page 229.

Light Requirement

Water

Beneficial Characteristic

There are plenty of Maples that make good shade trees, and the selection is increasing every year. They are deciduous, and all have red, yellow, orange, or a combination of colors for fall leaf coloration. All have lobed leaves with the exception of the Box Elder, which has a compound leaf of between three and seven leaflets, and the Paperbark Maple, which has three leaflets. The leaves are from 3 to 10 inches wide depending on the species, and leaves and branches are opposite each other. The flowers are small chartreuse-to-yellow blooms that cover the whole tree in the spring, and all have very interesting seeds called samaras. They look like little helicopters as they float down to the ground. (DP)

REGIONAL TIPS

Maples are limited to the high desert and mountainous regions of the state. They get leaf scorch in the hot region around Las Vegas, and the temperatures are too hot in the fall to develop good fall color.

WHEN, WHERE, AND HOW TO PLANT

As with most deciduous trees, Maples transplant best in the fall; but the best selection will be in the spring. Many are available in the late winter and early spring as bare root or balled and burlapped, but the majority are grown as container plants. Maples like full sun and grow best in a well-drained soil. Dig the hole as deep as the rootball and three to five times as wide, place the rootball in the hole, and backfill with the same soil that was removed. After planting, give it a good soaking.

CARE AND MAINTENANCE

All Maples need a deep watering to a soil depth of 12 inches about every ten to fourteen days, so use about 2 inches of water. All Maples tolerate pruning, and dead and diseased or broken branches should be removed when noticed. Maples do bleed (the sap runs out of the exposed cuts in the spring) so I like to prune them in the fall after the leaves drop, if shaping is needed. Care of Maples can vary greatly. Norway Maple is pretty much pest-free, while Box Elder has, you guessed it, box elder bugs, and the Japanese Maples get some winterkill in the colder regions.

LANDSCAPE MERIT

They are used as specimen trees, shade trees, and street trees. The Amur Maple is a large shrub or small tree and an excellent choice for the small lot. Some of the Japanese Maples are small enough to grow in pots—mine are staying at 2 feet high. All Maples have shallow roots, and the Silver Maple is the worst, so don't plant them next to sidewalks, patios, or driveways because the roots will crack the concrete.

ADDITIONAL SPECIES, CULTIVARS, OR VARIETIES

There are quite a few species to try and many cultivars. *A. campestre*, the Hedge Maple, is a nice tree that grows to 25 feet; *Acer rubrum*, the Red Maple, has great fall color; and *A. saccharum*, the Sugar Maple, is a very hardy large tree and has green leaves during the summer, which turn yellow to red in the fall. The fastest growing is *A. saccharinum*, Silver Maple. Schwedler Maple, *A. platinoides*, has bronzy-red leaves all season long. Norway Maple is a globe-shaped tree used throughout the state.

Did You Know?

The Sugar Maple is where maple syrup comes from. It has red fall color on the sunny parts of the tree and yellow on any part that is shaded.

Mexican Palo Verde

Parkinsonia aculeata

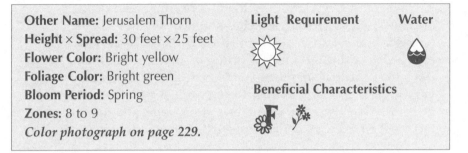

Other Name: Jerusalem Thorn
Height × Spread: 30 feet × 25 feet
Flower Color: Bright yellow
Foliage Color: Bright green
Bloom Period: Spring
Zones: 8 to 9
Color photograph on page 229.

Light Requirement

Water

Beneficial Characteristics

Palo Verde means "green tree" or "green stick." The Mexican Palo Verde covers itself in the late spring with radiant lemon-yellow flowers for a month, when the whole tree becomes a giant bouquet with fernlike foliage in the background. Although the subsequent seed-pods may be deemed messy, this is a small price to pay for the view of the striking mass of bright yellow flowers covering the entire canopy. This graceful, fast-growing deciduous tree has long, narrow leaves to 16 inches, each with numerous 1/8-inch-long, bright green leaflets that shed, creating a straw-colored thatch that helps conserve water under the tree. This is when the now leafless tree brings out its intricate branching patterns. Yellow-green bark covers the thorny trunk and branches, and as the tree ages the bark becomes rough and gray. It grows fast to 30 feet tall or more with a crown spread as wide or wider. Frost can injure Palo Verde, but it becomes hardier when you keep the soil dry during the winter. (LM)

REGIONAL TIPS

The Mexican Palo Verde comes from the deserts of the Southwest and is only hardy into temperatures to the high teens. It is only recommended for southern Nevada landscapes.

WHEN, WHERE, AND HOW TO PLANT

Plant it anytime from containers, but like most desert-native trees, it does best planted in the spring to early summer. It is tolerant of alkaline soils but prefers sandy soils with good drainage, and it needs full sun to thrive. Thoroughly loosen the soil at least three times as wide and as deep as the rootball to get good root growth. There is no need to add organic matter, although it does better if planted in a rich soil. Build a water basin around it to contain the water, and fill it to soak the surrounding soil, watering weekly until you see new growth emerging.

Care and Maintenance

This tree accepts tough growing conditions like alkaline soil, wind, dust, and low rainfall, and it thrives in heat. It will grow with minimal irrigation but does best with the moderate amounts you give your lawn. Leaf litter can be a problem in flower beds; if that's the case, irrigate longer. Remove the lower, drooping branches so people can walk underneath, and also to reveal the beauty of the interior parts of the tree. (Pruning also helps to form the crown, although the tree usually takes on a handsome shape naturally.) The tree's interior growth can become dense, so remove dead and crisscrossing branches to open the tree when it is dormant. If you can see through the tree, or as I often say, if a bird can fly through the tree without much twisting or turning, you did a great job. Maintain the tree's natural form by avoiding heavy pruning and stubbing. Because the Mexican Palo Verde is from the legume family, it doesn't require much fertilizer, but a pound of ammonium sulfate spread under the leaf canopy in February keeps a more lush appearance. It has no known pest problems.

Landscape Merit

This tree is a must for its flowers and beautiful green bark. Use it to make the yard feel tropical or desertlike. It will surprise people with the amount of shade it produces. Be sure to locate these trees in natural areas or in the background of a landscape, where leaf debris is not noticeable.

Mountain Ash

Sorbus scopulina

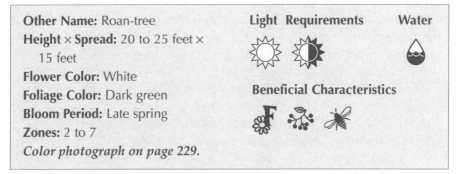

Other Name: Roan-tree
Height × Spread: 20 to 25 feet × 15 feet
Flower Color: White
Foliage Color: Dark green
Bloom Period: Late spring
Zones: 2 to 7
Color photograph on page 229.

Light Requirements

Water

Beneficial Characteristics

If you are looking for a small deciduous tree that will grow in the lawn and has great dark-green leaves, then Mountain Ash is the tree for you. It grows to about 25 feet at the most, and because it has erect branches, it will only spread to around 15 feet. The leaves come out first in the spring and are followed by the white flowers forming in flat clusters scattered throughout the tree, and they do have some fragrance. The fruit matures in the fall, red or orange, resembling a berry—it attracts lots of birds. The leaves are compound and made up of seven to fifteen narrow leaflets. In the fall the leaves turn yellow first, then change to orange and red if the temperatures stay cool but don't freeze. (DP)

REGIONAL TIPS
Mountain Ash is pretty much limited to the high desert and mountainous regions of the state, and they will withstand the coldest of winters with ease. This is a good flowering tree for Ely, which is at an elevation of 6,200 feet.

WHEN, WHERE, AND HOW TO PLANT
You can purchase Mountain Ash bare root, balled and burlapped, or containerized. Bare-root trees are available in the late winter and early spring and you can find them as packaged plants in the garden centers. Plant balled-and-burlapped trees in the spring, and any time during the growing season if you are planting from a container. They prefer full sun but will grow in part shade, and they grow in most any soil—mine is growing in good old clayey, adobe soil as if it were just another bad weed. Before planting, be sure to remove the container or the burlap and also any twine or wire that might be

wrapped around the roots or trunk. Dig the hole as deep as the rootball and about three to five times as wide, place the rootball in the hole, and backfill with the soil taken from the hole. Once the tree is planted, water until it puddles on the soil surface.

CARE AND MAINTENANCE

Water deeply every seven to ten days with about 2 inches of water. Mountain Ash is easy to maintain and it is not bothered by pests. It is occasionally attacked by fireblight, which can be pruned out if caught soon enough. Fireblight looks like the tips of the branches and leaves have been scorched by fire, and branches will often twist to look like a shepherd's crook. If the trees are planted in a sunny location, wrap the trunks the first few winters to prevent southwest injury. A symptom of this problem is when the trunk splits open on the southwest side. Sunlight causes the tree's tissues to thaw, then rapid freezing at night splits the trunk.

LANDSCAPE MERIT

Mountain Ash is very well adapted to the average city lot and can be used for framing the home, as a background tree, or as a specimen in the lawn. There are a few places you don't want to plant them because they tend to be a little messy. It's not large enough to damage anything, but when the fruit drops on the patio furniture or on your car, it rots and makes the surface sticky.

ADDITIONAL SPECIES, CULTIVARS, OR VARIETIES

'Fastigiata' is a tall, narrow-growing tree.

Northern Catalpa

Catalpa speciosa

Other Names: Western Catalpa,
Indian Bean
Height × Spread: 25 to 40 feet ×
20 to 40 feet
Flower Color: White
Foliage Color: Green
Bloom Period: Early summer
Zones: 5 to 9
Color photograph on page 229.

Light Requirement

Water

Beneficial Characteristics

The characteristics of Northern Catalpa that I like best are the extremely large leaves and the pattern they form as you look toward the sky. Northern Catalpa is a deciduous tree with leaves between 6 to 12 inches long, green and smooth on the tops and fuzzy underneath. The leaves may turn a little yellow in the fall, but for the most part, they turn brown and drop off. Even though Catalpa has large leaves, the branching pattern is very open and loose to allow you to look up through the tree. The flowers are really neat, too, large and white on 6-inch spikes that fully drape the tree when in bloom. The seedpods hang down like giant string beans, each about 1/2 inch in diameter and 20 inches long. The tree gets to 40 feet tall and will spread to about 40 feet. It is not bothered by the heat or cold and is very drought tolerant. (DP)

REGIONAL TIPS
Northern Catalpa grows in the high desert and hot regions of Nevada but is not hardy enough for the cold, mountainous regions.

WHEN, WHERE, AND HOW TO PLANT
Northern Catalpa, like most deciduous trees, will transplant best in the fall. There is no problem planting them anytime during the growing season if they are in containers, and they transplant best when they are young. (This is particularly true if transplanting them balled and burlapped.) Plant the trees in full sun in almost any soil; they even tolerate Nevada's alkaline soils. Do not amend the soil. Nevada's soils are mostly clayey and poorly drained; adding amendments creates an even bigger drainage problem because drainage

slows at the interface between the two soils. To plant, dig the hole only as deep as the rootball, but about three to five times as wide. Digging it this wide loosens the soil, allowing the roots to establish faster. Remove the container and place the rootball in the hole, backfilling around the roots using the soil you dug from the hole. Give it a good soaking after it is planted.

CARE AND MAINTENANCE
Northern Catalpa needs deep watering to a soil depth of 18 inches about every two weeks. Water with 2 inches of water. If it is growing in the lawn, there is no need to give it any more water then the lawn gets, and its fertilizer requirements are minimal. Prune to shape, but normally it doesn't need to be pruned. Northern Catalpa is a pretty pest-free tree in Nevada. The larvae of the sphinx moth (the moth is very large and looks and feeds like a hummingbird) occasionally attack the leaves.

LANDSCAPE MERIT

They develop into large trees, so plant them in areas where they will have room to grow. They have deep roots and so don't cause problems with walkways and drives. Avoid using Northern Catalpa as a street or shade tree; the litter from the large flowers and seedpods is quite messy.

ADDITIONAL SPECIES, CULTIVARS, OR VARIETIES
Another species is *C. bignonioides* 'Nana', an interesting old dwarf developed in France that looks like a mushroom, only gets to 6 feet high, and doesn't flower.

Did You Know?

Researchers crossed Desert Willow with Catalpa and we now have the Chitalpa tree. It is a smaller tree, with showy pink or white flowers throughout the summer, and leaves that are larger than those of Desert Willow. It needs to be used more.

Pine

Pinus species

Height × Spread: 10 to 100 feet × 10 to 30 feet	**Light Requirement**	**Water**
Flower Color: Cones		
Foliage Color: Green needles		
Bloom Period: Spring	**Beneficial Characteristics**	
Zones: 2 to 10		
Color photograph on page 229.		

Pines are a diverse group of trees in Nevada. All are evergreen and vary in height from 6 feet to over 100 feet tall and to a spread of over 30 feet. Pines are monoecious plants, which means they have male and female flowers on the same plant. They also vary in the number of needles they have in a cluster: some, like Bristlecone Pine, have five; Ponderosa Pine has three; Aleppo Pine and Mondel Pine have two; and the Nevada state tree, Piñon Pine, has only one. Needles are from 1 inch to over 6 inches in length, and all Pines have a pyramidal form as young trees and the tops become more rounded as they mature. Most Pines self-prune as they mature: the lower branches get shaded, die, and fall off. All have cones, and they range in lengths from 1 inch for a Mugo Pine up to 20 inches long for the Sugar Pine. There are also differences in the heights of Pines. Mugo Pine, *Pinus mugo,* grows to about 4 to 6 feet and Jeffrey Pine, *P. jeffreyi,* will get to 120 feet. (DP)

REGIONAL TIPS

The Aleppo Pine and Mondel Pine both thrive in the heat but will not survive temperatures below zero. The opposite is true of those Scotch and Austrian Black Pines used in the high desert and mountainous regions.

WHEN, WHERE, AND HOW TO PLANT

Plant Pines anytime during the growing season, but you'll have the best selection in the spring at the beginning of the planting season. (The Piñon Pine is hard to transplant and needs to be planted when very young, started in a container.) Give Pines plenty of sun for best growth, and though they are adaptable to adverse soils, they'll grow better in soils that are well drained. Pines are often sold as balled-

and-burlapped plants or container plants. Before planting, remove the container, or if it is a balled-and-burlapped plant, remove the burlap, twine, and wire. Dig the planting hole only as deep as the rootball and up to five times as wide, place the rootball in the hole, and backfill with the soil removed from the hole.

CARE AND MAINTENANCE

Deeply water Pines once every ten to fourteen days with about 2 inches of water. Pines are susceptible to borers when they get stressed. They can be shaped by light pruning and even maintained as a hedge. They don't have any special fertilizer requirements, so fertilization beyond what the plants around them are getting is unnecessary.

LANDSCAPE MERIT

Pines are used in a variety of situations in the landscape. Because most of them are very tall it gives you the sense of being out in the forest when they're planted around the house. Mugo Pine and Bristlecone Pine, *P. aristata*, are used in rock gardens and as foundation plants. If you have a two-story house, Austrian Black Pine, *P. nigra*, and Scotch Pine, *P. sylvestris*, will effectively frame it, but the Scotch Pine should not be planted on a windy site. Japanese Black Pine, *P. thunbergii*, makes a picturesque tree in the garden—the limbs all end up on the lee side of the tree and the tree eventually leans away from the wind. Consider *P. canariensis*, Canary Island Pine, for southern Nevada for its graceful, pyramidal shape. Another one to consider is *P. pinea*, Italian Stone Pine, for its classic umbrella-shaped growth.

Spruce

Picea species

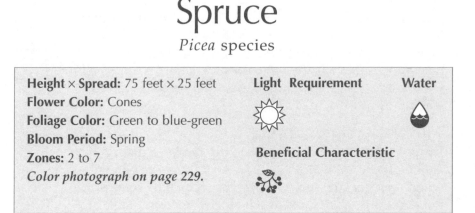

Height × Spread: 75 feet × 25 feet
Flower Color: Cones
Foliage Color: Green to blue-green
Bloom Period: Spring
Zones: 2 to 7
Color photograph on page 229.

Light Requirement

Water

Beneficial Characteristic

Spruce are very popular evergreen conifers in the high desert and mountainous regions of the state, pyramidal in shape, with foliage from the ground to the tips of the trees. The needles develop up to 1¹/₂ inches long, are diamond-shaped (if you were to look at a cross section), and have sharp points. The needles sit on top of short, ¹/₈-inch-long pegs. Cones of Spruce range in size from 2 inches to 6 inches long and about 1 to 1¹/₂ inches wide. The Colorado Spruce is the most popular of the Spruces and is used all over the state. Colorado Blue Spruce is the most sought after, and 'Hoopsii' is perhaps the bluest. 'Koster' is also blue, but its growth is irregular. There's a relatively new one known as 'Baby Blue Eyes'. Norway Spruce has a nice pyramidal shape, and as it matures, the branches hang down. (DP)

REGIONAL TIPS

Spruces grow best in the high desert and mountainous regions of Nevada. Most are somewhat sensitive to high temperatures.

WHEN, WHERE, AND HOW TO PLANT

Plant Spruce any time of the growing season. It is often sold as a living Christmas tree packaged in a bushel basket. This type should be planted in the very early spring unless new growth starts while it is still in the house; if that happens, it needs to be left somewhere in the house or garage where it will stay cool but above freezing. Then transplant into the yard when temperatures warm up in spring. Spruce seems to adapt to most soils but grows best in a well-drained one. (The trees have shallow roots, so avoid planting in windy sites.) Dig the hole as deep as the rootball and three to five times as wide, place the rootball in the hole, and backfill with the same soil that was removed. After it has been planted, give it a good soaking until the water puddles on the soil surface.

CARE AND MAINTENANCE

Water the trees deeply once a week with 2 inches of water, but they don't need any extra fertilizer other than what you give the rest of the yard. Don't prune them; it ruins their natural shape. Spruces are generally easy to maintain. If they get stressed they are often attacked by spider mites, and in some cases the tree is killed. Infested needles look dull and dusty; use an insecticide that is registered for mites. The other major problem they have is shallow roots, which allow them to topple in strong winds.

LANDSCAPE MERIT

Spruces are great accents for corners of lots and they can also be used as specimens. They need to be planted where they will have room to grow; more often than not, they are planted too close to a house or fence and then get butchered in attempts to keep them under control.

ADDITIONAL SPECIES, CULTIVARS, OR VARIETIES

An additional Colorado Spruce is *Picea pungens* 'Fat Albert', which gets to 12 feet tall and 10 feet wide. Cultivars of Norway Spruce, *P. abies*, include Bird's Nest Spruce, a small tree growing to 4 feet high, and 'Pendula', a spreading ground cover.

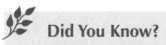

Did You Know?

Spruces have many members that are native to North America. They are also fragrant.

'Swan Hill' Olive

Olea europaea 'Swan Hill'

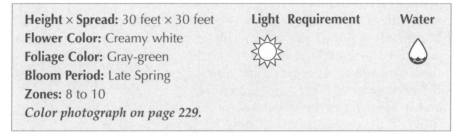

	Light Requirement	Water
Height × Spread: 30 feet × 30 feet		
Flower Color: Creamy white		
Foliage Color: Gray-green		
Bloom Period: Late Spring		
Zones: 8 to 10		
Color photograph on page 229.		

You cannot travel the Southwest without encountering an Olive Tree. They are durable, long-lived, and evergreen—all characteristics that people look for in trees. Anytime you see plants that are silver and gray it usually indicates a low-water-use tree, and the Olive meets that mark with its glossy gray-green leaves and the undersides painted silver. The gnarled gray trunks suggest durability despite all odds, and they become rough with age. European Olives generate a lot of pollen and that drives allergy sufferers out of town for three weeks in April; if you don't do anything about the pollen, the fruit becomes a real nuisance, staining walk entrances and carpets. Such problems have led to the abandonment of the tree in southern Nevada. But relief came with the discovery of the 'Swan Hill' Olive. It has all the beauty of the standard Olive but without the pollen and is sold as a fruitless, low- to no-pollen producer. (The UNLV Arboretum has tested additional pollenless cultivars.) It usually comes as the multitrunked tree that is so typical of desert-dwelling trees, with a round head growing slowly to 30 feet and a spread almost as wide. In fact, I find most desert-loving trees have rounded crowns that push the infrequent rains out to the drip line of the tree. (LM)

REGIONAL TIPS
'Swan Hill' Olive will only tolerate temperatures to the mid-teens. It is recommended only for southern Nevada.

WHEN, WHERE, AND HOW TO PLANT
Plant this durable tree anytime during the year it is available at the nursery. It does best planted from October through March, tolerating stony, alkaline soils and needing full sun to perform best. Open up the soil at least three times as wide and as deep as the rootball. Mix organic matter in the on-site soil and firm it around the ball. Build a

water basin around the tree and fill it twice a week until new growth emerges.

CARE AND MAINTENANCE

Do not cultivate too deeply under Olives, because they develop a dense mat of feeder roots near the ground's surface. The tree tolerates low-watering situations but looks best with weekly irrigations throughout the summer and occasional watering during the winter. If it gets too much water, it generates a proliferation of growth through-out the tree. Its lower limbs can't get light, they shed their leaves and develop what is known as "olive whiskers." Keep the tree thinned to avoid this, but avoid topping, as this creates excessive sucker growth and "poodling," which becomes an invitation for serious branch and trunk sunburn. Although fertilization is not necessary, trees respond to an annual feeding of nitrogen, and you can scatter a cupful of ammonium sulfate under the canopy each spring. Follow the feedings with a deep irrigation. Verticillium wilt may be a problem. It appears after a cool spring that is followed by rapidly rising temperatures. For a positive identification of this disease and its control, con-tact the Nevada Cooperative Extension. There are no insect problems.

LANDSCAPE MERIT

This picturesque tree is tolerant of most desert conditions even in lawns, in containers, or espaliered, and it makes an excellent silhouette against structures. It looks at home in a desert or normal gardens where it blends with other plants, especially gray-colored ones. Use it as a canopy tree with plants under it.

Sweet Acacia

Acacia smallii

Height × Spread: 20 feet × 30 feet	Light Requirement	Water
Flower Color: Yellow		
Foliage Color: Bright green		
Bloom Period: Late winter to early spring	**Beneficial Characteristics**	
Zones: 7 to 9		
Color photograph on page 229.		

Sweet Acacia is excellent as a shade or patio tree that produces lush, dense shade. Looking up through the tree, you may doubt its shade potential because of the feathery foliage, but it really does create an oasis. It is a wide-spreading deciduous tree or large shrub, depending on how you use it. A profusion of tiny, fragrant, yellow-to-golden flowers arrange themselves in fluffy balls like miniature pincushions; it is very striking when in full bloom. Blooms adorn the tree while the rest of the country is under snow from January and into April. Like other desert trees, Sweet Acacia shows off best as a multitrunked and branching tree, in a vase shape. Or be stubborn and take the desert out of this tree and make it single-trunked. These trees reach 20 feet high and spread out about 25 to 30 feet. *A. farnesiana* is nearly the same tree, but it is not as hardy due to its tropical origin. For those who love to savor the fragrance of this tree, plant it upwind from your lounging areas to take advantage of its pleasant odor. (LM)

REGIONAL TIPS

The Sweet Acacia will only tolerate temperatures in the low teens and therefore is only recommended for southern Nevada.

WHEN, WHERE, AND HOW TO PLANT

You can plant this tree any time from a container, but it does best planted in fall. Keep it away from frequented areas because of its thorns, and because of its flowers, which can be messy as they shed. It does best in full sun to partial shade, and like all desert-loving trees, it loves a well-drained soil. Since southern Nevada has compacted soils, dig a hole up to three times as wide and as deep as the rootball so the roots can freely move into their new surroundings. Add organic matter to the backfill to keep porous spaces open to accelerate root growth. Build a water basin out beyond the rooted area and fill it twice weekly until new growth emerges. To conserve water, cover the soil under the canopy of the tree with mulch.

CARE AND MAINTENANCE

Sweet Acacia grows best with weekly irrigations throughout the summer, and monthly watering throughout the winter. If you prune the tree often, you are watering too much, but if it begins shedding foliage, increase the waterings. You can forget about fertilizing this legume, as it generates its own nitrogen. Always wear gloves when pruning because of the thorns, and during the early stages of Acacia's life, thin out its interior growth. Do the major pruning after bloom to get more blossoms next season. Keep this tree growing happily and pests will not be a problem.

LANDSCAPE MERIT

Use Sweet Acacia as an accent for a situation, as a specimen, or as a spreading hedge, patio tree, or space divider. It certainly brings a tropical effect to the landscape.

ADDITIONAL SPECIES, CULTIVARS, OR VARIETIES

A. stenophylla, or Shoestring Acacia, is a winner. Once people see it they fall in love with its long, weeping, drooping, evergreen needles. It is a graceful vertical tree, making it very popular around yards on smaller lots. *A. greggi*, Catclaw Acacia, could be called "Wait-a-minute bush" to describe the frustration people feel as they back up to unhook clothing where the bush has caught them with its clawlike thorns. It is from our deserts and is the last to leaf out in the spring and the first to drop leaves in the fall.

Texas Honey Mesquite

Prosopis glandulosa

Height × Spread: 25 feet high × 35 feet wide	**Light Requirement**	**Water**
Flower Color: Yellow		
Foliage Color: Yellow-green		
Bloom Period: Late spring	**Beneficial Characteristic**	
Zones: 8 to 10		
Color photograph on page 229.		

Oh, how I love Texas Honey Mesquite. I love its fine-textured, fern-like leaves that closely resemble those of the California Pepper, and the swaying leaves branch to remind me of Weeping Willows—but both of those are messy trees and do not do well in southern Nevada. This tree makes an excellent deciduous substitute. It is native to the Mojave as well as the Sonoran, Lower Colorado, and Chihuahuan Deserts. Its dark-gray, thorny branches make it easy to identify, and in spring, fresh, lime-green, feathery leaves brighten the landscapes and contrast with the bark even more. Soon after, 2- to 3-inch-long, fragrant yellow flower spikes emerge. Bees make an excellent honey from its flowers, hence the tree's name. Later, creamy seedpods hang like Christmas ornaments on the tree. Flower arrangers seek the pods to add to arrangements. Bonus: You don't have to feed it, which is welcome news to organic gardeners. (LM)

REGIONAL TIPS

Texas Honey Mesquite is an excellent tree for southern Nevada growing conditions. The winters of the north will prove too harsh for it.

WHEN, WHERE, AND HOW TO PLANT

For best results, plant in the early spring to give it plenty of time to root before the heat arrives. It tolerates a wide range of soils but does best in one that is open and well drained. You don't need to amend the soil for Mesquites; the key is to loosen the soil so roots can push out for long-term survival. And because it comes from the desert, it needs a constant source of sunlight. To plant from a container, dig a hole three to five times as wide and as deep as the rootball. Check for drainage by filling the hole with water, and if it drains away within 8 hours, plant the tree. After placing the rootball in the hole, refill it while allowing water to settle the soil surrounding the ball. Build a water basin and fill weekly until new growth emerges.

CARE AND MAINTENANCE

Water twice weekly the first year to encourage root growth, and then weekly throughout the heat of the summer. If you are pruning your Mesquite three to four times a year, you are watering too much. Cut back on the water and you'll cut back the maintenance pruning. As the tree matures, remove the twiggy growth to allow the wind to flow through the tree, and lift the branches so people can move freely under it; this also allows you to see the interesting inner structure of the tree. Fertilizer is not an issue, as this tree is a member of the legume family. Pests are not a problem.

LANDSCAPE MERITS

Use Texas Honey Mesquite to make a bold statement in a desert setting or the traditional landscape. But it has thorns, so keep it away from sidewalks, paths, play areas, and patios to avoid snags. There are some thornless selections, though.

ADDITIONAL SPECIES, CULTIVARS, OR VARIETIES

You'll find many other Mesquites at your nursery. *P. chilensis*, found on the shelves as Chilean or South American Mesquites, are known for their feathery green leaves that endear gardeners to them. The *P. velutina*, or 'Velvet' Mesquite, is unique with its velvety soft, gray-green foliage. *P. pubescens*, or 'Screwbean' Mesquite, is famous for the twisted bean pods decorating the branches in winter.

Thornless Honey Locust

Gleditsia triacanthos 'Inermis'

Height × Spread: 50 feet × 40 feet
Flower Color: Insignificant
Foliage Color: Medium green
Bloom Period: Spring
Zones: 5 to 8
Color photograph on page 229.

Light Requirement

Water

Beneficial Characteristic

Thornless Honey Locust is a large shade tree that does great in small landscapes. It is a large tree, but it does not occupy much space because of its upright growing habit. This tree is the last to leaf out in the spring, unfolding in lemon-lime color, and beautiful yellow-gold leaves follow in autumn; in fact, the Locust is the first signal that winter is on its way. But when leaves drop, the glossy branches take center stage with their upright, vase-shaped frames. Now here's a plus: their long dormant period prevents new leaves from being damaged by late-spring frosts. Many of the native species are thorny, so look for species with *inermis* in the name. This thornless cultivar makes it very desirable in landscapes, and because it is deciduous, the winter sun is allowed to peek through the canopy and warm the patio or landscape throughout the colder months. (LM)

REGIONAL TIPS

Thornless Honey Locust grows in the western and southern parts of the state.

WHEN, WHERE, AND HOW TO PLANT

Plant Thornless Honey Locust from containers anytime, although it does best planted in the fall for more root growth through the winter and less twig dieback the next summer. Thornless Honey Locust will grow in any soil, provided it has good drainage, and it needs full sun. Open up a hole that is three to five times as wide and the same depth as the rootball—this ensures that new roots will have an easy time breaking ground. Amend the backfill soil by working in some organic matter. After placing the rootball in the hole, fold the soil around the roots for good soil-to-root contact, build a water basin around the tree, and fill the basin to thoroughly soak the rooted area. Cover the soil with generous amounts of mulch to conserve water and to cool the soil to accelerate more root development.

CARE AND MAINTENANCE

Water new trees twice a week until established, then weekly until the foliage drops. After that, water monthly until the new leaves unfold, and give trees near sidewalks extra water to keep surface roots from heaving walks in search of moisture. Because Thornless Honey Locust is from the legume family it doesn't require much fertilizer, but a pound of ammonium sulfate spread under the tree's canopy in February will keep it lush. In alkaline soils, Thornless Honey Locust sometimes needs iron to prevent leaves from yellowing. The only pruning it needs is the removal of crisscrossing branches; it naturally develops a vase shape of strong branches. Borers may attack weakened trees if the bark sunburns. To deter them, paint the trunks with a white water-based paint (this also prevents the bark from burning).

LANDSCAPE MERIT

Because so many landscapes are smaller, consider this upright, vase-shaped tree, as it takes less space and its filtered light allows a beautiful lawn to grow under this beauty. And in the fall, the golden-yellow foliage brings on a welcome change to Nevada yards.

ADDITIONAL SPECIES, CULTIVARS, OR VARIETIES

'Moraine' is the oldest of the cultivars and a rapid grower with upward-growing branches. The 'Inermis' cultivar was the first thornless tree. 'Shademaster' is more open and arching in habit with a wineglass shape and is somewhat reminiscent of the American Elm at maturity. 'Sunburst' has yellow new foliage, gradually turning green, but it suffers because the yellow foliage doesn't manufacture food to keep the tree robust. 'Ruby Lace' offers a splash of red-purple when new leaves emerge, becoming green with age.

Washington Hawthorn

Crataegus phaenopyrum

Height × Spread: 20 to 30 feet × 20 to 25 feet
Flower Color: White
Foliage Color: Varies by season
Bloom Period: Late spring
Zones: 5 to 8
Color photograph on page 230.

Light Requirement

Water

Beneficial Characteristics

One of the features of Washington Hawthorn is that it has a more rounded, upright form than some of the other Hawthorns. But like all Hawthorns, it has thorns. The white flowers are about 1/2 inch in size and bloom in late spring on flat corymbs at the ends of the twigs. You might want to plant 'Lustre' Washington Hawthorn because the flowers are larger; when this tree is in bloom, it looks like layers of flowers from top to bottom, and this cultivar does have fewer thorns. The fruit of Washington Hawthorn is a small pome, which looks like a miniature apple when you cut one in half. The fruit turns scarlet in the fall and is about 1/4 inch in diameter, hanging in clusters. When they ripen, the birds move in for lunch. The flowers of Washington Hawthorn are spectacular as are the fruits. The deltoid-shaped leaves on these deciduous trees have from three to five lobes and turn scarlet in the fall. (DP)

REGIONAL TIPS

Washington Hawthorns are better adapted to the high desert and mountainous regions of the state because winter cold is needed for flower development.

WHEN, WHERE, AND HOW TO PLANT

Washington Hawthorn can be planted any time during the growing season if container grown, but it must be planted in the late winter or early spring if purchased bare root. Balled-and-burlapped plants are available mainly in the spring. Plant where it will get full sun, in any kind of soil, but it will grow faster in a well-drained one. (If you are planting it to use as a hedge, space the plants about 4 feet apart.) If you are planting as a balled-and-burlapped tree, remove the burlap and any twine or wire used to support the rootball—the burlap will rot in our dry climate, and the twine or wire will eventually girdle the trunk and kill the tree. Dig the hole only as deep as the rootball, but up to five times as wide, place the rootball in the hole, and backfill using the soil that came from the hole. Give the tree a good soaking after planting.

CARE AND MAINTENANCE

Water deeply about every ten to fourteen days with 2 inches of water. The tree can be pruned if it becomes necessary, but with those thorns, I would leave it alone. Hawthorns generally are plagued with fireblight, a bacterial disease that can seriously injure the tree and even kill it, but Washington Hawthorn is resistant to the disease. When it gets hot and dry, check for spider mites.

LANDSCAPE MERIT

Because of its size, this tree makes a great specimen for any yard. The thorns can be a real nuisance, and many gardeners prefer to use it as a barrier hedge for that reason. Because of its dense growth, it will stop most everything.

ADDITIONAL SPECIES, CULTIVARS, OR VARIETIES

'Paul's Scarlet' Hawthorn, *C. oxycantha* 'Paulii', is one of the showiest, with double, bright-red flowers. The English Hawthorn, *C. oxycantha*, has white flowers and is very good for hedges.

White Fir

Abies concolor

Other Name: Silver Fir
Height × Spread: 50 to 60 feet ×
   25 to 35 feet
Flower Color: Cones
Foliage Color: Blue-green
Bloom Period: Spring
Zones: 3 to 7
Color photograph on page 230.

Light Requirements

Water

Beneficial Characteristic

White Fir is one of the common native evergreen plants in the Sierra Nevada Range, used in the landscape where a nice, pyramidal-shaped tree is wanted. It is very hardy and will take temperatures way below zero. The needles are often only 1 1/2 inches long in the wild but grow to almost 3 inches long under landscape conditions. The needles range from a dark-green to a silvery-green color. One of the interesting characteristics is the way the needles attach to the twigs: they have little suction cups that hold them tightly to the stem. The needles of White Fir are also very fragrant and flat, are blunt at the ends, and have a tendency to curve upwards on the sides and undersides of the twig. Another interesting point about all Firs is that the cones never fall off the tree intact, unless the wind knocks them down or a squirrel gets them. The 5- to 6-inch cone forms and matures on the top of the branch and stands upright. When fully ripe, the scales of the cone fall off, letting the seed drop out and leaving a peg standing upright, still attached to the branch. White Fir is an attractive landscape tree that withstands heat and drought very well and still looks good. (DP)

REGIONAL TIPS
White Fir is best adapted to the mountainous regions of the state and will not survive at all in southern Nevada.

WHEN, WHERE, AND HOW TO PLANT
Plant White Fir in the spring and summer for best results, but if container grown, it can be transplanted any time during the growing season. It can be purchased balled and burlapped in the spring, or in containers. White Firs grow in full sun or part shade. Dig the hole

only as deep as the rootball and about three to five times as wide, and remove the container or burlap. Place the root-ball in the hole, backfill with the soil you took from the hole, and give it a good soaking.

CARE AND MAINTENANCE

Water White Fir about every seven to ten days. It will get all the fertilizer it needs when you fertilize other plants in your garden. You can give it a light shearing to make it a little bushier, but it is pretty much carefree.

LANDSCAPE MERIT

Use White Fir as a focal point in the landscape or for framing a view. It can develop into a very large tree, so plant it where it can grow to occupy a spot 35 feet in diameter.

ADDITIONAL SPECIES, CULTIVARS, OR VARIETIES

The Sub-Alpine Fir *A. lasiocarpa* is sometimes used for rock gardens because it is a very slow-growing plant. It gives the feeling of a scene high up in the mountains.

 Did You Know?

White Fir is one of the major trees sold for Christmas in northern Nevada. It has a lot of fragrance when you bring it into the house, and it holds its needles well.

CHAPTER ELEVEN

Turf Grasses

W HEN SOMEONE SUGGESTS ELIMINATING TURF in Nevada to conserve water, we may get the feeling a civil war is about to break out. We all bring with us memories of our own expansive turf area where we played football and baseball. Turf makes a great place to play, to lounge, to party, to cool off and just enjoy life. For some reason, we forget about the monotonous times spent chasing a mower over the grass.

Did you ever walk through a lawn on a hot summer day? As you walk from pavement onto grass something is very obvious—the difference in temperature between the two surfaces. Of course, turf is much cooler. And is there any better reason for utilizing turf in the desert?

Historically, Europeans used turf for lawn bowling, and the game of golf became popular in the British Isles. Villages established lawns, which served as meeting places and recreational areas. Lawns became common with wealthy landowners. They didn't have lawn mowers, so they cut the grass with a scythe or "mowed" it using grazing livestock such as sheep.

The real birth of the modern turf grass industry occurred in the United States after World War II. The rapid growth of the economy resulted in a housing boom that had a revolutionary effect. As millions of houses were built, millions of lawns were planted, and recreational activities became increasingly popular.

There are many reasons why turf grass is the leading ornamental plant in the American landscape. It is a superior ground cover. Grass plants have an extensive root system that knits the soil together rather than being blown around or washed away. Turf grass also releases significant amounts of oxygen into the air (for us) and through the transpiration process cools our environment. It also

Chapter Eleven

reduces the glare from the sun and helps remove air pollutants and dust particles from the atmosphere.

The technological revolution has accelerated the pace of life so that a peculiar contrast exists: Individuals face increased pressure to make a living on one side, and on the other, they have more free time available. This has led to a demand for additional "green space." Homeowners show the increased emphasis on the use of plants by creating attractive, soothing backgrounds for recreational activities, with turf being used most often.

A pleasing landscape for the home adds enjoyment for all who see it. In fact, a well-groomed lawn will generate a fifteen percent increase in the resale price of a home. A community with a high percentage of attractive home lawns enhances the quality of living for all inhabitants.

As residents migrate to Nevada, they bring with them an appreciation for grass. But in the Southwest, turf must be adjusted to the environment. Nature rarely occupies the soil with a single type of plant, but rather with a mixture of different species. We insist on planting one type of grass alone, and those grasses (Bermudagrass and Fescue) we do grow are not found growing wild. Therefore, matching the climate and growing conditions to the appropriate grass is a major factor in turf grass selection.

Turf grass is the major vegetative ground cover in the American landscape. Some may be mowed regularly, which is the case in Nevada. Some are able to withstand hard use and can provide an ideal surface. But whatever the type, we Americans love our turf. In the United States, there are more than 50,000,000 lawns and over 12,000 golf courses. Wow!

Bermudagrass

Cynodon dactylon

Recommended Mowing	Light Requirement	Water
Height: 1 inch		
Foliage Color: Green; brown in winter		
Zones: 8 to 10	**Beneficial Characteristic**	

B elieve it or not, Bermudagrass is southern Nevada's most impressive lawn grass. It is a vigorous warm-season grass that spreads three ways: by aboveground stems called "stolons," underground stems called "rhizomes," and by seed. Old-timers like the fine texture and dense growth this grass offers in a lush green carpet so durable that golf courses and athletic complexes use it. Some varieties, like Tifgreen, Tifway, and Tifdwarf, further refine these virtues, as they are denser, finer textured, and more tolerant of cultural conditions. One of the drawbacks of Burmudagrass is that it browns out in the winter. Let's call it "golden brown" to put a positive twist on it in an effort to get people to return to it as a water-conserving grass. (LM)

REGIONAL TIPS

In southern Nevada, it makes an excellent turf and is very water efficient. It will not withstand northern Nevada's harsh winters.

WHEN, WHERE, AND HOW TO PLANT

Plant Bermudagrass from April through August in an area receiving full sun. You must decide if you are going to seed or sod the lawn. If you choose sod, order it from the nursery to insure a fresh supply. Soil preparation is the same for both methods. Clean away all debris. Next, rototill 3 to 4 inches of organic matter into the top 6 inches of soil. Smooth out the area and spread 1 to 2 pounds of seed over a 1000-square-foot area of soil. Then lightly rake in the seeds and cover with mulch. Keep the soil moist until the seedlings emerge. If you want instant sod, stagger the strips as a brick mason staggers the pattern of the bricks. Keep the sodded area moist with five to six light sprinklings a day. After about a week, pull up a corner and check the roots. If it looks like an unshaven man, the zillions of white roots reaching into their new surroundings, then you are off to a great start.

CARE AND MAINTENANCE
Bermudagrass needs twice-weekly sprinkle irrigations in the spring and fall, running for 15 minutes. In summer, run the sprinklers every other day for 15 minutes to keep this grass vigorous and lush. Fertilizer is a key issue. Spread 5 pounds (10 cups) of ammonium sulfate per 1000 square feet over the lawn area around Valentine's, Memorial, and Labor Days, and water in. To get the finest looking turf, mow frequently, cutting the grass an inch high with a reel mower. Bermudagrass has a tendency to develop a thatch layer (or, dead grass) just above the soil surface. It impedes water and fertilizer movement into the soil. Remove the thatch periodically with a vertical mower. Grubs plague Bermudagrass. If the grass dies for no apparent reason, dig in the infected area and look for grubs. If you find them, contact your local garden center for an appropriate control.

LANDSCAPE MERIT
Bermudagrass is a very tough grass, tolerating heavy football traffic. After a game, give it a good irrigation and it will be ready for the next game. Bermudagrass uses 50 percent less water than other lawns and turns a golden-brown in winter. I hope it catches on.

ADDITIONAL SPECIES, CULTIVARS, OR VARIETIES
Tifdwarf is rich-green and spreads slowly. Tifgreen is fine textured, rich-green, and a vigorous grower producing a heavy thatch. Tifway is fine textured and makes an excellent lawn with good frost resistance.

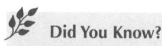 **Did You Know?**

Tifdwarf, Tifgreen, and Tifway do not produce seeds, so they are not allergy-producing plants.

Fescue

Festuca arundinacea × hybrid

Other Name: Tall Turf Fescue	**Light Requirements**	**Water**
Recommended Mowing		
Height: 3 inches	☀ ☀	💧
Foliage Color: Dark green		
Zones: 4 to 8		

A revolution began back in the early 1980s. People by the thousands were coming to southern Nevada, and they all wanted an ever-green lawn. Bermudagrass didn't fit the bill because it browned out through the winter. Old-timers overseeded theirs, but that didn't go over with the newcomers. Breeders developed new cultivars and suppliers couldn't keep the seed in stock, as all wanted to make the switch to an evergreen lawn. These new Fescues have finer leaf blades, more resistance to insects and disease, better shade-tolerance, and make better use of soil moisture. Add to that their deep root characteristics and wearability. And through it all, the improved Fescues came closer to the Bluegrasses. (LM)

REGIONAL TIPS:

Fescue is a transition grass. It will grow in both the north and the south. In southern Nevada, heat restricts the growth of Kentucky Bluegrass and Fescues became an alternative.

WHEN, WHERE, AND HOW TO PLANT

Lay sod anytime, but you'll get the best results laying it in spring and fall. Seeding is best done during the same times. Fescue does best when grown in full sun but tolerates dappled shade. Take time to work organic matter in the soil prior to seeding or sodding the lawn to eliminate problems later. Follow directions on the package for the amount of seed to spread, then lightly rake seed into the soil surface and cover with mulch. Set the sprinklers to run a few minutes to keep the surface moist. Repeat the sprinklings three to five times a day, gradually reducing the number of times and lengthening the duration. If you use sod, calculate the square footage and order your sod so it will be fresh—then you and your nursery will be happy. Keep the sod moist, but also run the sprinklers long enough to penetrate into the soil below and encourage deep rooting.

CARE AND MAINTENANCE

Mow your grass at 2 to 3 inches, with the taller height in the summer. Grass requires at least three feedings a year: Memorial and Labor Days for the entire state, Columbus Day in the north, and Thanksgiving in the south with a fertilizer high in nitrogen and potassium. Follow each feeding with a deep irrigation. Distribute the fertilizer evenly over the grass to avoid the zebra look. Water is critical to a happy lawn. Let the sprinklers run 15 minutes at a time twice a week, but as the temperatures increase (90 degrees Fahrenheit), switch to three times a week. Because Nevada has compacted soils, aerate in the spring and fall to assist the growth of the grass. Lawn diseases are hard to identify, and by the time you send a sample off, the disease is either gone or has become so bad you need to replace the lawn. I recommend the shotgun approach. Translation: If you suspect a disease, go after it with Daconil, but follow the directions. Leafhoppers flourish in the grass but they don't cause much damage. I ignore them or use Neem.

LANDSCAPE MERIT

Fescue is an evergreen lawn grass that allows homeowners to have a green lawn throughout the winter. It is a very drought-hardy plant.

ADDITIONAL SPECIES, CULTIVARS, OR VARIETIES

Seed companies are coming out with new and improved varieties every day. Your nursery has the best of those that are now available. Rebel and Mustang are but two—new varieties are released each year, causing a lot of changes. Avoid coarse pasture Fescues such as Kentucky 31.

Kentucky Bluegrass

Poa pratensis

Recommended Mowing	Light Requirements	Water
Height: 3 inches		
Foliage Color: Dark green		
Zones: 3 to 8		

Kentucky Bluegrass is the standard against which all other lawn grasses are measured. It is the most widely grown and recognized grass across the United States. It looks and feels the way most people think a lawn is supposed to look—dark green, dense, with a medium texture. It is the grass that took my falls while I played baseball and football in my youth. It grows faster in the spring and fall and slows during the summer but remains green if given ample water. It does stop growing during the winter. Kentucky Bluegrass propagates by stolons (aboveground runners rooting down as it spreads) and rhizomes (underground runners as it spreads) and by seed. If properly cared for, it fills in bare spots. (LM)

REGIONAL TIPS

It is easy to grow in northern Nevada but struggles in southern Nevada with the increased heat.

WHEN, WHERE, AND HOW TO PLANT

You can plant it from early spring until early fall. It loves full sun but takes some shade. If the shade becomes too strong, it will decline. To plant, clean away all debris and rototill organic matter in the top 6 inches of soil. Smooth out the area and spread the variety of your choice at the rate recommended on the package. Lightly rake in the seeds and cover with mulch, keeping it moist with five to six sprayings a day until grass emerges. If you want instant lawn, lay sod tightly together. Stagger the sod as a bricklayer staggers bricks, then roll the sod to bring the rooted area in firm contact with the soil. Keep the planted areas moist, and provide a first feeding in about a month.

CARE AND MAINTENANCE

Kentucky Bluegrass is a high-maintenance grass. Mow your grass at 2 to 3 inches with the taller height in the summer. Kentucky

Bluegrass requires at least three feedings a year: Memorial and Labor Days for the entire state, Columbus Day in the north, and Thanksgiving in the south, with a fertilizer high in nitrogen and potassium. When you follow this schedule, there is no need to give the lawn an earlier feeding. Follow each feeding with a deep irrigation and be sure to distribute the fertilizer evenly over the grass to avoid the zebra look. Water is critical to a happy Bluegrass lawn. Let the sprinklers run 15 minutes at a time twice a week, but as temperatures increase (90 degrees Fahrenheit), switch to thrice-weekly waterings. In winter, give Kentucky Bluegrass lawns a monthly watering in the south. Because Nevada has compacted soils, aerate in the spring and fall to assist the growth of the grass. Kentucky Bluegrass brings with it many problems. You can expect billbugs, sod webworms, grubs, and a host of fungi. Since each has its own unique trait, call your Extension office for proper identification of the problem and its controls.

LANDSCAPE MERIT

Most people prefer Kentucky Bluegrass because it is the ultimate ground cover. It is tough and wearable, withstands foot traffic, and provides a serene expanse of green—lovely to look at and pleasant to walk or play upon. It has the ability to mend divots we create, with its stolons and rhizomes. These same features hold the sod together during transport, and sod growers use this trait, planting Bluegrass with Fescue to help it hold.

ADDITIONAL SPECIES, CULTIVARS, OR VARIETIES

Seed companies are coming out with new and improved varieties. Your nursery has the best of those now available.

CHAPTER   TWELVE

Vines

THE "IVY LEAGUE" COLLEGE, a backbone of American higher education, owes its name to vines. From Harvard, founded in 1636, to Yale and to the many universities that have followed, the humble vine has played an important role in the nostalgia for American universities. To this day many old, majestic homes along the East Coast have an ivy-covered exterior. Even in our rapidly expanding Western area, vines can be utilized to preserve a cultural and historic image.

Whether used to create a cooling effect, provide privacy, establish a boundary, or just produce flamboyant flowers, vines offer many options for landscape designs. An important characteristic of a vine is its ability to adapt to the environment. This means "training" is possible—the vine can grow up walls, trellises, arbors, and posts and can even arch a gate. Even aggressive vines can be curtailed with selective pruning and "pinching back." Most vines have a natural tendency to grow upward and branch into a tangled mass while leaving the bottom of the plant bare. To prevent these growth habits, train and tie the vine branches horizontally until the desired plant width is reached. To promote multiple branching, pinch back regularly just above the buds. As you might guess, the vine can become just as creative as you desire it to be. One of the unique ways to utilize a vine is as a hedge that can define garden or landscaping areas.

In a desert area, a vine placed on the south or west side of a home will significantly reduce the amount of sunlight and heat reaching the structure. This is nature's air conditioning. While providing heat relief in the summer, a vine that drops its leaves in winter allows the sun to provide heat for a home. Since vines are vertical plants, they take up very little land area. The vine can also be a beautiful,

Chapter Twelve

blooming shade provider for any outdoor people-area. Lattice over a deck or patio can be turned into a Garden of Eden by planting vines to cover the lattice.

Different vines have different ways to cling. Some have their own methods for attaching themselves to a structure; others need our assistance to remain upright. But vines do not grow vertically in thin air. Whether the vine is self-clinging or not, a structure is needed to provide support. That structure could be the side of a house or a wooden or plastic trellis or arbor. Support may be provided by soft twine attached to something at both ends. Even a chain-link fence might be used to support a vine. All vines will create a ground cover when they are not furnished with support.

Never plant self-attaching vines next to a house with wood siding. The vines hold moisture and can cause rapid deterioration of painted wood. Most homes in an urban, desert environment have cinder-block walls around their yards. These walls create an opportunity for vines to help deflect some of the intense summer heat that can be generated by concrete surfaces. In this situation, vines also produce a way to extend the garden or yard area to include an exterior wall.

Some vines will produce flowers with sweet nectar that can be used to attract winged visitors such as butterflies, bees, and hummingbirds to the yard. A vine that sheds its foliage in winter provides a great opportunity to reduce the temperature in a green-house during the summer months, when the foliage is present.

Boston Ivy

Parthenocissus tricuspidata

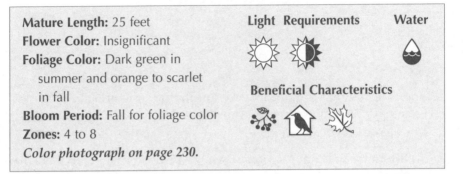

Mature Length: 25 feet

Flower Color: Insignificant

Foliage Color: Dark green in summer and orange to scarlet in fall

Bloom Period: Fall for foliage color

Zones: 4 to 8

Color photograph on page 230.

Light Requirements

Water

Beneficial Characteristics

Boston Ivy brings a striking array of fall color to our landscapes—something those of us from colder climes truly miss. In winter, bare twigs trace the wall with interesting patterns. The glossy three-lobed leaves (up to 8 inches wide) are bright green in spring, dark leathery green in summer, and a brilliant scarlet-red in fall. Boston Ivy is a deciduous vine, which is more easily controlled than English or Algerian Ivies and doesn't scorch if properly watered, and variegated cultivars are available. Use this deciduous vine to conserve energy by shading sun-exposed walls in summer and allowing winter sun to warm the home. The inconspicuous flowers produce BB-like berries in the fall, and birds feed on the berries through the winter. (LM)

REGIONAL TIPS

Boston Ivy is a good vine to grow in either northern or southern Nevada, as it survives virtually all weather conditions. In the south, it does need some protection from the afternoon summer sun.

WHEN, WHERE, AND HOW TO PLANT

Plant Boston Ivy any time from containers but it makes its most aggressive growth when planted in the spring. Plant it in full sun to partial shade—it takes sunlight to really cause the fall foliage to make the beautiful colors. Boston Ivy will tolerate a wide range of soils but prefers a slightly acidic soil. (Add sulfur yearly, to keep the soil within the acid range.) Open up the soil by making a hole three times wider than and as deep as the rootball. Mix in organic matter with the on-site soil to help keep our compacted soils open, to get the most out of this vine. Fold the prepared soil in and around the rootball, adding water at the same time for good soil-to-root contact.

Build a basin around the plant and fill twice weekly until established. Mulch under this vine will aid in getting the plant off to a good start and also helps to cool the soil and conserve water.

CARE AND MAINTENANCE

Water the plant at least three times a week throughout the summer, and more if the leaves begin to scorch. As the weather cools, water once a week and only monthly during winter. Without adequate moisture, the leaves become sensitive to direct sunlight. Boston Ivy needs a balanced fertilizer at some time around Valentine's Day and again near Labor Day. It is a plant that doesn't need a lot of pruning to keep it handsome; prune only to maintain it within the bounds you desire. Be aware that the vine clings tightly to buildings with disklike attachments that are hard to remove. It is disease- and insect-free with the exception of the grape leaf skeletonizer, which strips the greenery from each leaf, leaving only the veins. This pest is easy to control with *Bacillus thuringiensis*.

LANDSCAPE MERIT

Use this beauty primarily as a wall covering. It looks great climbing fences, masonry, or stone. Plants are somewhat aggressive and may cause some problems with their disklike attachments if they are using wooden structures for support.

ADDITIONAL SPECIES, CULTIVARS, OR VARIETIES

P. tricuspidata 'Veitchii' leaves turn an intense orange to scarlet in fall. 'Beverly Brooks' has similar leaves and turns brilliant shades of scarlet-red in fall. Tightly clinging stems quickly cover walls and fences.

 Did You Know?

In Nevada, we can plant the same Boston Ivy that covers the walls of Wrigley Field.

Cat's Claw Vine

Macfadyena unguis-cati

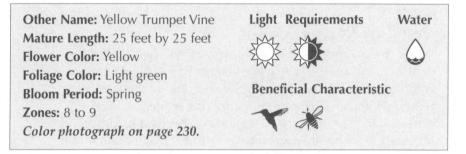

Other Name: Yellow Trumpet Vine	**Light Requirements**	**Water**
Mature Length: 25 feet by 25 feet		
Flower Color: Yellow		
Foliage Color: Light green	**Beneficial Characteristic**	
Bloom Period: Spring		
Zones: 8 to 9		
Color photograph on page 230.		

Try planting Cat's Claw Vine in your entryway and see what happens. It's fun to watch people gazing at the spreading vine above. Stems head off in one direction and then, with no apparent reason, head another way. Soon other stems are overlapping each other to totally cover the ceiling. As plant density thickens, new stems can't find anything to attach to and hang down from the silhouette, festooning the area beneath. It's like they're saying, "Help me find someplace to sink my cat claws into so I can do wondrous things too!" This is a fast-growing semievergreen vine that can cover walls, fences, and shade structures if it finds someplace to attach itself. Its claws (officially called tendrils) literally look like cat's claws and are used to hook on surfaces like stucco, plaster, brick, or concrete. This remarkable vine is one of the best vines for southern Nevada's hot walls. In the spring, trumpet-shaped butter-yellow colored flowers about 3 inches deep bloom impressively but are short-lived. This is when you'll see hummingbirds and bees frequenting the flowers. Foot-long beans follow, to become very showy as they hang well below the silhouette. The tendrils release easily and don't mark the surface where attached—providing you push rather than pull to remove the vine. It releases just like cat's claws! Heaviest growth is usually at the top of the vine where it gets the most sun. (LM)

REGIONAL TIPS
This vine will only survive temperatures down to 22 degrees Fahrenheit. This means it will only grow in the southern Nevada climate.

WHEN, WHERE, AND HOW TO PLANT
Because it is frost-sensitive, plant it after the last frost, which is around March 15. And because it is such an aggressive vine, only

purchase the 1-gallon containers, as Cat's Claw will fill in fast. It does best in full sun but will do well in partially shaded conditions, and it loves an open, well-drained soil. Dig a hole three times wider than and as deep as the rootball. Enrich the on-site soil by adding generous amounts of organic matter. Build a water basin around it and keep soil moist until you see new growth emerging from the plant. Cover the soil under the canopy with a 3-inch layer of mulch to cool the roots for better plant growth and to conserve water.

CARE AND MAINTENANCE

Cat's Claw thrives against hot walls, and it needs weekly waterings throughout the summer and monthly waterings when it's cold. Water more if you want fast, lush growth. It is not a big eater, but with the spring flush of growth and flowers coming on, feed it around Valentine's Day and again Labor Day using a balanced fertilizer. If it gets rank, prune to the ground in the late winter to stimulate new growth and create density. (This doesn't have to be done every year.) You may need to tie higher stems to supports in windy areas. Cat's Claw Vine doesn't have any pest problems.

LANDSCAPE MERIT

Cat's Claw Vine is a wonderfully durable, self-climbing covering for walls, trellises, posts, and fences. Use it to assist energy conservation when it's planted on the southwest side of a home. It certainly accents whatever it covers.

ADDITIONAL SPECIES, CULTIVARS, OR VARIETIES

There are no additional varieties.

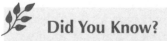

Did You Know?

Cat's Claw Vine develops tuberous roots that store a lot of water and nutrients.

Chinese Wisteria

Wisteria sinensis

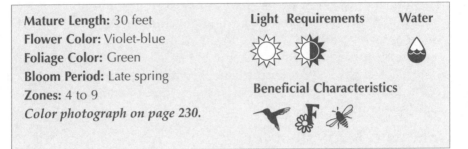

Mature Length: 30 feet
Flower Color: Violet-blue
Foliage Color: Green
Bloom Period: Late spring
Zones: 4 to 9
Color photograph on page 230.

Light Requirements

Water

Beneficial Characteristics

There is nothing more spectacular than Chinese Wisteria in bloom. The pendulous clusters of flowers look like bunches of grapes hanging down as one solid mass of color. The blooms are lavender to blue and have a slight but very pleasant fragrance. They bloom in late spring before the leaves emerge. It is a very aggressive vine that can grow 20 feet or more in a single season. It needs a support to grow on, but will also latch onto anything and start twining around it—it's not unusual to see Wisteria flowers blooming up in trees. But Chinese Wisteria only twines counterclockwise, and why it does, I don't know. (Japanese Wisteria twines clockwise.) The leaves are compound and are made up of between seven and thirteen deciduous leaflets; so in the summer it's a very full-looking plant, and in winter it just looks like a lot of twining stems. The fruit is a brown bean-shaped pod about 6 inches long. (DP)

REGIONAL TIPS

Chinese Wisteria will grow almost anywhere in the state, but in colder regions plagued by late killing frosts, the flower buds are usually killed.

WHEN, WHERE, AND HOW TO PLANT

Chinese Wisteria is usually planted in the spring but can be planted any time during the growing season. It grows best in a well-drained, slightly alkaline soil. Some gardeners have trouble transplanting it, but in my experience it's not any different from planting any other shrub or vine. Wisteria vines flower best in full sun and produce fewer flowers in part shade; they are a little temperamental as far as flowering goes. (Mine flowers pretty much all the time. In fact, one spring it flowered about three times in the spring and then again in the late summer. My Grandpa's doesn't want to flower at all, and that could be because it was planted from a seedling and not grafted.) Dig the hole only as deep as the rootball and about three times as wide. Place the plant in the hole, backfill around the roots with the same soil that came out, and give it a good soaking. You can use a little complete fertilizer, high in phosphorous and low in nitrogen, at the time of planting.

CARE AND MAINTENANCE

Chinese Wisteria needs to be pruned and trained continually and also root-pruned to maintain the best flowering. You can root-prune by shoving a spade down into the root zone in a few places under the plant. This seems to stimulate blooming the following year. In the winter, cut it back to about four flower buds per stem. Fertilize in the spring, but not after it has started flowering. Give it 1 inch of water twice a week. Foliage may become yellow (chlorotic) in alkaline soils. Adding sulfur may correct this problem.

LANDSCAPE MERIT

Chinese Wisteria Vines are ideal for patio covers as long as you're not afraid of bees. I have seen them used to drape over garage doors and grow on fences and, of course, on arbors. The most effective use I've seen was on a trellis covering a garden walkway, which allowed the plant to spread out.

ADDITIONAL SPECIES, CULTIVARS, OR VARIETIES

If you want white flowers, try *W. sinensis* 'Alba'. 'Jako' is a white one with very fragrant flowers.

Did You Know?

Chinese Wisterias are so aggressive, they will strangle everything they come in contact with—so keep them out of your trees.

Coral Vine

Antigonon leptopus

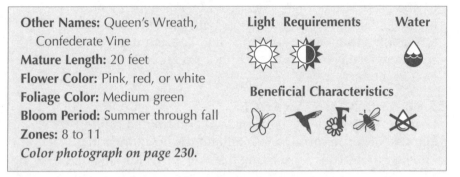

Other Names: Queen's Wreath, Confederate Vine
Mature Length: 20 feet
Flower Color: Pink, red, or white
Foliage Color: Medium green
Bloom Period: Summer through fall
Zones: 8 to 11
Color photograph on page 230.

Light Requirements

Water

Beneficial Characteristics

A festive summer vine with a tropical appearance, Coral Vine festoons fences, trellises, and walls in even the hottest situations. It is a Southwestern favorite. It grows bigger every year, dazzling observers with its shocking pink flowers. This tendril-climbing vine sends out shoots in late spring and blooms throughout the summer until frost until the vine freezes to the ground. Warm weather brings sprays of pink, red, or white blossoms (depending on the selection), concentrated where they get the most sun and lasting until the weather cools. Coral Vine's captivating color and the heart-shaped leaves serve the garden well during summer and fall. It is the ideal vine to screen sun from the hot side of a house. When frost hits, the vine dies back to the ground, but it is easy to pull down and discard. The foliage is very attractive, offering bright green leaves 4 inches long, and the vine covers supports rapidly without training. Once established, plant and root growth continue in greater abundance with each spring's renewal. (LM)

REGIONAL TIPS

Coral Vine is hardy in only the warmest areas of the state.

WHEN, WHERE, AND HOW TO PLANT

Plant Coral Vine from containers in March and April. Because it is an aggressive grower, there is no need to purchase large container plants. Plant it where it will get full sun to partial shade. The more sun it gets, the more blooms you will enjoy. Next, provide a trellis or something to support the initial stages of growth. It can tolerate many kinds of soils—growing in virtually untouched soil—but will perform much better in amended soil. Make a hole three times as wide and as deep as the rootball; then mix in an organic material with the on-site soil and nestle the plant into its permanent bed. Build a water basin under the vine and thoroughly soak the rootball twice a week until you see new growth emerging. Mulch the area under the plant to stop the evaporation of water from the soil by the southerly breezes. You can grow Coral Vine in containers, but you must provide a trellis and a backdrop to show off the vine as it develops.

CARE AND MAINTENANCE
Because of the hot and dry southerly winds, this vine needs thrice-weekly waterings throughout the summer to look its best. It will need daily watering if planted in a container. Fertilize the plant Valentine's, Memorial, and Labor Days with a balanced fertilizer high in phosphorous to help it produce flowers. (A high-nitrogen fertilizer will generate foliage at the expense of flowers.) You must provide supports for it to climb. If we have a mild winter, Coral Vine is deciduous, but if frost gets to the plant, prune the vine back to the ground; after, mulch over the underground parts of the plant to protect it from further frost damage. Insects and diseases don't find this beauty to their liking.

LANDSCAPE MERIT
Coral Vine brings a tropical effect in the landscape with loads of summer color. It is a good trellis and patio plant for the hot sides of homes, or use it as a shade screen for a patio.

ADDITIONAL SPECIES, CULTIVARS, OR VARIETIES
'Album' has white flowers; 'Baja Red' now comes to us with watermelon-red flowers.

Creeping Fig

Ficus pumila

Other Names: Climbing Fig, Trailing Fig
Mature Length: 40 feet
Flower Color: Inconspicuous
Foliage Color: Bright Green
Bloom Period: Insignificant
Zones: 8 to 11
Color photograph on page 230.

Light Requirement

Water

Beneficial Characteristic

If you want a vine that will paint an intricate design on your stucco walls or fence, plant Creeping Fig. It has many of the attributes found in English Ivy but is prized for the delicate tracery formed by its young leaves. They start out small to eventually become the size of a quarter. But don't be fooled by the innocence of the small stems and leaves; the leaves eventually mature to 2 inches to give the plant a completely different appearance. Creeping Fig will cover walls and ceilings, attaching itself tightly with aerial rootlets. Stems intertwine, crisscrossing to form a dense mat. I saw a situation where the vine covered an entire patio, and it was awesome. As the stems reach out into the air, the leaves become darker green on top and lighter green below. Sometimes you need to cut back the vines to renew the charming young ones, which will start up the wall yet again. The vine develops woody branches, which become unsightly and need removing. (A note of caution: Getting the rootlets off the wall is hard.) Once in a while some edible figs come along, so enjoy them. Creeping Fig can be used as a ground-cover vine, but its real virtue is climbing walls and generating intricate vine designs. (LM)

REGIONAL TIPS

Creeping Fig is not hardy enough for northern Nevada weather conditions.

WHEN, WHERE, AND HOW TO PLANT

Plant this vine anytime, but you'll get the best results when planted in fall from containers. Creeping Fig tolerates partial shade but would rather have plenty of sunlight; it will tolerate most soil conditions, provided it gets good drainage, although it prefers a highly organic soil. Mix in a generous amount of organic matter with the on-site soil before planting. Purchase 1-gallon containers, as the vine grows quickly. Fold the soil around the rootball, adding water at the same time to settle the soil next to the roots. Build a water basin and fill with water three times a week to get started, as Creeping Fig requires constant moisture.

CARE AND MAINTENANCE

Water three times a week throughout summer and monthly during winter. It loves a balanced fertilizer around Valentine's, Memorial, and Labor Days. Follow each feeding with a good irrigation to move nutrients to the roots. Creeping Fig isn't a highly demanding vine, but stragglers need to be thinned and older wood removed when it becomes exposed. Every few years, cut the vine back to the ground to see juvenile leaves at their best and to control its size. It is pest-free.

LANDSCAPE MERIT

By planting Creeping Fig, you achieve a deep green, woodsy feeling with a minimum of care. It does well on north-facing walls and partly shaded pillars. You'll find Creeping Fig useful as a patio specimen, and it's also very popular as a houseplant grown on stakes or small trellises. You might get the feeling that it will overrun a container, but the way it attaches and hangs on to the exhibit is what makes it so pretty.

ADDITIONAL SPECIES, CULTIVARS, OR VARIETIES

'Minima' is smaller, with leaves that appear to stay juvenile longer; the leaves are only 1/2 inch long or less, making it an especially useful houseplant. 'Quercifolia' has leaves that are somewhat oak leaf–shaped. 'Variegata' has very attractive variegated leaves but it is less hardy.

Grape

Vitis vinifera

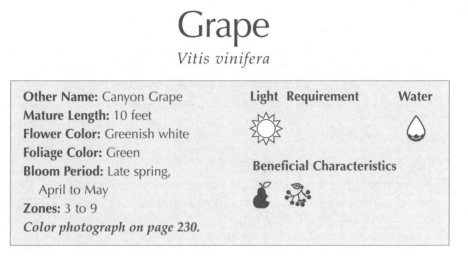

Other Name: Canyon Grape
Mature Length: 10 feet
Flower Color: Greenish white
Foliage Color: Green
Bloom Period: Late spring,
  April to May
Zones: 3 to 9
Color photograph on page 230.

Light Requirement

Water

Beneficial Characteristics

I love Grapevines in my yard. They cover those famous, ugly block walls in landscapes. This wallpaper of vines cools the surroundings and livens up the yard, adding to their glamour by producing an abundance of grapes. To me, Grapevines have a show going on all year. In the winter, I enjoy the gnarled canes and use them for Christmas wreaths. In spring, lush foliage unfolds and the blooms follow shortly thereafter; then clusters of berries size up and ripen in the summer for eating (Nevada's sunshine generates high concentrations of sugars to make them very sweet). As fall sets in, the foliage turns golden-yellow and drops, finally revealing the twisted canes. Grapes grow with great vigor, putting on several feet of new growth a season. Use this trait to cover a patio or make an arbor. Clusters of fruit hang below the foliage to become an awesome sight. If fruit is not harvested, let the birds eat some and then clean up the rest. (LM)

REGIONAL TIPS

Grapes in general perform well throughout Nevada. Some varieties are more tolerant of cold winters than others; select a variety best for your area.

WHEN, WHERE, AND HOW TO PLANT

Plant grapes grown in containers anytime you find them in the nurseries. Grapes do best in full sun yet will tolerate partial shade and poor soil conditions. But to perform best, they prefer a well-drained soil. Make a hole three times as wide and as deep as the rootball, and work some organic matter into the on-site soil. Place the plant in the hole and fold the prepared soil around the ball, using water to help settle the soil; then give the plant good soakings until established. Once established, Grapes have a deep root system.

CARE AND MAINTENANCE

Grapes respond quickly to water. You will know they are overwatered if the vines run rampant, but if leaves are small and sparse, add water. Grapes get by on very little nitrogen fertilizer; add it after pruning. Do not use manure, as it induces iron chlorosis or yellowing of leaves. You must rejuvenate your Grapes by removing the old wood each spring. First select four light brownish–colored canes that grew last year to keep for this year, and remove all other canes. Count out fifteen buds along the saved canes and clip at that point; then tie the canes to supports, as they will be carrying this summer's grapes. Grapes have two real pests: grapeleaf skeletonizers and leafhoppers. Skeletonizers strip all the foliage from leaves, leaving only the veins. Use *Bacillus thuriengensis* as a control. Leafhoppers cause blotchy spots on leaves as they remove sugars, causing the grapes to be bitter. Use insecticidal soap to control these pests.

LANDSCAPE MERIT

Use Grapevines to screen, to espalier, to cover an arbor, and to produce fruit to eat and for raisins, wine, juices, and jellies. I use the canes to make Christmas wreaths.

ADDITIONAL SPECIES, CULTIVARS, OR VARIETIES

When selecting vines for fruit, consult your Cooperative Extension Office. The following are some favorites of mine. To cover a fence with no emphasis on fruit, chose *V. arizonica*, a sprawling, scrambling woody vine with tendrils, often covering entire trees. It flowers greenish white, followed by juicy purple-black grapes. *V. vinifera* 'Red Flame', 'Lady Fingers', and 'Muscate' are familiar table grapes good for the home garden.

Hall's Honeysuckle

Lonicera japonica 'Halliana'

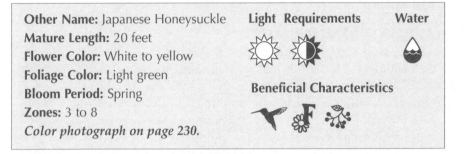

Other Name: Japanese Honeysuckle
Mature Length: 20 feet
Flower Color: White to yellow
Foliage Color: Light green
Bloom Period: Spring
Zones: 3 to 8
Color photograph on page 230.

Light Requirements

Water

Beneficial Characteristics

It's time to revert to the oldies. Back home, Honeysuckle covered an ugly fence with the corral just beyond it. My mother planted Hall's Honeysuckle, an aggressive vine, along the fence in an attempt to hide the corral. In the spring, the vine's fragrance filled the yard and suppressed those "other" smells. Some consider it an invasive weed, but to us in the desert it is a staple. Soft green foliage dresses the vine, and its flowers become the cherry on the sundae. White flowers pair themselves along gnarled stems as they unfold, only to turn yellow as they age. You end up with a mixture of yellow and white clusters and they turn into a haven for the birds because of the sweet nectar. The flowers are shaped like trumpets, making Hall's Honeysuckle especially attractive to hummingbirds. (To me, the flowers resemble Columbine flowers.) As the fruit comes on, other birds frequent the vine, and as summer progresses, flowers become less profuse. The aggressive vine, once established, can cover a large piece of real estate. If left to spread, it becomes a ground cover, and I have often wondered why we don't use Hall's Honeysuckle more this way? If we have warm winters, vines retain their leaves; otherwise, they becomes deciduous. Hall's Honeysuckle is a twining climber, so give it something to hang onto near a patio so you can enjoy its fragrance. (LM)

Regional Tips
It is a deciduous vine in the north and semievergreen in the south.

When, Where, and How to Plant
Plant Hall's Honeysuckle from containers all through the year, but it is best planted in the spring. It does well in most soils, providing they drain, and it prefers full sun to partial shade. Because our soils are so compacted, we need to make a hole three times as wide and as

deep as the rootball. Mix organic matter in with the onsite
soil and plant; also build a water basin to keep it soaked
until established. Add a mulch to conserve water and to
add to the beauty of the setting.

CARE AND MAINTENANCE

Hall's Honeysuckle will go without water for a while, but
if it becomes woody, that's a signal to water more; it will
come back quickly. Water it three times a week throughout
summer and monthly during winter. Its aggressiveness
requires a balanced fertilizer on Presidents' Day, Memorial
Day, and Labor Day. You must vigorously prune Hall's
Honeysuckle right back to the ground in the early spring
or the gnarled branches will become exposed. Don't worry;
it will come back with a vengeance. Throughout the summer, prune back the extending branches to keep the plant
in check. Aphids are about the only bug that bothers the
vine. (A honeydew substance on the leaves is a good indication you have aphids.) Spray the plant, making sure you
direct a strong jet of water to the undersides of the leaves.
This will wash off most aphids, or you can use insecticidal
soap or Neem.

LANDSCAPE MERIT

Hall's Honeysuckle is fragrant for a long time. It provides
shade, but you must provide supporting trellises. Use it
to conserve energy by letting it climb up the west side of
a home.

ADDITIONAL SPECIES, CULTIVARS, OR VARIETIES

'Aureo-reticulata' is a golden Honeysuckle with leaves
veined in yellow. 'Halliana' is vigorous and bears flowers
that attract bees. 'Purpurea' has leaves with purple-tinged
undersides and flowers that are purplish-red outside,
white inside.

Lady Bank's Rose

Rosa banksiae

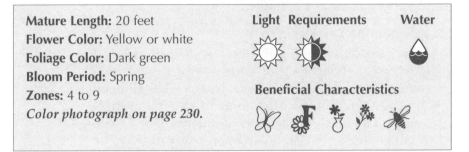

Mature Length: 20 feet
Flower Color: Yellow or white
Foliage Color: Dark green
Bloom Period: Spring
Zones: 4 to 9
Color photograph on page 230.

Light Requirements

Water

Beneficial Characteristics

"I looked out the window and what did I see? Popcorn popping on the apricot tree." Will you let me insert the Lady Bank's Rose into this old song? It fits the Lady Bank's Rose so well. In spring a profusion of small, 1-inch, pale yellow or white flowers adorn the long stems. The blossoms have crinkled petals that appear in clusters along thornless branches. From a distance the blooms look like popcorn popping along the canes. Lady Bank's Rose has glossy, leathery, rich green leaves. They become an excellent background to accent the flowers. Use this climber to cover fences, arbors, or housetops, or for other screening effects. Given support, it will also grow as a small tree. For a dense covering, shear the rose as needed. Lady Bank's Rose is one of the best-known climbers and is suitable as a vine. (LM)

REGIONAL TIPS

In northern Nevada, plant Lady Bank's Rose in the early spring when it becomes available. In southern Nevada, you can plant it before Valentine's Day, but it will have better establishment if planted in fall.

WHEN, WHERE, AND HOW TO PLANT

Spring is the time to plant Lady Bank's Roses in Nevada. If you find some available in the fall in southern Nevada, plant to become established before the heat sets in. Lady Bank's Rose does best in a soil highly amended with organic matter and loves full sun to partial shade. The "upstairs" part of the plant does only as well as the roots. By opening up a hole at least three times as wide and at least as deep as the rootball, you will get this plant off on the right track. Mix in copious amounts of compost with the on-site soil, and work the prepared soil in and around the rootball. Water to further settle the soil, build a water basin around the plant, and thoroughly soak the rootball two to three times a week until established.

CARE AND MAINTENANCE
Water this beauty at least three times a week through the heat and weekly as temperatures cool. In southern Nevada, it will need monthly waterings through the winter, especially if there is a lot of a wind to dry out the soil. Feed in the early spring around Valentine's Day, Memorial Day, and Labor Day to encourage new growth. If it shows iron deficiency, or yellowing of the leaves, feed it some chelated iron so the alkaline soils cannot hold it back. Lady Bank's Rose is a rapid grower and once established may require pruning or shearing several times during the growing season. Prune after the spring bloom to avoid flower loss. It is aphid-resistant and immune to disease.

LANDSCAPE MERIT
Lady Bank's is an attractive spring bloomer with masses of yellow or white flowers covering it, making it excellent for borders, specimen, or ground cover; or as a covering for fences, arbors, trellises, or ugly eyesores.

ADDITIONAL SPECIES, CULTIVARS, OR VARIETIES
Nevadans use two Bank's Roses a lot. One is 'Alba Plena', or White Banksias Rose. It climbs about 20 feet, has light apple-green leaves, and is virtually thornless. Double white flowers up to 1 1/2 inches across bloom profusely in late spring. 'Lutea', or Yellow Banksias Rose, does about the same, except flowers are double canary yellow. It needs full sun to bring out the most in them. 'Fortuniana', sometimes sold as Double White Banksias, has larger flowers that bloom individually rather than in clusters on thorny canes.

Lilac Vine

Hardenbergia violacea

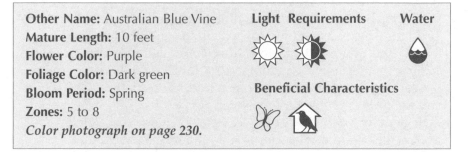

Other Name: Australian Blue Vine
Mature Length: 10 feet
Flower Color: Purple
Foliage Color: Dark green
Bloom Period: Spring
Zones: 5 to 8
Color photograph on page 230.

Light Requirements

Water

Beneficial Characteristics

In Salt Lake City, where I lived before I moved to Nevada, Lilacs are everywhere. Lilacs lined my yard, creating a living fence between my neighbors. It was everywhere in the valleys and we enjoyed it. When I came to Las Vegas, in went a Lilac bush. The nursery told me not to plant it, but as Missourians say, "They had to show me." Well, they were right! We don't get enough cold weather for them to bloom like the Lilacs of my dreams. Finally, I met Lilac Vine. It is a prolific flowering vine that produces deep, intense, bright blue-purplish pea-type flowers on dangling clusters in the early spring, followed by small gray-to-brown pods. Under these flowers are twining stems covered with dark green, narrow, pointed leaves about 4 inches long. If you see this vine at its maturity, you get the feeling it is very fast growing. But it starts out slow, gaining momentum as its roots sink deep into the surrounding soil. As this happens, the Lilac Vine will then cover a patio, wall, or gazebo in short order. (LM)

REGIONAL TIPS

It is only hardy enough for southern Nevada weather conditions. So, you northerners can enjoy Lilacs, instead.

WHEN, WHERE, AND HOW TO PLANT

Plant anytime from containers, with emphasis on fall planting for better plant establishment. It loves full sun but does well in partial shade. I know of a planting under a tree; it is now occupying about a third of the tree, and they both are doing fine. The vine tolerates poor soils but must have good drainage. The wider you make the hole, the better the plant will perform; I suggest a hole at least three times as wide and as deep as the rootball you are about to plant. Mix some organic matter in the on-site soil and fold the soil in around the rootball, using water to further settle it. Build a basin around the plant and thoroughly water Lilac Vine three times a week until you see new growth emerge.

CARE AND MAINTENANCE

Twice-weekly waterings keep the plant healthy during the summer, but it only needs monthly waterings through the winter. It doesn't take much fertilizer to keep this beauty happy, but to keep it lush, feed it a balanced fertilizer around Valentine's and Labor Days. To show it off best, provide a trellis or let it climb on nearby plants. It really doesn't take much trimming to keep it under control, just a little pruning to keep the new growth in check. Do the major pruning after blooming to regenerate the plant. If you like the tangling effect of the vine, let it go. Spider mites can be a real problem. They cause the plant to look dry and unthrifty, working on the older leaves (where it's dusty). Direct a strong jet of water to these areas. If they persist, use insecticidal soap or Neem.

LANDSCAPE MERIT

Lilac Vine is an excellent vine to cover walls and fences, and it grows under filtered shade. It does need some support on walls, and once latched to a tree, it will climb. It creates a delicate tracery on walls and covers trellises, or it can be turned loose to become a dense ground cover.

ADDITIONAL SPECIES, CULTIVARS, OR VARIETIES

H. comptoniana is a more widely used species than *H. violacea*. It has pinkish-blue flowers but is not as drought resistant or cold hardy. The *H. violacea* 'Happy Wanderer' cultivar is more vigorous than the Lilac Vine species.

Silver Lace Vine

Fallopia baldschuanica

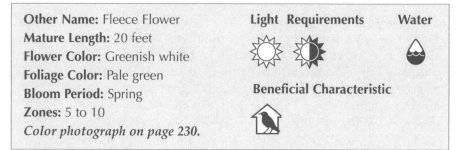

Other Name: Fleece Flower
Mature Length: 20 feet
Flower Color: Greenish white
Foliage Color: Pale green
Bloom Period: Spring
Zones: 5 to 10
Color photograph on page 230.

Light Requirements

Water

Beneficial Characteristic

The profusely blooming Silver Lace Vine will hide an unsightly area, screen out a junky yard, or cover a broken fence in a short time. It gets its name from the billowy, small flowers that blanket the vine. It becomes especially striking as the vine cascades over walls, with blooms frothing like white foam when backlit. Silver Lace Vine blooms from late summer into the fall, when other plants have finished their blooming season. Greenish-white blossoms are held in dense, upright clusters above the stems. Distinctive arrow-shaped leaves, up to 2 inches long, have wavy margins and glossy surfaces that appear pale green and darken with age. It grows rapidly to 20 feet and quickly turns a troubled setting into a heavenly oasis. If you have tough growing conditions, call on Silver Lace Vine. For years I have watched a Silver Lace Vine that gets absolutely no attention or water and to this day looks beautiful as the vine keeps covering the old stems. The vine becomes deciduous if it experiences a cold winter. It is an excellent accent plant to choose for sites where other vines will suffer from the rigors of strong winds or adverse growing conditions. Stems twine quickly over their supports to turn an ordinary pergola, arbor, or patio into a lovely shaded area. (LM)

REGIONAL TIPS

This tough vine will take temperatures down to the high teens. As a result, it tolerates the winters of Reno and Sparks.

WHEN, WHERE, AND HOW TO PLANT

Plant any time from containers, with emphasis directed toward fall planting for better plant establishment. It loves full sun but does well in partial shade, and it tolerates poor soils if there is good drainage. The wider you make the hole, the better the plant will perform—I suggest a hole at least three times as wide and as deep as the rootball you are about to plant. Mix some organic matter in the onsite soil and fill in around the rootball using water to further settle in the soil. Build a basin around the plant and thoroughly water twice a week until you see new growth emerge.

CARE AND MAINTENANCE

Through the heat of the summer, water twice a week, but as the weather cools, revert to weekly waterings. During the winter, water monthly. If the plant experiences a hard freeze, it will die to the ground and you'll need to remove the damaged stems; the resilient vine will send up new stems in the spring. It is a plant that doesn't require many nutrients, but a feeding in the early spring will bring on a luster and increase the quality of blooms. Newly established plants will need branches tied to a support for early training to maintain an attractive form. Prune off growing tips to increase bushiness and control the shape, although flowering will be delayed. Silver Lace Vine is free of pests.

LANDSCAPE MERIT

It is an excellent accent plant for tough growing conditions, especially if it is located in an area receiving constantly strong winds. It's a vine you can forget about—it will still look manicured and will do so on very little water. Silver Lace Vine makes a splendid choice to cover a fence.

ADDITIONAL SPECIES, CULTIVARS, OR VARIETIES

There are no other varieties.

Trumpet Vine

Campsis radicans

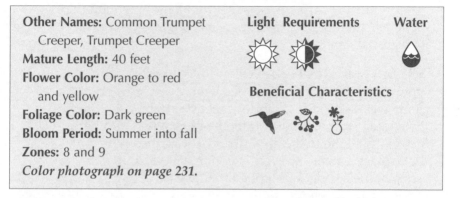

Other Names: Common Trumpet Creeper, Trumpet Creeper

Mature Length: 40 feet

Flower Color: Orange to red and yellow

Foliage Color: Dark green

Bloom Period: Summer into fall

Zones: 8 and 9

Color photograph on page 231.

Light Requirements

Water

Beneficial Characteristics

If you want to hide an unattractive scene, create a shade screen for your patio, or hide a towering light pole (fast!), plant Trumpet Vine. How can you go wrong with large clusters of brilliant orange, trumpet-shaped flowers cascading down a dark-green backdrop of lush foliage to hide an unwanted scene? During the growing season, hummingbirds frequent the flowers to feast on the sweet nectar. Although Trumpet Vine is self-clinging, it's best to tie it in a few places to prevent it from being blown off its supports. It will grow horizontally or vertically by self-attaching aerial rootlets, but be cautious, as they can damage stucco and structures where attached. You'll get the most good from this vine on a southwest-facing wall or shielding a patio from the blistering sun. Stunning clusters of trumpet-shaped flowers are 1 to 2 inches wide and up to 3 inches deep, developing into clusters of six to twelve. Pods follow that turn brown and, as they mature, disperse small seeds with velvety white hairs. Unfortunately, the seeds germinate easily—but for once, Nevada's poor soils become the best management tool to control the vine. (LM)

REGIONAL TIPS

This tough vine will take temperatures down to the high teens and is hardy in most of northern Nevada.

WHEN, WHERE, AND HOW TO PLANT

Plant Trumpet Vine anytime from containers, with emphasis directed toward planting in the fall for better establishment. It thrives in full sun, but you can subject it to some shade, and to poor soil conditions if it drains well. The wider you make the planting hole, the better

Trumpet Vine will perform; I suggest a hole three times as wide and as deep as the rootball. Because southern Nevada soils are so compacted, mix in some organic matter with onsite soil to open it up, and fold the prepared soil back in around the rootball, adding water to settle the soil. Build a water basin around the plant, and soak roots three times a week until new growth emerges.

CARE AND MAINTENANCE
Throughout the summer, water the vine twice weekly. Scorched leaves, smaller leaves, and a reduction in blooms will be an indication to water more. During the winter, keep the soil moist with monthly waterings. Trumpet Vine is a plant that doesn't require many nutrients, but a feeding in the early spring will generate a lush vine and quality blooms. As new branches emerge and reach out from the wall or trellis, you will need to redirect them back into the trellis. Thereafter, thin and guide branches to maintain an attractive form, and prune regularly to increase bushiness. While it is free of pests, the plant and its roots can become invasive if not maintained.

LANDSCAPE MERIT
Trumpet Vine can cover unsightly areas, fences, walls, arbors, and trellises in a hurry, which makes it useful as quick shade for porches and patios. Its bold vine is often used for rustic or large-scale situations. Those with a knack for flower arranging use the vines, flowers, and seedpods in their designs.

ADDITIONAL SPECIES, CULTIVARS, OR VARIETIES
C. radicans 'Flava' is a selection with bright-yellow flowers. *C. × tagliabuana* 'Madame Galen' has salmon flowers deeply infused with red. It is more frost-tender than the other species during establishment.

NURSERIES

Nevada Nurseries

Nurseries listed are for identification only and this list does not imply an endorsement by the authors or by Cool Springs Press, nor does it imply criticism of similar nurseries that are not listed here. The following list is organized by nursery name in alphabetical order by city.

Blue Diamond:
Cactus Joe's, 12470 Blue Diamond Road, Blue Diamond, NV 89004

Boulder City:
Ladybug Nursery, 1674 Nevada Highway, Boulder City, NV 89005

Carson City:
Greenhouse Garden Center, 2450 South Curry Street, Carson City, NV 89703
Native Plant Farm and Tree Movers, 5005 Old US 395 North, Carson City, NV 89506

Dayton:
Dayton Valley Floral and Nursery, 209 Dayton Valley Road, Dayton, NV 89403

Elko:
Elko Garden and Landscape Center, 2222 Last Chance Road, Elko, NV 89801
Kimberly Nurseries and Gift Shop, 2223 North 5th Street, Elko, NV 89801

Ely:
Flowers Unlimited, 1500 Great Basin Blvd, Ely, NV 89301

Fallon:
Flower Tree Nursery, 2975 Reno Highway, Fallon, NV 89406
Garden of Edith, 3900 Sheckler Road, Fallon, NV 89406
Green Team Growers, 5975 Bottom Road, Fallon, NV 89406
Workman Farms, 4990 Reno Highway, Fallon, NV 89406

Fernley:
Mirage Garden and Gifts, 350 East Main, Fernley, NV 89408

Gardnerville:
A and B Tree Sales, 1650 Lombardy Road, Gardnerville, NV 89410

Nurseries

Carson Valley Garden/Ranch, 1144 Highway 395, Gardnerville, NV 89410
Highland Nursery,1167 Kimmerling Road, Gardnerville, NV 89410

Hawthorn:
Dutch Creek Tree Farm, Highway 95, Hawthorn, NV 89415
T L C Nursery, 929 G Street, Hawthorn, NV 89415

Henderson:
Hafen Nursery, 1740 North Boulder Highway, Henderson, NV 89015
Vista Nursery, 20 North Gibson Road, Henderson, NV 89014

Incline Village:
High Sierra Gardens, 866 Tahoe Boulevard, Incline Village, NV 89451

Las Vegas:
Corey Nursery, 3112 North Nellis Boulevard, Las Vegas, NV 89115
Davis Nursery, 2700 East Bonanza Road, Las Vegas, NV 89101
Desert Garden Center, 6221 West Charleston Boulevard, Las Vegas,
    NV 89146
Howard's Nursery, 3340 North Rancho Drive, Las Vegas, NV 89130
Las Vegas Garden Center, 5050 North Rainbow, Las Vegas, NV 89130
Oasis Palms, 2685 North Nellis Boulevard, Las Vegas, NV 89115
Plant It Earth, 3070 West Ford Avenue, Las Vegas, NV 89139
Plant World Nursery, 1250 East Tropicana Avenue, Las Vegas, NV 89119
Plant World Nursery, 9040 South Eastern Avenue, Las Vegas, NV 89123
Plant World Nursery, 5311 West Charleston Boulevard, Las Vegas,
    NV 89146
Promise Land Nursery, 3020 West Wigwam Avenue, Las Vegas,
    NV 89139
Rancho True Value, 3535 North Rancho Drive, Las Vegas, NV 89130
Star Nursery, 5340 Boulder Highway, Las Vegas, NV 89122
Star Nursery, 8725 South Eastern Avenue, Las Vegas, NV 89123
Star Nursery, 8170 West Charleston Boulevard, Las Vegas, NV 89117
Star Nursery, 7330 West Cheyenne Avenue, Las Vegas, NV 89129
Star Nursery, 4810 Wynn Road, Las Vegas, NV 89103
Turner Greenhouse, 4455 Quadrel Street, Las Vegas, NV 89129

Lovelock:
Pitt Mill and Elevator, 1210 Cornell Avenue, Lovelock, NV 89419

Minden:
Genoa Lane Trees, 2181 US Highway 395, Minden, NV 89423
Northern Nevada Nursery, 3190 Highway 395, Minden, NV 89423
Spikes Trees, 1321 Judy, Minden, NV 89423

Nurseries

Reno:
Comstock Nursery, 3270 War Paint Circle, Reno, NV 89506
Dayton Valley Turf, 290 Kietzke Lane, Reno, NV 89502
Discount Nursery, 190 West Moana Lane, Reno, NV 89509
Dry Creek Garden Company, 7250 South Virginia Street, Reno, NV 89511
Flower Farm, 510 Zolezze Lane, Reno, NV 89511
Garden Shop Nursery, 4690 Longley Lane, Reno, NV 89502
Garden Spot Nursery, 300 Lemon Drive, Reno, NV 89506
Highland Roses, 4250 Longknife Road, Reno, NV 89509
Interpretive Gardens, Inc., 7777 White Fir Street, Reno, NV 89523
Moana Nursery, 1100 West Moana Lane, Reno, NV 89509
Mountain Valley, 3390 White Lake Parkway, Reno, NV 89506
Nature's Gifts, 10475 Red Rock, Reno, NV 89506
Nevada Native Plants, 2150 Dickerson Road, Reno, NV 89506
Pioneer Landscape Materials and Nursery, 4685 Gold Strike Court,
    Reno, NV 89511
Springtime Gardens, 3295 East Second Street, Reno, NV 89502
Truckee River Rock and Nursery, 5200 West Fourth Street, Reno,
    NV 89523
Virginia House Nursery, 1350 Geiger Grade, Reno, NV 89511
Weekend Gardener at Arlington, 606 West Plumb Lane, Reno, NV 89509
Western Turf & Nursery, 5200 Grass Valley Road, Reno, NV 89510

Silver Springs:
Mother Earth Growers, 1500 Ebony Avenue, Silver Springs, NV 89429
Nevada Green Nursery/Greenhouse, 2450 Highway 95A South, Silver
    Springs, NV 89429
Reed's Seeds, 1665 East 5th Street, Silver Springs, NV 89429
Tiffany Plants, 2960 East 4th Street, Silver Springs, NV 89429

Sparks:
G and H Nursery, 1425 Hymer Avenue, Sparks, NV 89431
Kitchens and Gardens, 3059 Meadowlands Drive, Sparks, NV 89431
Legends Landscaping and Nursery, 324 South 18th Street, Sparks,
    NV 89431
Rail City Garden Center, 1720 Brierley Way, Sparks, NV 89434

Springcreek:
Colorscapes Greenhouse, HC 36 PVE 167-5, Springcreek, NV 89815

Stateline:
Sunbasin Landscape and Nursery, 276 Kingsberry Grade, Stateline,
    NV 89449

Nurseries

Washoe Valley:
Stony Acres Nursery, 1468 Eunice Way, Washoe Valley, NV 89704
Washoe Valley Tree Farm, 7635 Old Highway 395, Washoe Valley,
NV 89704

Wellington:
Home Again, 2805 Highway 208, Wellington, NV 89444
Nevada's Own, 267 Artesia Road, Wellington, NV 89444

Winnemucca:
Miller Hay and Farm, 720 East 4th Street, Winnemucca, NV 89445
Northern Nevada Turf Farms, 9505 South Buffalo Road, Winnemucca,
NV 89445
Ron's Seed and Supply, 710 Grass Valley Road, Winnemucca,
NV 89445
Winnemucca Nursery and Landscape, 7305 South Grass Valley Road,
Winnemucca, NV 89445

Yerington:
Country Flower Shoppe, 19 West Bridge, Yerington, NV 89447
Draper Landscape and Nursery, 120 North Main Street, Yerington,
NV 89447
High Desert Turf, 186 Highway 208, Yerington, NV 89447
Minute Man Nursery, 2 Penrose Lane, Yerington, NV 89447

Zephyr Cove:
Round Hill Nursery, 212 Elks Point Road, Zephyr Cove, NV 89448

CHARTS

Lawn Watering Chart
for Northern Nevada Grasses

	AVERAGE WATER DEPTH FROM CAN TEST						
TENTHS OF INCH	.25"	.31"	.375"	.44"	.50"	.56"	.625"
FRACTION OF INCH	1/4"	5/16"	3/8"	7/16"	1/2"	9/16"	5/8"
AMOUNT NEEDED PER WEEK	MINUTES TO WATER EACH WATERING DAY (twice-a-week watering)						
April .98 inch/week	29	23	20	17	15	13	12
May 1.18 inch/week	35	28	24	20	18	16	14
June 1.45 inch/week	43	35	29	25	22	20	17
July 1.60 inch/week	47	38	32	28	24	22	19
August 1.50 inch/week	46	37	30	26	23	20	18
September 1.12 inch/week	34	27	23	20	17	15	13
October .96 inch/week	29	23	19	17	15	13	12

Minutes based on a 15-minute cup test and ET data. If runoff occurs, water more frequently. For example: Water twice for 10 minutes each time instead of once for 20 minutes, allowing water to soak in between cycles.

Source: Data collected by University of Nevada Cooperative Extension and Nevada Agricultural Experiment Station.

Lawn Watering Chart for Carson City Grasses

	AVERAGE WATER DEPTH FROM CAN TEST						
TENTHS OF INCH	.25"	.31"	.375"	.44"	.50"	.56"	.625"
FRACTION OF INCH	1/4"	5/16"	3/8"	7/16"	1/2"	9/16"	5/8"
AMOUNT NEEDED PER WEEK	MINUTES TO WATER EACH WATERING DAY (twice-a-week watering)						
April .98 inch/week	15	12	10	9	8	7	6
May 1.18 inch/week	18	14	12	10	9	8	7
June 1.45 inch/week	22	18	15	13	11	10	9
July 1.60 inch/week	24	19	16	14	12	11	10
August 1.50 inch/week	23	19	15	13	12	10	9
September 1.12 inch/week	17	14	12	10	9	8	7
October .96 inch/week	15	12	10	9	8	7	8

Minutes based on a 15-minute cup test and ET data. If runoff occurs, water more frequently. For example: Water twice for 10 minutes each time instead of once for 20 minutes, allowing water to soak in between cycles.

Source: Data collected by University of Nevada Cooperative Extension and Nevada Agricultural Experiment Station.

Southern Region Watering Guide

LAWN

Winter	Spring / Fall	Summer
Nov., Dec., Jan., Feb.	Mar., Apr. / Sept., Oct.	May, June, July, Aug.
2 days per week	**4** days per week	**7** days per week
3 times a day	**3** times a day	**3** times a day
4 minutes each watering	**4** minutes each watering	**4** minutes each watering

PLANTS

Winter	Spring / Fall	Summer
Nov., Dec., Jan., Feb.	Mar., Apr. / Sept., Oct.	May, June, July, Aug.
1 day per week	**2** days per week	**3** days per week
1 time a day	**1** time a day	**1** time a day
1 hour* each watering	**1** hour* each watering	**1** hour* each watering

*The time provided is for low-flow emitters.

Source: Reproduced courtesy of the Southern Nevada Water Authority

DRIP EMITTER GUIDE

12 minutes each watering	1 hour each watering	2 hours each watering
High-flow emitters (Up to 20 gph)	Low-flow emitters (Up to 4 gph)	Low-flow emitters (Up to 2 gph)

To find out how fast your emitter waters, measure how many seconds it takes to fill a tablespoon:

14 seconds = 1 gph   7 seconds = 2 gph   4 seconds = 4 gph
gph = gallons per hour

PLANT WATERING TIPS

- The three most common emitters are above. If you're not sure what type you have, use the above test to find their rate of flow.

- If your plants appear stressed, check the soil moisture.

- If the soil is wet, your plants may be overwatered. Water less often or for less time.

- If the soil is dry, check that all emitters are working. If they are, increase the watering time or add emitters only near the stressed plants.

- Flush the drip irrigation lines and filters every time you change your irrigation schedule.

- If your **irrigation clock** has a "skip day" mode, water:
  - Every 2 to 3 days in summer
  - Every 4 to 6 days in spring and fall
  - Every 8 to 12 days in winter

Source: Reproduced courtesy of the Southern Nevada Water Authority

Home Garden Insect Control

Pest	Physical					Biorationals[1]						
	Barriers (Tanglefoot)	Hand Pick	Pruning	Trapping	Wash or Syringe Off	BT/Thrucide/Dipel	Diatomaceous Earth	Insecticidal Soap	Neem	PDB/Moth Crystal	Superior/Supreme Oil	Ultrafine Summer Oil
Aphids			×		×			×	×		×	×
Armyworms or Cutworms	×	×				×			×		×	×
Borers, Flat Headed											×	
Boxelder Bugs												
Corn Earworms						×			×		×	×
Earwigs				×				×	×			
Elm Leaf Beetles	×					×						
Flea Beetles							×		×			
Grasshoppers								×	×			
June Beetle, Fruit Beetles							×					
Lawn Insects								×				
Leafhoppers					×			×	×			
Leafminers		×				×			×			
Leafrollers		×				×					×	×
Loopers and Caterpillars		×				×	×				×	×
Mealybugs					×			×	×		×	
Mites					×			×	×	×	×	×
Root Weevils												
Rose or Pear Slug (Sawfly)		×		×	×			×	×			

Biologicals						Traditional Insecticides[1]								
Lace Wing	Ladybird Beetle	Predatory Mite	Parasitic Nematode	Parasitic Wasp	Viral Disease	Carbaryl (Sevin)	Dimethoate (Cygon)	Endosulfan (Thiodan)	Kelthane or Tedlon	Lindane	Malathion (Cythion)	Meta-Systox-R[2]	Orthene[1]	Pyrethrins[2]
×	×			×		×	×	×			×	×	×	×
				×		×		×					×	
			×							×				
													×	×
				×		×		×			×		×	
				×		×								
						×					×		×	×
			×			×		×			×		×	×
						×	×				×		×	
			×			×					×		×	
						×				×				
	×			×		×	×	×			×	×	×	×
				×		×	×	×		×	×	×	×	
×				×		×					×	×	×	
×			×			×		×			×		×	×
×	×			×			×				×		×	
		×		×		×	×	×	×		×	×		
			×			×		×		×	×		×	×
×						×								×

Home Garden Insect Control

Pest	Physical					Biorationals[1]						
	Barriers (Tanglefoot)	Hand Pick	Pruning	Trapping	Wash or Syringe Off	BT/Thrucide/Dipel	Diatomaceous Earth	Insecticidal Soap	Neem	PDB/Moth Crystal	Superior/Supreme Oil	Ultrafine Summer Oil
Scales (crawler stage)			×					×	×		×	×
Silverfish							×	×				
Slugs/Snails	×	×		×			×		×			
Southern Fire Ants												
Sowbugs				×				×				
Spittlebugs								×				
Squash Bugs		×		×			×	×	×			
Tent Caterpillars			×			×		×	×			
Thrips				×[3]	×		×	×	×			×
Tomato Fruitworms		×				×					×	×
Tomato Hornworms		×				×			×			
Whiteflies				×[3]				×	×			

[1] Use of trade names is only for convenience of the reader, and does not constitute an endorsement of a product or criticism of a similar product. Orthene can cause leaf damage to cottonwoods.

[2] Use only on ornamentals, do not use on home vegetables. Many synthethic pyrethrins are available.

[3] Thrips—use blue sticky cards, Whiteflies—use yellow sticky cards.

Source: University of Nevada Cooperative Extension

| Biologicals | | | | | | Traditional Insecticides[1] | | | | | | | | |
Lace Wing	Ladybird Beetle	Predatory Mite	Parasitic Nematode	Parasitic Wasp	Viral Disease	Carbaryl (Sevin)	Dimethoate (Cygon)	Endosulfan (Thiodan)	Kelthane or Tedlon	Lindane	Malathion (Cythion)	Meta-Systox-R[2]	Orthene[1]	Pyrethrins[2]
	×			×		×	×				×	×	×	×
														×
													×	
						×								
						×		×					×	
						×		×						×
						×					×		×	×
×	×	×				×	×				×	×	×	×
					×	×					×			
				×		×								
				×			×	×			×		×	×

G LO S S A R Y

Alkaline soil: soil with a pH greater than 7.0. It lacks acidity, often because it has limestone in it.

All-purpose fertilizer: powdered, liquid, or granular fertilizer with a balanced proportion of the three key nutrients—nitrogen (N), phosphorus (P), and potassium (K). It is suitable for maintenance nutrition for most plants.

Annual: a plant that lives its entire life in one season. It is genetically determined to germinate, grow, flower, set seed, and die the same year.

Balled and burlapped: describes a tree or shrub grown in the field whose soilball was wrapped with protective burlap and twine when the plant was dug up to be sold or transplanted.

Bare root: describes plants that have been packaged without any soil around their roots. (Often young shrubs and trees purchased through the mail arrive with their exposed roots covered with moist peat or sphagnum moss, sawdust, or similar material, and wrapped in plastic.)

Barrier plant: a plant that has intimidating thorns or spines and is sited purposely to block foot traffic or other access to the home or yard.

Beneficial insects: insects or their larvae that prey on pest organisms and their eggs. They may be flying insects, such as ladybugs, parasitic wasps, praying mantids, and soldier bugs, or soil dwellers such as predatory nematodes, spiders, and ants.

Berm: a narrow raised ring of soil around a tree, used to hold water so it will be directed to the root zone.

Bract: a modified leaf structure on a plant stem near its flower that resembles a petal. Often it is more colorful and visible than the actual flower, as in dogwood.

Bud union: the place where the top of a plant was grafted to the rootstock; usually refers to roses.

Canopy: the overhead branching area of a tree, usually referring to its extent including foliage.

Cold hardiness: the ability of a perennial plant to survive the winter cold in a particular area.

Composite: a flower that is actually composed of many tiny flowers. Typically, they are flat clusters of tiny, tight florets, sometimes surrounded by wider-petaled florets. Composite flowers are highly attractive to bees and beneficial insects.

Compost: organic matter that has undergone progressive decomposition by microbial and macrobial activity until it is reduced to a spongy, fluffy texture. Added to soil of any type, it improves the soil's ability to hold air and water and to drain well.

Corm: the swollen energy-storing structure, analogous to a bulb, under the soil at the base of the stem of plants such as crocus and gladiolus.

Crown: the base of a plant at, or just beneath, the surface of the soil where the roots meet the stems.

Glossary

Cultivar: a CULTIvated VARiety. It is a naturally occurring form of a plant that has been identified as special or superior and is purposely selected for propagation and production.

Deadhead: a pruning technique that removes faded flower heads from plants to improve their appearance, abort seed production, and stimulate further flowering.

Deciduous plants: unlike evergreens, these trees and shrubs lose their leaves in the fall.

Desiccation: drying out of foliage tissues, usually due to drought or wind.

Division: the practice of splitting apart perennial plants to create several smaller-rooted segments. The practice is useful for controlling the plant's size and for acquiring more plants; it is also essential to the health and continued flowering of certain ones.

Dormancy: the period, usually the winter, when perennial plants temporarily cease active growth and rest. **Dormant** is the verb form, as used in this sentence: *Some plants, like spring-blooming bulbs, go dormant in the summer.*

Established: the point at which a newly planted tree, shrub, or flower begins to produce new growth, either foliage or stems. This is an indication that the roots have recovered from transplant shock and have begun to grow and spread.

Evergreen: perennial plants that do not lose their foliage annually with the onset of winter. Needled or broadleaf foliage will persist and continues to function on a plant through one or more winters, aging and dropping unobtrusively in cycles of three or four years or more.

Foliar: of or about foliage—usually refers to the practice of spraying foliage, as in fertilizing or treating with insecticide; leaf tissues absorb liquid directly for fast results, and the soil is not affected.

Floret: a tiny flower, usually one of many forming a cluster, that comprises a single blossom.

Germinate: to sprout. Germination is a fertile seed's first stage of development.

Graft (union): the point on the stem of a woody plant with sturdier roots where a stem from a highly ornamental plant is inserted so that it will join with it. Roses are commonly grafted.

Hands: the female flowers on a banana tree; they turn into bananas.

Hardscape: the permanent, structural, nonplant part of a landscape, such as walls, sheds, pools, patios, arbors, and walkways.

Herbaceous: plants having fleshy or soft stems that die back with frost; the opposite of **woody**.

Hybrid: a plant that is the result of intentional or natural cross-pollination between two or more plants of the same species or genus.

Low water demand: describes plants that tolerate dry soil for varying periods of time. Typically, they have succulent, hairy, or silvery-gray foliage and tuberous roots or taproots.

Glossary

Mulch: a layer of material over bare soil to protect it from erosion and compaction by rain, and to discourage weeds. It may be inorganic (gravel, fabric) or organic (wood chips, bark, pine needles, chopped leaves).

Naturalize: (*a*) to plant seeds, bulbs, or plants in a random, informal pattern as they would appear in their natural habitat; (*b*) to adapt to and spread throughout adopted habitats (a tendency of some nonnative plants).

Nectar: the sweet fluid produced by glands on flowers that attract pollinators such as hummingbirds and honeybees for whom it is a source of energy.

Organic material, organic matter: any material or debris that is derived from plants. It is carbon-based material capable of undergoing decomposition and decay.

Peat moss: organic matter from peat sedges (United States) or sphagnum mosses (Canada), often used to improve soil texture. The acidity of sphagnum peat moss makes it ideal for boosting or maintaining soil acidity while also improving its drainage.

Perennial: a flowering plant that lives over two or more seasons. Many die back with frost, but their roots survive the winter and generate new shoots in the spring.

pH: a measurement of the relative acidity (low pH) or alkalinity (high pH) of soil or water based on a scale of 1 to 14, 7 being neutral. Individual plants require soil to be within a certain range so that nutrients can dissolve in moisture and be available to them.

Pinch: to remove tender stems and/or leaves by pressing them between thumb and forefinger. This pruning technique encourages branching, compactness, and flowering in plants, or it removes aphids clustered at growing tips.

Pollen: the yellow, powdery grains in the center of a flower. A plant's male sex cells, they are transferred to the female plant parts by means of wind or animal pollinators to fertilize them and create seeds.

Raceme: an arrangement of single stalked flowers along an elongated, unbranched axis.

Rhizome: a swollen energy-storing stem structure, similar to a bulb, that lies horizontally in the soil, with roots emerging from its lower surface and growth shoots from a growing point at or near its tip, as in bearded iris.

Rootbound (or potbound): the condition of a plant that has been confined in a container too long, its roots having been forced to wrap around themselves and even swell out of the container. Successful transplanting or repotting requires untangling and trimming away of some of the matted roots.

Root flare: the transition at the base of a tree trunk where the bark tissue begins to differentiate and roots begin to form just before entering the soil. This area should not be covered with soil when planting a tree.

Glossary

Self-seeding: the tendency of some plants to sow their seeds freely around the yard. It creates many seedlings the following season that may or may not be welcome.

Semievergreen: tending to be evergreen in a mild climate but deciduous in a rigorous one.

Shearing: the pruning technique whereby plant stems and branches are cut uniformly with long-bladed pruning shears (hedge shears) or powered hedge trimmers. It is used when creating and maintaining hedges and topiary.

Slow-acting fertilizer: fertilizer that is water insoluble and therefore releases its nutrients gradually as a function of soil temperature, moisture, and related microbial activity. Typically granular, it may be organic or synthetic.

Succulent growth: the sometimes undesirable production of fleshy, water-storing leaves or stems that results from overfertilization.

Sucker: a new growing shoot. Underground plant roots produce suckers to form new stems and spread by means of these suckering roots to form large plantings, or colonies. Some plants produce root suckers or branch suckers as a result of pruning or wounding.

Tuber: a type of underground storage structure in a plant stem, analogous to a bulb. It generates roots below and stems above ground (example: dahlia).

Variegated: having various colors or color patterns. The term usually refers to plant foliage that is streaked, edged, blotched, or mottled with a contrasting color, often green with yellow, cream, or white.

White grubs: fat, off-white, wormlike larvae of Japanese beetles. They reside in the soil and feed on plant (especially grass) roots until summer when they emerge as beetles to feed on plant foliage.

Wings: (*a*) the corky tissue that forms edges along the twigs of some woody plants such as winged euonymus; (*b*) the flat, dried extension of tissue on some seeds, such as maple, that catch the wind and help them disseminate.

BIBLIOGRAPHY

Benson, Lyman, and Robert A. Darrow, *Trees and Shrubs of the Southwestern Deserts*, Tucson, AZ: University of Arizona Press, 1981.

Cobourn, John, Bill Carlos, John Christopherson, Wayne Johnson, Richard Post, JoAnne Skelly, and Ed Smith, *Home Landscaping Guide for Lake Tahoe and Vicinity*, Reno, NV: University of Nevada, 2000.

Duffield, Mary, and Warren D. Jones, *Plants for Dry Climates: How to Grow and Enjoy*. Tucson, AZ: H.P. Books, 1981.

Everett, Thomas H., *Readers Digest Complete Book of the Garden*, Pleasantville, NY: The Readers Digest Association, 1968.

Ferguson, Barbara, Project Editor, Deni W. Stein, Project Writer, and James Stockton, Art Director, *Ortho's Complete Guide to Successful Gardening*, San Francisco, CA: Ortho Books, Chevron Chemical Company, 1983.

Greelee, John, *The Encyclopedia of Ornamental Grasses*, Emmaus, PA: Rodale Press, 1992.

Johnson, Eric, *Johnson's Guide to Gardening Plants for the Arid West: Pruning, Planting, and Care*, Tucson, AZ: Ironwood Press, 1997.

Johnson, Eric, and Scott Millard, *The Low Water Flower Gardener*, Tucson, AZ: Ironwood Press, 1993.

Knopf, Jim, *The Xeriscape Flower Gardener*, Boulder, CO: Johnson Books, 1991.

McPhearson, E. Gregory, and Gregory H. Graves, *Ornamental and Shade Trees for Utah*, Logan, UT: Cooperative Extension Service, Utah State University, 1984.

Mielke, Judy, *Native Plants for Southwestern Landscapes*, Austin, TX: University of Texas Press, 1993.

Perry, Robert, *Landscape Plants for Western Regions*, Claremont, CA: Land Design Publishing, 1992.

Phillips, Judith, *Natural by Design: Beauty and Balance in Southwest Gardens*, Santa Fe, NM: Museum of New Mexico Press, 1995.

Post, Richard L, Plant Information Class Notes, Bozeman, MT: Montana State University, 1960.

Robinson, Florence, *Useful Trees and Shrubs*, Champaign, IL: Garrard Publishing Company, 1960.

Sierra Pacific Power Co., *Your Guide to Landscaping in the Truckee Meadows*, Reno, NV: Sierra Pacific.

Bibliography

Stark, N., *Review of Highway Planting Information Appropriate to Nevada*, Reno College of Agriculture Bulletin No. B.7, University of Nevada, 1966.

Stead, Susan, and Richard Post, *Plants of the Tahoe Basin: A Collection for Fact Sheets*, University of Nevada and Soil Conservation Service, 1989.

Sunset Books and *Sunset Magazine, Sunset Western Garden Book*, Menlo Park, CA: Sunset Publishing Corporation, 1995.

Wasowski, Sally, and Andy Wasowski, *Native Gardens for Dry Climates*, New York, NY: Clarkson Potter Publishers, 1995.

Weinstein, Gayle, *Xeriscape Handbook: A How-to Guide to Natural, Resource-wise Gardening*, Golden, CO: Fulcrum Publishing, 1999.

Winger, David, ed., *Xeriscape Plant Guide, Denver Water, AWWA*, Golden, CO: Fulcrum Publishing, 1998.

Younker, Gordon, L., Craig W. Johnson, Fred A. Baker, and Wayne S. Johnson, *Urban and Community Forestry, a Guide for the Interior Western United States*, Ogden, UT: USDA Forest Service Intermountain Region, 1990.

SEED AND NURSERY CATALOGS
Thompson and Morgan, Inc., Jackson, NJ, 2000
Wayside Gardens, Hodges, SC, 1999
W. Atlee Burpee and Co., Warminster, PA, 2000

INDEX

Index

Index

Index

Index

Index

Index

Index

MEET DICK POST

Dick Post

Dick Post has shared his knowledge with Nevada readers and listeners for more than thirty years. His long and varied career spans all mediums from print, to radio, to television. Post hosted the popular radio program, "Nevada Gardener", on KSRN (Reno) daily for 20 years. In 1986, Post began broadcasting from station KGVN (Gardnerville) as host of "Carson Valley Gardener" 5 times weekly until 2001. He hosted the "Gardening Talk Show" on KPTL for 5 years. Post's television experience includes "The Extension Connection" produced by the University of Nevada Cooperative Extension. As a columnist for the *Nevada Rancher* and the *Nevada Appeal*, as well as other western Nevada newspapers, Post reached readers to answer all types of gardening questions.

As a teacher, Post founded several degree programs at University of Nevada's College of Agriculture. Post reaches over 20,000 people annually through the horticulture programs he developed. He also founded the Master Gardener Program in Nevada, which has more than 1,000 volunteer members. A few of the many societies to which he belongs include, The American Horticulture Society, National Arbor Day Foundation, Trees Nevada, Nevada Shade Tree Council, and the North Lake Tahoe Demonstration Garden. Currently, Post is Western Area Director of the Nevada Cooperative Extension, and he is an Associate Professor at the University of Nevada. Post received his undergraduate and graduate degrees in Horticulture from the University of Montana, Bozeman. Currently, Post and his wife, Shirley, and their family live in Reno.

MEET LINN MILLS

Linn Mills

A much sought-after lecturer and horticulture expert, Linn Mills has been both a student and teacher of Nevada plant life for more than thirty years. Currently, Mills is an anchor for "Water Ways" on Government Access Channel TV 4. He is also the producer for "Gardening in Las Vegas" on station KLAS TV 8. Mills also contributes to Las Vegas Life, Southwest Trees and Turf, and he writes a weekly garden column for the *Las Vegas Review Journal*. Mills reaches more than 400,000 listeners and readers weekly!

For his work, Mills has been awarded the annual "Tomyiasu Award" from the Green Industry, the Extension "Agent of the Year" award for the state of Nevada, an "Extension of Merit" award from Gamma Sigma Delta, and numerous other awards. Mills was honored as the "Outstanding Faculty Member" by the University of Nevada, Reno for his contributions to the Las Vegas community. Mills earned his undergraduate and graduate degrees in horticulture from Utah State University. He joined the University Extension Service, based in Las Vegas, where he served the public for 24years. Mills was the Southern Area Director of the Extension service from 1992 to 1997, and received emeritus status after his retirement from active service. Currently, Mills serves on the Southern Nevada Water Authority, and focuses on youth education, water conservation and teaching at the Desert Demonstration Garden. Mills and his wife, Barbara, live in Las Vegas.